THE CENTENNIAL EDITION

OF THE WORKS OF

SIDNEY LANIER

GENERAL EDITOR

CHARLES R. ANDERSON

BRONZE BUST OF LANIER BY EDWARD POTTER, 1915

Piedmont Park, Atlanta, Georgia

CENTENNIAL EDITION

VOLUME VI

SIDNEY LANIER

FLORIDA

AND

MISCELLANEOUS PROSE

••

BIBLIOGRAPHY

EDITED BY

PHILIP GRAHAM

THE JOHNS HOPKINS PRESS

BALTIMORE AND LONDON

CONTENTS

INTRODUCTION

O N MARCH 24, 1875 Lanier wrote from Baltimore to his wife
at Brunswick, Georgia:

Here hath come a letter from one A. Pope, the same being a high
functionary in the net-work of railroads . . . the Great Atlantic Coast
Line . . . and he wisheth me to write,—By Homer and Lucretius, By
Dan Chaucer and John Keats and Will Shakespeare,—he wisheth me
to write a —, a — — (Choke, choke, choke) a — ch— (gulp, gulp,
gulp) a Guide book to Florida Travellers. He proposeth, By Pegasus,
to pay my hotel-bills and travelling expenses, and to give me one
hundred and twenty-five dollars a month—By Croesus, in addition
thereto: and I am to take from April to the last of June for the work.[1]

In these bantering words there is evidence of struggle and pain, but
nevertheless Lanier promptly accepted Mr. Pope's offer. The result
was to be *Florida*.

It is not strange that he accepted the offer, and it is not strange,
either, that there was pain associated with that acceptance. For after
the war Lanier's experiences had narrowed themselves into three related struggles: his effort to preserve his health against the ravages of
consumption, his effort to make a living for his growing family, and
his effort to preserve his self-respect as an artist in spite of conditions
imposed by economic necessity. All three of these struggles are
involved in his acceptance of Mr. Pope's invitation to write *Florida*.

The fight for health and economic survival had begun as early as
1865, when he wrote that consumption had laid its bony finger upon
his life.[2] The Prattville Academy venture of 1867-1868 ended dis-
astrously, with the first hemorrhage of the lungs and a persistent
cough that left little doubt as to the nature of his malady,—all against
the sad background of serious financial difficulties. He would be
compelled, he decided, to devote himself to hard work with the pen,
or with whatever else gave promise of money.

From school teaching he turned to his father's law office, where for
five years he tried futilely to find a vocation. But his physical condition, fast approaching an advanced stage of tuberculosis, dictated travel,
not work. He spent nervous and anxious weeks at resorts in Tennessee
and West Virginia and then went to New York, where, under Dr.

---

[1] All letters by Lanier quoted or cited in this Introduction are printed in the
present edition, vols. VII-X.
[2] Letter to Clifford A. Lanier, July 24, 1865.

Marcy's care, he drank cream, lifted weights, and rested in the home of his journalist-friend, Salem Dutcher. His father, his brother Clifford, and his father-in-law generously contributed to his and his family's support. October (1870) found him again in Georgia, at Macon, Brunswick, and Marietta, fighting his disease with all the then-known remedies—the milk cure, the beef-blood cure, the grape cure, the raw-beef cure, the whiskey cure, the health-lift cure, the climate-change cure, the horseback-riding cure, and one method earnestly recommended by Lanier, the flute-playing cure. A second visit to New York resulted only in disappointment and Lanier's admission, " I must crawl home by the easiest way."

By the summer of 1872 his battle for health seemed so definitely going against him, that he was persuaded to consider a trip to Texas, a suggestion that his father had been urging on him for two years.[3] The journey would be expensive and arduous, and, worst of all, would mean long miles and months of separation from his wife. But the promise of health for his work justified even these hardships, and on November 13 he left Macon for the long journey to San Antonio, traveling via Montgomery, New Orleans, Galveston, Houston, and Austin.

If he had expected surcease from struggle in Texas, he was dis-appointed. For though his physical condition gradually improved, he became more than ever acutely conscious of matters of health, and worried much also about his financial dependence. He was in a strange land, without his family, and homesickness rendered him weak.

Thinking perhaps of how his friend Salem Dutcher would have capitalized on the novel surroundings, Lanier wrote a series of three letters for the New York *World* (Dec. 27, 1872; Feb. 6, 1873; March 13, 1873), describing conditions in Texas (see pp. 187-201, below). The first of these recounts the experiences of his recent Austin-San Antonio stage journey, tracking closely his first letter from San Antonio to his wife, November 25, 1872—the stage driver, the crossing of the Colorado, the fellow-passengers, the German supper at New Braunfals—and ending with a treatise on the mesquit, " the apparitions of all the leafless peach-orchards in Georgia." The editor of the *World*, much to Lanier's disgust, cut all the letter except the section on the mesquit.[4]

[3] Letter of Aug. 26, 1870, from R. S. Lanier.
[4] See letter to Robert S. Lanier, Jan. 15, 1873. Edward King, in " Glimpses of Texas " (*Scribner's*, VII, 302 ff., Jan. 1874, later republished as Ch. XIII of *The Great South*, Hartford, 1875), writes a strikingly similar description of his stage journey over the same route, with mention of the fording of the Colorado, New Braunfals, the mesquits, and the passengers.

The second letter describes Indian raids in the Medina section, within fifty miles of Lanier, during January of 1873, the account following news stories in current issues of the San Antonio *Herald*. The third letter pictures Mexican and cattle troubles on the Rio Grande border, and likewise draws part of its material from the *Herald*. Lanier planned " to write up the Texas Legislature and Texas generally," but the " trifling compensation " paid by the *World* changed his plans.[5]

The three Texas letters represent Lanier's first frankly journalistic work, written to boil the pot rather than to further the art. It is therefore significant that they were anonymously published over the pen-name of " Otfall."

Since his arrival in San Antonio, Lanier had been engaged on a project more pretentious than the letters for the *World*.[6] This was an article on San Antonio, descriptive and historical, in which he hoped to picture the grotesquely mixed scene before him as well as to trace its romantic past. He worked industriously, relying for his information chiefly (1) on Frederick Law Olmsted's *A Journey through Texas*, a copy of which his father sent him from Georgia; [7] (2) on current issues of the San Antonio *Herald* and the *Texas Almanac* for 1873; (3) on his observation during desultory strolls and horseback rides in and about the city, and, most important of all, (4) on Henry Yoakum's *History of Texas*. From the Olmsted he picked up only scattered details, and from the *Herald* only statistics and news items that seemed to support his statements. But from the Yoakum he paraphrased and quoted extensively, the result sometimes suggesting skillful condensation rather than familiarity with the robust idiom of the frontier. Here is a typical example of Lanier's handling of material from Yoakum:

Yoakum writes:

They [the Americans] moved by file, and in the most profound silence, until they approached sufficiently near to hear the enemy's advanced guard. Here they sat down, with their arms in their hands, until they heard the Spaniards at matins. Orders were given that, on notice, the Americans should charge. This notice was to be given by a check from the right of each company, and in silence. The signal was given, and they all marched forward with a firmness and regularity becoming veteran soldiers. The enemy's pickets were surprised and taken prisoners. The Americans advanced to the works, mounted them, hauled down the Spanish flag, and ran up their own tri-color, before they were discovered by the Spanish camp. This was just at the dawn of day.

[5] Letters to Robert S. Lanier Jan. 7, 15, 1873.

[6] The day after his arrival he had written of " a magazine article I am concocting." See letter of Nov. 26, 1872.

[7] Requested in letter to Robert S. Lanier, Jan. 1, 1873.

Lanier writes:

In the darkness of the night of June 4th the Americans marched quietly out of town, by file, to within hearing of the enemy's pickets, and remained there until the enemy was heard at matins. The signal to charge being given—a cheer [sic] from the right of companies— the Americans advanced, surprised and captured the pickets in front, mounted the enemy's work, lowered his flag and hoisted their own, before they were fairly discovered through the dim dawn.[8]

Similar instances abound. Lanier frankly borrowed also Spanish phrases and even footnote translations of them from Yoakum. Whenever he quoted from another historical source, such as Henry S. Foote's *Texas and the Texans*, the same quotation usually appears in Yoakum.[9]

"San Antonio de Bexar," as Lanier decided to name his article, may be informally divided into three unequal sections. The first few paragraphs call attention to the strange contrasts and incongruous juxtapositions on every hand—in people, in architecture, even in climate—a theme to which Lanier recurred often in the essay. The main section is the historical sketch, from the beginnings of San Antonio in 1715 through its checkered fortunes of war, to the date of writing, 1873; the fullest treatment is accorded the years covered by Yoakum, 1715-1846. The last section, brief and catalogue-like, shows us the novel panorama passing before Lanier's eyes: the squatted Mexican woman washing her clothes on the banks of the many-bridged river, the Indian-fighter with his swagger and his scalps, the Mexican huts with their fringes of children, the promenading *cabellero* intent upon the subjugation of his womankind. It is genuinely disappointing to know that Lanier viewed these scenes and yet devoted most of his space to such topics as the La Harpe-D'Alarconne controversy or the San Antonio climate. It is the same disappointment that one feels when one realizes that Lanier listened to the music of the negro and the cracker, and yet often chose the more traditional patterns.

Lanier completed "San Antonio de Bexar" about the middle of February, 1873, and soon thereafter submitted it to William Hand Browne, of the *Southern Magazine*, which had two years before published "Retrospects and Prospects." It was accepted, and appeared five months later at about the same time that Lanier received his check for sixty-three dollars.[10]

[8] Yoakum, *History of Texas*, I, 172; Lanier, "San Antonio de Bexar," p. 219 of the present volume.

[9] For an instance, see the quotation attributed to Foote in "San Antonio de Bexar," p. 223 of the present volume; Yoakum (*History of Texas*, I, 366) quotes the same, with the source.

[10] *Southern Magazine*, XIII, 83-99, 138-152 (July-Aug., 1873); see letter from Turnbull Brothers, Aug. 9, 1873.

Lanier's final judgment on the essay was, " 'Tis but a poor piece." [11]
He could not know at that time that its value to him was far more
than the intrinsic worth of the essay itself. For it furnished practice
in assembling facts, interesting to the public, concerning an unfamiliar
locality, and thus prepared for the writing of *Florida*, to come two
years later. Furthermore, nothing could have been more wholesome
for his ornate prose style than commercial writing.

Even before the completion of " San Antonio de Bexar " Lanier
was planning to return to Georgia. He had gained strength slowly
but steadily, and his homesickness suggested many reasons for an
immediate return to his loved ones and to familiar scenes: the change-
able climate of San Antonio, his reluctance to accept further support
from kinsmen, the possibility of making " so much money with the
flute in the great cities," his belief that San Antonio was " doomed to
dwindle away," and even the danger of Indians! [12] Before the middle
of March he was back in Georgia, abandoning an environment that
might have brought him robust health, and with it a faster developing
artistic independence.

His most immediate need was money. The birth of a third son
soon after his return from Texas brought new debts, and his father's
second marriage complicated the family finances. There was talk of a
contract to write a history of Georgia, but the project never materialized.
Periodically he resolved to return to the law office, but his health
dictated otherwise. His subsequent engagement as first flutist in the
Peabody Orchestra, Baltimore, in December, 1873, at a salary of sixty
dollars a month only meagerly relieved the financial stress. He considered a college chair in metaphysics and also one in the physics of
music. He planned a series of articles in the style of Isaac Bickerstaff,
but none of these was ever published.[13] In a search for publishable
material, he resurrected a burlesque essay called " Peace " (pp. 247-
253, below), written four years earlier (October, 1870), and sold it
to the *Southern Magazine*, where it was duly published.[14] It is a
facetious description of the author's plight when he volunteered, for
one afternoon, to play nurse-maid to his two-year-old son Charlie and
his nephew Eddie Shannon of similar age, while their mothers " went
out,"—perhaps upon the occasion of the birth of Lanier's second son.[15]

[11] Letter to Virginia Hankins, July 17, 1873.
[12] See Letters, Jan. 12-Feb. 18, 1873.
[13] Two short MSS, perhaps incomplete, entitled " The Tatler," are preserved
in the Charles D. Lanier Collection, Johns Hopkins University. See also letter
of Sept. 13, 1874.
[14] *Southern Magazine*, XV, 406-410 (October, 1874).
[15] Almost a year later he wrote: " Charlie seems to have utterly lost his

The spring of 1875 brought serious reverses in the fight for health, and with each relapse the deepening discouragement of added debts.

Coming at such a moment of stress, Mr. A. Pope's proposal of a guide book to Florida seemed to Lanier like the Hand of Providence stretched out barely in time. The agreement was this: Lanier was to write a book descriptive of Richmond, Petersburg, Wilmington, Raleigh, Charlotte, Columbia, Augusta, Charleston, Savannah, Jacksonville, St. Augustine, and Florida generally—the territory served by Mr. Pope's railways,—recounting their histories, products, great men, and points of interest; it was to be at once a guide-book and a literary attraction. Mr. Pope was to pay for the work a salary of one hundred and twenty-five dollars per month for three months (April-June), plus all expenses. Here was a comfortable living wage for Lanier, with opportunity to travel, perhaps with his wife, in a region that promised health. No wonder that he exclaimed, with characteristic exuberance, " It doth soberly seem to me that God hath arranged this matter." [16] Recent publicity resulting from the publication of " Corn " and of a review of Paul Hamilton Hayne's Poems, as well as a winter of flute-playing in Baltimore, explains the selection of Lanier for this thinly disguised advertising project. His name was sufficiently well known to insure public notice, and the nature of his work thus far guaranteed that the proposed book would be more than the conventional travel-guide.

The " Poet-in-Ordinary to a long line of Railroad Corporations," as Lanier styled himself, lost little time. After a brief visit with his wife and sons in Brunswick, Georgia, he proceeded at once to Jacksonville, Florida, expecting his wife to follow in a few days to assist him in the actual writing down of his material, since this exercise often caused severe pain in his right lung. But circumstances rendered such assistance impracticable, and alone Lanier soon began a series of systematic fact-finding campaigns, using Jacksonville as the center of his operations.

His most enjoyable stay was in St. Augustine, where he fell into a " rage of delight " over old Fort Marion, and, as he walked the seawall, gave himself up to re-creating the ancient French-Spanish encounters on this very soil. He had been here only three days when (in a letter of May 14, 1875, to his wife) he reported progress: " I have

warlike disposition, and I think he will shortly retire from the army to resume the peaceful walks of life. The fatigues of his last campaign with Edward I appear to have given him an inclination for the gentler arts of peace." (Letter to Robert Lanier, Aug. 13, 1871.)

[16] Letter to Mary D. Lanier, Mar. 28, 1875. Lanier actually received the salary for six months, April-September.

written the first fifteen pages,"—probably the section which was to be Chapter XIII, " Historical," in the final arrangement. " I put on great airs therein," he added, " as if I were going to sum up and conclude the whole business, and forever remove the necessity of any more being said anent this country:—but 'tis hard work." Five days later he had well under way " On the Climate of Florida," to become Chapter XII. " St. Augustine in April," to become Chapter III, followed closely, undoubtedly the best section of the book. Lanier's witnessing the arrival of seventy-two Indians for imprisonment in old Fort Marion, and his sympathy for the sixteenth century atmosphere of the city lend to this chapter a noble interest and dignity of emotion not to be found elsewhere in the book.

His next excursion carried him up the St. John's River to Pilatka, to gather information for " The St. Johns and Indian Rivers " (to be Chapter VII), and thence up the Oclawaha, on the river-steamer *Marion*, among potentially the most vital materials he had yet encountered,—Florida crackers, negro boatsmen, alligator-infested swamps, and at the end of the journey the Silver Spring, concerning all of which he made careful notes for " The Oclawaha River," Chapter II. The section was actually written almost a month later at Savannah.[17]

A journey westward took him, now accompanied by his wife, to Gainesville (" The Lake City and Gainesville Country," Chapter VIII), Cedar Keys (" The Gulf Coast," Chapter V), and Tallahassee (" The Tallahassee Country," Chapter VI), where he was the guest of ex-Governor David S. Walker and his daughter, Florida. He did not visit the western portion of the state, but depended on information gathered in Tallahassee for Chapter IX, " West Florida," and used a similar method for Chapter XI, " The Key West Country," probably not going farther south than the lake region in Central Florida (" Lake Okeechobee and the Everglades," Chapter X).

" For Consumptives," Chapter XIV, though not directly the result of Florida travel, is more intimately associated with the author than any other portion of the book. Lanier begins the chapter with a frank statement that he is writing from the experience of his own apparently successful fight with the disease, and ends with sundry prescribed remedies, ranging from the " whiskey cure " to the flute-playing cure. The tinge of over-frankness here suggests a strong defensive attitude. He is so afraid of being charged with undue reticence that he sometimes unnecessarily sacrifices delicacy.

After much of the Florida portion of the book had gone to press, he wrote the brief sections on Charleston, Savannah, Augusta, and

[17] Letter to Mary D. Lanier, June 22, 1875.

other Atlantic Coastal cities ("Other Winter Resorts on the Route to Florida," Chapter XV), his wife and his friend Salem Dutcher assisting in this work, especially with reference to Augusta.

Lanier did not depend entirely on observation for his information about the localities he visited, but made use of much material from books. The most important of these—he carried it with him—was George R. Fairbanks, *History of Florida* (Philadelphia, 1871), which he quotes and paraphrases quite extensively, often citing his source. He draws material also from the same author's *History and Antiquities of the City of St. Augustine, Florida* (New York, 1858).[18] Virtually all the material for the chapter entitled "Historical" is drawn from Fairbanks, as well as substantial passages for other chapters.

Soon after his arrival in Florida, Lanier wrote to his wife (May 14, 1875), "Every day I find new books about Florida." His starting point was probably Daniel G. Brinton, *Florida and the South* (Philadelphia, 1869). In general plan and method Lanier owes more to this one hundred and thirty-six-page guide-book than to any other source. Headings read: "Historical," "Physical Geography of Florida," "The St. Johns River and St. Augustine," "Jacksonville to Tallahassee," "The Oklawaha River and the Silver Spring," "Fernandina to Cedar Keys," "Key West . . . and the Gulf Coast," "Chapter to Invalids," and "What Climate Shall be Chosen?" A comparison with Lanier's table of contents reveals a striking similarity in both plan and material. Furthermore, Brinton suggests a list of eight books, including Fairbanks's *The Spaniards in Florida*,[19] Sprague's *History of the Florida War*, McCall's *Letters from the Frontiers*, and Bache's *The Young Wrecker of the Florida Reef*, from all of which Lanier drew material. He was familiar also with a number of other guide-books concerning the region, especially with Charles Jones's *Appleton's Hand-Book of American Travel—Southern Tour* (New York, 1874), R. K. Sewall's *Sketches of St. Augustine* (New York, 1848), and Ledyard Bill's *A Winter in Florida* (New York, 1869). In addition, he drew from current newspapers and magazines, notably from the New York *Evening Post* and from Edward King's series of articles on the South in *Scribner's Monthly*.[20] Blodget's *Climatology of the United States* and Maury's *The Physical Geography of the Sea*[21] were particularly useful to him in the preparation of the chapter on climate.

---

[18] All known sources are cited in footnotes to the text in the present edition.

[19] The second edition of the author's earlier *The History and Antiquities of the City of St. Augustine, Florida* (N. Y., 1858).

[20] The *Post*, May 21, 1875; see p. 87 of the present volume. *Scribner's*, VII-IX, Nov. 1873-Dec. 1874; the entire series later appeared in book form, *The Great South* (Hartford, 1875).

[21] Lorin Blodget, *Climatology of the U. S.* (Phila., 1857); Lanier's copy, well

Lanier leaned heavily on a few reliable books concerning the Caro-
lina-Georgia regions. His chief sources here were George White's
Historical Collections of Georgia, B. R. Carroll's *Historical Collections
of South Carolina*, F. D. Lee and J. L. Agnew's *Historical Record of
the City of Savannah*, Francis S. Holmes's *Phosphate Rocks of South
Carolina*, and T. S. Arthur's *History of Georgia.* To the casual reader,
however, he seems to draw from far more numerous sources, since
Lanier in re-quoting from an author almost invariably assigns the passage to its original source: thus he assigns passages to the *Georgia
Gazette* which he is really re-quoting from George White, some to
Thomas Ashe or Oldmixon which he is re-quoting from Carroll, and
others to Francis Moore which he is re-quoting from Lee and Agnew.
It is significant that most of the serious digressions in *Florida* are
apparently caused by Lanier's desire to quote at length. It is so of his
digression on love and lovers, when he quotes Chaucer; of his digression on the pines, when he quotes Ruskin; of his digression on
infinity, when he quotes a medieval Latin song.[22]

Undoubtedly Lanier knew the classic Bernard Romans's *Natural
History of East and West Florida*, William Bartram's *Travels*, and
William C. Bryant's account of Florida,[23] but he apparently avoided
their materials. He did not include any kind of map, a rather strange
omission, it seems, especially when one remembers that every source
that Lanier consulted—from the cheapest guide-book to the most
authoritative history—contained at least one map. Perhaps Lanier
wished to avoid the appearance of a commercial guide-book, or perhaps
he felt that he might be obligated to indicate on a map only the
railways represented by his employers.

Before mid-July (1875) Lanier was ready to submit the Florida
material. He met Mr. Pope in Columbia, S. C., with the result: " I
read him much of the book,—here and there—and he seems greatly
pleased with my handiwork." [24] It remained to negotiate a contract
with a publisher. Though Lanier had earlier consulted Hurd and
Houghton, who had printed *Tiger-Lilies*, Lippincott's offer seemed
now more advantageous. The final contract stipulated: Mr. A. Pope,

annotated by him, bears the inscription, " For Mr. Pope's work in N. Carolina
and Georgia." Matthew F. Maury, *The Physical Geography of the Sea*, N. Y.,
1857; Lanier's copy was presented by ex-Governor David S. Walker, in whose
house Lanier had been a guest in Tallahassee. Both volumes are preserved in
Lanier's library, Johns Hopkins University.

[22] Pp. 27, 46, and 49, below.

[23] The last of these Lanier had found appended to George R. Fairbanks's
History and Antiquities of St. Augustine, Florida.

[24] Letter to Mary D. Lanier, July 13, 1875.

representing the railways, to pay for all plates and illustrations, and to continue Lanier's monthly salary ($125.00) until the completion of proof-reading; Lippincott to pay all other publishing and marketing costs; Mr. Pope to receive twenty-five per cent of the wholesale receipts, Lippincott the remaining seventy-five per cent.[25]

So much work remained to be done in finishing and revising the manuscript that Lanier decided to find a quiet boarding place in New York, where he remained during most of August. Matters were considerably complicated by Lippincott's agreement to publish chapters II ("The Ocklawaha River") and III ("St. Augustine in April") as articles in *Lippincott's Magazine*.[26] The arrangement meant a small additional sum of money for Lanier, and much additional labor. The illustrations also proved a source of worry. Mr. Pope had been so insistent that the book be richly adorned with local scenes that he had agreed to pay the entire illustrating cost of the book and half of that of the magazine articles, to insure that this feature of the work would not be restricted. *Florida* contains forty illustrations, all of them wood engravings, six of them full-page, and most of them signed by the firm of Van Ingen-Snyder.[27]

When Lanier lacked only "five days of steady work, more, in order to be freed from the dreadful bonds of the Florida book," he collapsed from over-exertion, with the usual serious hemorrhages.[28] His recovery was so slow that the completed manuscript was not in the printer's hands until the middle of October (1875), and Lanier read the last page of proof almost a month later.

After Lippincott released the book in November (1875), Lanier's family in Georgia sent reassuring praise. Mary Day Lanier reported that on Christmas night Clifford read *Florida* aloud to the family group in Montgomery, with Virginia Hankins also present:

Clifford is in a land of pure delight in reading "Florida." I think it a noble work and will live when "Florida travel" has passed away. In it I review our happy journey and sojourn in that land, and thus have a double delight in it.

Brother Clifford wrote: "*Florida* charms me and I have devoured the whole state, Saurians and all." [29]

[25] Letter to Mary D. Lanier, July 22, 1875.
[26] These appeared in the October and November (1875) issues, XVI, 403-413 and 537-550, identical with the chapters in *Florida* except for very minor verbal differences. The same chapters, with slight revisions, were reprinted in *Some Highways and Byways of American Travel*, by Edward Strahan and others (Phila., 1878).
[27] All except one omitted from the present edition (see vol. IX, facing p. 260).
[28] See letters to Mary D. Lanier, Sept. 5 and Sept. 9, 1875.
[29] See letters of 1876, note 1.

Lanier's own opinion of his book was undoubtedly colored by its associations with painful illness and work under strain. Upon receiving his first copy, he wrote to his wife (December, 1875):

It is very handsomely printed, bound and illustrated:—but I hate it with intense hatred, and I have no pleasure in it.

A little later, on February 12, 1876, he wrote to Mrs. Laura Boykin:

The book has been like a wound to me ever since I was engaged to write it; for, aside from the inherent difficulties of the commission (my instructions from my employers were simply to write them a guide-book which should be also a poem), I did not wish ever to appear before the public again save in the poetic character, and it was like being stabbed with a dull weapon to be compelled to put forth any more prose.

He had called it, in an earlier letter to Paul Hamilton Hayne (October 16, 1875), "a kind of spiritualized guide-book."

Lanier showed considerable anxiety concerning the forth-coming reviews. These were neither so numerous nor so favorable as Mr. Pope had hoped. The *Atlantic* and *Harper's* carried no notices at all. The reviewer of the *Nation*, writing of the chapter "St. Augustine in April," was not favorable:

It is more historical than descriptive, and Mr. Lanier's poetical licenses in prose are accordingly fewer than usual. . . . Even here his rhetorical-poetical foible of seeing "God in everything" displays itself once too often, in the passage where he speaks of "a morning which mingles infinite repose with infinite glittering, as if God should smile in his sleep." [30]

Then followed a comparison with the minor writer Mrs. Rebecca Harding Davis, a juxtaposition that angered Lanier. The criticism offered in the Chicago *Tribune* (Dec. 18, 1875) was better balanced, though Lanier found it most distasteful:

A writer who falls into ecstasies . . . over a running stream, a bit of still water, a passage in a forest, a wild turkey swimming, a negro plaintively whistling,—any thing under heaven that may possibly be considered romantic,—is not likely to be reckoned a safe guide through a foreign country. Yet if one has patience enough to bear with his frequent fits of frenzied raving, Mr. Lanier will, in the course of his book, impart a useful amount of intelligence concerning Florida. . . . His book, notwithstanding the merriment provoked by its exaggerated style, is really what it professes to be,—a serviceable guide-book to Florida.

[30] *Nation*, XXI, 277 (Oct. 28, 1875). See Lanier's comments in his letter of Oct. 29, 1875, to Bayard Taylor.

The Macon *Telegraph and Messenger* (Jan. 26, 1876), on the other hand, extravagantly praised the very quality condemned in most of the Northern notices:

It is impossible for Mr. Lanier to be commonplace in anything. The light of genius irradiates his thoughts and invests with grace and interest the simplest narrative of passing scenes and events. Ever wielding the pencil of the accomplished artist, also, not a forest picture, retired nook, glorious waterview, mossy grove, or picturesque group of human habitations escapes a place in his sketchbook.

The author's " accuracy of thought and clearness of expression which are characteristic of the legal profession," his " good sense and sound judgment," as well as his " cheerful talk given to consumptives " bring forth more praise. The Boston *Literary World* called the author " an easy and sometimes brilliant writer." [31]

No reviewer seemed to realize that *Florida* was the inevitable result of two conflicting desires in Lanier: on the one hand he was striving to make more palatable a task which was by its nature distasteful to him; on the other hand, he was too honest to shirk in any way the drudgery of fact-recording which his employers had a right to expect of the salaried writer of a guide-book. Thus he sought to render his work more agreeable and more sustaining of his fast growing reputation as a poet by indulging in flights of the imagination and sometimes absurdly extended figures, by expounding some of his favorite doctrines (as " progress toward etherealization," the " fever of the unrest of trade "), by quoting some of his favorite authors, and paying tribute to some of his new-made friends,—in short, by putting much of himself into *Florida*. If he had not done just this he would have been temperamentally unable to complete the disagreeable task assigned him. And yet he satisfied his conscience by including much appropriate factual information, such as weather charts, tables of distances, train schedules, and hotel lists.

The first edition of *Florida* carries the title-page:

FLORIDA / ITS / SCENERY, CLIMATE, AND HISTORY./ WITH / AN / ACCOUNT OF CHARLESTON, SAVANNAH, / AUGUSTA, AND AIKEN, AND A CHAPTER / FOR CONSUMPTIVES;/ BEING / A COMPLETE HAND-BOOK AND GUIDE./ BY / SIDNEY LANIER./ WITH NUMEROUS ILLUSTRATIONS./ PHILADELPHIA:/ J. B. LIPPINCOTT & CO./

It bears 1875 on its copyright notice, and has a four-page (263-266) appendix entitled " General Itinerary."

[31] *Literary World*, VI, 116 (Jan., 1876). No other reviews have been located.

The second edition, published in March, 1876, carries the title page:

FLORIDA:/ ITS SCENERY, CLIMATE, AND HISTORY./ WITH / AN ACCOUNT OF CHARLESTON, SAVANNAH,/ AUGUSTA, AND AIKEN; A CHAPTER FOR / CONSUMPTIVES; VARIOUS PAPERS / ON FRUIT-CULTURE;/ AND / A COMPLETE HAND-BOOK AND GUIDE./ BY / SIDNEY LANIER./ WITH NUMEROUS ILLUSTRATIONS./ PHILADEL-PHIA: / J. B. LIPPINCOTT & CO./ 1876./

For this second edition Lanier revised his earlier criticism concerning Henry Timrod, probably at the suggestion of his friends,[32] and added

[32] See p. 160 of the present edition. More than a year after the publication of this second edition, Paul Hamilton Hayne wrote to Lanier:

" Now, don't misunderstand, or be offended, Lanier, if I have a small, and not particularly black crow to pick with you!!, concerning a passage in your able book on *Florida*, a passage which has just caught my attention.

" *Involuntarily*, no doubt, your criticism on Timrod's poetry does it less than justice; at least, in the particular of *art*.

" One but slightly acquainted with his verse, or who had never read it, would derive from your remarks the impression that he was a half rustic-Bard, who never in the course of his thirty eight years of mortal life, had enjoyed the opportunity of associating with men eminent in letters, & was wholly ignorant of the great rules of poetic art.

" ' It is *thoroughly evident* from these (his lyrics)' you say, ' that he had never had time to learn the *mere craft of the poet*,—the *technique of verse* & that a broader association &c &c &c.'

" I must confess my astonishment at such a view as this!! Glancing over the many critiques, English & American, which were published on his vol., I find a remarkable agreement upon *one* point, (viz), in the Language of the *Athaeneum*, ' the singular delicacy & finish of T's versification; the unpretentious, but *exquisite art which conceals itself*!'

" Are ' Ethnogenesis,' ' The Cotton Boll,' ' Katie,' ' The Exotic,' and many other pieces, *not* admirable illustrations of the truth of this opinion?

" Moreover, let me tell you, that I have heard Timrod, for hours, discuss with scholars of the ' first water,' such men as Prof. Gildersleeve, formerly of *Göttingen*, now of the U. of Virginia,—the *profoundest* questions associated with both English & Latin prosody; displaying a subtle & minute acquaintance with his subject, which surprised those with whom he conversed. Excepting *Edgar Poe*, I don't believe the Southerner, nay, the American has ever existed, whose knowledge of the ' technique of verse' surpassed Timrod's. It is exemplified in his . . . [six lines cut out] it, to invest your notice with . . . well . . . what shall I call it? . . . a certain air of *posthumous patronage*, as if you had said: ' Come here my bonny lad; my clever " child," and let me pat you on the head! do you know that your " native wood-notes wild," are very graceful & musical? they please me much;—but oh! my sweet boy, what a pity it is you sing so completely by ear! If you had only been blessed with the chance of learning that poetry is not altogether confined to spontaneous bird-warblings! Oh, dear! how sad to reflect, that, probably, the " technique of verse," is a phrase you but dimly comprehend!'

" Upon my soul, Lanier, such is the impression produced by your notice, not on my mind merely (you may deem me *prejudiced* unduly in T's favor), but an elaborate appendix (pp. 263-336, treatises on horticulture, by various authorities, and a gazetteer of rivers and towns), which was stripped from copies sold at a reduced price.

Reprints were run off in 1877 and in 1881, all identical with the second edition.

The text of the present edition is that of 1876, without the appendix and with only one of the " numerous illustrations " (see IX, facing 260). No manuscript is known to exist except eight pages of notes in Lanier's hand, now in the Johns Hopkins University Library.

Before Lanier had finished proof for *Florida*, he had received a contract for the articles that were to be *Sketches of India* (pp. 254-323, below). On October 4, 1875, he wrote to Mary Day Lanier:

Mr. Kirk [editor of *Lippincott's Magazine*] has given me a job, of four ten-page articles on India to be richly illustrated from French plates sent over by J. B. Lippincott from Europe. I will have about $300 for the four papers: the first one to come out in January next.

The following month he devoted to feverish reading, for all his information must come from books. He found in the Philadelphia Free Library such sources as Appleton's *The Annual Encyclopedia* (1873), John Malcolm's *A Memoir of Central India* (London, 1823), Bayard Taylor's *India* (New York, 1859), and Charles Dilke's *Greater Britain* (Philadelphia, 1869). He was appalled at "a great French book, of a thousand pages, to be read." [33] His father sent a copy of John Hobart Caunter's *The Oriental Annual* (Vol. I, London, 1834). When Lanier was visiting Charlotte Cushman in Boston he found still other sources in the Public Library of that city, and it was here, as the guest of the actress that he began, at the Parker House, the actual writing of the first installment of the India Papers, on November 4. A week later he had completed it, and early in December it was in proof. By " toiling day and night " he completed the second article in time to receive pay for it before Christmas, and " with great labor and strain " he finished the third the first week of January.[34] On February 7, 1876, he wrote to Mary Day Lanier that he had finished the last one:

upon the minds of several highly cultivated persons—Northern men of letters—, to whom I showed your paragraph. . . ." (Letter from Hayne to Lanier, July 25, 1877. MS in the Charles D. Lanier Collection, Johns Hopkins University. No reply by Lanier has been found.)

[33] Letter to Mary D. Lanier, Oct. 12, 1875. The book referred to was probably François Bernier (1620-1688), *Histoire de la derniere revolution des etats du Grand Mogol* (Paris, 1670—published also under title *Voyages de*).

[34] Letters to Gibson Peacock, Nov. 4, 10, 1875; to Mary D. Lanier, Dec. 2, 15, 1875, and Jan. 8, 1876; to Clifford A. Lanier, Dec. 21, 1875.

The burden of it has been on my back so long that I still perceive it though it is now off, and I do not expect to feel otherwise than hump-back'd for several days.[35]

Almost immediately he fell seriously ill, again the victim of lung hemorrhages. This *tour de force*, "executed under the greatest imaginable disadvantages and under the leaden weight of limited time," had been too much for him.

In order to avoid any semblance of literary dishonesty in writing an account of a country which he had never seen, Lanier was careful to explain in the final paragraph of the last article that Bhima Gandharva was only another name for *Imagination*, the only traveling companion that honesty would permit under such circumstances. This embarrassing lack of first-hand information explains why he published the articles anonymously; it explains also why his Presbyterian conscience dictated meticulous care and unusual thoroughness, even for Lanier, in assembling his array of facts, all gleaned from books, in this case his only possible source. The result is a surprisingly entertaining and accurate, though very incomplete, account of India—its history, art, religion, and customs. When one gets through being amazed that Lanier accepted such a commission, especially in view of his condemnation of "trade," one has time to wonder why *Lippincott's* should have selected for the task a writer who had never visited India. Financial pressure is probably the explanation for Lanier; sympathy and friendship, for the editor of *Lippincott's*.

Though there is marked improvement in Lanier's prose style in the India sketches,—more restraint and more directness than in *Florida*—one looks in vain here for the real Lanier. He seems rather to be reserving all personal interest: he carefully avoided his favorite topic of Trade and its evils, so eloquently expounded in "The Symphony," and he missed all the contemplative opportunities of his earlier "Nirvana." Perhaps he felt that the creed of Hindooism, chiefly fear and horror, was far removed from his own philosophy of love. Instead of giving himself, he substituted a superficial and popular appeal, the result of a quick gleaning.

The spring of 1876 was a most difficult season for Lanier. Exhausting train trips to New York, Montgomery, Macon, Baltimore, and Boston sapped most of his remaining strength. The bitter criticism of his Centennial Cantata was an emotional ordeal for him, and when his project of writing a memoir of Charlotte Cushman failed to materialize he faced the prospect of actual want. He borrowed again from both his father and his brother, and tried to negotiate another

[35] The four articles appeared, without a break in the sequence, in *Lippincott's Magazine*, XVII, 37-51, 172-183, 283-301, 409-427 (Jan.-April, 1876).

loan from his New York kinsman, J. F. D. Lanier. When in June he retreated to the village of West Chester, not far from Philadelphia, those who saw him felt that he might not live out the month. But gradually he drew from the surrounding country the bodily strength and the emotional calm to begin his struggle all over again.

It is quite fitting that "The Story of a Proverb," I (pp. 324-330, below) should belong to this period of recuperation and re-building of hope, when, with his boys and his wife, he was enjoying for a few weeks respite from his usual struggle.

Lanier called the piece a little *extravaganza* that "one might ' make up as he went along' for a lot of children about his knees." [36] It relates the story, with many intentional incongruities, of how a wise young poet, gifted with common-sense, found royal favor by shoeing the royal feet—entirely the invention of Lanier's imagination. He sold it to *St. Nicholas Magazine* for twenty-four dollars, and the next spring he was reading the proof at Tampa, Florida, and praising enthusiastically the elaborate illustrations—wood-cuts—by E. B. Bensell.[37]

"The Story of a Proverb," II, sub-titled "A Fairy Tale for Grown People" (pp. 331-339, below), continues the success-story of the young poet, now called Genius, who wisely rules the kingdom as the Grand Vizier. The child-machinery only thinly disguises Lanier's evident purpose of roundly scolding his critics. For he wrote it during the summer of 1877, when the wounds of the Centennial Cantata controversy were still fresh; and perhaps, too, he was becoming a little self-conscious about the importance of the Poet. *Lippincott's Magazine* paid twenty-five dollars for it.[38]

"Bob: The Story of our Mocking Bird" (pp. 340-349, below) belongs in the same category as the two proverbs. It was inspired by Charles Day Lanier's pet, which for two years had been chief entertainer for the family.[39] While the delicately humanized story of the mocking bird is written for Lanier's own small boys, the appended moral is not for children. The lesson—that the greater the genius the more willing he is to cage himself in the conventions as a means of attaining his high goal—suggests that Lanier had been wrestling with the problem of Walt Whitman, whose *Leaves of Grass* he had lately read. Apparently conventions had become irksome enough to need justification, and so they are compared to the cage which has

---

[36] Letter to Gibson Peacock, Apr. 26, 1877.

[37] *St. Nicholas Magazine*, IV, 468-472 (May, 1877).

[38] *Lippincott's*, XXIII, 109-113 (Jan., 1879).

[39] See letter to Richard Malcolm Johnston and accompanying note, May 21, 1878; also the sonnet written on the occasion of the bird's death, printed in vol. I of the present edition.

enabled the bird-artist to carry his songs into the hearts of human beings.

To this same group of ephemeral prose pieces belong also the two "letters" to J. F. D. Lanier [40] of New York, in which Lanier attempts to trace the family genealogy (see pp. 350-376, below). A long series of personal favors, beginning with the underwriting of the publication of *Tiger-Lilies* in 1867 and ending with a two-thousand-dollar loan in 1878, peculiarly obligated Sidney Lanier. Knowing his kinsman's interest in matters of ancestry, he spent many hours during July, 1877, in collecting from such books as Horace Walpole's (1717-1797) *Anecdotes of Painting in England*, and Charles Burney's (1726-1814) *History of Music* in the Peabody Library (Baltimore) information concerning former Laniers. Though the claims of descent from Queen Elizabeth's court musicians and from George Washington are in error,[41] the letters contain valuable facts concerning the nineteenth century family. The first of these letters was printed as an appendix to the second edition (1877) of his kinsman's brief autobiography.[42] The second letter was inspired by Lanier's stumbling across additional information concerning Jerome and Nicholas Lanier while he was preparing the lectures to be delivered at Mrs. Edgeworth Bird's home.[43]

So ends the list of Lanier's prose pot-boilers of the 1870's.[44] Through them all runs one characteristic, in most cases their best claim to importance: they contain the unmistakable evidence of the struggle going on in Lanier. These prose pieces are the record of the battle he waged. The conflict springs primarily from physical causes—the fight for life against tuberculosis; but financial matters become inex-

[40] James Franklin Doughty Lanier (1800-1881), born in North Carolina, practised law in Indiana. He later became one of New York's chief bankers and financiers after extensive speculation in Western railroads. He was financial advisor to Lincoln, and lent large sums to the Federal Government during the War Between the States. He consistently befriended Sidney Lanier, making loans and urging political appointment.

[41] See L. E. Jackson and A. H. Starke, "New Light on the Ancestry of Sidney Lanier," *Virginia Historical Magazine*, XLIII, 160-168 (April, 1935).

[42] *Sketch of the Life of J. F. D. Lanier*, New York, 1871. John S. Mayfield states (*Sidney Lanier in Texas*, Dallas, 1932), without citing authority, that Lanier received twenty-five dollars for this letter.

[43] Letter to J. F. D. Lanier, Apr. 30, 1878. An account of these lectures is given in the introduction to vol. III of the present edition.

[44] The four books that Lanier edited for boys, though in a sense pot-boilers, grew out of his studies in the history of English literature preparatory to his lectures at the Peabody Institute and Johns Hopkins. Hence they are treated in vol. IV of the present edition.

tricably involved,[45] and even the deeper matter of a conflict between the new and the old channels of thought.

Lanier's imprisonment at Point Lookout hastened the possibility of tuberculosis into the reality, and the death of his mother from the disease in 1865 made him acutely aware of the shadow. The remainder of his life may be divided into seven periods—climaxed by the years 1868, 1870, 1872, 1876, 1877, 1879, and 1881—each marked by a desperate attack of the disease, with hemorrhages, followed (except the last) by an increasingly slow recovery.

Such a condition inevitably colored Lanier's outlook, and his point of view became at times that of an invalid, keenly conscious of health and death. Thus he describes his first son as " rare-lunged "; and he writes to Paul Hamilton Hayne of making " Death dainty," and to Virginia Hankins of death and himself " waging a mighty war." [46] His " The Stirrup Cup " is evidence of the same emphasis.

Furthermore, his illness altered directly the facts of his life, as well as its extent. It dictated that this man, by tradition so peculiarly localized, should become more broadly traveled, from Texas to Florida, from Tennessee to Boston. It certainly caused the wasteful dissipation of his energies over areas foreign to his genius, and, through enforced work on such projects as *Florida* and *India*, led him to attempt what he called " research," an activity for which he was not fitted either by training or by temperament.[47]

But most of all, this prolonged struggle for life seriously affected Lanier's thinking and his art. It curtailed the boldness of his thought, at times almost to the point of timidity, for it is doubly difficult for a man with one foot in the grave to propose a serious disturbing of the well marked paths.[48] As a result, what promised at times to be a very daring imagination too often became merely ornate fancy. His ill health fostered an alignment with the past and so opened the door to sentimentalism; one may sometimes even suspect that his interest in medievalism was partly due to his willingness to escape from a present

[45] " I am perfectly clear in my own mind that a steady income of a hundred dollars a month . . . would make me a well man, comparatively."—Lanier to his father, Oct. 21, 1877; see also letters of Sept. 11, 1877, and Feb. 17, 1879.

[46] See letter to Milton H. Northrup, Mar. 15, 1869; to Paul Hayne, Mar. 5, 1870; to Virginia Hankins, Nov. 30, 1869.

[47] Cf. letter to Daniel C. Gilman, Sept. 26, 1877. The later Peabody and Hopkins lectures, however, give evidence of considerable skill as an amateur scholar.

[48] It was not until 1875 that Lanier could write: " In this little song I have begun to dare to give myself some of the freedom in my own peculiar style," and even as late as 1876 he recorded that he shrank " from the criticism which I fear my poem will provoke." See letter to Buck, Feb. 1, 1876.

that defied traditional patterns.   Certainly his fear of pity and charity caused him to be over-sensitive to both favorable and adverse criticism, and caused him also to take himself far too seriously, thus marring what otherwise would have been a robust sense of humor.   His desire not to appear sensitive, especially about matters of health, often led him into naïve frankness.

And yet there remains one compensation for all the dreary struggle: the simple fact of conflict.   Without it, Lanier's life would lack much of dramatic power; his message might even sink to the level of insipid effusion.   It is this conflict, definitely associated with his health and with his prose " pot-boilers," yet reaching beyond physical boundaries, that in the last analysis lines up in the life and work of Lanier the forces of his real battle,—on one side, tradition, on the other, progress.

FLORIDA

FLORIDA:

ITS

SCENERY, CLIMATE, AND HISTORY.

WITH

AN ACCOUNT OF CHARLESTON, SAVANNAH,
AUGUSTA, AND AIKEN; A CHAPTER FOR
CONSUMPTIVES; VARIOUS PAPERS
ON FRUIT-CULTURE:

AND

A COMPLETE HAND-BOOK AND GUIDE.

BY

SIDNEY LANIER.

WITH NUMEROUS ILLUSTRATIONS.

PHILADELPHIA:
J. B. LIPPINCOTT & CO,
1876.

[Title-page of the second edition, the text here followed.]

CONTENTS *

* [Reproduced from the original edition, except that the page numbers have been altered to refer to the present edition and the appendices have been omitted, since they were not written by Lanier.—ED.]

CONTENTS

CHAPTER I

INTRODUCTORY

IF JUST before crystallization the particles of a substance should become a little uncertain as to the precise forms in which to arrange themselves, they would accurately represent a certain moment of lull which occurs in the formation of popular judgments a little while after the shock of the beginning, and which lasts until some authentic *résumé* of the facts spreads itself about and organizes a definite average opinion.

Such a moment—what one might call the moment of molecular indecisions—would seem to have now arrived in the course of formation of an intelligent opinion upon that singular Florida which by its very peninsular curve whimsically terminates the United States in an interrogation-point. Among the fifteen to twenty thousand persons who visited the State during this last winter of '74-5 there are probably fifteen to twenty thousand more or less vague — and therefore more or less differing—impressions of it.

How, indeed, could it be otherwise? Florida is the name as well of a climate as of a country; and — all commonplace weather-discussions to the contrary notwithstanding—no subject of investigation requires more positive study, more patient examination of observed facts, more rigorous elimination of what the astronomers call the personal equation, than a climate.

It is not in a month, in a year, in ten years, that a climate reveals itself. To know it, one must collate accurate readings, for long periods, of the thermometer, of the rain-gauge, of the instruments that record the air's moisture, of the weathercock, of the clouds; one must consider its relations to the lands, to the waters, to the tracks of general storms, to the breeding-places of local storms, to a hundred circumstances of environment, soil, tree-growth, and the like; and, finally, one must religiously disbelieve every word of what ordinary healthy people tell one about it. The ignorance of intelligent men and women about the atmospheric conditions amid which they live is as amazing to one who first comes bump against it as it is droll to one who has grown familiar with its solid enormity. But a

7

little time ago a former resident of San Francisco, in reply to
my question about its climate, declared it was noble, it was
glorious, it was fit for the gods; and another, answering the
same interrogatory, informed me it was perfectly beastly. Which
is, in truth, as it should be. What business have healthy people
with climates? Thomas Carlyle long ago remarked that in our
political economies, as in our physical ones, we only become
conscious of things when they commence to go wrong.* Indeed,
this truth was not wholly outside of the experience of Carlyle
himself: for he—whom, with all his faults, one cannot call
otherwise than the magnificent old earnest man—once related
to an American visitor how in the course of a long and bitter
religious struggle of his early manhood, which lasted for weeks,
and during which his dietary was left to shift for itself, he became mournfully aware that he, too, was personally the owner
of what he called in his sturdy Scotch a *stammock*, and had
never since been at all able to forget this dyspeptic addition
to his stock of learning.

When one's lungs or one's nerves get sick, one acquires the
sense of lungs or of nerves: and then also one becomes for
the first time aware of climate. But not by any means truthfully
aware of it; for if, as has been said, a man ought religiously to
disbelieve all that healthy people tell him about climates, he
should absolutely take to his heels and flee afar off when an
invalid begins to discourse on this topic, unless that invalid
talks strictly by the thermometer.

There was poor Slimlegs, for instance (this present writer
used to be a "consumptive," and out of the very fervor of his
desire to do something towards lessening the wretchedness of
those who are now being or to be "consumed," he draws the
right to speak of them as he likes, even to a little tender abuse),
—there, I say, was Slimlegs: we all saw him here in Florida
last winter, on Bay Street in Jacksonville, or on the Plaza at
St. Augustine, or somewhere else and we all know how, after
he had arrived and had his breakfast and taken his poor little
shambling stroll around the square, he would go to his room
and write back home to Dr. Physic what he thought of the
Florida climate. Now, it is not in the least extravagant to assert
that, in nine cases out of ten, Slimlegs's opinion of the climate

* ["Characteristics," in *Critical and Miscellaneous Essays.*—Ed.]

was based upon one solitary observation of one solitary gastronomic circumstance, to wit, the actual rareness of the steak at breakfast as compared with the ideal rareness which suits Slimlegs's individual taste,—or some other the like phenomenon. Of course, it cannot be denied that these two are enormous factors in daily human life: nor that, if they are equal to each other—which is to say, if the actual steak coincides with one's idiosyncratic ideal steak—the weather is apt to be pleasant; and to this extent beef and gridirons are meteorological elements.

But, my honest Slimlegs, Reclus does not mention them, nor does Blasius, nor Doggett, nor any other of the recognized authorities in these matters.* Here is what Reclus defines a climate to be: " All the facts of physical geography, the relief of continents and of islands, the height and direction of the systems of mountains, the extent of forests, savannas, and cultivated lands, the width of valleys, the abundance of rivers, the outline of the coasts, the marine currents and winds, and all the meteoric phenomena of the atmosphere, vapors, fogs, clouds, rains, lightnings, and thunders, magnetic currents, or as Hippocrates said more briefly, ' the places, the waters, and the airs.' "

These invalids' letters are not, it is true, the only things that have been written about Florida. The newspapers have abounded with communications from clever correspondents who have done the State in a week or two; the magazinists have chatted very pleasantly of St. Augustine and the Indian River country; and there are half a dozen guide-books giving more or less details of the routes, hotels, and principal stopping-points.

But it is not in clever newspaper paragraphs, it is not in chatty magazine papers, it is not in guide-books written while the cars are running, that the enormous phenomenon of Florida is to be disposed of. There are at least claims here which reach into some of the deepest needs of modern life.

The question of Florida is a question of an indefinite enlargement of many people's pleasures and of many people's existences as against that universal killing ague of modern life—the fever of the unrest of trade throbbing through the long chill of a seven-months' winter.

For there are some who declare that here is a country which,

---

* [J. J. Élisée Reclus (1830-1905), Johann H. Blasius (1809-1870), and David S. Doggett (1810-1880), all authorities on physical geography and related matters.—ED.]

while presenting in its Jacksonville, its St. Augustine, its Green
Cove Springs, and the like, the gayest blossoms of metropolitan
midwinter life, at the same time spreads immediately around
these a vast green leafage of rests and balms and salutary
influences.

Wandering here, one comes to think it more than a fancy
that the land itself has caught the grave and stately courtesies
of the antique Spaniards, and reproduced them in the profound
reserves of its forests, in the smooth and glittering suavities of
its lakes, in the large curves, and gracious inclinations of its
rivers and sea-shores. Here one has an instinct that it is one's
duty to repose broad-faced upward, like fields in the fall, and
to lie fallow under suns and airs that shed unspeakable fertiliza-
tions upon body and spirit. Here there develops itself a just
proportion between quietude and activity: one becomes aware
of a possible tranquillity that is larger than unrest and contains
it as the greater the less.

Here, walking under trees which are as powerful as they are
still, amidst vines which forever aspire but never bustle, by large
waters that bear their burdens without flippant noise, one finds
innumerable strange and instructive contrasts exhaling from
one's contemplations; one glides insensibly out of the notion
that these multiform beauties are familiar appearances of vegetable growths and of water expanses; no, it is Silence, which,
denied access to man's ear, has caught these forms and set forth
in them a new passionate appeal to man's eye; it is Music in a
siesta; it is Conflict, dead, and reappearing as Beauty; it is
amiable Mystery, grown communicative; it is Nature with her
finger on her lip,—gesture of double significance, implying that
one may kiss her if one will be still and say nothing about it;
it is Tranquillity, suavely waving aside men's excuses for chafferings and for wars; it is true Trade done into leafage—a multitudinous leaf-typification of the ideal *quid pro quo*, shown forth
in the lavish good measure of that interchange by which the
leaves use man's breath and return him the same in better condition than when they borrowed it, so paying profitable usuries
for what the lender could not help loaning; it is a Reply, in all
languages, yet in no words, to those manifold interrogations of
heaven which go up daily from divers people—from business-
men who, with little time for thinking of anything outside of
their rigorous routines, do nevertheless occasionally come to a

point in life where they desire some little concise revelation of the enormous Besides and Overplus which they keenly suspect to lie beyond all trade; from families stricken into terror by those sudden gulfs which in our tempting hot modern civilization so often crack open and devour sons and daughters, and fathers and husbands; from students, who dimly behold a world of the inexplicably sweet beyond the field of conquerable knowledge; from the sick man, querulously wondering if he can anywhere find companions who will not shudder when he coughs, and friends who will not coddle him with pitiful absurdities nor sicken him with medicines administered not because they are known to cure but on the dismal principle of *lege artis*; from pleasure-seekers, who never quite succeed in ignoring a certain little secret wish that there might be Something Else after the hop is over at the hotel.

When one finds one's commission reading simply, *where there are trees and water, to persuade men to go to them,* two methods of discharging it present themselves. These are the poetical or descriptive and the practical or guide-book methods. It would seem that one need not hesitate to adopt both: they have the singular advantage that if successful they merge into each other; for if the poetical method draw men to nature, then it becomes practical, and if the practical method draw them there, it becomes, at least in its results, poetical.

In view of many absurdly hysterical utterances which have been made touching the tropical ravishments and paradisaical glories of Florida, it is proper to say at this point that the State is not remarkable for beauty of landscape, and that persons— particularly those from hill-countries—who should go to Florida for this sole end would certainly be disappointed.

There *are* places where ecstasies are legitimate, as one may hope will fully appear hereinafter; but, with the exception of the beautiful Tallahassee region, the land is either level or only very gently rolling, and as seen from the railways or the country-roads it always shows even the most unpicturesque aspect of its levelness, owing to the fact that the roads run usually through the open pine barrens, instead of the much more interesting hammocks which are pierced by the road-makers with difficulty in consequence of the very magnificence of growth that renders them beautiful.

Nor is the whole earth in Florida simply one tangle of tube-
roses and japonicas, as the guide-books fable. It seems even
ruthless to break up the popular superstition that Florida was
named so because of its floweriness. But truth is, after all, the
most beautiful thing under heaven; and there does not seem to
be the least doubt that Ponce de Leon named this country
Florida because the day on which he made the land was the
day called in his calendar *Pascua Florida*, or Palm-Sunday.

But so much being said in abundant protection of strict truth,
one can now go on to detail (without the haunting fear of being
classed among the designing hysterical ones) the thousand
charms of air, water, tree, and flower which are to be found in
Florida, and which remain there practicable all the winter days.

With these views, the next eleven chapters contain some account of the Ocklawaha River in May, St. Augustine in April,
Jacksonville in January, the Gulf Coast, the Tallahassee country
or Piedmont Florida, the St. Johns and Indian Rivers, the Gainesville country, West Florida, Lake Okeechobee and the Everglades, and the Key West country; these being disposed in separate and unconnected chapters, and in an order for which there
is no particular reason why there should be any reason. Chapter
twelve discusses those physical conditions existing in the nature
and environment of Florida which go to make up its very remarkable climate, and presents tables of temperatures, frosts,
winds, cloudy days, and the like, for various portions of the
State. Chapter thirteen is devoted to a historical sketch. Chapter
fourteen concerns itself particularly with invalids, and chapter
fifteen with accounts of the other winter-resorts which lie on
the route—Charleston, Savannah, Augusta, and Aiken. To these
is added an Appendix which contains papers from various
authoritative hands on the culture of Florida tobaccos, oranges,
strawberries, figs, bananas, and sugar-cane; such portions of the
last report of Hon. Dennis Eagan, Commissioner of Lands and
Emigration, as are of interest to intending purchasers or settlers;
an Itinerary, showing the routes to and in Florida; and an alphabetically arranged Gazetteer which embodies various items of
information as to the towns, rivers, and counties of the State....*

* [The original text further explains the Gazetteer, which is omitted from the
present edition along with the Itinerary and the Appendices, since none of them
were written by Lanier.—ED.]

CHAPTER II

THE OCKLAWAHA RIVER

FOR A PERFECT journey God gave us a perfect day. The little Ocklawaha steamboat *Marion* * — a steamboat which is like nothing in the world so much as a Pensacola gopher with a preposterously exaggerated back — had started from Pilatka some hours before daylight, having taken on her passengers the night previous; and by seven o'clock of such a May morning as no words could describe unless words were themselves May mornings we had made the twenty-five miles up the St. Johns, to where the Ocklawaha flows into that stream nearly opposite Welaka, one hundred miles above Jacksonville.

Just before entering the mouth of the river our little gopher-boat scrambled alongside a long raft of pine-logs which had been brought in separate sections down the Ocklawaha and took off the lumbermen, to carry them back for another descent while this raft was being towed by a tug to Jacksonville.

Observe that man who is now stepping from the wet logs to the bow of the *Marion*—how can he ever cut down a tree? He is a slim native, and there is not bone enough in his whole body to make the left leg of a good English coal-heaver: moreover, he does not seem to have the least idea that a man needs grooming. He is disheveled and wry-trussed to the last degree; his poor weasel jaws nearly touch their inner sides as they suck at the acrid ashes in his dreadful pipe; and there is no single filament of either his hair or his beard that does not look sourly, and at wild angles, upon its neighbor filament. His eyes are viscidly unquiet; his nose is merely dreariness come to a point; the corners of his mouth are pendulous with that sort of suffering which does not involve any heroism, such as being out of tobacco, waiting for the corn-bread to get cooked, and the like; his—— But, poor devil! I withdraw all these remarks. He has a right to look disheveled, or any other way he likes. For

* [For a picture of the *Marion* on the Ocklawaha see *Scribner's Monthly*, IX, 1 (Nov., 1874). The same picture became the frontispiece in Edward King, *The Great South* (Hartford, 1875), a copy of which Lanier owned.—ED.]

listen: "Waal, sir," he says, with a dilute smile, as he wearily leans his arm against the low deck where I am sitting, "ef we did'n' have ther *sentermentillest* rain right thar last night, I'll be dad-busted!"

He had been in it all night.

Presently we rounded the raft, abandoned the broad and garish highway of the St. Johns, and turned off to the right into the narrow lane of the Ocklawaha, the sweetest water-lane in the world, a lane which runs for more than a hundred and fifty miles of pure delight betwixt hedgerows of oaks and cypresses and palms and bays and magnolias and mosses and manifold vine-growths, a lane clean to travel along for there is never a speck of dust in it save the blue dust and gold dust which the wind blows out of the flags and lilies, a lane which is as if a typical woods-stroll had taken shape and as if God had turned into water and trees the recollection of some meditative ramble through the lonely seclusions of His own soul.

As we advanced up the stream our wee craft even seemed to emit her steam in more leisurely whiffs, as one puffs one's cigar in a contemplative walk through the forest. Dick, the pole-man —a man of marvelous fine functions when we shall presently come to the short, narrow curves—lay asleep on the guards, in great peril of rolling into the river over the three inches between his length and the edge; the people of the boat moved not, and spoke not; the white crane, the curlew, the limpkin, the heron, the water-turkey, were scarcely disturbed in their quiet avocations as we passed, and quickly succeeded in persuading themselves after each momentary excitement of our gliding by that we were really after all no monster, but only some day-dream of a monster. The stream, which in its broader stretches reflected the sky so perfectly that it seemed a riband of heaven bound in lovely doublings along the breast of the land, now began to narrow: the blue of heaven disappeared, and the green of the overleaning trees assumed its place. The lucent current lost all semblance of water. It was simply a distillation of many-shaded foliages, smoothly sweeping along beneath us. It was green trees, fluent. One felt that a subtle amalgamation and mutual give-and-take had been effected between the natures of water and leaves. A certain sense of pellucidness seemed to breathe coolly out of the woods on either

side of us; and the glassy dream of a forest over which we
sailed appeared to send up exhalations of balms and odors and
stimulant pungencies.

"Look at that snake in the water!" said a gentleman, as we
sat on deck with the engineer, just come up from his watch.
The engineer smiled. "Sir, it is a water-turkey," he said, gently.

The water-turkey is the most preposterous bird within the
range of ornithology. He is not a bird, he is a neck, with such
subordinate rights, members, appurtenances and hereditaments
thereunto appertaining as seem necessary to that end. He has
just enough stomach to arrange nourishment for his neck, just
enough wings to fly painfully along with his neck, and just big
enough legs to keep his neck from dragging on the ground; and
his neck is light-colored, while the rest of him is black. When
he saw us he jumped up on a limb and stared. Then suddenly
he dropped into the water, sank like a leaden ball out of sight,
and made us think he was drowned,—when presently the tip of
his beak appeared, then the length of his neck lay along the
surface of the water, and in this position, with his body submerged, he shot out his neck, drew it back, wriggled it, twisted
it, twiddled it, and spirally poked it into the east, the west, the
north, and the south, with a violence of involution and a con-
tortionary energy that made one think in the same breath of
corkscrews and of lightnings. But what nonsense! All that labor
and perilous asphyxiation—for a beggarly sprat or a couple of
inches of water-snake!

But I make no doubt he would have thought us as absurd as
we him if he could have seen us taking *our* breakfast a few
minutes later: for as we sat there, some half-dozen men at table,
all that sombre melancholy which comes over the American at
his meals descended upon us; no man talked, each of us could
hear the other crunch his bread *in faucibus*, and the noise thereof
seemed in the ghostly stillness like the noise of earthquakes
and of crashing worlds; even the furtive glances towards each
other's plates were presently awed down to a sullen gazing of
each into his own: the silence increased, the noises became intolerable, a cold sweat broke out over at least one of us, he felt
himself growing insane, and rushed out to the deck with a sigh
as of one saved from a dreadful death by social suffocation.

There is a certain position a man can assume on board the

steamer *Marion* which constitutes an attitude of perfect rest, and leaves one's body in such blessed ease that one's soul receives the heavenly influences of the Ocklawaha sail absolutely without physical impediment.

Know, therefore, tired friend that shall hereafter ride up the Ocklawaha on the *Marion*—whose name I would fain call Legion—that if you will place a chair just in the narrow passage-way which runs alongside the cabin, at the point where this passage-way descends by a step to the open space in front of the pilot-house, on the left-hand side facing to the bow, you will perceive a certain slope in the railing where it descends by an angle of some thirty degrees to accommodate itself to the step aforesaid; and this slope should be in such a position as that your left leg unconsciously stretches itself along the same by the pure insinuating solicitations of the fitness of things, and straightway dreams itself off into an Elysian tranquillity. You should then tip your chair in a slightly diagonal position back to the side of the cabin, so that your head will rest thereagainst, your right arm will hang over the chair-back, and your left arm will repose on the railing. I give no specific instruction for your right leg, because I am disposed to be liberal in this matter and to leave some gracious scope for personal idiosyncrasies as well as a margin of allowance for the accidents of time and place; dispose your right leg, therefore, as your heart may suggest, or as all the precedent forces of time and the universe may have combined to require you.

Having secured this attitude, open wide the eyes of your body and your soul; repulse with a heavenly suavity the conversational advances of the drummer who fancies he might possibly sell you a bill of white goods and notions, as well as the polite inquiries of the real-estate person who has his little private theory that you are in search of an orange-grove to purchase; then sail, sail, sail, through the cypresses, through the vines, through the May day, through the floating suggestions of the unutterable that comes up, that sink down, that waver and sway hither and thither; and so shall you have revelations of rest, and so shall your heart forever afterwards interpret Ocklawaha to mean repose.

Some twenty miles from the mouth of the Ocklawaha, at

the right-hand edge of the stream, is the handsomest residence
in America. It belongs to a certain alligator of my acquaintance,
a very honest and worthy saurian, of good repute. A little cove
of water, dark green under the overhanging leaves, placid,
pellucid, curves round at the river-edge into the flags and lilies,
with a curve just heart-breaking for the pure beauty of the
flexure of it. This house of my saurian is divided into apartments—little subsidiary bays which are scalloped out by the lily-
pads according to the sinuous fantasies of their growth. My
saurian, when he desires to sleep, has but to lie down anywhere:
he will find marvelous mosses for his mattress beneath him;
his sheets will be white lily-petals; and the green disks of the
lily-pads will straightway embroider themselves together above
him for his coverlet. He never quarrels with his cook, he is not
the slave of a kitchen, and his one house-maid—the stream—
forever sweeps his chambers clean. His conservatories there
under the glass of that water are ever and without labor filled
with the enchantments of strange under-water growths; his
parks and his pleasure-grounds are bigger than any king's. Upon
my saurian's house the winds have no power, the rains are only
a new delight to him, and the snows he will never see. Regarding fire, as he does not employ its slavery, so he does not fear its
tyranny. Thus, all the elements are the friends of my saurian's
house. While he sleeps he is being bathed. What glory to
awake sweetened and freshened by the sole careless act of
sleep!

Lastly, my saurian has unnumbered mansions, and can change
his dwelling as no human householder may; it is but a filip of
his tail, and lo! he is established in another place as good as the
last, ready furnished to his liking.

For many miles together the Ocklawaha is a river without
banks, though not less clearly defined as a stream for that
reason. The swift, deep current meanders between tall lines of
trees; beyond these, on each side, there is water also,—a
thousand shallow rivulets lapsing past the bases of multitudes
of trees. Along the immediate edges of the stream every tree-
trunk, sapling, stump, or other projecting coign of vantage is
wrapped about with a close-growing vine. At first, like an
unending procession of nuns disposed along the aisle of a

church these vine-figures stand. But presently, as one journeys, this nun-imagery fades out of one's mind, and a thousand other fancies float with ever-new vine-shapes into one's eyes. One sees repeated all the forms one has ever known, in grotesque juxtaposition. Look! here is a great troop of girls, with arms wreathed over their heads, dancing down into the water; here are high velvet arm-chairs and lovely green fauteuils of divers pattern and of softest cushionment; there the vines hang in loops, in pavilions, in columns, in arches, in caves, in pyramids, in women's tresses, in harps and lyres, in globular mountain-ranges, in pagodas, domes, minarets, machicolated towers, dogs, belfries, draperies, fish, dragons. Yonder is a bizarre congress— Una on her lion, Angelo's Moses, two elephants with howdahs, the Laocoön group, Arthur and Lancelot with great brands extended aloft in combat, Adam bent with love and grief leading Eve out of Paradise, Cæsar shrouded in his mantle receiving his stabs, Greek chariots, locomotives, brazen shields and cuirasses, columbiads, the twelve Apostles, the stock exchange. It is a green dance of all things and times.

The edges of the stream are further defined by flowers and water-leaves. The tall, blue flags; the ineffable lilies sitting on their round lily-pads like white queens on green thrones; the tiny stars and long ribbons of the water-grasses; the pretty phalanxes of a species of "bonnet" which from a long stem that swings off down-stream along the surface sends up a hundred little graceful stemlets, each bearing a shield-like disk and holding it aloft as the antique soldiers held their bucklers to form the *testudo,* or tortoise, in attacking. All these border the river in infinite varieties of purfling and chasement.

The river itself has an errant fantasy, and takes many shapes. Presently we come to where it seems to fork into four separate curves above and below.

"Them's the Windin'-blades," said my raftsman. To look down these lovely vistas is like looking down the dreams of some pure young girl's soul; and the gray moss-bearded trees gravely lean over them in contemplative attitudes, as if they were studying—in the way strong men should study—the mysteries and sacrednesses and tender depths of some visible reverie of maidenhood.

And then, after this day of glory, came a night of glory. Down in these deep-shaded lanes it was dark indeed as the night drew on. The stream which had been all day a baldrick of beauty, sometimes blue and sometimes green, now became a black band of mystery. But presently a brilliant flame flares out overhead: they have lighted the pine-knots on top of the pilot-house. The fire advances up these dark sinuosities like a brilliant god that for his mere whimsical pleasure calls the black impenetrable chaos ahead into instantaneous definite forms as he floats along the river-curves. The white columns of the cypress-trunks, the silver-embroidered crowns of the maples, the green-and-white of the lilies along the edges of the stream, —these all come in a continuous apparition out of the bosom of the darkness and retire again: it is endless creation succeeded by endless oblivion. Startled birds suddenly flutter into the light, and after an instant of illuminated flight melt into the darkness. From the perfect silence of these short flights one derives a certain sense of awe. Mystery appears to be about to utter herself in these suddenly-illuminated forms, and then to change her mind and die back into mystery.

Now there is a mighty crack and crash: limbs and leaves scrape and scrub along the deck; a little bell tinkles; we stop. In turning a short curve, or rather doubling, the boat has run her nose smack into the right bank, and a projecting stump has thrust itself sheer through the starboard side. Out, Dick! out, Henry! Dick and Henry shuffle forward to the bow, thrust forth their long white pole against a tree-trunk, strain and push and bend to the deck as if they were salaaming the god of night and adversity, our bow slowly rounds into the stream, the wheel turns, and we puff quietly along.

Somewhere back yonder in the stern Dick is whistling. You should hear him! With the great aperture of his mouth, and the rounding vibratory-surfaces of his thick lips, he gets out a mellow breadth of tone that almost entitles him to rank as an orchestral instrument. Here is his tune:

It is a genuine plagal cadence. Observe the syncopations marked in this air: they are characteristic of negro music. I have heard negroes change a well-known melody by adroitly syncopating it in this way, so as to give it a *bizarre* effect scarcely imaginable; and nothing illustrates the negro's natural gifts in the way of keeping a difficult *tempo* more clearly than his perfect execution of airs thus transformed from simple to complex accentuations.

Dick has changed his tune: *allegro!*

Da capo, of course, and *da capo* indefinitely; for it ends on the dominant. The dominant is a chord of progress: no such thing as stopping. It is like dividing ten by nine, and carrying out the decimal remainders: there is always one over.

Thus the negro shows that he does not like the ordinary accentuations nor the ordinary cadences of tunes: his ear is primitive. If you will follow the course of Dick's musical reverie—which he now thinks is solely a matter betwixt himself and the night, as he sits back yonder in the stern alone—presently you will hear him sing a whole minor tune without once using a semitone: the semitone is weak, it is a dilution, it is not vigorous like the whole tone; and I have seen a whole congregation of negroes at night, as they were worshiping in their church with some wild song or other and swaying to and fro with the ecstasy and the glory of it, abandon as by one consent the semitone that *should* come according to the civilized *modus*, and sing in its place a big lusty whole tone that would shake any man's soul. It is strange to observe that some of the most magnificent effects in advanced modern music are produced by this same method, notably in the works of Asger Hamerik of Baltimore, and of Edward Grieg of Copenhagen. Any one who has heard Thomas's orchestra lately will have no difficulty in remembering his delight at the beautiful *Nordische Suite* by the former writer and the piano *concerto* by the latter.*

* [Asger Hamerik (1843-1923) was the conductor of the Peabody Orchestra,

And then it was bed-time. Let me tell you how to sleep on an Ocklawaha steamer in May. With a small bribe persuade Jim, the steward, to take the mattress out of your berth and lay it slanting just along the railing that incloses the lower part of the deck, in front, and to the left, of the pilot-house. Lie flat-backed down on the same, draw your blanket over you, put your cap on your head in consideration of the night air, fold your arms, say some little prayer or other, and fall asleep with a star looking right down your eye.

When you awake in the morning, your night will not seem any longer, any blacker, any less pure than this perfect white blank in the page; and you will feel as new as Adam.

At sunrise, I woke, and found that we were lying with the boat's nose run up against a sandy bank which quickly rose into a considerable hill. A sandy-whiskered native came down from the pine cabin on the knoll. " How air ye? " he sung out to the skipper, with an evident expectation in his voice. " Got any freight fur me? "

The skipper handed him a heavy parcel, in brown paper. He examined it keenly with all his eyes, felt it over carefully with all his fingers; his countenance fell, and the shadow of a great despair came over it.

" Look-a-here," he said, " *hain't* you brought me no terbacker? "

" Not unless it's in that bundle," said the skipper.

" Hell! " he said, " *hit's* nuthin' but shot; " and he turned off into the forest, as we shoved away, with a face like the face of the Apostate Julian when the devils were dragging him down the pit.

I would have let my heart go out in sympathy to this man— for his agonizing after terbacker, ere the next week bring the *Marion* again, is not a thing to be laughed at—had I not be-

Baltimore, in which Lanier had been first flutist since Dec., 1873; Theodore Thomas (1835-1905), who had organized his own orchestra in New York in 1862, later invited Lanier to join it but the invitation never materialized (see letter to Gibson Peacock, Jan. 25, 1876, and Starke, p. 259). Lanier's observations on negro music were put to further use in *The Science of English Verse* (see II, 146), and his admiration of the modern compositions of Hamerik and Grieg continued through life.—ED.]

lieved that he was one of the vanilla-gatherers. You must know that in the low grounds of the Ocklawaha grows what is called the vanilla-plant—a plant with a leaf much like that of tobacco when dried. This leaf is now extensively used to adulterate cheap chewing-tobacco, and the natives along the Ocklawaha drive a considerable trade in gathering it. The process of this commerce is exceedingly simple: and the bills drawn against the consignments are primitive. The officer in charge of the *Marion* showed me several of the communications received at various landings during our journey, which accompanied small shipments of the spurious weed. They were generally about as follows:

" Deer Sir

" i send you one bag Verneller, pleeze fetch one par of shus numb 8 and ef enny over fetch twelve yards hoamspin.

" Yrs trly

" &c."

The captain of the steamer takes the bags to Pilatka, barters the vanilla for the articles specified, and distributes these on the next trip to their respective owners.

In a short time we came to the junction of the river formed by the irruption of Silver Spring (" Silver Spring Run ") with the Ocklawaha proper. Here new astonishments befell. The water of the Ocklawaha, which had before seemed clear enough, now showed but like a muddy stream as it flowed side by side, unmixing for some distance, with the Silver Spring water.

The *Marion* now left the Ocklawaha and turned into the Run. How shall one speak quietly of this journey over transparency? The Run is very deep: the white bottom seems hollowed out in a continual succession of large spherical holes, whose entire contents of darting fish, of under-mosses, of flowers, of submerged trees, of lily-stems, and of grass-ribbons revealed themselves to us through the lucent fluid as we sailed along thereover. The long series of convex bodies of water filling these white concavities impressed one like a chain of globular worlds composed of a transparent lymph. Great numbers of keen-snouted, blade-bodied gar-fish shot to and fro in unceasing motion beneath us: it seemed as if the underworlds were filled with a multitude of crossing sword-blades wielded in tireless thrust and parry by invisible arms.

The shores, too, had changed. They now opened out into clear savannas, overgrown with a broad-leafed grass to a perfect level two or three feet above the water, and stretching back to boundaries of cypress and oaks; and occasionally, as we passed one of these expanses curving into the forest, with a diameter of a half-mile, a single palmetto might be seen in or near the centre,—perfect type of that lonesome solitude which the German names *Einsamkeit*—onesomeness. Then again, the cypress and palmettos would swarm to the stream and line its banks. Thus for nine miles, counting our gigantic rosary of water-wonders and lovelinesses, we fared on.

Then we rounded to, in the very bosom of the Silver Spring itself, and came to wharf. Here there were warehouses, a turpentine distillery, men running about with boxes of freight and crates of Florida cucumbers for the Northern market, country stores with wondrous assortments of goods—fiddles, clothes, physic, groceries, school-books, what not—and a little farther up the shore, a tavern. I learned, in a hasty way, that Ocala was five miles distant, that one could get a very good conveyance from the tavern to that place, and that on the next day—Sunday—a stage would leave Ocala for Gainesville, some forty miles distant, being the third relay of the long stage-line which runs three times a week between Tampa and Gainesville, *via* Brooksville and Ocala.

Then the claims of scientific fact and of guide-book information could hold me no longer. I ceased to acquire knowledge, and got me back to the wonderful spring, drifting over it, face downwards, as over a new world of delight.

It is sixty feet deep a few feet off shore, and covers an irregular space of several acres before contracting into its outlet—the Run. But this sixty feet does not at all represent the actual impression of depth which one receives, as one looks through the superincumbent water down to the clearly-revealed bottom. The distinct sensation is, that although the bottom there *is* clearly seen, and although all the objects in it are of their natural size, undiminished by any narrowing of the visual angle, yet it and they are seen from a great distance. It is as if depth itself—that subtle abstraction—had been compressed into a crystal lymph, one inch of which would represent miles of ordinary depth.

As one rises from gazing into these quaint profundities and glances across the broad surface of the spring, one's eye is met by a charming mosaic of brilliant hues. The water-plain varies in color, according to what it lies upon. Over the pure white limestone and shells of the bottom it is perfect malachite green; over the water-grass it is a much darker green; over the sombre moss it is that rich brown-and-green which Bodmer's * forest-engravings so vividly suggest; over neutral bottoms it reflects the sky's or the clouds' colors. All these views are further varied by mixture with the manifold shades of foliage-reflections cast from overhanging boscage near the shore, and still further by the angle of the observer's eye.

One would think these elements of color-variation were numerous enough; but they were not nearly all. Presently the splash of an oar in a distant part of the spring sent a succession of ripples circling over the pool. Instantly it broke into a thousand-fold prism. Every ripple was a long curve of variegated sheen. The fundamental hues of the pool when at rest were distributed into innumerable kaleidoscopic flashes and brilliancies, the multitudes of fish became multitudes of animated gems, and the prismatic lights seemed actually to waver and play through their translucent bodies, until the whole spring, in a great blaze of sunlight, shone like an enormous fluid jewel that without decreasing forever lapsed away upward in successive exhalations of dissolving sheens and glittering colors.

* [Karl Bodmer (1805-1893), Swiss landscape-artist and etcher.—Ed.]

CHAPTER III

ST. AUGUSTINE IN APRIL

A sailor has just yawned.

IT IS SEVEN o'clock, of an April morning such as does not come anywhere in the world except at St. Augustine or on the Gulf Coast of Florida,—a morning woven out of some miraculous tissue, which shows two shimmering aspects, the one stillness, the other glory,—a morning which mingles infinite repose with infinite glittering, as if God should smile in his sleep.

On such a morning there is but one thing to do in St. Augustine: it is to lie thus on the sea-wall, with your legs dangling down over the green sea-water, lazaretto-fashion; your arms over your head, caryatid-fashion; and your eyes gazing straight up into heaven, lover-fashion.

The sailor's yawn is going to be immortal: it is reappearing like the Hindoo god in ten thousand avatars of echoes. The sea-wall is now refashioning it into a sea-wall yawn; the green island over across the water there yawns; now the brick pillars of the market-house are yawning; in turn something in the air over beyond the island yawns; now it is this side's time again. Listen! in the long pier yonder, which runs out into the water as if it were a continuation of the hotel-piazza, every separate pile is giving his own various interpretation of the yawn: it runs down them like a forefinger down piano-keys, even to the farthest one, whose idea of this yawn seems to be that it was a mere whisper.

The silence here in the last of April does not have many sounds, one observes, and therefore makes the most of any such airy flotsam and jetsam as come its way.

For the visitors—those of them who make a noise with dancing of nights and with trooping of mornings along the Plaza de la Constitucion—are gone; the brood of pleasure-boats are all asleep in "the Basin"; practically the town belongs for twenty-three hours of each day to the sixteenth century. The twenty-fourth hour, during which the nineteenth claims its own, is when the little locomotive whistles out at the depot three-quarters of a mile off, the omnibus rolls into town with the mail —there are no passengers—the people gather at the post-office, and everybody falls to reading the Northern papers.

Two months earlier it was not so. Then the actual present took every hour that every day had. The St. Augustine, the Florida, the Magnolia, three pleasant hotels, with a shoal of smaller public and private boarding-houses, were filled with people thoroughly alive; the lovely sailing-grounds around the harbor were all in a white zigzag with races of the yacht-club and with more leisurely mazes of the pleasure-boat fleet; one could not have lain on the sea-wall on one's back without galling disturbance at every moment; and as for a yawn, people do not yawn in St. Augustine in February.

There are many persons who have found occasion to carp at this sea-wall,* and to revile the United States Government for having gone to the great expense involved in its construction, with no other result than that of furnishing a promenade for lovers. But these are ill-advised persons: it is easily demonstrable that this last is one of the most legitimate functions of government. Was not the encouragement of marriage a direct object of many noted Roman laws? And why should not the Government of the United States "protect" true love as well as pig-iron? Viewed purely from the stand-point of political economy, is not the former full as necessary to the existence of the State as the latter?

Whatever may have been the motives of the federal authorities in building it, its final cause, *causa causans*, is certainly love; and there is not a feature of its construction which does not seem to have been calculated solely with reference to some phase of that passion.   It is just wide enough for two to walk side by side with the least trifle of pressure together; it is as smooth as the course of true love is *not*, and yet there are certain reentering angles in it (where the stair-ways come up) at which one is as apt to break one's neck as one is to be flirted with, and in which, therefore, every man ought to perceive a reminder in stone of either catastrophe; it has on one side the sea, exhaling suggestions of foam-born Venus and fickleness, and on

* [Built 1835-1842 as a protection against tidal waves and storms, at a cost of $100,000; Lanier probably consulted R. K. Sewall, *Sketches of St. Augustine* (N. Y., 1848).—ED.]

the other the land, with the Bay Street residences wholesomely whispering of settlements and housekeeping bills; it runs at its very beginning in front of the United States barracks, and so at once flouts War in the face, and pursues its course, — happy omen! — towards old Fort Marion, where strife long ago gave way to quiet warmths of sunlight, and where the wheels of the cannon have become trellises for peaceful vines; and finally it ends— How shall a man describe this spot where it ends? With but a step the promenader passes the drawbridge, the moat, the portcullis, edges along the left wall, ascends a few steps, and emerges into the old Barbican. What, then, is in the Barbican? Nothing: it is an oddly-angled inclosure of gray stone, walling round a high knoll where some grass and a blue flower or two appear. Yet it is Love's own trysting-place. It speaks of love, love only: the volubility of its quietude on this topic is as great as Chaucer has described his own:

> For he hath told of lovers up and down,
> Moo than Ovid made of mencioun
> In his Epistelles that ben so olde.
> What schuld I tellen hem, syn they be tolde?
> In youthe he made of Coys and Alcioun,
> And siththe hath he spoke of everychon,
> These noble wyfes, and these lovers eeke
> Whoso wole his large volume seeke
> Cleped the seints legendes of Cupide,
> Ther may he see the large woundes wyde
> Of Lucresse, and of Babiloun Tysbee;
> The sorwe of Dido for the fals Enee;
> The dree of Philles for hir Demephon;
> The pleynt of Diane and of Ermyon,
> Of Adrian, and of Ysyphilee;
> The barren yle stondyng in the see;
> The dreynt Leandere for his fayre Erro:
> The teeres of Eleyn, and eek the woe
> Of Bryxseyde, and of Ledomia;
> The cruelté of the queen Medea,
> The litel children hanging by the hals
> For thilke Jason, that was of love so fals.
> O Ypermestre, Penollope, and Alceste,
> Youre wyfhood he comendeth with the beste.
> But certaynly no worde writeth he

Of thilke wikked ensample of Canace,
That loved her owen brother synfully!
On whiche corsed stories I seye fy! *

Thus the Barbican discourses of true love to him who can hear. I am persuaded that Dante and Beatrice, Abelard and Heloise, Petrarch and Laura, Leander and Hero, keep their tender appointments here. The Barbican is love-making already made. It is complete *Yes*, done in stone and grass.

The things which one does in St. Augustine in February become in April the things which one placidly hears that one *ought* to do, and lies still on one's back on the sea-wall and dangles one's legs.

There is the pleasant avenue, for instance, by which the omnibus coming from the depot enters the town after crossing the bridge over the San Sebastian River. It runs between the grounds of Senator Gilbert on the right (entering town), and the lovely orange-groves, avenues, cedar-hedges, and mulberry-trees which cluster far back from the road about the residences of Dr. Anderson and of Mr. Ball. The latter gentleman is of the well-known firm of Ball, Black & Co., of New York, and has built one of the handsomest residences in Florida here on the old "Buckingham Smith Place."

Or there are the quaint courts inclosed with jealous high coquina-walls, and giving into cool rich gardens where lemons, oranges, bananas, Japan plums, figs, date-palms, and all manner of tropic flowers and greeneries hide from the northeast winds and sanctify the old Spanish-built homes. One has to be in St. Augustine some time before one realizes, as one passes by these commonplace exteriors of whitish houses and whitish walls, the unsuspected beauties stretching back within.

Then there are the narrow old streets to be explored—Bay Street, next the water, Charlotte, St. George and Tolomato Streets running parallel thereto; or the old rookery of a convent, where the Sisters make lace, looking ten times older for the new convent that is going up not far off; or the old cathedral on the Plaza to peep into, one of whose bells is said to have once hung on the chapel beyond the city gates where the savages

---

* [From Chaucer's Introduction to the "Man of Law's Prologue," *Canterbury Tales*.—ED.]

murdered the priests; or the Plaza itself—*Plaza de la Constitu-cion*—where certain good and loyal persons burned the effigies of Hancock and Adams some hundred years ago; * or the Confederate monument on St. George Street, near Bridge, where one may muse with profit in a Centennial year; or the City Gate, looking now more like an invitation to enter than a hostile defense as it stands peacefully wide open on the grassy banks of the canal which formerly let the San Sebastian waters into the moat around Fort Marion; or a trip to the hat-braiders', to see if there is any new fantasy in palmetto-plaits and grasses; or an hour's turning over of the photographic views to fill out one's Florida collection; or a search after a leopard-skin sea-bean.

Or there is a sail over to the North Beach, or to the South Beach, or to the high sand-dunes from which General Oglethorpe once attempted to bombard the Spanish governor Monteano out of the fort; or to the coquina-quarries and the lighthouses on Anastasia Island, the larger of which latter is notable as being one of the few first-class light-houses in the country. Or there is an expedition to Matanzas Inlet, where one can disembark with a few friends, and have three or four days of camp-life plentifully garnished with fresh fish of one's own catching and game of one's own shooting. Or, if one is of a scientific turn, one may sail down to the Sulphur Spring which boils up in the ocean some two and a half miles off Matanzas. This spring rises in water one hundred and thirty-two feet deep, though that around the fountain is only about fifty feet, and its current is so strong that the steamer of the Coast Survey was floated off from over the "boil" of it. It is intermittent, sometimes ceasing to flow, then commencing another ebullition by sending up a cloud of dark-blue sediment, which can be seen advancing to the surface. It has been recently explored by a Coast Survey party. Such a spring is mentioned by Maury ** in a report made many years ago to the Navy Department. I am informed that a similar one exists in the Upper St. Johns; and

* [John Adams and John Hancock, during the American Revolution, when Spain owned Florida.—ED.]

** [Matthew Fontaine Maury (1806-1873) in appendix to *Report of the Secretary of the Navy* (Washington, 1840). Lanier had read also R. M. Bache, *The Young Wrecker of the Florida Reef* (Phila., 1869), which concerns the Coast Survey, and Maury, "The Gulf Stream and Currents of the Sea" in *Southern Literary Messenger,* X, 393-409 (July, 1844).—ED.]

a gentleman told me at Cedar Keys that having applied some
years ago to a sponging-vessel out in the Gulf for water, one
of the crew took him in a small boat to a spot where he dipped
up several buckets full of fresh water in the midst of the brine.

Or late in the afternoon one may drive out St. George Street
through the Gate, and passing the Protestant burying-ground
ride down a clean road which presently debouches on the beach
of the San Sebastian, and affords a charming drive of several
miles. Soon after getting on this beach, one can observe running
diagonally from the river in a double row the remains of an old
outer line of palisades which connected Fort Moosa with a
stockade at the San Sebastian. This row runs up and enters
the grounds of the residence formerly occupied by George R.
Fairbanks, author of an excellent history of Florida.*

Or one may visit Fort Marion—that lovely old transformation
of the seventeenth century into coquina, known in the ancient
Spanish days as Fort San Juan and as Fort San Marco—and peep
into the gloomy casemates, the antique chapel, the tower, the
Barbican; and mayhap the fine old sergeant from between his
side-whiskers will tell of Coacoochee, of Osceola, and of the
skeletons that were found chained to the walls of the very dun-
geon in whose cold blackness one is then and there shivering.
The old sergeant might add to his stories that of a white prisoner
who once dragged out a weary five years in these dungeons,
and who was a man remarkable for having probably tasted the
sweets of revenge in as full measure as ever fell to human lot.
I mean Daniel McGirth. He was a famous partisan scout in
the early part of the American Revolution, but having been
whipped for disrespect to a superior officer, escaped, joined the
enemy, and thereafter rained a series of bloody revenges upon
his injurers. He was afterwards caught by the Spanish—it is
thought because he had joined William Augustus Bowles in his
dreadful instigation of the Indians against the Floridian Spaniards—and incarcerated in this old fort for five years.

If, indeed, the fine old sergeant of Fort Marion be still there:

---

* [Lanier's marked copy of Fairbanks, *History of Florida* (Philadelphia,
1871) is preserved in the Charles D. Lanier Collection, Johns Hopkins University. This volume was apparently his source for the accounts in the following
paragraph of the historic prisoners at Fort Marion—Daniel McGirth and the
Seminole chiefs.—ED.]

it may be that he has ceased to be *genius loci* since the Indians arrived.

For, alas! and alas! the old lonesome fort, the sweet old fort, whose pyramids of cannon-balls were only like pleasant reminders of the beauty of peace, whose manifold angles were but warm and sunny nooks for lizards and men to lounge in and dream in, whose ample and ancient moat had converted itself with grasses and with tiny flowers into a sacred refuge from trade and care, known to many a weary soul,—the dear old fort is practically no more: its glories of calm and of solitude have departed utterly away. The Cheyennes, the Kiowas, the Comanches, the Caddoes, and the Arapahoes, with their shuffling chains and strange tongues and barbaric gestures, have frightened the timid swallow of romance out of the sweetest nest that he ever built in America.

It appears that some time about the middle of 1874 the United States Government announced to the Indians in Northwest Texas that they must come in and give a definite account of themselves, whereupon a large number declared themselves hostile. Against these four columns of troops were sent out from as many different posts, which were managed so vigorously that in no long time the great majority of the unfriendly Indians either surrendered or were captured. Some of these were known to have been guilty of atrocious crimes; others were men of consequence in their tribes; and it was resolved to make a selection of the principal individuals of these two classes, and to confine them in old Fort Marion, at St. Augustine.

And so here they are—" Medicine Water," a ringleader, along with " White Man," " Rising Bull," " Hailstone," " Sharp Bully," and others, in the terrible murder of the Germain family, and in the more terrible fate of the two Germain girls who were recently recaptured from the Cheyennes; " Come See Him," who was in the murder of the Short surveying-party; " Soaring Eagle," supposed to have killed the hunter Brown, near Fort Wallace; " Big Moccasin " and " Making Medicine," horse-thieves and raiders; " Packer," the murderer of Williams; " Mochi," the squaw identified by the Germain girls as having chopped the head of their murdered mother with an axe. Besides these, who constitute most of the criminals, are a lot against whom there is no particular charge, but who are confined on the principle that prevention is better than cure. "Gray Beard," one of this latter class of chiefs, leaped from a car-window at Baldwin, Florida, while being conveyed to St. Augustine, and was shot, after a short pursuit, by one of his guards. "Lean Bear," another, stabbed himself and two of his guards, apparently in a crazy fit, when near Nashville, Tennessee, *en route,* but has since recovered and been sent to join those in the fort. One of the Kiowas died of pneumonia shortly after arriving at St. Augustine, leaving seventy-three, including two squaws and a little girl, now in confinement. Their quarters are in the casemates within the fort, which have been fitted up for their use. During the day they are allowed to move about the interior of the fort, and are sometimes taken out in squads to bathe; at night they are locked up.

They seem excessively fond of trying their skill in drawing, and are delighted with a gift of pencil and paper. Already, however, the atmosphere of trade has reached into their souls: I am told they now begin to sell what they were ready enough to give away when I saw them a few weeks ago; and one fancies it will not be long before they are transformed from real Indians into those vile things, watering-place Indians.

Criminals as they are, stirrers-up of trouble as they are, rapidly degenerating as they are, no man can see one of these stalwart-chested fellows rise and wrap his blanket about him with that big, majestic sweep of arm which does not come to any strait-jacketed civilized being, without a certain melancholy in the bottom of his heart as he wonders what might have become of these people if so be that gentle contact with their white neighbors might have been substituted in place of the unspeakable maddening wrongs which have finally left them but a little corner of their continent. Nor can one repress a little moralizing as one reflects upon the singularity of that fate which has finally placed these red-men on the very spot where red-men's wrongs began three centuries and a half ago; for it was here that Ponce de Leon landed in 1512, and from the very start there was enmity betwixt the Spaniard and the Indian.

Nor, finally, can one restrain a little smile at the thought that not a hundred years ago nearly this same number of the

most illustrious men in South Carolina were sent down to this
same St. Augustine to be imprisoned for the same reason for
which most of these Indians have been—to wit, that they were
men of influence and stirrers-up of trouble in their tribes. After
the capture of Charleston by the British, during the American
Revolution, between fifty and sixty of the most distinguished
South Carolinians were rudely seized by order of the English
commander and transferred to St. Augustine for safe-keeping,
where they were held for several months; one of their number,
Gadsden, being imprisoned for nearly a year in this very old
fort, refusing to accept the conditions upon which the rest were
allowed the range of the city streets. The names of these
prisoners are of such honorable antiquity, and are so easily
recognizable as being names still fairly borne and familiarly
known in South Carolina, that it is worth while to reproduce
them here out of the dry pages of history. They are—John
Budd, Edward Blake, Joseph Bee, Richard Beresford, John
Berwick, D. Bordeaux, Robert Cochrane, Benjamin Cudworth,
H. V. Crouch, J. S. Cripps, Edward Darrell, Daniel Dessaussure,
John Edwards, George Flagg, Thomas Ferguson, General A.
C. Gadsden, Wm. Hazel Gibbs, Thomas Grinball, William
Hall, Thomas Hall, George A. Hall, Isaac Holmes, Thomas
Heyward, Jr., Richard Hutson, Noble Wimberley Jones, Wil-
liam Johnstone, William Lee, Richard Lushington, William
Logan, Rev. John Lewis, William Massey, Alexander Moultrie,
Arthur Middleton, Edward McCready, John Mouatt, Edward
North, John Neufville, Joseph Parker, Christopher Peters, Ben-
jamin Postell, Samuel Prioleau, John Ernest Poyas, Edward
Rutledge, Hugh Rutledge, John Sanson, Thomas Savage, Josiah
Smith, Thomas Singleton, James Hampden Thompson, John
Todd, Peter Timothy, Anthony Toomer, Edward Weyman,
Benjamin Waller, Morton Wilkinson, and James Wakefield.*
    As you stand on the fort, looking seaward, the estuary pene-
trating into the mainland up to the left is the North River,
which René de Laudonnière in 1564 called the " River of Dol-
phins"; across it is the North Beach; in front you see the
breakers rolling in at the harbor-entrance. The stream stretching down to the right is Matanzas River, communicating with

* [Lanier's source was probably George R. Fairbanks, *History of Florida.*—ED.]

open water at Matanzas Inlet, about eighteen miles below. Another estuary, the San Sebastian, runs behind the town, and back into the country for a few miles. The bar there is said to be not an easy one to cross; and once in, sometimes a nor'-easter springs up and keeps you in a week or so. In the old times of sailing vessels these northeast winds used to be called orange-winds—on a principle somewhat akin to *lucus a non*— because the outside world could not *get* any oranges, the sailboats laden with that fruit being often kept in port by these gales until their cargoes were spoiled.* In rummaging over old books of Florida literature, I came across the record of *A Winter in the West Indies and Florida, by An Invalid*, published by Wiley & Putnam, in 1839, whose account of one of these nor'-easters at St. Augustine so irresistibly illustrates the unreliableness of sick men's accounts of climates that I cannot help extracting a portion of it:

A packet-schooner runs regularly from here to Charleston, at ten dollars passage, but owing to northeast winds it is sometimes impossible to get out of the harbor for a month at a time. I was detained in that manner for ten days, during which period I wrote this description, in a room without fire, with a cloak on, and feet cold in spite of thick boots, suffering from asthma, fearing worse farther North, still burning with impatience on account of the delay.

Such a proem is enough to make a St. Augustine person shiver at the " description " which is to follow it; and well he might, for my " Invalid," after giving some account of the climate from a thermometric record of one year, and drawing therefrom the conclusion that invalids had better go to St. Augustine in the summer than in the winter, proceeds:

But the marshes in the vicinity harbor too many musquitoes in summer, . . . which rather surprised me, as it seemed from the state of the weather in April *that musquitoes would freeze in summer*. These marshes, too, in warm weather must produce a bad effect upon the atmosphere.[1]

---

* [The anecdote is apparently paraphrased from the anonymous work cited immediately below.—Ed]

[1] Showing our invalid to be an unmitigated landlubber. The only marsh about St. Augustine is salt-water marsh, which is perfectly healthy. It is only freshwater marsh that breeds miasma.

At the time of writing the above, [he proceeds,] I suppose the wind was coming about, so as to take me along to some place—if no better, at least free from pretensions to a fine climate. Nothing can be worse than to find oneself imprisoned in this little village, kept a whole week or more with a cold, piercing wind drifting the sand along the streets and into his eyes, with sometimes a chance at a fire morning and evening, and sometimes a chance to wrap up in a cloak and shiver without any, and many times too cold to keep warm by walking in the sunshine: with numbers of miserable patients hovering about the fire telling stories of distress, while others are busily engaged in extolling the climate. It is altogether unendurable to hear it. Why, a man that would not feel too cold here would stand a six years' residence in Greenland or send an invalid to the Great Dismal Swamp for health. The truth is, a man in health [and I am sure nothing more naïve than this is to be found in literature] can judge no better of the fitness of a climate for invalids than a blind man of colors: he has no sense by which to judge of it. His is the feeling of the well man, but not of the sick. I have been healthy, and now I am sick, and know the above remark is correct. No getting away. Blow, blow, blow! Northeast winds are sovereigns here, forcibly restraining the free-will of everybody, and keeping everything at a stand-still except the tavern-bill, which runs against all winds and weather. Here are forty passengers, besides a vessel, detained for ten days by the persevering obstinacy of the tyrant wind, while its music roars along the shore to regale us by night as well as by day, and keep us in constant recollection of the cause of detention.

Oh for a steamboat, that happiest invention of man, that goes in spite of wind and tide! Talk of danger! Why, rather than be detained in this manner, I would take passage on board a balloon or a thunder-cloud. Anything to get along.

The city of St. Augustine * is built on the site of the old Indian town of Seloy or Selooe. It was probably a little north of this that Ponce de Leon made his first landing in Florida in 1512. The tragic mutations of the town's early fortunes are so numerous that their recital in this limited space would be little more than a mere list of dates. Instead of so dry a skeleton of history, the reader will be at once more entertained and more instructed in all that is the essence of history by this story

* [Lanier's historical sketch of St. Augustine in the following pages is closely paraphrased from Fairbanks, *History of Florida,* and his quotations are drawn from this volume except where otherwise indicated.—ED.]

—thoroughly representative of the times—of the brief wars between Menendez, the then Spanish governor, or *adelantado,* of Florida, on the one side, and Jean Ribaut and René de Laudonnière, French Huguenots, on the other. Already, in 1562, Ribaut has touched the shore of the St. Johns, and then sailed northward and planted a short-lived colony. In 1564, Laudonnière has come over and built Fort Caroline, not far above the mouth of the St. Johns. He had previously landed at the present site of St. Augustine, and had amicable entertainment from a *paracoussi,* or chief, and his attending party of Indians. These Frenchmen appear to have had much more winning ways with them than the Spaniards. Laudonnière declares that the savages " were sorry for nothing but that the night approached and made us retire into our ship," and that " they endeavored by all means to make us tarry with them," desiring " to present us with some rare things."

But presently queer doings begin in Fort Caroline, which it is probable was situated at St. Johns Bluff, on the south side of the St. Johns River. A soldier who professes magic stirs up disaffection against their leader. Laudonnière manages to send seven or eight of the suspected men to France, but while he is sick certain others confine him, seize a couple of vessels and go off on a piratical cruise. Most of them perish after indifferent success as freebooters: one party returns, thinking that Laudonnière will treat the thing as a frolic, and even get drunk as they approach the fort, and try each other, personating their own judges and aping Laudonnière himself. But Laudonnière turns the laugh: he takes the four ringleaders, shoots them first (granting so much grace to their soldierships) and hangs them afterward.

So, Death has his first course in Fort Caroline, and it is not long before he is in midst of a brave feast. The garrison gets into great straits for lack of food. One cannot control one's astonishment that these people, Spaniards as well as Frenchmen, should so persistently have fallen into a starving condition in a land where a man could almost make a living by sitting down and wishing for it. Perhaps it was not wholly national prejudice which prompted the naïve remark of the chronicler of the party of Sir John Hawkins, who, with an English fleet, paid Fort Caroline a visit at this time, and gave the distressed Frenchmen a generous allowance of provisions:

The ground, [says the chronicler,] doth yield victuals sufficient if they would have taken pains to get the same; but they [the Frenchmen], being soldiers, desired to live by the sweat of other men's brows.

This chronicler's ideas of hunger, however, are not wholly reliable. Hear him discourse of the effect of tobacco upon it:

The Floridians, when they travel, have a kind of herbe dried, who, with a cane, and earthen cup in the end, with fire and the dried herbes put together, doe suck throu a cane the smoke thereof, which smoke satisfieth their hunger, and therewith they live four or five days without meat or drinke; and this all the Frenchmen used for this purpose; yet doe they hold withal that it causeth them to reject from their stomachs, and spit out water and phlegm.*

The fate of Fort Caroline rapidly approaches. In 1565, Captain Jean Ribaut comes back again from France, with workmen and five hundred soldiers, to relieve and strengthen the colony on the St. Johns. Meantime, news gets from France to Spain that he is coming, and one Menendez is deputed by the Spanish Government to checkmate him. With much delay and loss by storms, Menendez ardently pushes on, and makes land near St. Augustine harbor within twenty-four hours of the arrival of Jean Ribaut in the St. Johns, fifty miles above. They quickly become aware of each other. Menendez tries to catch Ribaut's ship, but fails, and sails back to St. Augustine; to which, by the way, he has just given that name, in honor of the saint's day on which he landed. Ribaut in turn resolves to attack, and, sailing down with his whole force for that purpose, is driven southward by a great storm. Meantime, Menendez sets out, under the discouragements of a tremendous rain and of great difficulty in keeping his people up to the work, to attack Fort Caroline by land. No difficult matter to take it if they only knew it, for Menendez has five hundred men, and there are in Fort Caroline but two hundred and forty souls (Ribaut being away with all the available force), of whom many are people still seasick, workmen, women and children, and one is " a player on the virginals." Laudonnière himself, who has been left in charge, is sick, though trying his best to stimulate his people.

* [Lanier used this same anecdote several years later in his Peabody lectures on Shakespeare (see III, 246, of the present edition).—Ed.]

After three days Menendez arrives at dawn. It is but a shout, a rush, a wild cry of surprise from the French, a vigorous whacking and thrusting of the Spanish, and all is over. A few, Laudonnière among them, escape. Many, including women and children, were killed. It was at this time that Menendez caused certain prisoners to be hung, with the celebrated inscription over them, " *No por Franceses, sino por Luteranos.*"

Meantime, poor Jean Ribaut has met with nothing but disaster. His vessels are wrecked a little below Matanzas Inlet, but his men get ashore, some two hundred in one party, and the balance, three hundred and fifty, in another. Menendez hears of the first party through some Indians, goes down to the main shore, and discovers them across the inlet. After some conference this Delphic Menendez informs them that if they will come over he will " do to them what the grace of God shall direct."

Not dreaming that the grace of God is going to direct that they be all incontinently butchered, the poor Frenchmen, half dead with terror and hunger, first send over their arms, then come over themselves, ten at a time, as Menendez directs. And this is the way that the grace of Menendez's God directs him to treat them, as related by his own brother-in-law, De Solis:

The adelantado then withdrew from the shore about two bow-shots, behind a hillock of sand, within a copse of bushes, where the persons who came in the boat which brought over the French could not see; and then said to the French captain and the other eight Frenchmen who were there with him, " Gentlemen, I have but a few men with me, and they are not very effective, and you are numerous, and going unrestrained it would be an easy thing to take satisfaction upon our men for those whom we destroyed when we took the fort; and thus it is necessary that you should march with hands tied behind a distance of four leagues from here, where I have my camp." [Very well, say the Frenchmen, and so each ten is tied, without any other ten seeing it;] for it was so arranged in order that the French who had not passed the river should not understand what was being done, and might not be offended, and thus were tied two hundred and eight Frenchmen. Of whom the adelantado asked that if any among them were Catholic they should declare it. [Eight are Catholics, and are sent off to St. Augustine,] and all the rest replied that they were of the new religion, and held themselves to be very good Christians. . . . The adelantado then gave the order to march with them; . . . and he directed one of his captains who marched with his vanguard that at a certain distance from there he would observe a mark made by a lance, . . . which would be in a sandy place that they would be obliged to pass in going on their way toward the fort at St. Augustine, and that there the prisoners should all be destroyed; and he gave the one in command of the rearguard the same order, *and it was done accordingly; when leaving there all of the dead, they returned the same night before dawn to the fort at St. Augustine, although it was already sundown when the men were killed.**

The next day, in much the same way and at the same spot, Menendez causes a hundred and fifty more Frenchmen to be butchered. Among them was their commander, Jean Ribaut, who dies like a hero, without fear, triumphant. Some say Menendez cut off Ribaut's beard and sent it to Spain.

There are still two hundred men of Ribaut's, who get down the coast to a place they name Canavaral, and set to work to build a boat; but Menendez soon captures the party, and thus puts an end for the time to the Huguenot colonization in Florida, for Laudonnière's party have gone off across the ocean back to France.

But after many months—during which Menendez has been very busy building up the Indian town of Selooe or Seloy into the city of St. Augustine, planting garrisons and establishing priests in various parts of the country, and finally going back to Spain for succor—the French have their revenge. One Dominic de Gourgues sets out from France in 1567, and after much trial gets into the harbor of Fernandina. A favorable angel seems to have charge of the man from this time on. He is about to be resisted by a great crowd of Spaniard-hating Indians at Fernandina, when one of his men who had been with Laudonnière discovers to the Indians that they are Frenchmen. Thereupon they are hailed with joy, alliance is made with Satourioura, a chief with deadly feelings towards the Spaniards, and De Gourgues soon finds his army increased by several thousand good fighters. They straightway move down upon the Spanish forts on the St. Johns, completely surprise

---

* [Lanier's source for this quotation was apparently George R. Fairbanks, *The History and Antiquities of the City of St. Augustine.*—ED.]

them, and kill or capture the inmates. With these captives De Gourgues devises that piece of vengeance which has become famous in history. He leads a lot of them to the same spot where Menendez had hung his Frenchmen, harangues them first, hangs them afterward, and then replaces Menendez's tablet with a pine board upon which letters have been seared with a hot iron, setting forth how he does this " not because they were Spaniards, not because they were castaways, but because they were traitors, thieves, and murderers."

Early in 1568, Menendez gets back to Florida, and one fancies that one would not like to have been the body-servant of that same *adelantado* when he learned what De Gourgues had done in his absence, and how the latter was now gone back to France, quite out of his reach. Menendez thereupon turns his attention towards converting the country to his religion, but the inhabitants do not seem to appreciate its sublimity. It is stated that in one place four priests succeeded in baptizing seven people in one year; but three of them were dying, and the other four were children. The Indians, however, if they refuse Menendez's precepts, certainly accept his practice; for one of them, pretending to be converted, manages to get nine or ten priests on a religious errand away up into the Chesapeake country, and there does to them what the grace of his god directs—to wit, plays traitor and gets the whole party (except one who is kept captive) massacred incontinently. In truth, these friars do not seem to have ingratiated themselves with the Indians; and in the year 1578 the son of the chief of Guale organized a very bloody crusade against them especially. At Tolomato (an Indian suburb of St. Augustine), in the night, he kills Father Corpa; at Topiqui, another suburb, he finds Father Rodriguez, yields to the good father's entreaties that he may say mass before he dies, hears him say it, then kills him; at Assapo, kills Father Auñon and Father Badazoz; waylays Father Velacola, who is trying to escape from them, and kills him; carries off Father Davila into captivity (this Father Davila is twice saved from a cruel death during this captivity by Indian women); and finally gives over after being repulsed at the mission on San Pedro Island.

Meantime, in 1586, Sir Francis Drake has made a landing at

St. Augustine, scared everybody away from the fort, captured a couple of thousand pounds of money in the same, and pillaged and burnt the town. Some years later the priests got on better, and by the year 1618 had established twenty missions at various points, and begun to see some fruit springing from their blood and toil. About this time they had printed a catechism in the Timuqua (Tomoka) language, a copy of which was seen by Mr. Buckingham Smith some years ago in Europe.*

In 1638 the Appalachee Indians attacked St. Augustine, but were repulsed with the loss of many captives, who were put to work on the fortifications, and kept at it, with their descendants, for sixty years together. The buccaneers, however, were more successful, and in 1665, Captain John Davis, a pirate, pillaged the town.

And then followed wars and troubles, wars and troubles, until, finally, the cession of the State of Florida to the United States in 1821 ** gave the people rest from that long battle-door-life during which they had been bandied about from king to king.

That portion of the town near the fort is known as the Minorcan quarter, and is inhabited by persons—mostly sailors and fishermen—who are descendants of the colonists brought over by Dr. Turnbull to New Smyrna in 1767. These colonists were originally introduced to engage in the culture of indigo, mainly near New Smyrna, on the Halifax River, some sixty miles south of St. Augustine; but after working for eight or nine years, they disagreed with their employers, caused their contracts to be rescinded by the courts, and moved up to St. Augustine, where lands were assigned them.

The town has a resident population of about two thousand, but is swelled during the winter by probably six to ten thousand visitors. These were formerly landed by the St. Johns steamboats at Picolata, and thence transferred by stage to St. Augustine; but this cumbrous method gave way to the demands

* [Buckingham Smith, a Georgian, had before the Civil War built a home near St. Augustine, still known in 1875 as the " old Buckingham Smith Palace." In 1860 he published studies of the Apalachian and Timuquan languages.—ED.]

** [The treaty ceding Florida to the United States was concluded Feb. 22, 1819, and ratified Feb. 19, 1821. The flags at St. Augustine were changed July 10, 1821.—ED.]

of the increasing travel, and a tramway was then constructed to Tocoi, a landing on the St. Johns only fifteen miles distant, over which travelers were brought in horse-cars. In its turn the tramway has now given place to a railway, and a neat little locomotive pulls the train across the barren pine-flats that lie between St. Augustine and the river.

There are here a telegraph-office; post-office; a public library and reading-room, open to strangers, located in the rear portion of the post-office building on the Plaza; Catholic, Episcopal, Presbyterian, and Methodist churches; and a colored Baptist church.

Most consumptives, particularly those who have passed the earlier stage of the disease, are said to find the air of St. Augustine too "strong" in midwinter, but to enjoy its climate greatly in April and May. There are those, however, who have found benefit here during the winter; and it must be said that the needs of consumptives vary so much with the particular temperament and idiosyncratic condition of each patient that no certain prophecy, within the limits of climates at all suitable for consumptives, can be made beforehand.

St. Augustine is much resorted to by asthmatics: one of these has found the North Beach so pleasant that he has built a dwelling on it; and the visitor will discover many charming residences recently erected in various parts of the city by persons from the North seeking health.

The mean temperature of St. Augustine, calculated upon twenty years' readings of the thermometer, is—for spring, 68.54° Fahrenheit; for summer, 80.27°; for autumn, 71.73° and for winter, 58.08°. This would seem authoritatively to show a charming temperature; and the temperature *is* charming, except when the northeast wind blows in the winter. This is the wind that sets everybody to swearing at his coffee of a morning, to calling for his hotel-bill, and to howling in right Carlylese at humanity in general. It is not severe intrinsically: people here always want to kick a thermometer when they look at it during a nor'-easter and find it only about fifty-five or sixty, whereas they had every just ground for expecting any reasonable thermometer to show at least ten degrees below zero. The truth is, there is a sense of imposition about this wind which poisons its edge; one feels that one has rights, that this is Florida, and that the infernal thing is the very malignity of pure aerial persecution. It blows as if it had gone out of its way to do it; and with a grin.

Let, however, but a mere twitch of the compass happen— let but the east wind blow—and straightway the world is amiable again. For here the east wind, of such maleficent reputation in the rest of the world, redeems all its brethren. It is bland as a baby's breath: it is, indeed, the Gulf Stream's baby. And if it breathed always as it does on the day of this present writing— a sweet and saintly wind that is more soothing than a calm could be—one finds no difficulty in believing that in the course of a few years the entire population of the earth and of the heavens above the earth and of the waters beneath the earth would be settled in and around this quaint, romantic, straggling, dear and dearer-growing city of St. Augustine.

Chapter IV

JACKSONVILLE IN JANUARY

J ACKSONVILLE AND St. Augustine are two cities not fifty
miles apart; but the difference between them is just the distance from the nineteenth century to the sixteenth. In truth, if
you take them as they are herein described, the one in January
and the other in April, nothing can seem more appropriate than
their names; for the former strikes you with all the vim of
Andrew Jackson, after whom it is called, while about the latter
you cannot fail to find a flavor of saintly contemplation which
seems to breathe from out the ancient name of the good old
father whom Menendez selected for its patron saint.

Jacksonville not only belongs to the nineteenth century, but
practically to the last ten years of that; for previous to the war
between the States it was a comparatively insignificant town,
and even after the war, in the year 1866, I am informed that a
careful census made under the auspices of the Freedman's Bureau revealed but about seventeen hundred inhabitants in it, a
majority of whom are said to have been negroes drawing their
main subsistence from the charities of the nation. The resident population is now between twelve and fourteen thousand,
and this number is largely increased during the winter. It bears
all the signs of a city prospering upon the legitimate bases of an
admirable commercial location and of an enterprising body of
citizens; and in midwinter offers to the Northern visitor a pleasant surprise, which coming after the railway journey through
the pines is almost like a romantic adventure after a long
stretch of quiet life. The train comes to a stop on the wharf: as
one steps from the car, one hears a pleasant plash among the
lily-pads underneath the platform, and, lifting the eyes at this
suggestion of waters, perceives the great placid expanses of the
St. Johns stretching far away to the south and east. A few
yards from the railway-station, across Bay Street, the long
façade of the Grand National Hotel elevates itself; wherefrom, if the traveler's *éntrée* be at night, he is like to hear

44

sounds of music coming, through brilliantly-lighted windows opening upon a wide balcony where many people are promenading in the pleasant evening air. Farther back in the town a few hundred yards, situated among fine oaks which border a newly-planted open square, is the St. James Hotel; where the chances are strong that as one peeps through the drawing-room windows on the way to one's room, one will find so many New York faces and Boston faces and Chicago faces that one does not feel so very far from home after all.

The Grand National and the St. James are open only during the winter; and when we came along back this way in the late spring we found rough planks barring their hospitalities up— a clear case, in fact, of roses shutting and being buds again. Of course, one feels that this simile needs justification; for a hotel is *primâ facie* not like a rose: but what would you have? This is Florida, and a simile will live vigorously in Florida which would perish outright in your cold carping clime.

The Metropolitan Hotel, a quarter of a mile downtown from the depot, between Bay Street and Forsyth, blooms all the year round.

These hotels are really well appointed in all particulars. The Metropolitan has been recently enlarged; and the St. James is probably receiving additions at this writing. Besides the quarters they offer, pleasant abiding-places can be found in the smaller public houses and among private families taking boarders. These minor hostelries of various sorts are said to amount to one hundred in number. The National and St. James charge four dollars a day, the Metropolitan three; the smaller houses from one and a half to three a day, and from ten to twenty dollars a week. As one emerges from one's hotel in the morning, upon those springy plank sidewalks which constitute a sort of strolls-made-easy over a large part of the city, one is immediately struck with the splendid young water-oaks which border the streets, sometimes completely arching them over. Their foliage is dense, and, what with the brilliance of the sun, the lights and shadows are right Rembrandt. These trees contrast greatly with the pines through which one has been traveling ever since one left Wilmington, and in the midst of great forests of which Jacksonville itself is situated. While we walk

under the oaks, let us discuss the pines. Presently the best reason in the world will appear to support the propriety of the
association.

Never was a tree more misunderstood, æsthetically, than the
pine. As we came down through the great pine-forests which
fringe the coasts of North Carolina, South Carolina, Georgia,
and Florida, I frequently heard not only Miss Pertly, but her
father also, turn lazily in the car-seat, and yawn out of the
window and speak maledictions upon the eternal pines.

Nay, oftentimes the very yeomanry of the pine-countries
themselves utter disrespect and irreverence upon these trees:
insomuch that " piney-woods " has come to be a phrase conveying a certain idea of inferiority.

But let us consider a moment. Once John Ruskin, in the
noble days before his mournful modern insanity, wrote thus:

The Pine—magnificent! nay, sometimes almost terrible. Other trees,
tufting crag or hill, yield to the form and sway of the ground, clothe it
with soft compliance, are partly its subjects, partly its flatterers, partly
its comforters. But the pine rises in serene resistance, self-contained;
nor can I ever without awe stay long under a great Alpine cliff, far
from all house or work of men, looking up to its companies of pines, as
they stand on the inaccessible juts and perilous ledges of the enormous
wall, in quiet multitudes, each like the shadow of the one beside it—
upright, fixed, spectral, as troops of ghosts standing on the walls of
Hades, not knowing each other, dumb forever. You cannot reach them,
cannot cry to them: those trees never heard human voice: they are far
above all sound but of the winds. No foot ever stirred fallen leaf of
theirs: all comfortless they stand, between the two eternities of the
Vacancy and the Rock; yet with such iron will, that the rock itself
looks bent and shattered beside them—fragile, weak, inconsistent, compared to their dark energy of delicate life and monotony of enchanted
pride—unnumbered, unconquerable. Then note further their perfect-
ness. The impression on most people's minds must have been received
more from pictures than reality, so far as I can judge, so ragged they
think the pine; whereas its chief character in health is green and full
roundness. It stands compact, like one of its own cones, slightly curved
on its sides, finished and quaint as a carved tree in some Elizabethan
garden; and instead of being wild in expression, forms the softest of
all forest scenery, for other trees show their trunks and twisting boughs;
but the pine, growing either in luxuriant mass or in happy isolation,
allows no branch to be seen. Summit behind summit rise its pyramidal

ranges, or down to the very grass sweep the circlets of its boughs; so that there is nothing but green cone and green carpet. Nor is it only softer, but in one sense more cheerful than any other foliage, for it casts only a pyramidal shadow. Lowland forest arches overhead, and checkers the ground with darkness; but the pine, growing in scattered groups, leaves the glades between emerald bright. Its gloom is all its own; narrowing into the sky, it lets the sunshine strike down to the dew.*

And only hear the same John Ruskin commenting on this passage of his own after many years: "Almost the only pleasure I have myself in re-reading my old books, is my sense of having at least done justice to the Pine."

But—not to interfere in the least with such slender solace— this "justice" is, after all, only justice to the pines of the mountains; the pines of the plains still remain in disgrace. It is time to break another lance for them.

The pines of the plains are inexplicably oppressive to most people. Can it be for the same reason that a powerful sermon makes a sinner feel uncomfortable? For indeed these pines always preach. They are religion carven into trunks and branches and cones. All the similes they suggest are religious. You shall hear the school-boy and the poet alike picturing them as solemn priests, or as the stately pillars of a temple; and the most heedless ear finds organ-tones in the singing of the winds through their multitudinous leaves. Solemnities, mysteries, time, death, eternity, birth, life, sex, faith, the bottoms of oceans, the individualities of plants and stones, the affinities of atoms, the realities of stars; why does a thing weigh? is gravity a kind of love? may we not all be—we men of the earth—but as animalcules in a drop of water *quoad* some higher race of beings? is not the sky, then, perhaps only the outer film of our little globule? why does a marble continue to move after your thumb has ceased to push it? cannot really two things be in the same place at the same time? in infinite space can there be any phenomena corresponding to our ideas of place and direction? will that fox-squirrel live after death? why does a familiar word sound wholly strange and unmeaning after one repeats it several times over to oneself? what is the meaning of the

* [Quoted from *Modern Painters*. Ruskin's later comment, given in the next paragraph, was added as a note to his *Frondes Agrestes*.—ED.]

Tower of Babel? why do not our dead friends tell us The Secret if they are still alive? what time of day will I die? what superior chemistry to man's is this within the pine-tree that out of water and dirt manufactures rosin and leaves and complicated cones? how does the root of a pine know potash from silex? what a marvel, to think that many of these steadfast tall figures will presently be converted into ship-spars, and perhaps this very royal pine against which I am leaning will in a few months be advancing over the sea as the mainmast of a great ship, and swaying and bending from side to side in colossal arcs between the sky and the water! is not Herbert Spencer a man drunk with facts, as Spinoza was said to be intoxicated with God? is it possible that the pine-tree feels the wounds and scarifications of its trunk? if it did feel, would it not have a mouth or some organ for expression? what determined the precise beveling of the edge of this pine-needle, and that there should be here eleven in a row and there thirteen? did God actually ever walk in the cool of the day? what is the proportion of strings to reeds in the orchestras of Heaven? what does Beethoven think of his symphonies now? how will the world be reinstated in Belief? will God write another Bible? is not nature the everlasting word? do the pine-trees say anything but God, God, always God?—these things vaguely follow each other through one's mind when one is under the pines, with no more law, or at any rate no more apparent law, than the seeming-whimsical fugue of the winds through the pine-tops.

As for the hill-pines, they stand upon the corrugations of the earth's brow. They represent pain, spasms, paroxysms, desperations. The pines of the plain have higher meanings if lower sites; theirs is the unwrinkled forehead of a tranquil globe, they signify the mystery of that repose that comes only from tested power and seasoned strength—a grandeur of tranquillity which is as much greater than the grandeur of cataclysms as Chaucer is greater than Byron, as Beethoven is greater than Berlioz, as Lee's manhood is greater than Napoleon's.

A subtle sense of multitude begins to reveal itself to him who stands among the great pine-forests. We are accustomed to speak of the multitude of the stars: the astronomers say there are only about six thousand of them visible on a clear night to the naked eye; but six thousand pines! Six thousand is only the insignificant content of a few acres: here are thousands of square miles of them. When one looks from this great trunk to that, from that to another, to another, to a thousand, as they stand, distinct units, ranged in circles, in squares, in rhomboid figures, in endless aisles, in myriad-fold ranks, almost making a continuity by mere multitude, yet individual and countable if one only had eternity to count them in—it is as if one saw infinity, and a noise goes about through the high pine-needles which seems to formulate itself into that lovely Latin song:

> Infinitas! Infinitas!
> Hic mundus est infinitas!
> Infinitas et totus est,
> (Nam mente nunquam absolveris;)
> Infinitas et illius
> Pars quælibet, partisque pars.
> Quod tangis est infinitas;
> Quod cernis est infinitas;
> Quod non vides corpusculum,
> Sed mente sola concipis,
> Corpusculi et corpusculum,
> Hujusque pars corpusculi,
> Partisque pars, hujusque pars,
> In hacque parte quicquid est,
> Infinitatem continet.
>
> .   .   .   .   .
>
> Quiesce mens, et limites
> In orbe cessa quærere.
> Quod quæris in te reperis:
> In mente sunt, in mente sunt,
> Hi, quos requiris, termini,
> A rebus absunt limites,
> In hisce tantum infinitas,
> Infinitas! Infinitas! *

A singular phenomenon is taking place all along this belt of pines which now borders the Southern States like the ciliary fringes along the lip of some prodigious seashell. The yellow pine does not seem to reproduce itself, except under very rare

---

* [A medieval song, the authorship of which has not been ascertained.—ED.]

conditions: when the forests of it are cut away for timber, there springs up in its place not a forest of young pines, but a forest of young oaks! This circumstance has baffled the scientific knowledge of our time, so far as I know. The traveler on the way to Florida can see many very striking circumstances of it. Just after he leaves Wilmington, N. C., for example, going southward, let him look from the car-window on either side. As far as the eye can reach, in many places, a thick forest of young oaks (" black-jacks ") about four to five feet in height has sprung up. Whence came the acorns from which each of these young oaks sprang? There is not an old oak within miles; and before these young oaks grew, the whole surface of the land hereabouts was covered with an unbroken growth of pines, which have now been wholly cut away, either in the course of clearing land for agricultural purposes, or of the manufacture of turpentine and lumber.

Whence—one may ask again in astonishment, as one's eye ranges over miles and miles of these vigorous oak-saplings— whence came the simultaneous sowing which has resulted in this plantation of trees whose tops are as level as wheat-heads?

Whatever may be its explanation, the phenomenon is visible to the traveler at many spots along the whole route from Weldon to Jacksonville, through Wilmington, Columbia (or Charleston), Augusta, and Savannah. Its effect has been already to revolutionize the appearance, and incidentally the pursuits, of the country in which it is taking place. For the concomitants of pine-growth are very different from those of the oak. The civilization of the pines is that of the timber-cutter and the turpentine-distiller: to-day they set up their shanties and " stills," quickly they cut down or exhaust the trees, to-morrow they are gone, leaving a desolate and lonesome land. But presently the young oaks, as I have said, begin to clothe the nakedness of the earth—their thicker foliage shades it more than the pine, their leaves fertilize it more richly; then comes the farmer, who substitutes the civilization of corn and cotton for that of timber and turpentine, and erects a permanent house in lieu of the ephemeral shanties.

The road from Weldon to Wilmington presents a cheerful example of this transforming process. Within the recollection of this writer *—who is not an old man—it was, during the days of the lumber-men and the " still "-men, a desolate and barren route such as one could not remember without a dismal feeling; the pines—majestic enough when left alone—were all stumped and scarified, and there was little sign of human life; but it is now dotted with comparatively thriving towns, at which much more traffic is carried on than one unused to the " ways " of these people would ever imagine, and I am told that something like seventy-five thousand bales of cotton were produced last season in this single section.

Of course this process goes on more rapidly in the immediate neighborhood of the lines of railway than elsewhere; and it will not be long, one fancies, before Miss Pertly will travel from Portsmouth, Virginia, to Jacksonville through a level park of oaks.

As a final clincher, in the discussion of pines, one may ask Miss Pertly if she did not go into raptures over those violin-variations of Brahm[s]'s (e. g.), which Theodore Thomas's orchestra played so divinely last winter; and—for of course she did—what would these variations—or indeed anything else the orchestra played—have been without the rosin on those broad fiddle bows?

There is no escape for the young lady,—except by declaring she was not aware that rosin came from pine-trees. Of course she could not be expected to know that besides rosin these pines contain celluline, lignin, starch, turpentine, tar, zylol, phosphoric acid, phosphate of lime, phosphate of magnesia, silicic acid, silicate of potash, carbonate of potash, sulphate of potash, chloride of sodium, sulphate of soda, carbonate of lime, and carbonate of magnesia.

At this hour of the morning in Jacksonville everybody is eating his ante-breakfast oranges, with as much vigor as if he saw himself growing suddenly wrinkled and flaccid, like the gods and goddesses in Wagner's *Rheingold* when they had in their agitation forgotten to eat their daily allowance of the golden fruit which grew in Freya's garden and which was the neces-

* [Lanier was stationed in the Wilmington-Weldon area of North Carolina on several occasions during the Civil War, 1862-1864, as revealed in his letters—ED.]

sary condition of their immortal youth. In truth, to eat one's oranges with some such thought as this would not be wholly absurd. These old metaphors which by a curious intersection of events and of lines of thought converge to a point here in Florida—the metaphors of Freya's youth-conferring fruit, of De Leon's youth-conferring Spring: are they not evolved out of a certain vague sense in the bottom of our hearts that trees and waters—Nature—are full of healing, and that the man will never die who wisely and lovingly reaches forth his hand and plucks nature as a fruit, and eats it and digests it and incorporates it with himself?

But the sight of your dripping fingers reminds one that while there are few pleasanter things than the eating of an orange, yet it is also in the order of nature that difficulty and delight—which are essentially birds of a feather—should fly together, and there are therefore few harder things than the eating of an orange dry-fingered. The stickiness of orange-juice seems somehow at once one of the most unavoidable and most disagreeable of the earthly bads that hang by the goods; and one can never help regretting that neither Mr. George Lewes in his *Problems of Life and Mind,* nor Mr. Greg in his *Rocks Ahead,* has thought fit to treat the question, How to eat an orange.*

Yet it can be done with great daintiness, if the proper appliances are at hand. By Appliances I mean a lady. It is notorious that women can manage an orange with their delicately-tactile fingers to a marvel. There is a tradition in Jacksonville of one who, with kid gloves on her hands, kept the same wholly unspotted during the entire process of peeling, dividing, and eating. However that may be, it is certainly æsthetic delight to see ten white lady fingers deftly coaxing apart the juicy orange-sectors. That *is* apples of gold in pictures of silver.

It has been suggested that the reason for this superior skill is longer experience: woman, though younger than man, commenced to handle fruit sooner. But it is a suggestion that I make a point of loudly and ostentatiously scorning; for, as has been said, the solution of the problem of How to eat an orange depends upon being on good terms with Woman.

* [Volumes just published in 1874 and 1875 by a popular psychologist (the husband of George Eliot) and a social scientist, respectively.—ED.]

First get your orange: and you will at least produce an im-
plication of your connoisseurship in the mind of the dealer if,
in doing so, you ask for Indian River oranges, which many
persons hold to be the typic fruit. Then get your sister or any
available womankind—other men's sisters beside your own
might do—to peel your orange, divide it into sectors, and hand
you these, each lying on its detached arc of peel as on a small
salver. The rest, as the old play says, can be done without book.

Thus the question how to eat an orange without stickiness
resolves itself, in the last analysis, into a question of morals and
of behavior; into, in other words, the question How to be very
good and amiable to your womankind before breakfast; insomuch that one may look to see the time—coincident with the
bearing-time of the millions of young orange-trees which the
recent activities of Florida have set growing—when the orange
shall transform the bearish husbands of the whole land into
knightly lovers, and when Growly's manner to Mrs. G. before
breakfast shall be as suave and bland as is the juice of the fruit
itself—like the dyer's hand, subdued to what it works in.

By this time, no matter in what direction we may have
started, we will have arrived in Bay Street, which runs parallel
with and next to the river. It is the main business street of the
city, and is a lively enough thoroughfare of a winter's morning.
The curious visitors are trooping everywhere along the sidewalks—to the post-office, to the fruit-stores, to the palmetto-
braiders', to the curiosity-shops, to the wharf for a sailboat, to
the fizzing steamboats for a trip up the St. Johns or the Ocklawaha. The merchants and shop-keepers are all busy. Along
with the noises of traffic comes the hum of the lumber-mills;
fitly enough, for the latter are said to conduce no little to the
prosperity of the former, in bringing about cheap freights. The
three-masted schooners that you see lying at the wharves there,
waiting for cargoes of lumber, will transport heavy goods at
almost any price when they come here, rather than sail in
ballast.

The visitor strolling down this street soon discovers that not
an inconsiderable item in the commerce of Jacksonville is the
trade in " Florida curiosities," to which he will find several establishments devoted. These curiosities are sea-beans, alliga-

tors' teeth, plumes of herons' and curlews' feathers, cranes'-wings, angel-fish, mangrove and orange walking-canes, coral branches, coquina-figures, and many others. The sea-beans are interesting in more particulars than one. For example, how do they get on the eastern coast of Florida? After extensive inquiry, I was unable to find any person who had ever seen them [1] growing on the Florida shore; and the universal testimony of the sailors I met was that they were washed over from vines on the coasts of the West Indies. But, if Maury's idea of the Gulf Stream's shape and of its effect upon drift-matter be true, they *could* not be washed over from the West Indies. That author declares that the Gulf Stream is higher in the centre than at its edges, and that a subsidiary current, like rain shed from the roof, runs from the middle to the sides with sufficient force to carry a boat in a lateral direction; for which reason the drift-matter on the eastern edge is not, and cannot be, found on the western. This being so, how could sea-beans, grown in the West Indies—that is, east or south of the Gulf Stream—be washed over to Florida—that is, to shores west or north of it? And, if they do not cross it, what route do they pursue?

There are many varieties of sea-beans, differing greatly in shape and color, from the small round red ones, much affected by some for vest-buttons, through the medium-sized agate ones, which are split and mounted with gold for sleeve-buttons, to the large, perfect heart-shaped ones, of rich lava brown, more than two inches in length. The most beautiful, *me judice*, are those rare ones whose surfaces show a polished similitude of velvety leopard skins.

The alligators' teeth are made into whistles, watch-charms, and the like. It may be that some poor half-invalid of limited means, but of independent disposition, might find his account at once as to health and purse, by wandering among the numerous small unfrequented streams in lower Florida and making a business of shooting alligators and gathering their teeth; for I heard one of the largest curiosity-dealers in Florida freely

[1] They are the fruit of a leguminous plant, and drop from their pods into the sea. [The source of Lanier's information on the Gulf Stream in the following sentence is obviously M. F. Maury, *The Physical Geography of the Sea*.—Ed.]

offering from four to eight dollars a pound for such teeth, in any quantities, however large or small. I was told that the process of gathering the teeth was simply to shoot the animal, leave the carcass lying for a couple of months, and then revisit it and draw the loosened teeth from their sockets. The variation in price depends upon the size, the large ones bringing much higher prices than the small.

Jacksonville is as it were a city built to order, and many provisions have been made for employing the leisure of its winter visitors. A very good circulating-library is to be found on the northern side of Bay Street, a short distance below the National Hotel, which is open to strangers for borrowing; and a lively news-vender in the same room supplies all the prominent current papers and magazines every morning. A pleasant sort of exchange for visitors is also to be found in the reading-room of Ambler's Bank, farther down Bay Street, on the opposite side. Beyond this, a few doors, is the post-office. At the sign " Boats to let," on the wharf, not far below the Grand National, one can find pleasant sailboats for hire at prices ranging from seventy-five cents an hour upward.

Several good livery-stables offer first-class turnouts, in the way of saddle-horses, buggies, and carriages; and there are two shell-roads which afford pleasant drives. A very good objective-point for a ride is

MONCRIEF'S SPRING

This is a mineral spring, not yet analyzed, but said to be of often-tested efficacy in the cure of intermittent fevers and of agues. It lies about four miles from town, near a creek also called Moncrief. There is a tradition—of somewhat filmy basis —that a Jew named Moncrief, who had married an Indian woman, was once murdered by the savages for his money on the banks of this creek and that its name is derived from that event. The spring has been recently taken in charge by a company and many improvements made in its environment. The water is unusually transparent, and is first received in a circular basin twenty feet in diameter. Below this, well-arranged bath-houses, separate for ladies and gentlemen, each sixty feet long by fifteen wide, are being built. A restaurant, bowling-alley, dancing-pavilion, and race-course of a mile in length are also in process of construction. On the way to this spring one passes through the pleasant suburb known as Springfield.

From the high ground here a good view may be obtained of Jacksonville and the river. The hill slopes down to Hogan's Creek, a boundary line of the city. Besides Springfield, the advancing growth of Jacksonville has developed several other named suburbs, such as East Jacksonville, Oakland, Wyoming, La Villa, Brooklyn, Riverside, South Shore, and Alexandria. A small boat plies between Jacksonville and the three last-named points, running also to Reed's Landing.

No traveler of proper sentiments in Jacksonville neglects to have all his womankind furnished with a braided palmetto-hat, trimmed with wild grasses; and this particular writer, with a profound ignorance of all millinery, declares without hesitation that some combinations of these lovely grass-plumes with richly-woven palmetto-plaits form quite the most beautiful coverings he has ever seen on the female head.

Jacksonville not only makes hats of palmettos, it makes champagne of wild oranges; and the drink is said to be palatable enough. From the refuse lees, after the wine is made, the same chemist extracts a valuable essential oil.

Persons can spend their winters in Jacksonville without interrupting the education of their children, and delicate young people can here enjoy the advantage of the mild climate while pursuing their studies. Notable among the schools are: the Episcopalian Academy of St. Mary's Priory, under the personal supervision of the bishop of the diocese, who resides with his family in the school-building: and the Catholic institution, St. Joseph's Academy, under the charge of the Lady Superior and several Sisters of the order of St. Joseph.

In this connection may also be mentioned the Conservatory of Music, just inaugurated in Jacksonville, which seems to be a really praiseworthy attempt to organize musical instruction in the city, and which is advertised as under the care of the Bishop of Florida as President, and of a large number of the prominent citizens of the State as Vice-Presidents.

The city has its full quota of churches, Catholic, Episcopal, Presbyterian, Methodist, and Baptist; and possesses all needful telegraph, express, and general ticket-offices, and other the like adjuncts of civilization.

Jacksonville is indeed the main gateway of the State; and while one is here, one will do well to get some general view of the

TRANSPORTATION SYSTEM OF FLORIDA

The northern breadth of the State is nearly crossed by two railway lines, which are now operated as one, viz.: the Florida Central, running from Jacksonville, westward, to Lake City, and the Jacksonville, Pensacola and Mobile, running from Lake City, farther westward, to Chattahoochee, its present terminus, where the Chattahoochee River and the Flint River unite to form the Apalachicola. The former line passes the important railroad point called Baldwin. The latter goes through Lake City, Live Oak, Madison, Monticello Junction, Tallahassee, and Quincy. It has two branches, one of twenty miles in length, from Tallahassee to St. Marks, on the Gulf Coast; and the other of five miles in length, from Monticello Junction to Monticello. It is intended to terminate at Pensacola, and is now running regularly to Chattahoochee, above named.

The Florida Central is crossed at the above-mentioned Baldwin—twenty miles from Jacksonville—by the railway line of the Atlantic, Gulf and West India Transit Company. This was formerly known as the Florida Railroad, and extends from Fernandina, in the extreme northeast of the State, to Cedar Keys, on the Gulf Coast, one hundred and fifty-four miles southwest. This road runs through the important point of Gainesville, a good winter resort for consumptives. From Gainesville a tri-weekly stage runs to Tampa, on the Gulf Coast, about one hundred and fifty miles distant, *via* Ocala and Brooksville, which are relay-stations about a day's journey apart. A hack also leaves Gainesville for Newnansville twice a week.

At Live Oak a branch of the Atlantic and Gulf Railroad (which runs from Savannah to Albany, Georgia) joins the Jacksonville, Pensacola and Mobile Road. Through trains run twice a day in winter from Savannah to Jacksonville over these roads. The Atlantic and Gulf also brings a through Louisville sleeping-car for Jacksonville daily, receiving it from the Macon and Brunswick Railroad at their crossing-point, Jessup, Georgia.

The Pensacola and Louisville Railroad connects Pensacola

with the Montgomery and Mobile Road, at Pollard, Alabama.
The St. Johns Railway runs from Tocoi (on the east bank of
the St. Johns River, fifty miles above Jacksonville) to St. Augustine. It is fifteen miles in length, and connects regularly with
steamers from Jacksonville plying up the St. Johns.

Returning now to Jacksonville, to begin a similar short
résumé of the lines of water-transportation within the State of
Florida, one finds that place to be the headquarters of a fleet
of steamboats of all sorts, shapes, and sizes, plying up the St.
Johns. A set of river-steamers make daily trips to Pilatka,
seventy-five miles, and to points above as far as to Mellonville
and Enterprise, two settlements on opposite banks of Lake
Munroe, two hundred and five miles from Jacksonville. From
Enterprise a small steamboat makes excursions to Lakes Harney
and Jessup, a few miles distant, for the scenery, the fishing, and
the shooting. Other steamboats convey the traveler from Jacksonville up the river past the points named to Salt Lake, whence
a short drive conveys him to Sand Point, and to Titusville, on
Indian River. The little steamboat *Pioneer* plies from Titusville
to Jupiter Inlet, along the great lagoon of Indian River. Still
other small steamboats run from Jacksonville up the Ocklawaha
River to Silver Spring, *via* Pilatka; and sometimes, on high
water, quite up to Leesburg and Okahumpka, or Okahumpkee,
the head of Ocklawaha navigation. Pilatka is the headquarters
also of a line up the Ocklawaha.

Down the western coast a weekly mail steamer leaves Cedar
Keys for Key West, touching at Manatee, Punta Rassa, and
Tampa. A weekly steamer from New Orleans also touches at
Cedar Keys and Key West, on the way to Havana.

From Cedar Keys a small steamer plies once a week to
Suwannee.

It is probable also that a steamer will leave Cedar Keys once
a week during the winter of 1875-6 for Sarasota Bay, on the
Gulf Coast, touching at several minor points which are specified
in what is hereinafter said under the head of "The Gulf Coast."

From Fernandina to Jacksonville water-communication is had
by ("outside line") the steamers *Dictator* and *City Point*,
which each leave Charleston once a week, touching at Fernandina and Jacksonville; and by ("inside line") the steamer
Lizzie Baker, which leaves Savannah once a week, touching at

Brunswick, Georgia, Fernandina and Jacksonville; both these lines extending up the St. Johns to Pilatka and intervening river-landings.

The details of all these matters will be found in the guide-book which constitutes the latter portion of this volume.

Jacksonville is in latitude 30° 19′ 38″ N., and longitude 81° 30′ 7″ W. Its climate and general meteorology are fully set forth in a subsequent chapter on The Climate of Florida. Twenty-five miles to the eastward is the mouth of the St. Johns. Here are two proposed places of resort: one to the northward, on Fort George Island, and one to the southward, at " Mayport," on the mainland.

But Jacksonville, although the main gate to Florida, is not the only one. Lying on the northern end of Amelia Island, at the extreme northeastern portion of the State, is the important seaport of

FERNANDINA

The natural advantages of this now flourishing little city were known for some time before they were permanently brought into practical use. The bar gives about nineteen feet of water reliably to incoming vessels; the harbor is exceedingly capacious and securely land-locked; an inside passage between the islands lying along the Georgia shore and the mainland affords a quiet water-way to Savannah; and a similar passage between Amelia Island and the Florida coast extends to within a few miles of the mouth of the St. Johns, thus facilitating water-communication with Jacksonville. The completion of the Florida Railroad (now the Atlantic Gulf and West India Transit Company's Railway) connected Fernandina with Cedar Keys, on the Gulf of Mexico, and made it the shipping-point for Gulf products, as well as for the lumber and turpentine staples of the great pine-forests through which this railroad runs. The raising of early vegetables for the Northern market can, it is said, be carried on in this neighborhood with unusual advantages, arising from the facilities for transportation afforded by a weekly line of steamers direct to New York, a semi-weekly line to Charleston, and a weekly line to Savannah, besides the daily railroad communication with Savannah. To strangers, and, indeed, to many of the " natives " of Florida, the sandy soils which are found about Fernandina would not seem to give much encouragement to the raising of vegetables, or of anything else. As they say in the South, the land "looks like you could not raise a row on it." But careful and extensive inquiry appears to establish that these white sands, not only of Fernandina, but of a great deal of the other Florida territory, have in them many of the fecundities which one usually associates with black soils. And to this conclusion have come all who have investigated the facts. "When I first came here, nine years ago," said the venerable Solon Robinson in the Convention of the Florida Fruit Growers, last January, "and saw the sandy soil, . . . I was inclined to be disgusted. The first thing that convinced me the soil was fertile was the abundance of weeds growing in the white sand. Then I saw large trees growing at the rate of an inch a year, and I said to myself, 'There is *something* in this sand not in my philosophy.' " *

Said ex-Governor Reed ** in the same Convention: "The truth is, we do not appreciate the productive capacity and value of our soil. . . . When I first landed on Amelia Island (Fernandina) I thought its sands barren and valueless. But I noticed that when the drifting sand formed a lodgment for a season, it was immediately overgrown by a rank vegetation," etc.

Fernandina has now a population of about three thousand; two hotels, the Riddell House and the Norwood House, besides a number of boarding-houses; seven churches, and a newspaper. A general idea of its climate may be obtained from the remarks on the climate of Florida in the chapter hereinafter devoted to that subject.

Amelia Island figures in the earlier chronicles of Florida history as the province of Guale. The dreadful crusade—a crusade *en revers*—of that bloody Indian, the son of the chief of Guale, in 1598, against the priests at St. Augustine and other places, is recounted in the historical sketch hereinbefore given. Fernandina was a port of some resort during the Spanish occupation, and came into considerable prominence during the war of 1812, when it was neutral as between the United States and

* [*Proceedings of the Florida Fruit Growers' Association,* Jan. 20-24, 1875 (Jacksonville, 1875). Summary also in *Appleton's Annual Cyclopedia,* 1875 (under *Florida*).—ED.]

** [Harrison Reed, Governor of Florida, 1868-1873.—ED.]

Great Britain. It was also brought into notice in the year 1812 as the base of operations of a very absurd though finally bloody attempt by a party of "patriots" from near the borders of Georgia and Florida to seize and occupy the latter State. The United States had for its own purposes placed nine gunboats in the harbor of Fernandina; with the co-operation of these, the "patriots" under Colonel Ashley compelled the Spanish garrison of the town to surrender it, and then proceeded to march against St. Augustine. It was not long, however, before they retired, having effected nothing more than the massacre of several of their men by the negroes of St. Augustine, and the imposition upon the United States Government of a very difficult and delicate matter to explain to the Spaniards.

A shell road leads out of Fernandina to its celebrated beach, where for fifteen or more miles the visitor can drive over one of the smoothest roads in the world.

Dungeness (called hereabout Dun-je-néss), on Cumberland Island, separated by the inlet only from Amelia Island, is an interesting objective-point for an excursion. Here is the seat of General Nathaniel Greene, upon the estate which was presented him by the grateful State of Georgia in recognition of his Revolutionary services. The olives, the gardens, the great oaks, the trailing mosses, are well worth seeing; and the grave of Henry Lee, the father of Robert E. Lee—him who was called "Light-Horse Harry" — lies some half-mile from the house, speaking many eloquent things there, betwixt the sea and the woods, to every man who loves knightly honor and manliness.

CHAPTER V

THE GULF COAST

FLORIDA POSSESSES a coast line of about twelve hundred miles, of which greatly the larger half is washed by the Gulf of Mexico. There seems to be literally no end to the oysters, the fish, the sea-birds, the shells, the turtles, along these waters; and the shore and islands abound in the bear, deer, turkey, opossum and raccoon, and in smaller game. The most marvelous stories are told—ceasing to seem marvelous when one has really seen something of the multitudinous piscine life of these parts—of the hosts of the fish, even to the stoppage of vessels that have sailed into shoals of them. For mere variety these fish are wonderful. Here are the black-fish, white-fish, yellow bream, blue bream, silver bream, grouper, porgy, barracooter, trout, perch, eel, mullet, herring, flounder, gar, sheep-head, bass, grunt, yellow-tail, jew-fish, king-fish, pompino,* amber-fish, angel-fish, red-snapper, drum, whiting, sturgeon, whipperee (whip-jack), skate, and one knows not how many more. Here, too, one can follow that most sardonic of all sports, turtle-catching. You walk along the lovely beach at night, when the turtle has come up from the waters to deposit her hundreds of eggs; you see one: you advance, and coolly turn it over on its back,— and that is all. You leave it, leisurely pursue your stroll, turn another on its back, leave it, and so on, till you are tired. When you come again on the morrow, there they are. To walk up to a turtle of a morning, after having treated him in this manner overnight, and look steadily in the eye thereof without certain titillating sensations at once in your diaphragm (where you laugh) and in your conscience (where you do not laugh), re-quires more grim rigidity of the former and more supple elasticity of the latter than *some* people possess.

Nor can there be anything in life—considered without refer-ence to your own act in making it so—more preposterous than an upturned turtle, lying, poor innocent, on its mildly-convex

* [Lanier was apparently relying on his ear only in his spelling of *pompano* and *barracuda* (or *barracouta*), above.—ED.]

back, with its mildly-white obverse staring blearly at heaven, and its flippers wriggling in flabby helplessness toward the four quarters of the earth. It seems the very self-assertion of feeble wish-wash; it looks like mere Zero sick. The beholder's mind appears to resolve itself into a tepid pool of vapid lymph, in the shallow depths whereof one perceives slowly drowning out of sight any possible faith in the ancient fable which, through the sinew-strung tortoise-shell, connects the divine art of music with these inane creatures.

Yet there have been men who found pathos in this same situation of the turtle. In the year 1682 one " T. A.," [1] " Clerk on board his Majestie's ship *The Richmond*," among many other sprightly lucubrations, wrote from these Western parts of the world an account of the turtle, wherein he says:

Before they [the butchers] kill them [the turtles] they are laid on their Backs, where, hopeless of Relief, as if sensible of their future Con-dition, for some hours they mourn out their Funerals, the tears plenti-fully flowing from their eyes, accompanied with passionate sobs and sighs, in my Judgment nothing more like than such who are surrounded and overwhelmed with Troubles, Cares, and Griefs, which raise in strangers both Pity and Compassion.

Somewhat less overdrawn is T. A.'s description of another and better authenticated peculiarity of the turtle.

This I am assured of, [says he,] that after it's cut to pieces, it retains a sensation of Life three times longer than any known creature in the Creation. . . . Compleatly six hours after the Butcher has cut them up and into pieces mangled their bodies, I have seen the Callope [2] when going to be seasoned, with pieces of their Flesh ready to cut into Steaks, vehemently contract with great Reluctancy, rise against the Knife, and sometimes the whole mass of Flesh in a visible Tremulation and Concussion: to him who first sees it seems strange and admirable;

a tenacity of life which T. A. doubtless connected in his own mind with a certain superfluity of vital organs possessed by the turtle: he records that " it has 3 Hearts."

---

[1] Supposed by some to have been Thomas Ashe. [The passages concerning turtles and sea-cows are quoted and paraphrased from " A Compleat Discovery of the State of Carolina," as printed in B. R. Carroll, *Historical Collections of South Carolina*.—ED.]

[2] *Callipee*: a part of the flesh.

T. A. gives also a lively description of the Manatee, or Sea-
Cow, of these regions; from which, it may be remarked in
passing, Manatee County—one of the Gulf Coast counties of
Florida with a charming climate—derives its name.

The Manacy, or Sea-Cow, [he declares to be] a Fish of an extraordinary
Bigness, sometimes of a 1000 pound Weight: it feeds on the Banks and
Shoar Sides on the grassy Herbage, like a Tortoise; but that which is
more wonderful of this Creature is that she gives her young ones suck
from her Duggs; she is indeed like a Cow, of a green Colour, her Flesh
esteemed by some the most delicate in the world. It hath a Stone in
the Head, which is a gallant Remedy against the Pains and Dolours of
the Stone; . . . and its Skin makes excellent whips for Horses, if
prudently used, which are very serviceable and lasting; with one of
these Manaty straps I have seen a bar of iron cut and dented.

To the tourist and sportsman desiring a mild flavor of adventure, this portion of Florida offers a charming field; and
any invalid who is able to endure the comparative rudeness of
this manner of life cannot but find benefit from the liberal
air and genial appetites which range together along these quiet
shores.

It is probable that the air here is somewhat milder (getting
more so, of course, the farther down one goes) and dryer than
on the eastern coast in midwinter; and it is to be greatly hoped
that increased facilities for reaching these favorable regions will
soon render them practicable to those who now find the journey
too trying. It is in contemplation to send a weekly steamer from
Cedar Keys, touching at all the points which are hereinafter
named in detail, as far down as to Sarasota Bay, at which latter
location some Northern gentlemen have projected a colony.
Information as to this steamer can be obtained by letter addressed to Captain A. E. Willard, at Cedar Keys, Florida,—of
whom more presently.

At the extreme northwest end of the Gulf Coast is the city
of Pensacola, on Pensacola Bay, ten miles inland from the
Gulf. It is the county-site of Escambia County, and has about
four thousand inhabitants. It is noted for its bar which admits
vessels of twenty-two feet always and of twenty-four feet at
high tide, and for the breadth and directness of the harbor-
entrance. Seven miles down the bay is the United States Navy-

yard, with its two settlements, Woolsey and Warrington. The channel is defended by Fort Barrancas—which is on the mainland, a mile below the navy-yard—and Fort Pickens, on Santa Rosa Island. The latter, however, is little used at present.

The main activity of Pensacola is in the shipment of lumber, which is sent from here to the West Indies, South America, home ports, and other parts of the world. During the year ending September 30th, 1873, two hundred and fifty-nine vessels cleared here for various ports, carrying more than a hundred million feet of lumber and timber. There are here also small importations of liquors and cigars: and occasionally coal and salt are brought by ships coming for lumber.

The completion of the Pensacola and Louisville Railroad, running from Pensacola forty-four miles to Pensacola Junction, on the Mobile and Montgomery Railroad, has given the city a start, and it bids fair to become an important place.

The Perdido Railroad is a short line of nine miles, connecting Pensacola Bay with the large lumber establishments of Millview, on Perdido Bay.

During the old wars between the French, Spanish, and English, Pensacola was the scene of several animated contests. These are mentioned more particularly in the historical chapter of this book.

Cedar Keys, the western terminus of the Florida (or Atlantic Gulf and West India Company's) Railway, is a town of about five hundred inhabitants, in Levy County, one hundred and fifty-four miles from Fernandina. It is situated immediately on the Gulf, being built upon two " Keys " (from the Spanish *Cayo*, French *Quais*; same word as English, " Quay "), one of which is called Way Key, the other Atsena Otie. Between these a small sail ferry-boat plies, which you call to you—of course every one knows that a ferry-boat is always on the other side— by the hoisting of a flag on the pole which stands at the end of the wharf.

At Cedar Keys, and from there on in an increasing degree to the southward as one reaches the places hereinafter named, one finds that one has come into a country differing in many particulars from any part of Florida yet mentioned—a country of cedars, of sponges, of corals, of strange fish, of shells multi-

tudinous in shape and tint, of hundreds of quiet bays whose
circular waters lie embraced in the curves of their white beaches
as the old moon in the cusps of the new. There is a certain large
blandness in the atmosphere, a sense of far-awayness in the
wide water-stretches, an indefinable feeling of withdrawal from
harsh life, that give to this suave region, as compared with
others, the proportion which mild dreams bear to realities. It
is a sort of Arabian Nights vaguely diffused and beaten out into
long, glittering, sleepy expanses, and the waters presently cease
to be waters and seem only great level enchantments-that-shine.

The main commerce of Cedar Keys is in cedar and pine wood,
turtles, sponges, and fish.

These turtles are caught by the fishermen and kept in turtle-
"crawls," or inclosures staked off in the water, until ready for
shipment; and I am told that the turtle-crawl occupies much the
same relation in each private household along the Gulf Coast
that the chicken-coop does to inland dwellers.

The sponging-grounds are about sixty miles in a southerly
direction off Cedar Keys. The fishermen bring in their catch of
sponges to Cedar Keys, where they are baled and shipped to
market. Much of the product of these grounds, however, goes
to Key West, for lack of capital at Cedar Keys.

There are two places of accommodation at Cedar Keys, one
called the Gulf House, the other the Exchange. The accommodations at these are somewhat primitive; a fact which is to be
particularly regretted, for the reason that this would unquestionably be a pleasant headquarters for the most delightful excursions down the Gulf Coast if it were otherwise. The writer
mentions it with genuine pain, because the proprietor of the
house at which he stopped seemed anxious to do all in his
power to serve his guests, and there can be nothing but thanks
for his intentions; but with his materials, it was quite impossible
to accomplish much. Nevertheless, tourists—particularly those
fond of fishing and hunting—and invalids bent on the open
air and rude life cure, which can be pursued with great advantage farther down the coast, may come by this route with
no serious discomfort; and all that is meant by the strictures
above is simply to protect oneself against the just reprehension
of the daintier classes of pleasure-seekers and delicate invalids

who might be tempted by the charms—which are certainly great—of this portion of Florida to come to Cedar Keys for a prolonged stay. Possibly, too, better hotel-accommodations may be offered during the winter of 1875-6. A good hotel building was commenced a short time ago, on the shell mound which rises abruptly at one end of the town, but was blown down while in the frame, leaving the parties unable to proceed.

There is indeed at " Ford's "—the next station to Cedar Keys on the railway, going inland—a large house, which, I am told, was built by a gentleman who came there three or four years ago, seemingly far gone with consumption, but who has recovered his health and gone largely into the business of market-gardening. Here one could apparently be well lodged and fed: and it is but a few miles by rail to the Gulf.

The objective-points along the coast below Cedar Keys are, first, the Crystal River and Hamosassa settlements, Bayport, Anclote River, Clear Water Harbor, Law's Store (John's Pass), McMullen's Store, Philippi's Grove (a noted orange-grove), and Point Penales. In the course down to this point the mouths of the Withlacoochee, Crystal, Hamosassa, Chessawhiska, and Wecawachee (*alias* Wecaiwoochee) Rivers will have been passed, the last four of which are clear and splendid streams, formed by springs which break out ten or twelve miles from the coast. They are all set with numerous islands at their debouchments into the Gulf. One of the largest sawmills in Florida is situated at the mouth of the Withlacoochee, and is supplied with material from the timber floated down that stream. There is an inside passage from Cedar Keys to this point: and one of the most important projects, it would seem, that has been mooted in Florida, is one to connect the Withlacoochee River with the Ocklawaha by a canal, for which a charter has been already obtained by Colonel Hart, of Pilatka. An astonishingly small amount of labor would accomplish this end, and would thus render practicable a clear water-way across the entire peninsula of Florida from the Gulf to the Atlantic. Lake Panasofka, which has the Withlacoochee for its outlet into the Gulf, is but about thirteen miles from Lake Harris, whose outlet is the Ocklawaha, flowing into the St. Johns. Thus this new water-way would be: from the Gulf of Mexico, up the Withlacoochee, *via* Lakes Panasofka, Okohumpka, and Harris, into the Ocklawaha, thence into the St. Johns, to the Atlantic Ocean.

The enumeration above has brought us down to Tampa, the county-site of Hillsborough County, lying at the head of Tampa Bay just below the twenty-eighth parallel of north latitude. Here is a noble harbor, where De Soto landed in 1539, at the commencement of his wanderings.

Passing on southward from Tampa, the settlements are at Alafia (pronounced Alafeéa), Terrasea Bay, Little Manatee, Manatee, Sarasota, Charlotte Harbor and Punta Rassa: in the course of which occur the mouths of the Hillsboro', Alafia, Manatee, and Myakka Rivers, Pease Creek, the Tsalo-Papko-Hatchee, Halpata Hatchee, and Caloosatchee Rivers.

At all the settlements named board can be obtained, as I am informed: and it is said that the Orange Grove Hotel at Tampa, which has been temporarily closed, will be again opened during this winter of 1875-6.

Three of these points, to-wit, Tampa, Manatee, and Punta Rassa, are visited weekly by a mail steamer from Cedar Keys. Tampa, as has already been stated, is also the terminus of a tri-weekly hack line, from Gainesville, *via* Brooksville and Ocala.

The other points can be reached either by special contract for the steam-launch belonging to Captain A. E. Willard, of Cedar Keys, or by sail either from that point or Tampa. Any one making this excursion, would do well to communicate by letter beforehand with the gentleman just named, who is minutely informed as to this entire coast, is one of the most enterprising persons in this portion of Florida, and seems as courteous as he is active.

Below Tampa, these settlements I have named represent a belt of farming country, reaching a short distance inland, which contains fertile lands, sparsely cultivated, and forests of red cedar. Farther inland is a great cattle range, where the herds, belonging sometimes to far remote proprietors, feed at will the year round, without further attention from their owners than the annual expedition for the purpose of branding the newly-dropped calves, and of driving to the shipping port those which have been selected to be sold. The shipments are mainly to Cuba. One of the largest of these cattle-owners resides at Orlando, but ships his cattle from the port of Punta Rassa.

CHAPTER VI

THE TALLAHASSEE COUNTRY OR PIEDMONT FLORIDA

A S WE SAT in the railway car, steaming towards Tallahasse, a certain entomological adventure of an unknown lady and gentleman on the seat in front prepared us, in an indirect yet satisfactory way, for the fact that during a night of travel we had arrived in a different land from that about Jacksonville. Having settled themselves in their seats after a somewhat elaborate car-toilet, *his* gaze became suddenly fastened on the back of her neck; he grew contemplative, then earnest; a short stage of conviction followed; then he took action; plucking the Object from her neck betwixt his finger and thumb and regarding it seriously, he said, in a tone at once meditative and inquiring, " My dear, this is a *strange* flea; *this* is not a *Jacksonville* flea! "

So little mention has been made of this part of Florida, that many persons will be surprised at learning that there is any portion of the State which could justify an appellation ending in *mont*. But the counties of Madison, Jefferson, Leon, Gadsden, and Jackson, all lying in what is called " Middle Florida " except Jackson, which is in " West Florida," embrace as fair a set of arable hills as one would wish to see, some reaching to the height of four hundred feet. The important towns of these counties are Madison (Madison County), Monticello (Jefferson County), Tallahassee (Leon County), Quincy (Gadsden County), and Marianna (Jackson County), all of which except the last lie on the line of the Jacksonville, Pensacola and Mobile Railway.

Of these, the most important is the capital of the State,

TALLAHASSEE

In the year 1539, after De Soto had made his landing in Tampa Bay (or *Espiritu Santo* Bay, as he called it), he fared northward with his army for several days, and came to a " Great Morass," about which he made a *détour*; then marching four days longer through a fertile and well-inhabited country, he

69

arrived at the Indian village of Anhayca (or Anhayea), situated
in the midst thereof; and appears to have made his headquarters at that place for some little while, awaiting there the
return of the exploring expeditions which he sent in various
directions.

Several circumstances make it probable that this Anhayca
was near the present site of the city of Tallahassee; and I am
told that a complete suit of old Spanish armor was found not
long ago in a field in this vicinity.

At any rate, the ground upon which the city is built had, in
1823, long borne signs of Indian occupation; and in that year
the commissioners who had been charged with the duty of
selecting a seat of government for the then new Territory of
Florida, attracted by the general beauty of the location among
the hills as well as by the "noble growths" (according to
Fairbanks) "of live-oaks and magnolias, and . . . the vicinity
of a beautiful cascade, which has long since disappeared," *
pitched upon this spot.

And surely no one with an eye either for agricultural advantages or for the more spiritual beauties of hill-curves and tree-
arabesques can do other than praise the happiness of their
choice.

For several miles before reaching Tallahassee one begins to
see a country differing wholly in appearance from the lumber
and turpentine regions of Duval, Baker, Columbia, and Suwannee Counties, through which one will have passed on the way
from Jacksonville. Long fences, generous breadths of chocolate-
colored fields, spreading oaks, curving hills, ample prospects,
come before the eye.

As we shot out by an unusually open expanse some four or
five miles from Tallahassee, a little quick-drawn breath of
pleasure from my comrade made me look through the car-
window upon a lovely sight. We had emerged upon the shore
of Lake Lafayette; it was early in the morning, and the water
had that delicate sheen of distilled silver which it wears at no
other time, a sheen like an indefinite rolling out of the two
dainty cusps of the very newest moon, a sheen like the soft and
innocent childhood of a brightness which at maturity will be

* [Quoted from George R. Fairbanks, *History of Florida.*—ED.]

dazzling. Over the stirless plain of pleasant glory lay hundreds
and thousands and surely millions of virginal white water-lilies;
presently they thickened, there were yards and rods and acres
of them, until the whole surface of the water was covered without break; it was a long winding lake of round green lily-pads,
mysteriously upborne, and stretching away like a green heaven
in which were set the innumerable spherical stars of the lilies.
Occasionally, in shallow portions of the lake, young growths
of cypresses stood with slender stalks thickly in the water and
lifted their masses of tender green foliage a foot or two above
the surface. Under this canopy, between these many-figured
trunks, meandering away in the most charming galaxies and
vistas and labyrinths, ran the lilies; the eye did not have time
to regret the turning of one course of them out of sight ere
another presented itself; the ranges and involutions of them
seemed an endless fantasy of lilies involved in an endless dream
of lily-pads and cypress-stems. The sun was not yet up, the
perfect blue of the sky was in pellucid accord with the gentle
and unglaring white and green that reigned below, and the
noble and simple curves of the inclosing hills secluded this
Diana's-troop of freshnesses and lovelinesses and purities in a
firm yet velvety horizon.

Winding about among the hills for a few minutes longer, we
came presently to the Tallahassee depot; then a carriage took
us up the bold hill, about whose base we had just been steaming; and we found ourselves drawn up in front of a genuine
old-fashioned tavern, with a long double piazza running along
its entire front, with many nooks and corners here and there,
and with a general suggestion of old-timey ease and honest
comfort arising indefinably out of its aspect. These suggestions
took, as we entered, the more substantial shapes of well-
furnished apartments whose dimensions showed a Southern
amplitude, and of a neat colored "Auntie" who took charge
of our bags and ushered us into our quarters with a quiet respect
that formed the very perfection of unobtrusive courtesy.

In which quarters, however, not long did we stay; for in
ascending the long flight of stairs at the rear of the house we
had observed that a double-story piazza also ran around the
whole length of this side of it, ells and all, and an indistinct
view of ground sloping rapidly down from the back of the

building, and of a wide and much-notched horizon, had revealed itself as we passed. Upon re-emerging on the upper
story of the rear piazza, this vague promise fulfilled itself right
fairly. Toward every side the hills swelled up, colored with
colors that suggested fertility and abundance; their rounded
brows, their slopes, the valleys between them, were full of
green crops; comfortable homesteads and farm-buildings re-
posed in the distances, each cluster of which had its own protecting grove of oaks standing about it in the benignant attitudes of outer *lares* and *penates*; it was that sort of prospect
which the grave old English writers would have called " goodlye,
pleasaunt, and smylynge." These hills carried with them no
associations of hills. They did not in the least suggest agita-
tions or upheavals. They only seemed to be great level uplands,
distended like udders with a bounteous richness almost too
large for their content.

And this indeed has always been the tone of things—not only
of the hills, but of the social life—in Tallahassee. The repute
of these people for hospitality was matter of national renown
before the war between the States: and even the dreadful reverses of that cataclysm appear to have spent their force in vain
against this feature of Tallahassee manners; for much testimony
since the war—to which this writer cheerfully adds his own—
goes to show that it exists unimpaired. Genuine hospitality of
this sort is indeed as unconquerable as Zeno's problem of
Achilles and the Tortoise is unanswerable. The logic of it is
that if there is enough for ten, there is certainly enough for
eleven; and if enough for eleven, enough for twelve; and so on
ad infinitum; and this reasoning has such a mysterious virtue
in it, that it has compassed among good-hearted folk many a
repetition of the miracle of the loaves and fishes. It really appears to have been a serious question here, just after the war
had completely upset the whole productive system and stunned
every energy of the land, of what avail would so little be among
so many; but no one has starved, and albeit the people are poor
and the dwellings need paint and ready money is slow of circulation, yet it must be confessed that the bountiful tables looked
like anything but famine, that signs of energy cropped out here
and there in many places, and that the whole situation was but
a reasonable one for a people who ten years ago had to begin

life anew from the very bottom, with no capital, and with a set of laborers who had gone into politics to such an extent that their field-duties were often interrupted by taking their seats in the Legislature, or by other cares of office incompatible with the plow and the hoe.

Besides this City Hotel, which has been recently refitted and newly furnished, there are several boarding-houses in Tallahassee for the accommodation of travelers.

Opposite the City Hotel, in a well-kept square adorned with trees and flowers, is the Capitol Building. Here a visitor in the winter-time can study the working of Southern State Legislatures since the war.

Tallahassee abounds in beautiful groves of trees. There is a fourfold avenue of noble oaks diagonally across and down the street from the Capitol, next the residence of ex-Governor Walker,* whereof surely Dan Chaucer must have dreamed:

> And to a pleasaunt grove I 'gan to pass
>   Long or the brighte Sonne up-risen was;
>
> In which were okes greate, streight as a line,
>   Under the which the grasse, so fresh of hewe,
> Was newly sprong; and an eight foot or nine
>   Every tree well fro' his fellow grew,
>   With branches brode, lade with leves newe,
> That sprongen out ayen the sunne shene,
> Some very red and some a glad light grene;
>
> .   .   .   .
>
> And I, that all this pleasaunt sight ay sie,
>   Thought sodainly I felte so sweet an aire
> Com of the eglentere, that certainely
>   There is no heart, I deme, in such dispaire,
>   Ne with no thoughtes froward and contraire
> So overlaid, but it shoulde soone have bote,
> If it had ones felt this savour sote.**

Besides this, a walk or drive down the main street reveals

---

* [David Shelby Walker, Governor of Florida, 1866-1868, was Lanier's personal friend. See letter, Florida Walker to Mary Day Lanier, June 21, 1875 (MS, Charles D. Lanier Collection, Johns Hopkins University).—ED.]

** [From " The Flower and the Leaf," attributed to Chaucer in Richard Morris's edition, a copy of which Lanier owned.—ED.]

much other great wealth of leaf and flower loveliness clustering
about the spacious Southern homes.

The city has its post-office, telegraph- and express-offices,
two newspapers, and churches of all the main denominations;
with a population of between twenty-five hundred and three
thousand.

Lake Lafayette — so called from its situation on the estate
granted to the Marquis de Lafayette by the United States—
Lake Jackson, Lake Bradford, Lake Miccosukee, and Lake
Iamonia (pronounced with the *I* long and the accent on the
antepenult) all form charming objective-points for excursions,
and offer the substantial results of fine fish as well as lovely
views by way of invitations. Wild ducks, brent, and geese are
also found, often in great numbers.

One of these lakes—Lake Miccosukee—is supposed to be the
true origin of the St. Marks River. The lake contracts to a creek
at its southeastern end, and disappears in the earth through one
of the numerous " lime-sinks " of this portion of Florida. The
St. Marks (hereinafter referred to) rises abruptly from the
earth a short distance from here, and is thought to be only the
re-emergence of the waters of the lake.

The environment of these lakes is varied and beautiful. The
hills surround them now with gently-receding curves, now with
bolder bluffs, now with terraces rising one above another to the
height of a hundred feet in all; many growths of great glossy-
leaved magnolias, of water-oaks and live-oaks, of hickory, ash,
wild-cherry, mock-orange, glorify the shores; and between and
around and over these hang the clematis, the woodbine, the wild
grape-vines; while underneath appear the lesser growths of the
red-bud, the old man's beard, the sparkle berry, the dog-wood,
the wild plum; and still beneath these the yet more lowly but
not less beautiful forms of daisies, violets, primroses, spigelia,
bloodroot, and a thousand other delicate wild flowers and
grasses; and the great " bonnets," a foot and a half in diameter,
with their enormous white multiple stars, and the flags and
water-grasses purfle all the coves and bays in never-ending new
patterns and fantasies.

A mile and a half from town, on a commanding hill overlooking a broad sweep of cultivated farm-lands, is the unpre-
tending dwelling where used to cluster a circle of witty and

cultivated people about Murat* and his accomplished wife. The place is now owned by ex-Governor Bloxham,** whose own home-place one sees on the hill beyond, surrounded by a grove of oaks.

About fifteen miles from Tallahassee is one of the most wonderful springs in the world—the famous Wakulla Spring, which sends off a river from its single outburst. The easiest way to reach it is to cause a conveyance to be sent ahead from Tallahassee to Oil Station, on the St. Marks Branch Railway, to which point one proceeds by car, and takes carriage then for the spring, six miles distant. The road to the spring is uninteresting; but once arrived and afloat on its bosom, one renews the pleasures which have been hereinbefore described in what was said of Silver Spring. Like that, the water here, which is similarly impregnated with lime, is thrillingly transparent; here one finds again the mosaic of many-shaded green hues, though the space of the spring is less broad and more shadowed by overhanging trees than the wide basin of Silver Spring. In one particular, however, this is the more impressive of the two. It is one hundred and six feet deep; and as one slowly floats face downward, one perceives, at first dimly, then more clearly, a great ledge of white rock which juts up to within perhaps fifty feet of the surface, from beneath which the fish come swimming as if out of the gaping mouth of a great cave. Looking down past the upper part of this ledge, down, down through the miraculous lymph, which impresses you at once as an abstraction and as a concrete substance, to the white concave bottom where you can plainly see a sort of "trouble in the ground" as the water bursts up from its mysterious channel, one feels more than ever that sensation of depth itself wrought into a substantial embodiment, of which I have before spoken.

Three miles from the Oil Station just mentioned, in the opposite direction to that of Wakulla Spring, is the little village of

* [Achille Murat (1801-1847), a nephew of Napoleon, owned the plantation " Lipona " near Tallahassee. His wife was a grand-niece of George Washington.—ED.]

** [William Dunnington Bloxham served as governor of Florida 1881-1885, and again 1897-1901. " Ex-Governor " is here (1875) a courtesy title referring to his election in 1870 as lieutenant governor, though he was prevented from taking his seat by the carpet-bag legislature. See John Wallace, *Carpet-bag Rule in Florida* (Jacksonville, 1888).—ED.]

Newport. Here, in the old days of long ago, when Apalachicola shipped its hundred thousand bales of cotton and St. Marks was a busy port, grew a thriving country trading-point; but it now contains only a few families. A hotel has recently been opened, near which is a good sulphur spring, and a few feet from whose doors runs the St. Marks River, wherein there is good sport to be had with rod and gig. Not far off, also, is the Natural Bridge, where the St. Marks River sinks, and reappears after flowing some distance under-ground. The Rev. Charles Beecher resides at Newport.

This Tallahassee country, particularly Gadsden County, has been long noted for its tobacco-growing lands. The culture of tobacco in this region appears to owe its origin to Governor William P. Duval, who, in 1828, started the planting of a certain small-leafed variety of Cuba tobacco afterwards known as the "Little Duval." Then the "Florida Wrappers," a larger variety, came into demand. The county of Gadsden is said to have raised twelve hundred thousand pounds of tobacco in 1860, and many statements were made in the Florida Convention of Fruit-Growers last winter showing the great capacities of this region for the culture of fine-flavored tobacco.

But these lands really appear to have capacities for all things. Besides the great staples of cotton, corn, sugar-cane, wheat, tobacco, they produce market vegetables in prodigious abundance, and the growing of these for the Northern and Western markets appears to be rapidly becoming a great branch of profitable industry. A train from along the line of the Jacksonville, Pensacola and Mobile Railway, through to Chicago without break, has been recently inaugurated in the interest of those growing early vegetables and melons; and there seems nothing wanting to the development of this section into a prosperous and useful country save the muscles and the capital of the immigrants who must be attracted to it when once its genuine capabilities have become known authentically. These lands can be bought cleared for from five to thirty dollars an acre—in many instances at far less than the cost of their original preparation for the plow.

The climate of Tallahassee has been found exceedingly beneficial in consumption. One of the most active and enterprising citizens of the place is a gentleman who came to it a few years ago suffering with large and exhausting hemorrhages from the lungs. He presents every appearance of a well man, and all signs of hemorrhage have ceased entirely for a long time. The elevation of the city above the sea—probably from two hundred and fifty to three hundred feet—must make it colder than Jacksonville; and the invalid should here—as, indeed, in all the other portions of Florida—always wear warm woolen clothing, and have ample facilities for a fire even if it should be needed but a few times during a winter. Tallahassee is, however, but about twenty miles from the Gulf of Mexico, and must therefore often share the bland airs of that water.

The invalid can vary his location occasionally by changing to the easily-accessible towns of Quincy, Madison, and Monticello, which offer much the same characteristics of general soil and climate with Tallahassee. Or he can extend his hunting and fishing excursions to the Aucilla (or Ocilla) River, which forms the boundary-line between Jefferson County, on the west, and Madison and Taylor, on the east, and empties into the Gulf of Mexico a few miles southeast of St. Marks; or in various other directions, which will be cheerfully indicated by any of the citizens.

CHAPTER VII

THE ST. JOHNS AND INDIAN RIVERS

" THAT I may enter " — says the spirit of Heabani, the dead sage, crying from the Assyrian hell toward heaven — " the place of seers, *the place of abundant waters fed from eternal springs.*" *

That is a true St. Johns River sensation: of abundant waters fed from eternal springs. Below Pilatka—that is, for seventy-five miles above Jacksonville—it reaches breadths of six miles, and is never less than one in width, while, above, the wide lakes continue for a long distance. The Indians, indeed, called it the Welaka — " chain of lakes." When the Frenchmen came they called it the River May; and Menendez's Spaniards called it the San Mateo River.

As you start up the stream from Jacksonville, the first landing is an unimportant one, called Mulberry Grove, twelve miles from the city, on the right-hand side.

Three miles above, on the left, is Mandarin, a small but long-settled village. Here, in the early Indian wars, occurred a dreadful massacre. It is now most noted as the residence of Mrs. Harriet Beecher Stowe. Her house is a brown cottage, near the shore, nearly obscured by foliage. It is not nearly so imposing as her Tree—a magnificent king that overhangs her roof with a noble crown. It is well enough to remark, in this connection, that in steaming up the broad levels of the St. Johns, a close observer will find that his eye should be re-educated in some particulars. For most persons are not in the habit of coordinating heights with such great horizontal expanses as here meet the eye; and until one learns to make the proper allowance, the trees and shores appear lower than they should, in consequence of the disproportion thrown upon them by the long plane-lines of the water.

At Mandarin are a Catholic church and convent, a post-office, a store or two, and several fine orange-groves. There is no hotel, but travelers are accommodated at boarding-houses.

* [Babylonian " Epic of Izdubar," from Heabani's vision of heaven.—ED.]

Ten miles above, on the right-hand side, is Hibernia, a pleasant invalid resort. Mrs. Fleming's large boarding-house here usually attests its popularity by a state of repletion early in the winter.

Four miles beyond, on the same side, is Magnolia, where are a good hotel (The Magnolia) and private boarding-houses. Around Magnolia Point, a short distance beyond, is the mouth of Black Creek, a stream down which considerable quantities of lumber are floated to market, and along which a small steamer plies in the winter from Jacksonville as far as Middleburg.

Three miles beyond, on the same side, is Green Cove Springs, one of the most popular winter-resorts on the river. The springs, with the Clarendon Hotel adjoining, are but a short distance from the river-bank. Connected with this hotel are hot and cold baths, and swimming-baths, of the spring-waters. These waters contain sulphates of magnesia and lime, chlorides of sodium and iron, and sulphuretted hydrogen, and have a temperature of 76° F. They are used for the cure of rheumatism, gout, Bright's disease of the kidneys, and such affections. Besides the Clarendon, the Union House, a charmingly-located hotel, offers accommodations to visitors; and there are good private boarding-houses.

Five miles farther, on the left, is Hogarth's Landing, a wood-station and post-office.

Ten miles above, on the same side, is Picolata, a place formerly of some importance as the landing for passengers bound to St. Augustine, but now of only historic interest. Here in the old Spanish days was the crossing of the river on the thoroughfare from St. Augustine over towards St. Marks; and the remains of an old defensive work are still to be found on the opposite bank. Picolata was a considerable commercial Spanish settlement; and the Franciscans are said to have once erected a church and monastery here, of much architectural merit.

About five miles above (these river-distances are always to be regarded, indeed, as involving an "about" of a couple of miles or so) is Tocoi, where the St. Johns Railway takes on passengers for St. Augustine, fifteen miles distant. The name Tocoi is probably the same as Toccoa, the Creek name of the famous falls in Georgia, and indicates the derivation of the Seminoles (whose name is said to mean "runaway") from the

Creek tribe. Here is a factory for preparing the gray moss for market.

Thirteen miles above, on the same side, is Federal Point, a wood-station; three miles beyond this is Orange Hills; and one mile farther is Dancey's Place; the latter two noted for fine orange-groves.

Eight miles beyond, on the right—seventy-five miles from Jacksonville—is the important town of Pilatka (the Florida world is hopelessly divided as to whether it is spelled Pi- or Pa- latka), containing a population of about fifteen hundred inhabitants. It is on high ground, the surface of which is much mixed with shells. It is a considerable resort for consumptives. The Putnam House, St. Johns House, Pilatka House, and private boarding-houses give excellent accommodations to travelers. Pilatka is the terminus of the Charleston line of steamers (The *Dictator* and *City Point*) and of the Savannah line (The *Lizzie Baker*). From here steamers go up the Ocklawaha, and to Dunn's Lake. It has a telegraph-office, and a newspaper, the *Eastern Herald*, noted for alligator-stories to such an extent that its editor is universally known as Alligator Pratt.

Five miles above is San Mateo, a pleasant settlement lying on a high ridge a short distance back from the river. This place is the residence of Rev. P. P. Bishop, a Northern gentleman who has found health in Florida and is now one of the most intelligent and judicious of its citizens. He is President of the Florida Fruit-Growers' Association. San Mateo is a post-office. A good boarding-house is kept here by Mr. Miller; and there are other places where accommodations can be had.

Twenty miles above, on the east bank, one hundred miles from Jacksonville, is Welaka, the site of an old Indian village, and subsequently of a Spanish settlement. Here the St. Johns narrows to a third of a mile in width. Near Welaka, on the same side, is the opening leading into Dunn's Lake. The peninsula lying between Dunn's Lake and the St. Johns has been named Fruitland, from the number of recent settlers there engaged in fruit culture. Immediately opposite Welaka is the mouth of the Ocklawaha River, hereinbefore described.

The expanse of the river just above Welaka is called Little Lake George: it is four miles wide and seven long. The next expanse, above Little Lake George, is Lake George proper:

it is eighteen miles long by twelve wide. Not long after René de Laudonnière[1] with his Huguenots had built their fort on the St. Johns below Jacksonville, they made, among other excursions and explorations, one up the river as far as to this Lake George. The old chronicle gives a pleasant description of it, and of Drayton Island (which is called the "Island of Edelano"), near the entrance of the lake.

I sent my two barks to discover along the river, and up towards the head thereof, which went so far up that they were thirty leagues good beyond a place named Matthiaqua; and there they discovered the entrance of a lake, upon the one side whereof no land can be seen according to the report of the Indians, which was the cause that my men went no further, but returned backe, and in coming home went to see the Island of Edelano, situated in the midst of the river, as fair a place as any that may be seen through the world, for in the space of three leagues that it may contain in length and breadth a man may see an exceeding rich country and marvellously peopled. At the coming out of the village of Edelano to go unto the river's side, a man must pass through an alley about three hundred paces long and fifty paces broad, on both sides whereof great trees are planted: the boughs thereof are tied like an arch, and meet together so artificially that a man would think that it were an arbor made of purpose, as fair, I say, as any in all Christendom, although it be altogether natural.*

There are other islands here, one of which, Rembert's (by some called Rembrandt's) Island, is noted for a very large orange-grove on it. Lake George is noted for its birds—herons, white curlews, cranes, paroquets, etc.; and for its fish; and I am informed that some notable mineral springs have recently been discovered here.

Five miles above Lake George is Volusia. The settlement is some distance from the river-bank. This is supposed by some to have been the site of the colony brought over by Dennis Rolle from England in 1765; others suppose him, as is more probable, to have located at a point still called Rollestown, farther down the river. In the Spanish times Volusia was a point of importance on the road from St. Augustine to Mosquito Inlet; and later, during the Indian war of '36–'42, a fort was built

[1] See the historical chapter of this book.
* [Lanier's source is probably Fairbanks, *History of Florida.*—ED.]

here, which was the headquarters of the left wing of the army during the short campaign of General Scott.

Orange Grove and Hawkinsville are two wood-landings above Volusia. About thirty miles farther above is the large and transparent basin of Blue Spring, four hundred yards in length by twenty-five in breadth. The river made by this spring is large enough to float a steamboat at its confluence with the St. Johns. The water is said to be slightly sulphurous. There is a post-office here; and the fishing and hunting are excellent.

The traveler now comes to the two towns on Lake Monroe which are at the head of navigation for all except the very small steamers that go to Salt Lake, etc. These are Mellonville and Enterprise. Mellonville is on the right-hand side of the lake, and is in a neighborhood which is beginning to exhibit much activity in settlement and improvement. It has two hotels. Hereabout are many orange-groves, and in the neighborhood are Sanford (where is a money-order post-office, a sanitarium— The Onoro Hotel — etc.), the flourishing Swedish colony brought over by General Sanford in 1871, Eureka, Eauclair, Wekiva, Lake Jennie, Lake Maitland, Lake Conway, Fort Reid, and other settlements. Extensive interests have been established here in orange-groves. At the grove called St. Gertrude a large warm sulphur spring appeared in 1871. Adjoining General Sanford's lands are those of Mr. William Astor, consisting of eight thousand acres of timber- and orange-lands. Not far off is also the Fort Butler Grant—in which Mr. Astor is said to be interested—on which are numerous groves of wild oranges and the charming little Lake Schermerhorn. General Sanford seems to be a moving spirit of this side of Lake Monroe, and to be working wonders by far-reaching intelligence and energy in the location and development of judicious colonies. One also hears the name of B. F. Whitner mentioned often in connection with his own beautiful residence and his general energy.

On the opposite side of Lake Monroe is Enterprise, the terminus of the larger steamboat lines. The Brock House here is much renowned among travelers. From here excursion-parties are conveyed in a small steamer to Lakes Harney and Jessup, a few miles distant, and also to Salt Lake, from which conveyance is had across the tongue of land—some six miles wide —to Indian River. Conveyances can also be here procured for

New Smyrna, on Hillsboro' River, twenty-two miles distant. Other fishing and hunting routes are adopted by parties made up here, and it is the headquarters of those who desire to sport among the head-waters of the St. Johns. It is proper to mention, however, that parties are also made up at St. Augustine to go by yacht to Indian River.

Consumptives are said to flourish in this climate; and there are many stories told of cadaverous persons coming here and turning out successful huntsmen and fishermen, of ruddy face and portentous appetite, after a few weeks. Not far from the Brock House is the Green Sulphur Spring with a basin a hundred feet deep, filled with faint green but wonderfully transparent water.

Above Enterprise the St. Johns becomes much shallower than below. A project was on foot a short time ago to deepen it as far as to Lake Washington, and to dig a canal from the eastern edge of that lake across to Indian River, so as to give free water-communication with that stream. Above Lake Washington, somewhere near the middle of Brevard County, the St. Johns appears to have its origin in hidden springs. . . .*

INDIAN RIVER

"Indian River" is a term sometimes used to include the body of water which at its northern end is known as Halifax River, south of this as Hillsboro' River, and at the lower extremity as Mosquito Lagoon. The Indian River proper, however, is separated by a narrow isthmus from the lower end of Mosquito Lagoon as well as from the Halifax and Hillsboro'. From here it runs far to the southward, along the eastern edges of Volusia, Brevard, and Dade Counties, separated from the Atlantic by a narrow strip of land through which it communicates with open water by the two entrances of Indian River Inlet and Jupiter Inlet.

About forty miles south of St. Augustine the Halifax River commences. From this point southward for twenty-five miles, to Mosquito Inlet where it communicates with the Atlantic, it is about a half-mile wide and three or four feet in depth. South of the Inlet it commences to be called Hillsboro' River.

* [Lanier's table of distances from Jacksonville is here omitted.—ED.]

The Hillsboro' extends some thirty miles farther southward, its lower extremity (also called Mosquito Lagoon) lying parallel with the upper part of Indian River. For the first ten miles below the inlet it is said to be eight feet deep, and three feet for the next fifteen miles southward. At this distance—twenty-five miles south of the inlet—the "Haulover" canal, eight hundred yards long and twelve feet wide, connects its waters with those of Indian River, which thence extends, with a depth of three to four feet and a width of one to six miles, for a hundred and fifty miles southward.

On the Halifax and Hillsboro' Rivers are several settlements, most of which are due to the interest which has been excited within the last two or three years with regard to this portion of the State. This interest has resulted in the settlement, among others, of a party of people from New Britain, Connecticut, on the Henry Yonge grant; the Daytona settlement; the improvement of Port Orange; and the beginning of Halifax City. Judge Howell Robinson, of St. Augustine, is one of the principal promoters of this last-named settlement, and, I doubt not, would cheerfully furnish much valuable information to those wishing to visit this part of the country. I have before mentioned that parties are sometimes made up at St. Augustine, to go by boat from that place, for Indian River.

South of Halifax City is New Smyrna, the point to which Dr. Turnbull brought over his colony of Minorcans in 1767, whereof some account is given in the historical chapter of this book.

Farther south are the celebrated Dummitt and Burnham plantations, where large quantities of famous oranges, sugar and syrup are produced; still farther south, opposite Lake Washington, is Eau Gallie, which has recently been selected as the site of the Agricultural College of Florida.

The general character of the lands in the Indian River country appears to be a strip of "high, light, sandy" soil, lying immediately on the western shore, from a half-mile to a mile in width; then, coming westward, a belt containing "hammocks and savannas" of great fertility, from one to two miles in width; then ridges of "light hammock" and "scrub" lands; then, still westward, grazing lands.

Upon these lands oranges, sugar-cane, bananas, pine-apples,

lemons, limes, guavas, strawberries, blackberries, hay, corn, grapes, indigo, sweet-potatoes, and all manner of garden vegetables are said to yield profusely.

The fertility of this soil seems to have been better known a century ago than now. I have already alluded to the settlement of Dr. Turnbull at New Smyrna in 1767; besides this, many large and flourishing estates were commenced about the same period by wealthy English proprietors, and the ruins of these, frequently occurring through the woods that have since grown up, often attract the traveler's attention to the mutations of time. In those days the main products appear to have been sugar, rum, and indigo.*

Along this Indian River country is a marvelously bland air, and I have been told of many overworked men and incipient consumptives who have here found new life. The waters are full of fish in great variety; the woods abound in deer and other game; and the whole land amounts to a perpetual invitation to the overworked, the invalid, the air-poisoned, the nervously prostrate people, to come down with yacht and tent, with rod and gun, and rebuild brain, muscle, and nerve. Accommodations for travelers are found at the Bostrom House, some thirty miles above New Smyrna, and at the hotels of Port Orange, New Smyrna, and Daytona, besides private arrangements for board which almost all settlers' families are willing to make.

The following extract from the papers included in the report of Hon. Dennis Eagan, State Commissioner of Lands and Immigration, will be interesting in connection with this account of the Indian River country:

How good lands may be obtained and settled up will be seen by citing a single case. Last winter a company was formed of mechanics, in a machine-shop in New Britain, Connecticut, of which Lucas P. Summers is President, and Chester N. Penfield is Secretary, both of that city. They sent a party immediately to Florida to prospect for a place of settlement. The party reported favorably of the Henry Yonge grant of one thousand acres, lying on the west bank of the Halifax, and about six miles above Daytona, owned by the Swift Brothers, of New Bedford, Massachusetts. A more fortunate selection could not have been made. They have half a mile of most beautiful river front. The

---

* [Lanier treats the ruin of the indigo plantations more fully in "Sketches of India," in this volume, p. 308.—ED.]

land, commencing at once to ascend, gradually rises for some forty rods back, then retains its height, some twenty feet above the water, for a quarter of a mile to the westward. All this front is excellent land for gardens, for oranges, and other fruits. The best farming lands are in the hammock, about one mile west of the river. These were formerly well drained, and put under a high state of cultivation. Through the centre of this hammock, north and south, there is an old field of one hundred acres of the very best soil for orange-trees, and on which the clearing is worth more than the cost of the whole tract. To this place two of their party immediately returned, and commenced clearing the river front, all of which they alone have chopped down some twelve rods back, clearing off a part and planting sweet-potatoes. They have worked every day since the first day of March, and have enjoyed good health. There are fourteen families in their company, most of whom are expected out in the early fall.*

The price of lands ranges from five to fifty dollars an acre.

This section may be reached directly from Jacksonville by water; three schooners ply between Port Orange and Jacksonville, and, though not meant for passenger packets, offer tolerable accommodations. Further information of their movements can be had of Messrs. John Clark and John Foster, commission merchants at Jacksonville. Larger schooners also run from New York into Mosquito Inlet, during the winter, transporting live-oak; of which further information may be had from Messrs. Van Brunt & Brothers, 75 South Street, New York.

The common method of reaching the Indian River country, however, is by stage from Enterprise, on the St. Johns; or by small steamer from Enterprise to Salt Lake; thence by wheels to Sand Point or Titusville. It is in contemplation to establish a route from St. Augustine, by the steamer *Mayflower* down the Matanzas; thence by stage or tramroad along the shore to Halifax River; thence by small steamer along the Halifax and Indian Rivers. I am informed the little steamboat *Pioneer* has already been sent round into the Indian River, to ply along its entire length; and it may be that the *Mayflower* route, just mentioned, will have been consummated by the ensuing season of '75–6. These routes are being constantly improved, as the increasing needs of the winter tides of Florida travelers demand; and visi-

* [From the appendix of the *Sixth Annual Report of the Commissioner of Lands and Immigration* (Tallahassee, 1875), another portion of which Lanier reproduced in the appendix of *Florida* (1876).—ED.]

tors should make inquiry at the many ticket-offices in Jacksonville as to the best and latest routes in projecting any journey
into these regions of the upper St. Johns and Indian Rivers.

A letter has recently been printed in the New York *Evening
Post*, from "A Florida Housekeeper," which is so full of a pellucid truthfulness and of a certain undertone of brave vivacity,
as well as of common sense and precise information, that I am
going to close this sketch of the St. Johns and Indian River
countries by copying all except the opening paragraph of it,
verbatim et literatim.*

We live on the St. John's River, up and down which thousands of
people have gone this year and returned with very little more idea of
Florida than they had when they came from their homes. A hotel life,
a trip on a boat on the rivers, and a run to St. Augustine do not tell
much of life here. Our house is a good stone's throw from the river
bank, and is on a shell mound a good many feet above the water level.
These shell mounds are frequent on the river, are very high and dry,
and make lovely walks about the grounds. Our house is built of wood,
like a New England house, and has shingles for roofing.

For shingles we pay $3.50 per thousand, and $12 a thousand feet
for building lumber. [This is statistical.] Our house is very comfortable, and we live a pleasant life, I think. Much is written of "no
milk," of "tough beef," of "canned fruit," etc. Persons who have to
do with such things simply, do not know how to live. Cattle can be
bought for $15 a head, and live on the food in the woods. Our cattle
are branded and range for twenty miles. The milch cows are not bereft
of their calves, but we keep the calves at home, and the cows come up
to them every evening. We have from three cows, besides what their
calves take, about sixteen quarts of rich milk daily. Of course, this is
not like Northern cows, but it is good rich milk, and keeping cattle so
is no expense, so it is as easy to have a dozen as one. So much for "no
milk." In the spring we make our own butter. We have about sixty
cattle, most of them fat, and about once in two or three weeks we kill
one of them and have as good beef as you can get at the North anywhere. We eat some of the beef while fresh, and corn the rest, sell the
hide, make oil of the feet, and soap of the fat; and our fifteen dollar
beast has paid us well.

Chickens we get for thirty cents each. They lay well, so we have eggs
enough, and we kill them from time to time. About once a week our
man kills a wild turkey in the woods near the house. About once in two

* [The article, entitled "How We Live in Florida," appeared in the New
York *Evening Post*, May 21, 1875.—ED.]

weeks some one of the household shoots a deer, and we have venison. Let me here say that the reason so many Northerners do not like venison is because it is not properly cooked. Cooking venison is a thing not universally known—like some other things. Early in the morning we send a man with a net to the river, and he catches about twenty fish. A " cast net " costs six dollars. People do not know about them. That is why fish are scarce on many tables. Our hogs number about thirty, I believe, and we kill them off for lard, bacon and pork. (A grown pig is worth four dollars.) They range the woods and feed on what they find. Besides the above list of meats we have quail and ducks, pigeons and bear's meat. Bears are to be had in the woods. Sometimes they like our pigs and help themselves to one or two. So much for milk and beef, which our friends say cannot be had in Florida. Now as for canned things. We have had, all this last year round, Irish potatoes, sweet potatoes, cabbages, lettuce, tomatoes, peas, turnips and beets, all of which came from our own garden, and which the soil yielded with very little trouble and expense. We also had figs in the autumn, oranges (sweet, sour and bitter-sweet this winter), lemons and citrons, grapes and blackberries, huckleberries, and musk and watermelons, and peaches and bananas. All these were grown and not canned. We never saw a can. We expect another year to have raspberries and strawberries, but these expectations are not facts, and it is only with facts that I am dealing just now. We buy Florida made sugar; and have our own corn and hominy, also our own syrup of sugar cane grown here, and also our own rice. We have a mule to plow and work, as mules do better than oxen. Price $130. And we have a horse for family use. We have also one watch dog and ten hunting dogs, which eat sweet potatoes and keep us in venison and game. We have colored servants. We pay the men $10, and the women $8 per month, and they do well. I should not desire more faithful " help," as you call them at the North. You know about wood here, of course—pine for house fires, and oak for cooking in a stove. This is all picked up on the place. You know all about our fine air, and our bright sun, and how we sail and drive and walk. We are busy enough, early and late; and so we are not lonely, especially as we have nice neighbors.

Now, who of your readers who has sailed up to Enterprise and back knows all this? If I succeed in resenting the " beef, milk and canned food " slanders on Florida, I shall rest satisfied.

By the way, I heard a Northern party remark that they had seen no flowers in Florida but pumpkin Blossoms. I suppose some people go through the world with their eyes shut. Or what shall I suppose, with flowers all about me?

A FLORIDA HOUSEKEEPER

ON THE ST. JOHN'S, MAY 1ST.

CHAPTER VIII

THE LAKE CITY AND GAINESVILLE COUNTRY

G AINESVILLE LIES on the line of the Florida (or Atlantic, Gulf and West India Transit Company's) Railway, ninety-six miles from Fernandina and fifty-five miles from Cedar Keys. It is nearly equidistant from the Atlantic Ocean and the Gulf of Mexico, and the great forests which intervene between it and those waters appear to protect it in great measure from that rawness which seems to be inherent in some sea-winds. This circumstance, together with its accessibility and pleasant hotel-accommodations, has made it a place of much resort for invalids.

By the term "Gainesville Country" is meant to be specifically designated the inland and forest-protected portion of peninsular Florida: for example, those parts of Alachua (pronounced Al-la'sh-oo-ah), Lafayette, Putnam, Levy, Marion, Hernando, Sumter, and Orange Counties which lie so far removed both from the St. Johns and from the salt waters as not to partake of the river and sea-coast characteristics; to which may be added, in virtue of its similar position, Lake City, lying to the north of Gainesville some fifty miles, and fifty-nine miles to the westward of Jacksonville—the western terminus of the Florida Central and eastern terminus of the Jacksonville, Pensacola and Mobile Railroads, which are now operated as a single line, though not merged into one.

The associations proper for the general reader to connect in his mind with this division of Florida may be roughly outlined as follows: the lumber and turpentine business carried on along the lines of the two railroads mentioned, finding its outlets at Jacksonville and Fernandina; the growing industry of the culture of early vegetables, which continually increases along the two railroads mentioned, finding its transportation by steamer from Fernandina to New York, by rail to Savannah and Charleston and thence by steamer to New York, by steamboat from Jacksonville to Savannah and Charleston and thence by steamer to New York, or by all rail through to the West as mentioned

89

in the last chapter; the four lakes, Isabella, De Soto, Hamburg, and Indian—in the midst of which Lake City is situated, and from which it takes its name—together with the trout, bream, perch, and other fish, which they readily yield to hook and line, and the deer, partridges and ducks which thereabout abound; Lake City itself, a pleasant town of some two thousand inhabitants, county-site of Columbia County, with seven churches, three hotels (probably thirty rooms in each), a newspaper, and the terminal station of the Cuban telegraph line; Olustee, twelve miles eastward of Lake City, the site of a sanguinary battle in 1864 between General Seymour, commanding the Federal army, and Generals Finnegan and Colquitt, commanding the Confederates; Gainesville, the county-site of Alachua County, with fifteen hundred inhabitants, four churches, two newspapers, and three hotels; the celebrated Payne's Prairie and Sink, a short distance from Gainesville, the former about eighteen miles long and reaching a breadth of five miles, the latter a strange body of water therein, which is fed by a stream, but whose outlet is subterranean and probably communicates with the Gulf or the Atlantic Ocean; the two mail lines running from Gainesville, one to Newnansville, and one to Tampa *via* Micanopy, Ocala and Brooksville; the crates of cucumbers and cantaleups [*sic*] packed in slat-boxes stuffed with gray moss, the melons, and all the host of the early vegetables which one sees at the Gainesville station awaiting shipment; the uninteresting nature of the approach to the towns of Gainesville and Lake City, as compared with their interiors; the great Gulf Hammock, along which one travels for some distance just after leaving Gainesville, on the railroad to Cedar Keys, with its magnificent masses of oaks and magnolias and vines, and its rich soils awaiting the muscle of man; the numerous other portions of all the named counties above where are fine marls and fertile limestone hammocks, and where lands, which probably cost twenty-five dollars an acre to clear originally, having been abandoned in the vicissitudes of war and of new settlement can now be bought for from two to five dollars an acre; and finally the great natural groves of wild orange-trees about Orange Lake and Lakes Weir and Bryant, in Marion County, Lakes Griffin and Harris in Sumter County, and at other places in this belt of country.

Apropos of which wild orange groves is a story told by Judge Gillis, of Putnam County, to the fruit-growers of Florida last winter:

In 1863, [said he,] I was at the house of Mrs. McNabb [between Micanopy and Pilatka, on a very poor black-jack sand-ridge] and saw a few sour orange-trees in the yard, and inquired, Why do you not have these trees bearing sweet oranges? The answer was, How can this be? I replied, Bud or graft them with the sweet orange; that I could bud them. I did so. About two years since I passed her house with Colonel Baugh, of Atlanta. He pointed to a fine tree and inquired how many oranges it bore. She mentioned a large number, and said she sold the fruit from that tree last year for fifty dollars; that this was a good deal to a poor widow and her family. She turned, and pointing to me said, There is the man who budded that tree for me. I had forgotten my little service till then. I was repaid ten thousand times.

Of course it is not every orange-tree that will come thus to be worth fifty dollars a year in a short time. . . .*

In the southerly part of this belt of country is the growing town of Leesburg, to which the Ocklawaha steamers penetrate except when low water in the river prevents navigation above Silver Spring. It is considered the head of Ocklawaha River navigation, and is situated between Lake Griffin and Lake Harris, having practically a frontage on both. A few miles to eastward lie Buck Lake and Lake Eustis; southeastward, Lake Apopka; and westward, Lake Panasofka. Leesburg is the centre of an active and rapidly-improving fruit-growing section. It is estimated that within a distance of ten miles around the town fifty thousand orange-trees have been recently started, which will be in full bearing condition in five years' time. Besides oranges, the guava, citron, lemon, lime, grape-fruit (a fruit much like a very large pale-yellow orange, having a sweetish pulp but a very bitter white tissue between the pulp and the skin), banana, and pine-apple are being successfully raised; and experiments are being made, with much prospect of success, in

* [Five lines of the original text and Lanier's footnote to the preceding paragraph—referring to two papers in the Appendix entitled " Orange Culture " and " The Wild Orange Groves of Florida "—are here omitted. The passage is quoted from *Proceedings of the Florida Fruit Growers' Association,* Jan. 20-24, 1875 (Jacksonville, 1875).—ED.]

the culture of a native grape for wine. These products are
transported mostly down the Ocklawaha by steamer (or barge
to Silver Springs when the water is too low for the steamers
between there and Leesburg) to Pilatka, thence down the St.
Johns to Jacksonville.

Leesburg is the county-site of Sumter County, has a church,
court-house, post-office, Masonic hall, a hotel and private
boarding-houses, and a steam cotton-gin and grist-mill.

To the southeastward from Leesburg, a little beyond Lake
Apopka, and twenty-four miles southwest from Mellonville, is
Orlando, the county-site of Orange County. It is situated in a
high and rolling pine region, and, though not as near the routes
of transportation as Leesburg and Mellonville, seems to be a
growing place. Not far from Orlando is the residence of the
poet Will Wallace Harney,* whose dainty translations of his
sylvan environment into poetry must win friends for him among
all who love nature. The town has a new court-house, and there
are good boarding accommodations.

Of course no delicate invalid—I mean an invalid too weak,
for example, to try the open-air camp-life cure—will think of
taking the journey of twenty-four miles from Sanford or Mellonville to Orlando, by hack in winter, nor any similar journey in
Florida—a precaution which some sad experience (not of my
own) leads me always to repeat, even at the risk of being
tiresome.

Besides these general ideas, one associates with this region
the Suwannee and Withlacoochee Rivers, both emptying into
the Gulf of Mexico; and also the fearful Dade massacre—
referred to in the historical chapter of this book—which occurred
not far from Leesburg.

Fourteen miles from Lake City are the Suwannee White
Sulphur Springs, on the Suwannee River. They have considerable local reputation for efficacy in the cure of rheumatism.

The Register of the United States Land Office is located at
Gainesville. The State Land Office is at Tallahassee.

* [Journalist-poet (1831-1912), best known for his "South Florida Night"
and his volume, *The Spirit of the South* (Boston, 1909). Apparently Lanier
did not meet him. He wrote to Paul Hayne requesting a letter of introduction,
but Hayne replied that he only knew Harney through his poetry. (See Hayne
to Lanier, Apr. 7, 1875—MS, Charles D. Lanier Collection, Johns Hopkins
University—answering a lost letter by Lanier of Apr. 3, 1875.)—ED.]

Through this Gainesville country stretches down to the southward a series of hammock lands, including the great Gulf Hammock below Gainesville, and the celebrated Annuttelaga (pronounced An'nuttylah'ga) Hammock, in Hernando County, which is fourteen miles in length by seven in width.

There are also many marls and clay-soils to be found, and the river-mucks furnish great quantities of valuable fertilizing material.

CHAPTER IX

WEST FLORIDA

"WEST FLORIDA" is a term commonly used in the State to designate that portion of it lying west of the Apalachicola River, and has been brought to the attention of most news-readers in connection with a long-pending proposition to cede this part of Florida to the State of Alabama; to which, indeed, regarding it from the point of view of the geographical fitness of things, it seems rightly appurtenant.

It is comprised of the counties of Jackson (county-site, Marianna), Calhoun (county-site, Abe Spring Bluff), Washington (county-site, Vernon), Holmes (county-site, Cerro Gordo), Walton (county-site, Ucheeanna), Santa Rosa (county-site, Milton), Escambia (county-site, Pensacola), and part of Franklin (county-site, Apalachicola). Of these counties, the first-named, Jackson, is so much like the hill-country about Tallahassee that it was included in the account of that portion of Florida given in Chapter VI: and Pensacola, the principal town of this section, has been spoken of in the last chapter.

West Florida is sparsely inhabited; and the inaccessibility of it by rail causes it to be much less visited than the other portions of Florida. Its main industries are agriculture, the fish and oyster trade, and lumbering. It is abundantly watered by numerous creeks, rivers, and estuaries from the Gulf. These afford great facilities for getting out the logs and spar-timber, in which the country is enormously rich. Many portions of it are extremely fertile, and yield good crops of long- and short-staple cotton, ramie, tobacco, sugar-cane, turnips, sweet-potatoes, and garden vegetables. The principal growths of timber, besides the main product of the yellow-pine, are the magnolia, cypress, juniper, cedar, wild cherry, live-oak and water-oak. The coast abounds in beautiful bays, which those persons visiting Florida in their own steam-yachts might find well worth exploring! and the waters hereabout are noted for yielding fine fish and oysters, as detailed in the chapter on the Gulf Coast.

94

Apalachicola, on the bay of that name, near the mouth of the Apalachicola River, is a town of four or five hundred inhabitants, and is now little more than the shell of a once prosperous city. It was formerly the shipping port for large quantities of cotton sent down the Chattahoochee and Apalachicola Rivers; and even after the war it moved forward with much animation, until the building of the railroad across the northern portion of Florida together with the combinations of the Georgia railway system succeeded in diverting almost all of its trade. Its fish, and particularly its oysters, are celebrated for their excellent flavor. It is connected by weekly steamer along the Chattahoochee and Apalachicola Rivers with Columbus, Georgia, and there with the railway systems of Georgia and Alabama; and with the Gulf ports by occasional sail and steamer. Vessels are also brought from other points by its lumber-mills. Pleasant excursion-parties are sometimes made up in the spring at Columbus, for the purpose of descending the Chattahoochee and Apalachicola in a chartered steamer, fishing, hunting, and exploring the strange Dead Lakes of Calhoun County, as well as the brighter waters of St. Josephs, St. Andrews, and other beautiful bays of this coast.

The Scotch settlement along the Uchee Valley, in Walton County, centering about Ucheeanna, is worthy of mention; and the lands of the valley of Holmes Creek, about Vernon, the county-site of Washington County, are spoken of as particularly fertile.

Besides the steamboat line mentioned as running to Apalachicola, the other main line of transportation in this part of Florida is the Pensacola and Louisville Railroad, connecting Pensacola with the Montgomery and Mobile Railroad at Pensacola Junction. There is also a railroad, nine miles in length, connecting Pensacola Bay with Perdido Bay at Millview, where there are large sawmill interests.

Chapter X

LAKE OKEECHOBEE AND THE EVERGLADES

IN THE midst of the great cattle-ranges and prairies of Manatee, Monroe, Dade and Brevard Counties lies the large and lonesome sheet of water known as Lake Okeechobee. Its length is probably from forty to fifty miles, its width is about twenty miles, and its depth varies from eight to twenty feet. It is fed by the Kissimee River, which comes down from the north through Cypress and Kissimee Lakes; and likely also by internal springs. Its waters probably escape through the Everglades. This Kissimee River is but a short distance from the head-waters of the St. Johns, and flows parallel with them generally, though in the contrary direction. It is said to be deep enough for navigation by steamers of four feet. The country lying between it and the St. Johns, as well as that west of it, consists largely of prairies and savannas which afford fine ranges for cattle, and the business of stock-raising has been carried on here with great success by many parties.

Stretching off to the southward and southwestward is the great, shallow, island-studded lake called the Everglades. It is in many portions, indeed, not always under water; and, where covered, varies in depth from six inches to six feet. It is full of water-grasses and flowers, and abounds in islands containing from one to one hundred acres of dry land, covered with profuse growths of vines, palmettos, cocoa-trees, oaks, crab-wood, mastic, and cypress. These islands, as well as the shores of Lake Okeechobee, present inexhaustible resources to the huntsman and the fisherman. Deer, bears, panthers, wild-cats, alligators, wood-ducks, and many varieties of tropical water-fowl are to be found, with several sorts of fresh-water fish and turtles.

The space covered by water in the Everglades has in time contracted, owing to geological causes, and has left a belt of prairie varying from a half-mile to a mile in width around it, which contains a great quantity of dry and fertile land. The Fverglades have been found to be considerably higher than the level of the sea, and drainage could be easily effected, thus reclaiming a very large body of extremely fertile soil for agricultural purposes.

The Everglades run through a large portion of Dade County and a part of Monroe. To the westward, in the space inclosed between the Everglades and the Gulf Coast, in Monroe County, dwell the remnant of the Indians who for so many years defied Spaniard, Frenchman, Englishman, and American, in this bloody Florida. In the year 1842, at the close of his remarkable campaign against the Florida Indians, General Worth announced to the Government that there remained but about three hundred of them—men, women, and children—and suggested that these be allowed to stay, without further pursuit, within specified limits—being the space inclosed between Pease Creek, from its mouth along the southern fork of it, to Lake Istokpoga; thence down along that lake, the Kissimee River, Lake Okeechobee, and the Everglades to the Gulf Coast; thence along the coast back to the starting-point. This suggestion was finally acceded to, and with the exception of two insignificant disturbances quickly suppressed by State troops they have peacefully remained in their allotted territory, living mostly upon fish and game. They are said to retain their customs, and I met one resident of Florida who knew their old chief Tiger-tail, and had received an invitation to their Green-Corn Dance, then about to be held. Their number is now estimated to be about three hundred in all. They are seen by few whites, save the " cow-boys," and those dwelling in the lower portions of Orange County, and in Polk, Brevard, Manatee, and Dade.

CHAPTER XI

THE KEY WEST COUNTRY

A NARROW STRIP of high, rocky pine-land, varying from three to fifteen miles in width, intervenes between the southern margin of the Everglades and the waters of Biscayne Bay and Barnes' Sound. This strip, together with the numerous keys which inclose Biscayne Bay and Barnes' Sound and extend on a westward curve until they terminate in Key West, Marquesas Keys and the Dry Tortugas, constitutes the part of Florida which I mean to designate by the term "Key West Country." The strip of mainland is mostly in Dade County; the keys are partly in Dade, partly in Monroe.

Here one finds the land adapted to the cultivation of many tropical productions, and the warmth of the climate renders others available at seasons when they are impracticable farther north. Sea Island cotton, it is said, will grow throughout the year along the mainland about Biscayne Bay: and here also flourish the lime, lemon, citron, sapodilla, cocoanut, banana, plantain, maumee, tamarind, guava, pine-apple, fig, olive, grape, sisal hemp, sugar-cane, and tobacco. The maumee, sugar-apple, and avocado pear of this section are highly spoken of; and it is said to be extraordinarily productive of limes and to offer great facilities for the manufacture of citric acid from lime-juice.

The climate is happy in its effects upon rheumatism and consumption, and its details will be found in the climatic chapter of this book.

The "Coontee," a term, probably Indian in its origin, for a species of sago palm, grows profusely near Biscayne Bay, and yields a good commercial starch and farina.

It is in contemplation to connect the lower end of Indian River with the waters of Biscayne Bay and Barnes' Sound by a canal from Indian River to Lake Worth, and from the latter to Biscayne Bay. The same company (The Southern Inland Navigation and Improvement Company) propose to connect the St.

98

Johns with Indian River by a canal across the narrow strip between Lake Washington and the latter stream, and thus to afford an inland water-route from Jacksonville entirely down the length of the Florida peninsula to Biscayne Bay. It is said that twenty-five miles of canal-cutting would suffice for the whole line. A railway (The Great Southern) has also been projected to run from Jessup, Georgia (the intersection of the Atlantic and Gulf Railroad with the Macon and Brunswick), to Jacksonville, and thence down the centre of the peninsula to Turtle Harbor, between Biscayne Bay and Barnes' Sound. Some work has already been done on the northern end of this road.

There are settlements in Dade County, at the mouth of the Miami River, along Biscayne Bay and at Key Biscayne, the latter being the county-site. This Miami River is thought to indicate in its name a possible connection between the Indians of this region and those of the Miami country of Ohio. Three hundred years ago, when Menendez was sending out exploring-parties from St. Augustine, the Indians declared that the waters of the St. Johns could be reached in boats from a certain Lake Miami, and that this lake had also an outlet to the sea. Dade County is sparsely inhabited, and the facilities for reaching its settlements, outside of private boats, are confined mostly to occasional sail from Key West. Those desiring to know more of this portion of Florida would doubtless be cheerfully informed upon application by letter or otherwise to Rev. W. W. Hicks, at Fernandina, Florida, or Hon. W. Gleason, Miami, Florida, who seem to be stirring men of Dade County.

Key West, the county-site of Monroe County, is the most populous city in Florida next to Jacksonville, having about eight thousand inhabitants. It is situated on the western end of the island of the same name, which is about five miles long by one mile wide. It has a deep and ample harbor, whose entrance is defended by Fort Taylor, and is a prosperous city, with a large trade in cigar manufacturing and in the gathering and shipping of sponges. The sponge-gatherers inhabit mainly that quarter of the city called Conch-town.

Fish and turtle are shipped from here to New York and Cuba; and Florida cattle in large numbers are sent to the latter country from this point. It is headquarters also for the Florida wreckers, into whose hands the reefs throw many a prize. These industries, together with the influx of Cuban refugees, and the activities incident to its being a coaling station and naval depot, have contributed to build here a thriving city; and its position with relation to the West Indies and the Gulf must always make it an important point.

The great leaves of tall cocoa-palms, the feathery fronds of the date-palm, the almond-tree, and many varieties of the warmer-natured flowers and vines, reveal themselves about the town. There are excellent hotel and boarding accommodations at the Russell House and at boarding-houses. Very few of the other " keys " are at all inhabited, save by great numbers of white herons, spoonbills, cormorants, cranes, gulls, egrets, pelicans, and other water-fowl. The plumes of these herons are in much commercial demand for head-decorations. Indian Key is the residence of several wreckers, who cultivate its soil. Plantation Key is noted for the pine-apples which have been grown on it; and Key Largo, which is the most extensive of the group, being some forty miles in length, is said to possess a considerable quantity of soil available for the cultivation of cocoanuts and pine-apples. The ordinary growths on these keys are mangrove, crab-wood, palmetto, and sweet-bay. Their surfaces are generally not more than two feet above the water at high tide.

Key West can be reached by steamers from New Orleans and Havana, by the New York and Galveston steamers, and by the Baltimore and New Orleans steamers; all of which touch there. A steamer also runs weekly from Cedar Keys to Key West, carrying the mails, and touching at several intermediate points, as hereinbefore mentioned in the Gulf-Coast chapter.

CHAPTER XII

THE CLIMATE

PERHAPS NO more important initiatory observation could be urged upon the attention either of invalids or healthy people than that there is absolutely no such thing as a perfect climate. As surely—and perhaps upon the same awful economic principle at bottom—as the rose has its thorn, so your Nice has its *mistral*, your San Antonio its norther,* your Darjiling its monsoon.

The climate of Florida is perhaps more nearly a perfect consumptive's climate than either of these; but it has a northeast nick in it.

As well to advise the intending invalid faithfully of perfection and of imperfection, as because the presentation involves many curious matters which cannot but be of interest to the merely general reader, it is proposed first to give here—in a wholly unscientific way, for this author is not a scientific person—some account of the chief physical circumstances in the nature and environment of Florida which contribute to differentiate its very remarkable climate, and then to present a set of tables which have been prepared from digested records of all the important meteorological instruments for a period of from twenty to twenty-seven years, and which will enable invalids, physicians, and tourists to determine the nature of the climate with reference to all given exigencies.

The very first step in the investigation of this subject leads one into the presence of a phenomenon which still baffles the explanatory power of science, and the contemplation of which no man can approach without a fresh uprising of wonder.

For of the many circumstances not astronomical which tend to individualize the climate of Florida, the first in importance are without question

THE GULF STREAM AND THE ARCTIC CURRENT

Although under certain conditions the warm air from over the Gulf Stream may blow westward, and thus indirectly

---

* [For Lanier's account of a Texas norther see p. 236 of this volume.—ED.]

heighten the temperature of some unusually cold winter-day, yet this would be but a trifling variation from the main effect of the Gulf Stream upon the Florida climate—which is, to cool it. Why, indeed, should we have an Italian climate ten degrees nearer the equator than the Old-World Italy? Florida is entitled by its latitude to a climate considerably warmer than that it possesses. Why is it cooler? Unceasingly the Gulf Stream is employed in conveying heat away from the neighborhood of Florida, and thus of course in cooling it. "The quantity of heat daily carried off by the Gulf Stream from these regions and discharged over the Atlantic is sufficient to raise mountains of iron from zero to the melting-point, and to keep in flow from them a molten stream of metal greater in volume than the waters daily discharged from the Mississippi River." [1] What, then, is the Gulf Stream? The answer—such answer as is possible—to this question cannot be better begun than in the celebrated words of one who studied the sea as a lover studies his mistress, and who, in spite of many crudenesses and inconsistencies into which he was led to fall by the great mass of undigested and hitherto unclassified facts which his labors collected, must yet be held to have been the greatest expounder of this subject. Says M. F. Maury, at the beginning of the first chapter in the work just above quoted:

There is a river in the ocean. In the severest droughts it never fails, and in the mightiest floods it never overflows. Its banks and its bottoms are of cold water, while its current is of warm. The Gulf of Mexico is its fountain, and its mouth is in the Arctic Seas. It is the Gulf Stream. There is in the world no other such majestic flow of waters. Its current is more rapid than the Mississippi or the Amazon and its volume more than a thousand times greater.

Its waters are bluer than those of the surrounding sea, and the line of demarkation, for a long distance from the starting-point of the stream, is so sharp that a vessel has been distinctly

[1] *The Physical Geography of the Sea,* by M. F. Maury, p. 53. London: Samson Low, Son & Co., 1859. [A large portion of Lanier's account of the Gulf Stream in the following pages is paraphrased or quoted from this work, a copy of which he received as a gift from Ex-Governor David S. Walker of Florida. See letter, Florida Walker to Mary Day Lanier, June 21, 1875 (MS, Charles D. Lanier Collection, Johns Hopkins University).—ED.]

seen to be half in and half out of it. This deeper blue is probably owing to the fact that the Gulf Stream is also more salty than its neighbor water.

It is not only more blue and more salty, it is also warmer than the water about it by twenty or thirty degrees in a winter's day. Its maximum temperature is 86°, and after a run of three thousand miles over and between cold water it still retains a summer heat.

It runs out of the Gulf of Mexico and the Caribbean Sea, along the coast of the United States, in a northeastern direction to Newfoundland. Here it meets a cold under-current, which is forever coming down out of the Arctic waters and making its way under the ocean-surface to those points which are being depleted by the outflow of the Gulf Stream. Off the coast of Newfoundland this cold current runs under the warm one; icebergs whose great bases extend beneath the depth of the warm current are seen to make their way across it, under the influence of the cold one beneath, which is pushing them to the southward.

From this meeting of the warm vapor-exhaling waters and the cold vapor-condensing waters result the great fogs of that region. A still more wonderful effect of their meeting is that the animalcules of the warm stream are, as it were, frozen to death by the cold one, and those of the cold stream are, as it were, boiled to death by the warm one; as these minute creatures die their shells fall; and in the farther course of the Gulf Stream over the ocean towards Ireland these shells have been deposited until in the course of ages they have formed a great ridge in the bottom of the sea, upon which the Atlantic Telegraph Cable is laid. For after leaving Newfoundland the Gulf Stream—retaining probably the motion which it had acquired while whirling with the earth from west to east along the equator or greatest circumference—strikes across to the eastward and finally spreads itself over the European waters, giving out its genial warmth to modify and temper the climates of Western Europe. By so much, therefore, as the air of Western Europe is warmed through the agency of the Gulf Stream waters, by just so much has the climate of Florida been cooled.

It is not a great many years since people believed that the Gulf Stream was caused by, or was a mere prolongation of, the current of the Mississippi River, or perhaps of the Amazon. When it came to be found out that the volume of the Gulf Stream was a thousand times larger than that of its supposed progenitors this idea had to be abandoned. It gave way to the theory of Dr. Franklin: that the Trade Winds piled up a vast head of water in the Caribbean Sea, which, owing to the tendency of water to seek its level, must of necessity find some outlet, and that this outlet was the Gulf Stream. This theory is still extensively entertained, though Maury's objections to it would seem to be conclusive enough. To mention only two of them: The Trade Winds, which are supposed to pile up surplus water in the Caribbean Sea, only do so for six months in the year, since for the other six they blow in a different direction; what accounts for the Gulf Stream during the latter six months? And again, it is well known that there is an enormous submarine current setting southward out of the polar basin, and flowing opposite to the Gulf Stream toward the very head of waters supposed to originate it; and this cold current runs along at a distance beneath the surface of the ocean to which the winds do not reach at all: hence there is plainly some other agency than the wind which *does* originate currents. Indeed, the supposition that the Caribbean Sea and the Gulf of Mexico are at a higher level than the rest of the Atlantic seems to be rendered untenable by the probability—which Maury's researches appear to have developed—that there is a constant tendency of waters and of drift-matter from all parts of the Atlantic Ocean *into* the Gulf of Mexico, excepting of course the Gulf Stream, and that curious Sargasso Sea, lying between the Azores, the Canaries, and the Cape Verde Islands, which appears to be a sort of slow whirlpool in which the drift and sea-weed collect— a pivot upon which the whole Atlantic slowly turns, as Maury strikingly says. Without wholly denying that the winds may have some agency in the production of the Gulf Stream, and without professing to be able to detail the precise method of its formation by any other means, Maury assigns as active causes in the formation of ocean currents generally the three following agencies. Starting with the familiar principle that water will necessarily flow to or from any part of a body of it where its equilibrium has been disturbed, he finds disturbing causes in heat, evaporation and secretion.

Heat renders the waters of the tropical regions lighter: and as they rise to the surface and flow off—as, for instance, in the Gulf of Mexico—their place must be supplied by colder waters.

Evaporation—the second disturbing cause—takes place with enormous rapidity on the surface of the warm tropical waters. In the evaporation of sea-water, the salt contained in solution is not evaporated but left behind. The water which receives this surplus salt becomes heavier and sinks, and to supply its place water must flow in from somewhere. Any one who will take the pains to observe closely what occurs the next time he holds a lump of sugar half submerged in a cup of tea for the purpose of melting it more quickly may actually perceive currents set up by a process much like that which Maury believes to result from evaporation. One will see that as the particles of water immediately around the sugar-lump become saturated they grow heavier than their neighbors and sink; these neighbors then flow in from all directions, saturate themselves, sink, and are succeeded by *their* neighbors: and so on, the course of the currents being indicated by the progress of the bubbles from the sides of the tea-cup toward the place of the lump.

And lastly, the secretions of sea-animals from sea-water produce differences in the gravity of the water, and hence currents. All persons know that the shells of marine animals are made of lime, and that this lime is drawn from sea-water which holds it in solution. Now when, for example, each one of the corallines who built the great coral arches upon which Florida rests passed a drop of water through his little crucible and extracted its lime, it became lighter in consequence of this loss and rose toward the surface. Hence, along with the progress of the work of these busy creatures, must occur a constant uprising of light water and a constant compensating inflow of heavier water, the light water rising to the surface and flowing off. This cause of currents will appear at first insignificant; but it seems much less so as one tries to force one's mind to the proper estimation of the myriads of large and small shell-secreting animals who are daily causing these flights of lightened water toward the surface—animals whose minutest families have left such monuments of their multitude as the State of Florida itself, or as that enormous ridge hereinbefore referred to, which stretches its plateau entirely across the Atlantic Ocean for the cable to rest on.

Such are the theories of Maury, though it is proper to say that most scientific men, while according him the highest praise for the diligent collection of facts, reject most of his inferences from them, and attribute the Gulf Stream to the heating of the Indian Ocean, the inflow thereby set up from the neighboring waters, and the relative westward motion of these, coming as they do from the smaller circumferences toward the equator—thus producing a current which strikes across to the westward and splits on the central projecting point of South America, one branch flowing south, and the other north through the Caribbean Sea, out of which it emerges as the Gulf Stream.

Of course it is not the place here to discuss these matters, but it may be said that to the unscientific mind it is exceedingly difficult to find mental repose in either of these hypotheses, as explaining the eternal flow of the sharply-defined current of the Gulf Stream.

But it is not only by the Gulf Stream that Florida is cooled. The same magnificent scheme of oceanic circulation which sends out that great heated current to temper the cold of Western Europe brings down a counter cold current from the Polar seas to temper the heat of Florida. There are many circumstances which tend to show that the waters immediately bathing the coasts of Florida are shoalings of this Arctic stream.

In regarding Florida, therefore, with reference to its temperature, one must conceive it as a long pier running down nearly four hundred miles, having on the left, looking southward, first a band of cool water, then the warm band of the Gulf Stream, then the great expanse of the Atlantic—all these water-expanses of different temperatures—and on the right the reservoir of the Gulf of Mexico, constantly pouring off from its surface the heated volume of the Gulf Stream, and constantly receiving, beneath, the supplies of new water from the return Arctic current.

I shall have occasion, presently, to present the details of the temperature resulting from these circumstances, as well as to refer to some other indirect effects of these variously temperatured bands of water; reserving these, I go on to remark that a second important circumstance peculiarly affecting the Florida climate is *the position of the State with reference to the breeding-places and tracks of general storms in the United States.*

Any one who will run the most cursory glance over the storm-maps of the Signal Service Bureau will be immediately struck with the fact that the black lines, representing the courses of the storm-centres, or "low barometers," almost all originate in about the same spot on all the charts. There would seem to be indeed a definite breeding-place of storms in the United States, from which they issue as wasps from a hive. Not only so, but they mostly pursue the same general flight. No one can regard this sameness of origin and direction without astonishment.

This territory, which is the place of the beginning of storms, may be roughly indicated as lying not far to the eastward of the Rocky Mountains, and about on a line produced to the westward from New York. It would seem that there is here a sort of wild Debatable Land or Scottish Border of the winds. The cold blasts come down through that end of the wide Mississippi Valley which opens out toward the north; the warm, vapor-laden airs from the Gulf of Mexico blow freely into its lower end; thus alternately the wild forayers rush downward and upward; and when they meet, snows and rains and gales rage like running battles from west to east.

Such, at least, is the theory which has been suggested by Dr. A. S. Baldwin, of Jacksonville, Florida, a gentleman to whose courtesy in placing his accumulations of meteorological material and learning at disposal this writer desires freely to acknowledge obligations.

The influence of the Valley of the Mississippi, [says Dr. Baldwin, in a pamphlet containing his Address to the Medical Association of Florida, of which he is President,] upon the weather of the United States is much greater, in my opinion, than has been heretofore accredited to it. The valley is open on the south to the Gulf of Mexico, and is bounded on the west by the Rocky Mountain range, which has a direction from southeast in the lower end of the valley to northwest, and extends to the Polar basin in the north. At the lower and southern portion, it has the Alleghany range for a boundary on the east, which has a direction from southwest to northeast. . . . This valley, however, does not terminate at the sources of the Mississippi River, but extends still northward until it reaches the Polar basin; no ridge of mountains crosses the valley to separate the lower part from the Polar basin, or prevent the winds of the Polar regions from traversing its entire length, nor those from the Gulf of Mexico—winds which alternately move up and down this valley, the one cold and dry, and the other hot and loaded with moisture from the Gulf, the Caribbean Sea, and the equatorial regions farther south. . . . Professor Coffin . . . says, " In any well-defined valley of considerable extent, it is a well-known fact that the winds are influenced to take the direction of the valley." An example is given of the Hudson River Valley, where half of the winds or more follow the river up and down; and yet the mean direction of the winds of the whole is nearly at right angles to it. Now, if we make application of this well-established principle to the Mississippi Valley, which certainly is a well-defined one, what is the result? As the winds of the Polar belt have been shown to have a southerly direction by Professor Coffin, there is nothing to prevent their free entrance into that broad, northern mouth of this valley, and the high wall of the Rocky Mountains on the western boundary of the valley for its entire length would tend to continue this direction to the Gulf of Mexico, and even beyond, for the mountains of Mexico—the Sierra Madre—are but the continuation of the Rocky Mountain range, extending to Central and even South America, curving to the eastward so as to embrace the Caribbean Sea, and then taking a southern direction and joining the Andes. This is the course taken by the Polar winds. . . . The winds from the Polar basin would move close to the surface in consequence of their greater density. . . . If the rain-bearing winds from the south should meet those from the north with anything like equal force, there would necessarily be a conflict in opposing directions, . . . and some new direction would be given to the opposing currents. They could not return back upon themselves; they could not go far west on account of the barrier opposed by the Rocky Mountain wall. Now, what way or direction is open to them? They can go to the east or northeast. And in this conflict of winds from north and south, the mass might, and probably would be, elevated and carried up the eastern slope of the Rocky Mountains, until brought into the influence of the high westerly belt of winds [which Professor Coffin has shown to encircle the earth], and then would be swept across the States north of the Alleghanies, as storm-winds, which would pass up the coast of New England and follow the Gulf Stream, . . . or turn farther north and pass down the St. Lawrence. . . . The winds which come over the Rocky Mountains have hitherto been considered the great weather-breeders of the Mississippi Valley, and of the United States.*

Now, of the storms thus bred, all move to the eastward. The large majority trend north of east, and trouble the great lakes of the United States, giving them that stormy character

* [" Climatology of Florida," Jacksonville, 1875; sections of the pamphlet are summarized in *Appleton's Annual Cyclopedia*, 1875 (under *Florida*).—ED.]

for which they are noted. Out of about three hundred such general storms which I counted on these charts for two years, only thirteen passed across the State of Florida.

Doubtless some faint ticklings from the fringes of storms which did not pass centrally over the State must have been felt, but they were not vigorous enough to produce more than small variations of comfort.

Of course, what is here said applies purely to general storms; there are local and peculiar storms over and above these, of which I shall speak in the proper place.

Thirdly, the quantity of moisture in the atmosphere of Florida, while not great enough to render it a damp climate, appears to be sufficient to prevent the diurnal changes of temperature from being excessive. This is accomplished through the intervention of the principle that moist air allows the passage of direct rays from the sun to the earth, but prevents the re-escape of radiated rays from the earth into space. Direct heat seems to be readily transmitted through moist air; reflected heat, not. It is said that in the Desert of Sahara, where the superincumbent air is of course very dry, the radiation of the earth's heat is so rapid after sundown as to send the thermometer quickly down to freezing-point; [1] and Dr. Baldwin quotes General Emory as stating that he had observed a difference of 60° in temperature between the day and the night on the dry Western plains.

A fourth circumstance is the number of bands of unequally-heated land and water, of which Florida is one. The Gulf Stream, of a temperature of 86°, is one band; the intervening Atlantic water between the Gulf Stream and the coast (which the exploration of the Gulf Stream made under A. D. Bache * has shown to be itself broken up into two more bands, whose temperature differs considerably at the surface and very greatly at twenty fathoms below) is another of different temperature; the peninsula itself forms another of still different temperature; and finally comes the Gulf of Mexico, of yet different temperature, to which might be added the further complication of the

[1] See Dr. Baldwin's Address, above referred to.

* [Lanier is drawing from two studies of the Gulf Stream by A. D. Bache (1806-1867), in the *American Journal of Science and Arts*, XXIX, 199-205 (March, 1860), and XXX, 313-329 (Nov., 1860).—Ed.]

St. Johns River and its lakes, and of the expanse of the Atlantic Ocean. Every one is familiar with the phenomenon that air resting upon a warm surface grows lighter when heated, rises, and sets up thus an inflow of air of different temperature to supply its place; and it will be readily seen how the proximity of these varying bands of surfaces which I have specified must produce a constant circulation of fresh air in the highest degree beneficial.

Fifthly, there are no snow-capped mountain ranges within any such distance of Florida as to render it liable to any of those rawnesses and sudden variations which proceed from this cause.

Sixthly, the rainy season in Florida is in summer, and it does not consist of steady rains but of afternoon showers which come up in the heat of the day with purifying thunder and lightning. This disproportion of summer rain leaves the winter an agreeable excess of clear days, as will more definitely appear presently.

Lastly, I merely mention the plenteous pine-growth of the State, without going into details for the reason that Florida possesses this feature in common with the sea-coast of Virginia, the Carolinas, and Georgia. It is believed by eminent physicians that, aside from the purely meteorological effects of these masses of foliage, the terebinthine odors exhaling from pines form a healing and antiseptic constituent in the atmosphere. Such evidence as has come under my own observation is favorable to this idea. It is curious to note in this connection that Spenser appears to attest the antiquity of this opinion as to such remedial virtue, in the *Shepherd's Calendar.* In the July Eclogue, Morrell says:

> Here grows Melampode everywhere,
> *And terebinth, good for goats;*
> The one my madding kids to smear,
> *The next to heal their throats.*

Regarding these, then, as the main physical facts which go to modify the normal climate of Florida, it now remains to set forth the final result, in reliable figures, of this mixture of climatic ingredients which I have specified.

TEMPERATURE [1]

The mean temperature of Jacksonville (lat. 30° 19′ 38″),
calculated upon twenty-seven years' observations, is for spring
70.06° Fahrenheit; for summer 81.82°; for autumn 70.35°; for
winter 56.33°.

The mean temperature of St. Augustine (which is immediately on the eastern coast, about half a degree farther south
than Jacksonville), calculated upon twenty years' observations,
is for spring 68.54°; for summer 80.27°; for autumn 71.73°;
and for winter 58.08°.

These figures, it will be observed, show St. Augustine to be
slightly warmer in winter and cooler in summer than Jacksonville.

The mean temperature of Tampa Bay—which is on the
western coast, 1° 48′ farther south than St. Augustine—calculated upon twenty-five years' observations, is for spring 72.06°;
for summer 80.2°; for autumn 73.08°; for winter 62.85°.

The mean temperature of Key West (in latitude 24° 32′),
calculated upon fourteen years' observations, is for spring
75.79°; for summer 82.51°; for autumn 78.23°; for winter
69.58°.

These averages may be fairly considered to give a just view
of the range of the thermometer over the whole State; for
while I have been unable to gain any thermometric accounts of
points in the interior of the State based upon periods of time
sufficiently long to render them perfectly authentic, yet no information I have received has led me to infer more than such variations from the above means as one could easily approximate by
considering the distance of any given point from the localities
above specified.

It must be apparent to the most casual reader of the foregoing figures that the popular idea which conceives the Florida
climate as a tropical one is thoroughly erroneous. Surely 82½°
— which is the highest mean of summer temperature — and
69½°—which is the highest mean of winter temperature—
enumerated in the above table, for Key West, the point nearest

[1] The following figures are derived from Dr. Baldwin's above-quoted pamphlet,
and are believed to be thoroughly reliable.

the equator—surely, these are not tropical temperatures! No, the air, here, is bland, it is not hot: it is cool enough to retain some little bracing quality in itself and to prevent the invalid from that dangerous inanition which the tropical languors are so apt to superinduce; yet it is not so cool as to irritate the membranes or check the healthful exhalations of the body, if the plainest precautions of proper clothing and of proper freedom from exposure are taken. Let me, therefore, here earnestly desire all persons, whether invalids, or pleasure-seekers, who come to Florida with the expectation of spending their mid-winters in white linen blouses, lying on beds of roses under spice-trees and palms, to exchange this delusion for the finer and truer notion of a temperature just cool enough to save a man from degenerating into a luxurious vegetable of laziness, and just warm enough to be nerve-quieting and tranquillizing. Warm days there are, truly, in winter; and there are roses and palms, too; nevertheless, moderate flannels, moderate woolens, good reddening exercise,—these are the things for Florida, and he who knows how to use them properly will always think of the land with a lighter heart.

Again: it should be here said, before I leave the subject of temperature, that in general points in the interior of the State are warmer than those on the coast, because protected from the northwest and northeast winds. The northwest wind is dry-cold: the northeast wind is cold and raw.

I have already had occasion to speak of the insanity of that exodus of consumptives from Florida which begins to occur even so early as March. Suffice it to say here again that the plainest logic conceivable proves that no sick man should leave Florida, to go to any point more northerly than (say) Charleston, before the very last of May.

FROSTS

At Jacksonville frosts are possible in any month from October to April, inclusive. Dr. Baldwin found, from twenty-seven years' record, an average of 2.3 frosts for November; 5.2 for December; 5.4 for January; 3.1 for February; 1.3 for March. In April and October there is .2 of a likelihood of frost; none, between. As the traveler goes southward along the Peninsula the number of frosts of course diminishes; and at Key West and along the tier of southern coast counties they practically disappear. Much inquiry left me unable to fix any line north of this where it could be said that one had gotten below frost; but the phenomenon is rare at any rate below 28°.

RAINFALL AND HUMIDITY

During something over sixteen years the average rainfall at Jacksonville was 50.29 inches. Only 7.06 inches of this amount fell, on the average, in the winter; 9.19 inches during the spring; leaving 20.5 inches for the summer, and 12.98 inches for the autumn. I have not been able to find any records of rainfall at other points based upon a sufficient length of time to render them authentic. But it may be in general remarked that the yearly average given above for Jacksonville will probably serve as a fair basis for judging of the rainfall at other points, except that the amount should probably be decreased for points on the immediate eastern coast. There seems to be here somewhat less rain than farther inland. A gentleman at St. Augustine informed me it often occurred that the steady sea-breeze blowing in from the east would drive back rain-clouds advancing from the west, and prevent them from discharging over the city; and Dr. Baldwin mentions having repeatedly witnessed the same phenomenon on the eastern coast.

This brings me to say, however, that although there seems to be less precipitation of rain on the eastern coast than elsewhere, it is nevertheless probable that more humidity exists in the atmosphere of that region; for the reason that the northeast wind, which is the raw wind, has a fairer sweep there than at points which lie farther inland and which are consequently more sheltered by the forests from winds that come out of this quarter. The average annual amount of humidity at Jacksonville was found to be 5.7 grains of water to the cubic foot of air. This is said to be about enough to be pleasant for respiration. It is probable that this amount should be increased a little for the eastern coast and decreased for the interior and western coast.

Hereof asthmatics may take heed, who usually require more moisture in the air for free breathing than invalids with other diseases of the air-passages.

Yet—when a man thinks of it—what is the use of talking to the asthma? It is a disease which has no law, no reason, no consistency; it pulls logic by the nose, it spins calculation round with a crazy motion as of a teetotum about to fall; and as for the medical faculty, it deliberately takes that august personage by the beard and beats him with his own gold-headed cane. It is as whimsical-inconsequent as Mollie Sixteen; it is the capriccio in five-four time of suffering; it is Disease's loose horse in the pasture. I have a friend who begins to wheeze with asthma on reaching New York City, but recovers immediately on arriving at Philadelphia; and another who cannot exist in Philadelphia, but is comparatively a free-breather in New York. People are known who can live in London but are changed to gasping asthmatics five miles away from it; and their opposites are equally well known, who gasp in London but can live five miles out. Yonder is a man, over on the North Beach, within three miles of St. Augustine, who has gone to reside there, though whenever he comes over in the boat to St. Augustine he wheezes by the time he is half-way, and does not prosper at all in the city.

And I am told there are asthmatics in New York to whom Canal Street is a perfect barrier of asphyxia, and who can live below it, but would die above it. I know one who has to sleep part of each night in his chair, but cannot have his feet on a level with his body; and I have no doubt there are those who are obliged to elevate their feet at an angle of 45° in order to get a wink.

I obstinately refuse to repeat the story—which a friend has just told me for true—that there is a man here who sleeps standing every night before a window with the sash out.

NUMBER OF CLEAR DAYS

This is a matter of great importance to healthy pleasure-seekers as well as to sick people. The most unsentimental of vigorous folk respond to a sunny sky in a manner of which they are often wholly unconscious; and I have seen a car-load of people who had preserved a grim silence so long as we steamed along through the rain glide into a cheerful buzz of conversation in a few minutes after the sun came out.

During a period of twenty-two years (and some years longer

for several of the months hereinafter mentioned) it was found that at Jacksonville, January averaged about twenty clear days; February, nineteen; March, twenty; April, twenty-five; May, twenty-two; June, seventeen; July, eighteen; August, nineteen; September, seventeen; October, nineteen; November, twenty; and December, twenty. It is not to be understood by any means that the cloudy days in this calculation were rainy days; probably on something like half of them rain fell.

THE WINDS

I have before remarked that the northwest wind is the cold dry wind in Florida. It is the wind that kills the orange-trees; and its prevalence may be estimated from the statistics of frost, which I have given above. The northeast wind is the cold wet wind; and the reader is referred to what is said of it in the chapter on St. Augustine (Chapter III) for some account of its nature and habits, which are not pleasant. The east wind is a delightful wind; and the south wind is somewhat like in the temperature it brings and the sensation it produces.

It is proper to refer, in closing this account of the Florida climate, to the popular impression that malarial diseases render it unhealthy. Perhaps this impression will be most authoritatively corrected by the following extract from a report of U. S. Surgeon-General Lawson:

Indeed, the statistics in this Bureau demonstrate the fact that the diseases which result from malaria are a much milder type in the peninsula of Florida than in any other State in the Union. These records show that the ratio of deaths to the number of cases of remittent fever has been much less than among the troops serving in any other portion of the United States. In the Middle Division of the United States the proportion is one death to thirty-six cases of remittent fever; in the Northern Division, one to fifty-two; in the Southern Division, one to fifty-four; in Texas, one to seventy-eight; in California, one to one hundred and twenty-two; in New Mexico, one to one hundred and forty-eight; while in Florida it is but *one to two hundred and eighty-seven*.*

* [Thomas Lawson (Surgeon-General of the United States, 1836-1861), *Statistical Report on Sickness and Mortality in the Army from 1819 to 1839*, Washington, 1840. The same passage is quoted in Charles H. Jones, *Appleton's Hand-Book of American Travel, Southern Tour* (N. Y., 1874), probably Lanier's direct source.—ED.]

CHAPTER XIII

HISTORICAL *

THE HISTORY of Florida for some three hundred years is but a bowl of blood; and if a man could cast something into it, like the chemists, that would throw aside the solid ingredients from the mere water of it, he would find for a precipitate at the bottom little more than death and disappointment.

It reads like a bill of mortality; the writing of it can be done briefly, and almost on a formula.

As thus:

There seems to be no sufficient evidence that Sebastian Cabot, as has been claimed by some, went as far down as Florida in 1497.

In 1512, Ponce de Leon, a *caballero* then verging upon old age, who had been a comrade of Christopher Columbus, set forth from Porto Rico to find a certain island called Bimini, where was said to be a fountain of youth. He failed to discover it; afterwards sailed northwestward, made land on Palm-Sunday (a day called *Pascua Florida* in Spanish), and shortly afterwards effected a landing somewhere a little to the north of St. Augustine's present site. After two months of worry with fierce natives he went back home, not a day younger than when he came. Net result of the expedition: a multitude of jokes, which they of Spain cracked on the old searcher after the fountain of youth.

In 1516 comes Diego Miruelo, and goes back. Result: a little gold obtained from the natives, and a large bundle of lies manufactured aboard ship, which got spread over Cuba and grew out of all proportion by the time they flew to Spain.

In 1517 comes Fernandez de Cordova. Result: one killed and six hurt by the Indians; wherewith De Cordova goes back to Cuba, and dies of his own wounds.

Immediately afterwards comes one Alaminos with three ships.

* [The entire chapter follows closely George R. Fairbanks, *History of Florida.*—ED.]

116

He twice makes a landing; twice has immediately to unmake it by stress of Indians; and goes home. Result: nothing.

About 1520 comes De Ayllon, thinking to procure slaves from among the Indians. It appears that Las Casas, that magnificent patriot, had caused the Spanish Government to stop this business; but where there is a will there is a way. People are found who declare that some of the Caribs are cannibals: these De Ayllon may take. He does not succeed in getting any among the islands; the storms beat him about, and finally he comes to the land of Chicora—at present known as South Carolina. Here, by a wretched trick, he allures a hundred and thirty natives aboard and starts home. But he never got a lick of work from them: for they all to a man died of sorrow. Moreover, one of the ships is wrecked, and the whole crew drowned on the way home. Result: a pack of ludicrous lies (as, for instance, that they had found enormous giants among the natives—the kings of Xapida—who were made so when children by having their bones forcibly elongated, the bones having been treated with herbs to make them plastic; that they had also found men with tails, which they could lash fearsomely about, and the like), and a burst of indignation at De Ayllon's vile inveigling of the Chicora people.

In 1521 again comes Ponce de Leon, with two ships. Result: the Indians fall upon him, slaughter many of his people, and wound himself; whereupon he goes back to Cuba and straightway dies in bitterness.

In 1524 again comes De Ayllon, with further designs upon Chicora. It may be here remarked parenthetically that this expedition belongs to the history of Florida only in virtue of the fact that in these days of which we speak everything from the Chesapeake to the Gulf is called Florida. This time the natives play off his own trick upon him, and quite beat him at his own game. They deceive him with hospitable shows for some days; then suddenly massacre an unsuspecting party of two hundred men whom he has sent off from the main body, and fall upon the balance so fiercely that they have great difficulty in regaining their ships. Result: the death of De Ayllon, and afterwards of his son, who is commissioned to carry out the project of his father but appears not to have been able to command means to do so and to have died of disappointment.

Then comes Panfilo de Narvaez, in 1528. On the way, a hurricane wrecks two of his ships and drowns seventy men. He lands on the western coast of Florida, somewhere about present Tampa Bay, takes possession of the country, and, leaving a hundred men in the ships to coast along to the northward, marches with three hundred into the interior. Presently he is wiled by the Indians, with tales of gold, into the northern country of Apalachee. But he never finds the gold; after seeing his dreams of palaces and cities—he knows of Cortez's Mexican glories, revealed a year or two before—continually melting away into the disgusting realities of petty towns composed of a few Indian huts; after unspeakable fatigues, hungers, privations, ending in naught but disappointment; he gives up the gold-quest, long before he reaches the Georgia hills where he might have found it, and makes his way back to Auté (as the Indians call it), a point probably not far from Apalachicola. But here is no rest. They are starving; and when they fish or hunt, the Indians kill them. Ten men disappear in this way. The fevers help the Indians: forty more die. The ships never come. Finally, in despair they build five boats, rig them with cordage of palmetto-fibre and horsehair and with sails of clothing, tie up horse-skins for water-bottles, embark, and make westward. But they do not know their geography: they fare hither and thither; they live on the flesh of their own dead and endure all manner of suffering, till finally all but four (with one who had been previously captured, and of whom we shall hear more) are either drowned, starved, or killed by the Indians. The fate of Narvaez himself is particularly tragic. Arrived somewhere beyond the Perdido River, his men go ashore, leaving him with a sailor and a boy in the boat. In the night the wind comes, and blows them to sea, and they die a lonesome death. The four survivors become medicine-men among the Indians; and after six or seven years make their way westward by land to their countrymen in Mexico. These four cross the Mississippi River some years before De Soto "discovers" it. One of them, Cabeça de Vaca, writes an account of these matters, which, albeit it reports lions and kangaroos as among the fauna of Florida, nevertheless contains much valuable matter for the historians. The vessels originally left with the hundred men aboard finally return, having missed their land-party all through. Results: the narrative of Cabeça de Vaca.

In 1539, Hernando de Soto, brilliant with fame and wealth brought from Peru where he has been Pizarro's right-hand man, comes with a thousand men and lands in Tampa Bay, which he calls Espiritu Santo, after the Whit-sunday upon which he comes ashore. Here he is presently joined by one Juan Ortiz, the captive who has already been mentioned as one of the five survivors of the Narvaez expedition. About this man Ortiz hangs a noble story of salvation from death by an Indian maiden, which, for the pure unrewarded magnanimity of it, should compel the world to hold her in even higher reverence than the Virginian Pocahontas. It is the story of Hirrihigua's daughter. Early in the Narvaez expedition King Hirrihigua's Indians brought in two captives—Ortiz and a companion—whom they had decoyed ashore. The companion was quickly killed; but by the greatest ill-luck in the world, at that moment King Hirrihigua bethought him of having a roast; being all the more intent upon it through the remembrance of certain dreadful treatment which his mother had received from Narvaez. Her nose had been cut off by that commander in the pursuance of his bloody Spanish policies. Hirrihigua therefore caused Ortiz to be bound upon a sort of huge gridiron composed of wooden poles, under which a fire of hot coals was fiercely burning. At the instant when the poor boy—he was but eighteen years old—hovered upon the brink of death by fire, King Hirrihigua's daughter, a young girl (another account adds other females as assisting at this first intercession), fell at her father's feet, and by many persuasions —such as that Ortiz was but a youth, whom it was ignoble to fear and cowardly to kill, and the like sweet argument—prevailed upon him to release his victim. She ministered to the poor young man, and herself cared for his hurts. And finally married him, of course, you say? No; and this is the magnanimous part of the story. No long time passed before King Hirrihigua repented him of his clemency. His mother was not avenged. Ortiz must certainly die. The daughter discovered his intentions, apprised Ortiz thereof, and under the darkness of night guided him away herself (another version says, furnished him with a guide) into the forest, with minute directions how he should reach one Mucoso, a chief, who was her affianced lover. This Mucoso appears to have been a man that God made, a man rooted in honor. He consented to protect Ortiz; and, having once undertaken, carried out his word with fidelity under temptations that would have shaken a Christian mightily. For it was not long before King Hirrihigua demanded the return of Ortiz. Mucoso refused. Hirrihigua put on the screws: Mucoso should not have his daughter unless he gave up the prisoner. Still Mucoso refused. He refused to the end; to the end Hirrihigua's daughter upheld him in the refusal; and to the end this savage man and woman, for pure honor, expended their love's happiness to save a foreigner who had come to conquer them.

One turns with regret from this fair story to follow the long march of De Soto. Why, indeed, follow it? De Soto travels on and on for eighteen months; gets into South Carolina, Georgia, Alabama, and has great battles with the natives. One of these battles was with King Vitachuco, early in the march, not far from Ocali (modern Ocala) in Florida; and after the fight De Soto, finding himself run short of chains for his captives, causes all whom he cannot manacle securely to be shot. Sometimes he catches a lot and cuts off their hands. But cruelties to his enemies avail not; hungers and fatigues and deaths of his own avail not; and at the end of these eighteen months he has marched back southward to Mauvilla, a place likely on the Alabama River, and thought to have originated the name of Mobile. Here he fights another great battle with the Indians, has eighteen killed and a hundred and fifty wounded, and, alas! what is worst of all, in burning the Indian houses burns up with them the bushels of pearls which he had obtained through the kindness of the beautiful Indian queen—the Ladie of the Countrie, they call her—whom he had met in South Carolina.

At Mauvilla he learns that Maldonado with the ships is not far away—at Ochuse, or Pensacola. Here is a chance to get home. But he will not take it. He and Ortiz keep the news secret from the troops; and soon they all fare again into the interior, to the northwestward; they must have some gold, or die.

And presently, with poor De Soto, this last alternative comes to be plainly inevitable. After leaving Mauvilla they wander about: the summer, the fall, the winter, pass, and still they are wandering; they have crossed the Mississippi (*Rio Grande*— Great River—they call it) in cottonwood boats, have penetrated up into the White River country; until finally the spring is come again, and they have got back among the desperate cane-brakes, on the banks of the Great River.

And now De Soto, with his Ulysses' wanderings, is literally tired to death. A fever wears him away. One day in May of 1542 he calls his people together; in the presence of death he forgets about gold and plunder: he makes them a grave and noble speech, and appoints them a commander. Next day he dies; and for fear of the Indians they let his body down, in a dark night, to the bottom of the Mississippi River. This man has been one of the most brilliant of his brilliant time. He has been a great conqueror, he has brought a hundred and eighty thousand ducats out of Peru; and the sum and final good of it is,—a little pitiful water-gurgle in a May night.

The balance of the men start towards Mexico; and, after wild adventures, three hundred and forty out of the original thousand get back to Panuco.

As for the result of this expedition, it is far beyond all the others: for it is the story of Hirrihigua's daughter—a story to which, in comparison, the "discovery" of the Mississippi River is but as a dried fig.

One would think that this disastrous expedition was enough in all conscience to have been thoroughly satisfactory to these Spaniards. But it was not; the glamour of the riches of Mexico and of Peru still lay on their eyes; and so here, in 1559, comes the greatest expedition of all. Fifteen hundred men, with many priests bent on missionary work, under the command of Don Tristan de Luna, come up and land in the Bay of Santa Maria, or Pensacola. At the very start there is disaster: a hurricane destroys the whole fleet a few days after their arrival, with most of their provisions; but they send back for more and push into the country. They go through much the same experience with that of their predecessors. Sometimes the Indians are friendly, sometimes not. The priests do not convert any worth mentioning. It appears that even the friendly Indians do not always appreciate the pleasure of the Spaniards' company; and one day a party of savages who have been entertaining them, and who find themselves likely to be eaten out of house and home by their guests, devise a pretty trick to get rid of them. A very gorgeous person, with a retinue, appears in the Spanish camp, declares amid much ceremony and grave formality that he is ambassador from the King of Coca (likely Coosa, in Alabama) to invite them there, and desires that he may conduct them. They receive him with effusion; and march towards Coca. Next morning the ambassador and all his suite are nowhere to be found; and the caballeros discover that the whole thing is a grievous hoax. One fancies that these old Dons were villainously heavy persons, swashbucklers iron-clad as to their bodies and souls. If they had had the wit of Yankee soldiers or Confederates, then "going to see the King of Coca" would have been synonym for a hoax the world over.

They marched on, however, to Coca. It was the old story. Quarrels arose in the camp; disaffection and mutiny sprung up; hunger—even to the living upon acorns—weariness, and death, all worked together; and finally my Lord Tristan de Luna, having got back to Santa Maria with a few followers, was ordered by the Viceroy of Mexico to come home.

It would really seem that the Spaniards were now seriously thinking of letting Florida alone. But they were soon stirred up to fresh endeavor by the appearance of certain French Huguenots, who, under Jean Ribaut, came over in 1562, and after coasting along to the northward established a short-lived colony at Port Royal. In 1564 came René de Laudonnière, also of the Huguenot party in France, and built Fort Caroline on the St. Johns, after having landed at the present site of St. Augustine and had amicable entertainment from a *paracoussi*, or chief, and his attendant subjects.

The history of Florida now becomes the history of St. Augustine, for some years; and the reader is referred to the latter half of the chapter devoted to that city, where he will find some brief account of the wars between the Spaniards and the Huguenots in Florida; of the massacre of the priests at St. Augustine by the son of the chief of Guale; of the sacking of the town by pirates, and the like matters, bringing up this outline to 1670–1.

About this time certain English colonists get over to Port Royal, and soon thereafter to the Ashley River. One would think there was room enough between the Ashley and the St. Johns for these little bands of colonists. But no. People in these old days seem to have had a perfect mania of truculence upon them. No sooner does one man see another than he wants to fight him. They are not tamed and rendered social, as *a priori* one would conclude they might have been if even by the mere common brotherhood of the sensation of exile. So far from it, they land upon the shores of the New World ready, like Trinculo's party on the sands, to smite the very air for breathing in their faces.

And so the two colonies straightway fall into hostilities which continue a long time. The Carolinians accuse the Spaniards of harboring their runaway servants; the Spaniards accuse the Carolinians of harboring pirates; until, in 1676, they come to blows. The Spaniards on their first expedition encounter entrenchments, and retreat; but in 1678 they come up again from St. Augustine, pillage Lord Cardross's Scotchmen on Port Royal Island and other settlements, and commit many atrocities.

In 1696 the Spanish Government, roused to new energy by envy of the success of Monsieur de la Salle in exploring the Mississippi River, commenced colonizing the western coast of Florida, and build a fort at Pensacola (Pençacola).

The South Carolinians, in the mean time, have not forgotten the Port Royal barbarities; and, in 1702, they proceed to chastise the Floridian Spaniards. With about twelve hundred men, equally composed of white militia and red allies, they advance in two parties—one by sea under Governor Moore (then Governor of South Carolina), and another under Colonel Daniel moving in boats down the protected sounds on the coast and up the St. Johns to Picolata, thence across to St. Augustine, which is the objective-point of both columns.

This latter party reach their destination first, drive the Spaniards into their fort, and hold the town.

Governor Moore, on the sea-side, makes less headway. His guns are not big enough, he finds, after trying them; and Colonel Daniel is sent to Jamaica to get bigger ones. But while he is gone a couple of Spanish vessels appear, and Governor Moore seems to take a panic. He destroys his transports and extra supplies, burns poor St. Augustine (this burning of St. Augustine really appears to have acquired the force of a habit among all its conquerors, and the setting this ill-used town afire gets to be as much a matter of course as the lighting a cigar), and puts back to South Carolina, leaving Colonel Daniel, who returns from Jamaica in ignorance of this hasty departure, to come very near falling into the hands of the enemy.

And now the Indians, as if they had not quarrels enough of their own, embrace the whites'. Nine hundred Apalachees advance against Carolina in behalf of the Spaniards; five hundred Creeks oppose them in behalf of the Carolinians. When the two meet, the Creeks more than make up for their deficiency in numbers by a trick of war. They hang up their blankets, as if they were all asleep, and hide near by; the Apalachees plunge into the camp, thinking to surprise it, and are completely whipped in a short time by the ambushed Creeks.

Governor Moore is worried now about the St. Augustine *fiasco*, and gets together a thousand Creek Indians and a handful of militia to help him repair that failure. This time he lets St. Augustine alone, and moves down into the country about San Luis, a Spanish missionary station very near the present site of Tallahassee. He has better luck than last time. In his first serious battle he is so fortunate as to kill the Spanish commander, Mexia, who is in charge at San Luis, together with about half of the four hundred Apalachees who are Mexia's allies. Then he has no further trouble, and he proceeds to smite and spare not. Fort or church, arms or communion-plate—it makes no difference; all are burnt and plundered.

That such things could go on down among these green woods and streams—where any man in his senses must, one would think, be drawn by the very force of nature into large labors and peaceful dreams—is to me only another proof that the world has not nearly enough insane asylums.

Thus these neighbors, South Carolina and Florida, with their respective Indian sympathizers, continued to fare up and down for years, first one side, then the other, like so many shuttles weaving death and sorrow. Their expeditions and counter-expeditions were so numerous that in a meagre sketch like this one has not room even to specify their dates and commanders. On every side were heard the war-whoops, were seen the scalps. In one uprising of the Yemassees—although they were defeated finally and driven into Florida, where they had previously sent their wives and children to the protection of their Spanish friends — it is said that four hundred of the South Carolina people were slain.

As time goes on, too, here come some new neighbors to Florida, who of course straightway begin to fight; these are the

French who have made a settlement at Mobile. De Bienville, in charge there, about 1718, lands with a party on Santa Rosa Island, captures some Spanish soldiers, puts their uniforms on some of his Frenchmen, and, skillfully pursuing his stratagem, captures the Spanish fort at Pensacola with its commander and entire garrison, being probably assisted (so say the Spanish) by four French frigates with their guns. The prisoners are sent to Havana, according to the terms of capitulation; here the Spanish resort to treachery, seize the vessels De Bienville had dispatched with the prisoners, and straightway organize a party to retake Pensacola, which De Bienville had left in charge of the Sieur de Chateaugué with a garrison. This counter-party play their trick in turn; they deceive De Chateaugué by sending in one of their treacherously-taken French ships under her own flag; then suddenly dispatch another of their own vessels and open fire; and so, after some days of negotiation, recapture their fort. But the French do not let them have it long. They retake it in 1719, and, probably considering the game not worth the candle, shortly afterwards destroy the fort and burn the town and abandon the whole business. The Spanish made another settlement on Santa Rosa Island; though it was still some years before Pensacola was commenced. The present Pensacola is probably only about one hundred and twenty-five years old.

In these days it is this same mournful fugitive slave trouble that keeps the sore festering. When the Yemassees come up foraying from Florida, any negro that has a mind joins them and finds harborage with the Spanish. The absconding debtors and escaped criminals, too, find their Texas down in Florida; and altogether there is a grievous exodus of people who are wanted in South Carolina. In 1725 two Spanish commissioners come up and meet Governor Middleton in Charleston to settle these matters; but they do not succeed; and finally things become so intolerable that one Captain Palmer, in 1727, with three hundred militia and a party of Indian allies, fares down into Florida and strikes the enemies with the arm of a long-suffering and much-injured man, burning and killing, even destroying the Yemassee village of Macariz not more than a mile north of St. Augustine.

In 1732 came still another neighbor of Florida's on the scene; and, of course, again began to fight. The only thing in nature

which approaches these people in truculence is crabs. Bring one
crab near another, on shore; immediately they spit at each other,
and grapple. Thus with Georgia, under General Oglethorpe.
This time it was the Spaniards that commenced. They desired
politely that Oglethorpe would immediately withdraw from all
that portion of Georgia lying south of St. Helena's Sound, for
that the same was the land of the King of Spain. General
Oglethorpe refused; negotiations between England and Spain
followed: no settlement; and finally in May of 1740 we find
Oglethorpe, with a regiment of English regulars, a company of
Scotchmen from the Altamaha under Captain McIntosh and a
few Indians, at the mouth of the St. Johns on his way to attack
St. Augustine, forty miles below. He advances without trouble,
and captures and garrisons Fort Moosa, or the Negro Fort, a
sort of stockade and block-house some two miles to the north
of St. Augustine which the runaways had built and had been
occupying. Then planting three batteries on Anastasia Island,
and blockading, as he supposes, all the inlets by which supplies
could reach the Spaniards from their friends, he leisurely proceeds to bombard and starve out Monteano, who is in charge
of the fort.

But, as might have been expected, matters do not work well.
The three officers left at Fort Moosa (Colonel Palmer and
Captains McIntosh and McKay) begin to quarrel among themselves; and presently some three hundred Spaniards sally out,
surprise the place and retake it after killing and capturing many
of the garrison. Moreover, the men get discontented; the
weather is warm, and the mosquitoes—Spaniards by bloody instinct as well as by territorial nativity—shed a great deal of
English blood.

This Governor Monteano appears to have been a Spaniard
at once stout and stately. He keeps up an energetic defense;
in reply to Oglethorpe's demand that he surrender his fort, he
swears to defend it to the last drop of blood, " and hopes soon
to kiss his Excellency's hand within its walls." He maintains a
sharp look-out with small armed boats, which are very troublesome. Finally Oglethorpe hears that Monteano has just received
supplies through Mosquito Inlet—a hole which the general had
neglected to stop up; and then, after much discussion, abandons
the siege and carries back his men to Georgia, without having
acquired any very great reputation as a military commander.

But is was not long before Governor Oglethorpe proved himself to be really a man of many resources, who could learn by failure. For in 1742 his opponent Monteano in turn assumed the offensive, and set out from St. Augustine with thirty-six vessels and some three thousand men for the purpose of striking a decisive blow at the new English colony. Monteano sailed for the bar of Brunswick harbor, between St. Simon's and Jekyll Islands; and on arriving was stoutly resisted by batteries which Oglethorpe had placed on the shore of St. Simon's and on vessels stationed near, in a rude and hasty way. It was not long before Monteano had passed these; but here his triumph ended.

Proceeding some days afterwards to attack Frederica, where Oglethorpe had retreated, Monteano's people were so stoutly assaulted while crowded together on a narrow causeway that he was compelled to fall back with the loss of many killed and captured. A subsequent attack by water resulted in no better success for Monteano. At this stage of the expedition, one of those tricks which the reader of the Florida wars soon comes to expect as a matter of course turned the tide in favor of the English.

Governor Oglethorpe had resolved to profit by the causeway defeat, and had disposed his forces so as to attack the Spanish before they recovered from the demoralization of it; but a deserter from his forces to the Spanish carried the news and spoiled his plan. Oglethorpe at once avenged himself upon the deserter and mystified Monteano, by bribing a Spanish prisoner to carry a letter to the deserter in the Spanish camp, purporting to be written by a friend of his in Oglethorpe's camp, and offering him a large sum if he would represent to the Spanish commander that the English force was much weaker than it really was and would lead him upon an ambush after having thus induced him to attack. The Spanish prisoner, upon arriving at his own camp, was immediately searched, and Monteano was thrown into a muddle of profound bewilderment by the plot and counterplot which arose betwixt the letter and the poor deserter's stout denial of having any such friend as the writer of it. In this ripe moment of perplexity three vessels from Charleston, with succors for Oglethorpe, appeared, and gave the finishing stroke to Monteano's wavering resolution; he called together his forces and straightway made sail backwards

to St. Augustine. A few months afterwards Governor Oglethorpe completed his triumph by marching into Florida—to the
very walls almost of the fort at St. Augustine, where his men
captured and killed forty Spanish soldiers—and offering battle
to the Spaniards at their own stronghold. They refused; and
matters appear to have been much more quiet thereafter for
several years, except certain murderous forays of Indians, which
still continued. This peaceful state was confirmed by the treaty
of peace between England and Spain in 1748. In 1762, however, war broke out again, in the course of which England
captured Havana. Up to this time Florida had remained of a
consistent color, blood-red, as one may say—right Spanish. But
she now commenced to change like a chameleon, and for some
years thereafter the people must have been often in some un-
certainty whether they were Spaniards, Englishmen, Frenchmen,
or United States citizens. In the tripartite treaty of 1763, between England, France and Spain, the former ceded Havana to
the latter in exchange for Florida.

The cession was a melancholy blow, however, to the Spanish
in Florida; and it is said that all but five of the Spaniards in
St. Augustine hastily disposed of their possessions and left the
country, some of them being only prevented by compulsion
from even destroying the town.

A new era now dawned upon Florida, which placed in strong
relief the contrasted colonial policies of Spain and of Great
Britain. Upon reviewing this sketch, one reflects with astonishment that here these Spaniards have held this magnificent
country of Florida since 1512—two hundred and fifty years,
and over—and nearly the entire results of their labor are the
beggarly settlements at St. Augustine and Pensacola, — even
these mostly consisting of soldiers and office-holders! The
English at once commenced to infuse a more vigorous life into
Florida. The country called by that name was divided into East
Florida and West Florida; East Florida comprising all of the
present State of Florida except that portion lying to the westward of the Apalachicola River, and West Florida embracing
the country lying between the Mississippi and Lakes Pont-
chartrain and Maurepas on the west, and the Chattahoochee
and Apalachicola Rivers on the east, as far up as the thirty-first
parallel of north latitude. In the same year—1763—General

James Grant was appointed Colonial Governor of East Florida, and appears to have at once commenced to carry out wise plans. Immigration was invited; liberal grants of land were made to the soldiers in the late wars upon condition of settlement and of quit-rents after ten years, the field-officers getting five thousand acres, captains three thousand, subalterns two thousand, non-commissioned officers two hundred, and privates fifty acres, each. Books, pictures and other descriptive publications were issued and distributed; the production of indigo and of naval stores was stimulated by offering bounties thereon; good roads were constructed (among others, the road from Fort Barrington to St. Augustine, which still remains good, and is still called the King's Road), and every means was used to develop the country. Beresford and Spring Garden were settled; Dennis Rolle brought over a hundred English families and located a colony at a point still called Rollestown, a few miles above Pilatka, on the opposite side of the St. Johns; and Sir William Duncan and Dr. Turnbull established fifteen hundred Greeks and Minorcans, brought over from Smyrna, at a point called New Smyrna near Mosquito Inlet. This latter colony was fostered by great expenditures, and seemed likely to prosper at first in cultivating indigo; but quarrels arose between the settlers and Turnbull; the matter was carried into the courts, the contracts of service were rescinded, and the whole colony removed to St. Augustine, where their descendants still occupy what is called the Minorcan Quarter—that portion of the town lying next the fort.

The war of the Revolution now came on, and Florida became an asylum for the tories and loyalists of Georgia and South Carolina. It is said that in 1778 nearly seven thousand of these persons moved there. Several ineffectual attempts and counter-attempts at invasion were made between Florida forces on the one side and those of Georgia and South Carolina on the other; but it was not until the latter part of 1778 that General Prevost moved up from St. Augustine with the Florida troops to unite in the operations before Savannah. It was in this expedition that the celebrated Rory (Roderick) McIntosh figured, a redoubtable gentleman of Scotch ancestry, whose name is connected by dozens of droll stories with the cities of St. Augustine, Savannah, and Charleston during these days.

I recollect seeing, [says the venerable John Cowper in a letter published in White's *Historical Collections of Georgia*] in St. Augustine, on some public day, Rory, Colonel McArthur, and Major Small . . . parading the streets in full Highland costume, *attended by their pipers.* . . . In 1777 he must have been about sixty-five years of age, about six feet in height, strongly built, [with] white frizzled bushy hair, and large whiskers [then uncommon] frizzled fiercely out, a ruddy McIntosh complexion, handsome, large and muscular limbs. In walking, or rather striding, his step must have been four feet.*

Rory was keenly solicitous for the honor both of his country and of his dog. *E. g.,* he one day makes his appearance in Savannah and calls on Cowper & Telfair, his bankers, for money to bear his expenses to Charleston. He appears unusually agitated, and Mr. Cowper, after much difficulty, elicits the outburst:

" That reptile in Charleston, Gadsden, has insulted my country, and I will put him to death."

" What has he done? " says Mr. Cowper.

" Why," says Rory, " on being asked how he meant to fill up his wharf in Charleston, he replied, *with imported Scotchmen,* who were fit for nothing better! "

With repeated persuasions the irate Scotchman was finally induced to return to his home at Mallow.

He was fond of dogs, . . . one in particular named *Luath,* which he had taught to take his back scent. He laid a considerable bet that he would hide a doubloon at three miles' distance and that Luath would find it. Luath went off on his trail and returned panting, his tongue out, but no doubloon. " Treason! " cried Rory, and off he and Luath went. The log was turned over, and the dog had scratched under it. A man appeared at some distance splitting rails. Without ceremony Rory drew his dirk, and swore that he would put him to instant death unless he returned the money. The man gave it up, saying that he had seen Mr. McIntosh put something under the log, and on examining had found it gold. Rory tossed him back the money. " Take it," said he, " vile caitiff! It was not the pelf, but the honor of my dog I cared for."

One evening in Charleston, Rory marches into the house of

* [Lanier's source for this and all the following quotations and anecdotes concerning McIntosh was apparently George White, *Historical Collections of Georgia.*—ED.]

Captain James Wallace, attended by his piper. " I am come, madam," said he to Mrs. Wallace, who was from the Highlands, " to take a cup of tea and give you a taste of our country's music! "

This Rory had been in that melancholy Fort Moosa capture, hereinbefore related. During the expedition under Prevost to Savannah, just spoken of, Sunbury (in Liberty County, Georgia) was attacked. Among the Florida troops before the fort, there, was Rory McIntosh.

Early one morning, when he had made rather free with " mountain dew," he insisted on sallying out to summon the fort to surrender. His friends could not restrain him; so out he strutted, claymore in hand, followed by his faithful slave Jim, and approached the fort, roaring out, " Surrender, you miscreants! How dare you presume to resist his Majesty's arms? " . . . [The commander of the fort knew him, and seeing his condition forbade any one from firing on him. As Rory kept advancing, the commander, whose name was also McIntosh, and who seems to have been a man who understood how to carry a joke,] threw open the gate and said, " Walk in, Mr. McIntosh, and take possession." " No," said Rory, " I will not trust myself among such vermin, but I order you to surrender! " [This appears to have been too much for some of the men in the fort, and a rifle was fired at Rory, the ball from which passed through his face, below his eyes.] He stumbled and fell, but immediately recovered, and retreated backwards flourishing his sword. Several dropping shots followed, and Jim called out, " Run, massa! dey kill you! " " Run, poor slave," says Rory; thou mayst run, but I am of a race that never runs! " [and the redoubtable old hero got back safely into his own lines.]

Sunbury, which had been unsuccessfully attacked a short time before by an expedition from Florida, was this time captured, and the troops moved on and took part in the reduction of Savannah.

In 1780, Governor Tonyn called the first General Assembly of the province of Florida together.

Florida now seemed to have emerged upon a steady career of peaceful prosperity. The culture of indigo had succeeded admirably; forty thousand barrels of naval stores had been shipped in 1779; turpentine was worth thirty-six shillings a barrel; and the estimation of all the manifold agricultural capacities of the State was growing so rapidly abroad that there can be no doubt it would have received a very great accession of hard-working immigrants had not one of those sudden changes of fortune occurred which seem for three hundred years to have made this unhappy country a mere ball of fate to be tossed about from king to king. In the year 1783 the Government of Great Britain concluded suddenly that it was worthless to retain the province of Florida. Those constituting the United States had been taken away; and even a part of Florida was already gone; for in the year 1781, De Galvez, the Spanish Governor of Louisiana, had attacked Pensacola—which was at that time a strong post, garrisoned with a thousand men, under General Campbell—and after a stout resistance, which was finally rendered hopeless by the explosion of a shell in the magazine of Fort San Michel, had captured it. Florida being thus isolated, Great Britain ceded it to Spain in 1783, by a treaty which allowed the British inhabitants of the State eighteen months to move out; and the unhappy Floridians found all their labors brought to ignominious result. It was no small addition to the troubles of their situation that many of them, having been loyalists, could look to no very pleasant residence in the now independent States of the Union; and there was really great difficulty in finding a suitable place of refuge. Transportation was provided by the Government, and the inhabitants were carried to England, the Bahamas, Jamaica, Nova Scotia, some, not loyalists, returning to South Carolina.

Possession was taken by Spain, at St. Augustine, in 1784; a Spanish lethargy settled upon the land; the fine estates of the thrifty Englishmen mouldered into decay; few settlers came in from Spain; the activity of the State was principally confined to trading with the Indians, and to foiling the desperate attempts of adventurers like William Bowles and Daniel Mc-Girth, who were for some time moving about among the Indians and exciting them to bloody disaffections with ingenious stories against the Spanish. Those who desire to pursue further the arts and machinations of these singular men, and to learn more of the remarkable Alexander MacGillivray, who was chief of the great Creek Nation at this time, will find some interesting particulars of them collected in the *History of Florida,* by George R. Fairbanks: Lippincott & Co., Philadelphia, 1871.*

* [Lanier bases much of his account also on White, *Historical Collections of Georgia.*—ED.]

Florida continued now for a long time a mere border-land, torn with Indian fights, and with irregular conflicts of adventuring parties and of ill-advised republican frontiersmen. In the year 1812 a party of these latter went so far as to meet in Southern Georgia and adopt a constitution, which they proposed to set up over the benighted inhabitants of Florida. They elected General John H. McIntosh to be head of the new republic, and Colonel Ashley commander of the army, moved down upon Fernandina, then just growing to be a place of some commercial resort, and captured the fort and garrison, with the ill-advised assistance of some American gunboats which happened to be in the harbor of Fernandina at that time under special instructions from the United States Government. They then marched upon St. Augustine; but in the mean time protests were made by the Spanish Government, followed by disavowal and recall on the part of the United States; and the new republic had to take itself out of Florida, with the loss of eight men killed by bushwhacking negroes from St. Augustine. It was during this expedition that a party of one hundred and ten men, under Colonel Newnan, of Georgia, penetrated into the Alachua country to near Lake Pithlachocco, where, in a severe battle with the Indians, under their King Payne, the latter were defeated after the exercise of much clever strategy and stout bravery by Newnan and his party. Payne is said to have behaved like a hero in this fight, and to have ridden a white horse into action, urging his men forward with consummate bravery.

Bowlegs, a co-leader with Payne, kept up the fight with great vigor; and it was only after eight days, in which Newnan had been compelled to fortify and undergo a siege, that he managed to effect a retreat. During the retreat he was again attacked by the Seminoles, and lost several men. His command suffered greatly for food before getting back to Picolata, even eating alligators in their distress.

Florida could not have been a pleasant place of residence in these days. Some account of a singular fort which existed for several years on the Apalachicola River may illustrate the state of affairs at this time. During the war of 1812 between Great Britain and the United States, General Jackson moved down upon Pensacola and captured it by storm. Thereupon its former commander, Colonel Nichols, who had gotten away by water, proceeded with some British troops and friendly Indians up the Apalachicola River and caused a fort to be constructed on a bluff of that stream at the point now known as Fort Gadsden, in which was placed a garrison of British troops and Creek Indians. This fort was intended to be used as a rendezvous and base of operations for the runaway negroes, from which they might depredate upon the neighboring border. The war of 1812 having closed, the British troops left the fort; but a negro named Garcia retained possession of it, the runaways under his lead garrisoned it, and it became a really strong point of defense to that large colony of runaway outlaws who had settled on the banks of the Apalachicola. The walls of the fort were fifteen feet in height and eighteen in breadth; it had a swamp behind, and creeks above and below it; it was armed with nine cannon and three thousand small arms, and had amply-stored magazines. This fort existed until 1816, when Colonel Clinch of the United States army reduced it, after a set battle with the negro garrison which opened hotly enough and would have doubtless been a troublesome piece of work for the whites had not a lucky hot shot from one of the United States gunboats exploded a magazine in the fort, causing great slaughter and demoralization among those inside. Garcia, and a Choctaw chief who was aiding and abetting him, were executed after the capture; and property amounting to two hundred thousand dollars in value is said to have been recovered in the fort.

The extent of Indian depredations at this time may be gathered from the fact that in the course of the expedition under General Jackson in 1818 against the Seminoles he discovered at Miccosukee "three hundred scalps of men, women, and children, most of them fresh." [1] In this foray General Jackson severely punished the Indians, hanging their chiefs without hesitation and even executing two Englishmen who were supposed to be instigating the Indians and supplying them with munitions of war.

That portion of West Florida west of the Perdido had been already acquired by the United States, it having been ceded to France by Spain in 1795 and thus forming a part of the Louisiana

[1] Fairbanks. [*History of Florida.*—ED.]

purchase of 1803. The balance of Florida was ceded by Spain to the United States in the treaty of 1819, ratified in 1821, in which latter year the United States Government took formal possession.

In 1822 an act of Congress consolidated East and West Florida into the Territory of Florida, and organized a territorial government for it. Soon afterwards the site of the former Indian settlement of Tallahassee, a place distinguished for its beautiful trees, was selected for the capital.

As the rich agricultural capabilities of the State began more and more to invite immigration, the demand now became more and more urgent for the Indians to be removed, so that the lands might be worked in peace. These Indians, the Miccosukies and Seminoles, occupied some of the best portions of the State. The latter tribe was an offshoot from the powerful Creeks. (Their name is usually, but wrongly, pronounced Se'minole; in conversation with General Sprague,* who has a thorough acquaintance with this tribe, I observed that he always called them Semino'lehs, making four syllables and placing the accent on the penult.)

In the course of many "talks," a proposition was made to the Indians by the United States Government, offering them strong inducements to remove to the West; and finally a treaty was made at Payne's Landing on the Ocklawaha River in 1832 by which many of the chiefs agreed that if the proposed Western country should be acceptable to a delegation which they should appoint to examine it, and if the Creeks would reunite with them, they would remove. This delegation actually visited the proposed reservation, and after spending several months in examining it came back and made a favorable report to their people. But meantime the party which had originally opposed removal had grown stronger. It included Osceola, who was exceedingly violent in his denunciation of the project; and the negroes (of whom it is said there were a thousand living with the Indians, some of them being very prominent persons in the councils of the savages) were also hostile to the movement.

This party-feeling among the red men ran so high that in 1835 Osceola came upon the old chief Charley Emathla, who

* [John Titcomb Sprague (1810-1878), whose *The Origin, Progress and Conclusion of the Florida War* (New York, 1848) Lanier consulted.—Ed.]

was making his preparations for removal, and killed him. This taste of blood seems to have whetted Osceola's[1] appetite. About a month afterwards he secreted himself near the Florida Indian Agency, and after lying in wait for some days shot down General Thompson and a companion as they were strolling and smoking after dinner. On the same day (December 28, 1835), and partly by the contrivance of this same Osceola, occurred in another part of the State a massacre which was in some particulars one of the most remarkable in history. Major Francis L. Dade of the United States army, with one hundred and thirty-nine regulars and a six-pounder, while marching on his way from Tampa to Fort King through an open pine and palmetto country near the Withlacoochee River in Sumter County was fired upon suddenly by a band of one hundred and eighty Indians secreted in the palmetto. It is said that at the first fire nearly half the whites fell. The Indians fell back for a little while. The remainder of the command erected a hasty breastwork of pines, and in less than an hour the attack was renewed by the savages, and continued until the last man in the breastwork had fallen. After possessing themselves of the soldiers' arms, the Indians left. But the measure of cruelty was not then full; for in a short time a party of negroes rode up and butchered with knife and hatchet all who were not yet dead. One man had bribed an Indian to spare him; another successfully concealed himself and made his way to Tampa; and these two were the sole survivors. Osceola was to have been at this ambuscade; but he was busy on this day, as we have seen, at other similar work.

That such a band of savages should have been able to accomplish these results against a party of regular troops and under such circumstances shows a capacity for vigorous and persistent attack on the part of the Indians which must ever remain matter of astonishment.

This massacre opened the long and bloody Indian war which followed in Florida. General Clinch, who was in command in

---

[1] The real name of this remarkable Indian was As-se-se-ha-ho-lar. He was also called Powell. He was a brave man both in appearance and action, and was a brilliant leader. He was captured—some say inveigled—by General Hernandez in one of the ensuing campaigns, and imprisoned in Fort Moultrie, Charleston harbor, where he died of pure heart-break in a few weeks.

Florida, immediately called for volunteers after the Dade massacre, and defeated the Indians under Osceola and Alligator after a severe battle. He was compelled to abandon active operations, however, by the expiration of his volunteers' term. Meantime, General Gaines had come down from New Orleans, in the emergency, without waiting for orders; but General Scott, who had assumed command, appears to have treated him with the grossest discourtesy and to have managed to completely paralyze his movements. General Clinch soon retired in disgust, and General Scott's campaign resulted in nothing. The Indians were now devastating and burning the whole country east of the St. Johns between St. Augustine and New Smyrna, and putting the unhappy families to the knife. Toward the latter part of the year 1836, General R. K. Call, of Florida, commanding twelve hundred troops under General Armstrong and a small force of regulars, militia and friendly Creeks, conducted a short campaign on the Withlacoochee and defeated the Indians in one engagement; but he had to fall back for supplies, and at the end of the year the whole lower portion of the State was practically in the hands of the savages.

Early in 1837, General Jessup inaugurated an active campaign upon a plan of rapid movements, designed to prevent those annoying withdrawals for the purpose of obtaining supplies which had deprived the preceding campaigns of results. He prosecuted his plan with vigor. The Indians began to ask for "talks," and in a few weeks many of them were assembled at one post or another—among others Osceola, King Philip and his son Coacoochee, near Fort Mellon—ostensibly for the purpose of carrying out the old project of a Western exodus. A rendezvous was appointed near Tampa, and some seven hundred had actually come in for this purpose, when early in June Osceola arrived with two hundred Miccosukies and so worked upon the intending Western emigrants that the whole party took themselves off toward the southern morasses and left General Jessup to commence over again. Which he did in the following fall with great vigor, and with a largely-increased force amounting to about nine thousand in all. These were divided into several columns and detachments, with specified districts for operation. One body of eleven hundred came from Tampa, under General Taylor, and immediately encountered four hundred Indians near Lake Okeechobee. After a gallant charge, which was desperately resisted by the Indians, the latter retired; but in all substantial results it was an Indian victory, for they lost but eleven killed and nine wounded, while the whites lost twenty-seven killed and one hundred and eleven wounded, and returned to Tampa.

The other detachments captured and killed a considerable number of Indians. Meantime, John Ross with a party of Cherokees had gone down among the Seminoles to treat with them, much to the disgust of General Jessup, who regarded the time lost from active fighting as wasted. While the Ross negotiations were pending, Coacoochee escaped through the embrasure in a cell of the fort at St. Augustine where he had been confined, and so stirred up his people upon rejoining them that the "talk" resulted in nothing. Meantime, by hook or by crook, over fifteen hundred Indians had been captured, who were transferred in May and June of 1837 to the West.

General Jessup was succeeded in command by General Zachary Taylor, and that officer carried on an active campaign during the winter of 1838–9. It resulted in little, however. The Indians had found out wherein their true strength lay, and could not again be tempted into a set battle, confining themselves to their own peculiar system of bushwhacking in small parties. General Taylor then established block-houses at a great many points, each with mounted scouts who were always on the search in their respective districts. It is probable this plan might have been very efficient had not General Macomb been sent down at this time by the Government to have another peace "talk" with the Indians. It so happened that it was just at that time of the year when—as any one must observe in reading these Florida wars—the wily Indians were ready to "talk," to wit, in the spring, when, if they could get the whites to suspend hostilities by some show of peace, they could have an opportunity to rest awhile, draw rations, get some sort of crop raised by the squaws off in the woods, and thus recruit as it were for a renewal of hostilities whenever they got ready. So it proved in this instance. General Macomb actually issued a sounding General Order proclaiming that the war was over, upon the strength of an agreement he had made with Halleck-Tustenuggee, Tiger tail, and Chitto-Tustenuggee; and peaceful operations were being universally resumed, when suddenly, little more than a month afterwards, the Indians broke out more bloodily than ever, killing without mercy. It was now found so difficult not only to fight, but even to find the Indians, that over thirty blood-hounds were actually brought from Cuba, at an expense of several thousand dollars, to be employed in tracking up the invisible red-men. But they failed, and the Indians kept up their cunning fights.

In May, 1840, Brigadier-General Armistead took command, and during a terrible year, filled with tragic Indian revenges, did his best to hunt out the foe. Notwithstanding the blood which was flowing on all sides, continual "talks" were had with small bands of Indians, who would come in and draw rations for awhile, then disappear and levy war again. It was to have one of these "talks" that Coacoochee (Wild Cat) came in once to meet Colonel Worth, arrayed in a very remarkable dress which he had made up from the properties of some play-actors whom he had killed and plundered not far from St. Augustine a short time previously.

General Armistead's command ended in 1841, when he was relieved at his own request. During the year some four hundred and fifty Indians of both sexes and all ages had been secured by various means.

General Worth now took the field in command, and immediately succeeded in turning the aspect of affairs. The Indians had been in the habit of escaping from the very clutches of their pursuers, and of retiring to places thought to be inaccessible to the whites. I was told a story of their facility in these matters some days ago. During one of these campaigns a party of soldiers had surrounded an Indian in a small pool of swampy water, in such a manner that they thought it absolutely impossible for him to escape. Upon a minute search, however, they were unable to find him, and abandoned the quest. Some time afterwards he was captured; and upon being asked how he had managed to escape, declared that he was lying under the very log upon which one of their party had stood, with his entire body under water except the mere tip end of his nose. Perhaps this may account for the marvelous feat recorded in the account of one of the great battles of De Soto near Ocala with King Vitachuco—how that two hundred Indians, having been driven into the lake by stress of battle, remained swimming in it for twenty-four hours.

General Worth, at any rate, appears to have convinced the Indians that all places accessible to them were accessible to him also, and that he could campaign in summer as well as in winter. Having secured the person of Coacoochee, he used that chief to great advantage in capturing others; and managed matters so well, bringing in band after band of captives and deporting them to the West, that early in 1842 he suggested to the Government to allow the small remainder of the Indians to stay within specified limits on the extreme southern end of the peninsula. His suggestion was finally adopted, and in August of the same year he formally announced that hostilities had closed.

About three hundred Indians remained. They, with their descendants, still carry on a peaceful life in the lower portion of Florida, supporting themselves by hunting, fishing, cattle-driving and scanty planting.

Thus ended a war which had lasted nearly seven years, had taxed the resources of six or seven United States generals, and had cost the Government more than nineteen millions of dollars.

This was indeed not the last blood shed on the soil of Florida in battle. The war between the States has its record here. This is so recent that it would not be interesting now to detail what is still in most people's recollection.

One cannot close this outline without reflecting upon the singular fate of this land which for three hundred and sixty years has languished, and has now burst into the world's regard as if it had but just opened like a long-closed magnolia-bud.

Surely it ought to give us a great many oranges, a great many bananas, and a great many early vegetables, after having been so bloodily fertilized for such a time. Surely it ought to restore to us a great many sick men,—it has swallowed up so many well ones!

CHAPTER XIV

FOR CONSUMPTIVES

IN THE course of a desperate but to all appearances successful struggle with a case of consumption which had everything in its favor at the start—the prestige of inheritance on both sides and the powerful reinforcement of a bent student's habits—this present author finds remaining prominently in his recollection a few cardinal principles of action in this behalf which may possibly be of practical service to consumptives.* In view of such a possibility, one cannot hesitate upon the sacrifice of personal delicacy involved in referring to oneself. A pain that cures a pain justifies its being.

And it often happens that the recommendations of a fellow-sufferer insinuate themselves into a patient's acceptance when the injunctions of a physician fail; they come with more force, because with less formula. The gentlest of invalids is sometimes disheartened with the best of doctors; " it is his business to tell me these things: *lege artis,*" one says, wearily, and turns away in apathy and neglects all the advice.

First. *Set out to get well, with the thorough assurance that consumption is curable.*

Do not allow yourself to be fobbed off with well-meant but often ill-advised reiterations of your friends that there's nothing in the world the matter with your lungs, it's only your throat, or your bronchial tubes, and the like. There is really no time for the Pickwickian methods in consumption. Once suspecting that you have it, show to some capable physician that you are strong enough to bear the certainty of knowing the fact, and then get his honest opinion of your condition. Let it be said here that in hundreds of instances these opinions, even of the most skilled practitioners, have been proven mistaken; the methods of examination, the apparent facts revealed by them, and the humanly drawn inferences therefrom, are all three liable to divers sources of error, and there is always a large

---

* [For an account of Lanier's long battle with consumption, see the Introduction to the present volume.—ED.]

margin of doubt to be attached to the diagnosis of even the best physician in the early stages of this disease.

But the declaration of the physician being given that you have consumption, then the first cardinal principle above stated comes into play: set about curing it, and with the certain assurance that it *can* be cured. It is now too late for the superstition, prevalent some years ago, that consumption is an incurable disease. This writer has personally seen a score of persons in active health who had seemed hopelessly ill with it years before; and the instances of the formation of healthy cicatrix in the lung are so numerous as to leave no doubt that many serious lesions of that organ may be repaired.

Secondly. *Give faithful and intelligent trial to every apparently reasonable mode of cure suggested for the disease.*

As has been before remarked in this book, the personal equation is almost as great an element in the phenomena of consumption as of asthma. Individual idiosyncrasies of either physical or mental temperament become frequently just the weights that turn the scale in favor of life or death. The effects of these personal peculiarities cannot be forseen, and often develop themselves during treatment. Of course, it is quite out of the range of this short chapter to discuss these various modes of cure. The milk cure, the beef-blood cure, the grape cure, the raw-beef cure, the whisky cure, the health-lift cure, the cure by change of climate, and many more have been devised. It will be observed that none of these depend upon medicine. Most intelligent physicians rely nowadays upon medicines only to alleviate the immediately distressing symptoms; the *curative* powers of drugs, in this as in any other disease, are much doubted by many of the most eminent persons in the faculty. In taking a general view, however, of all the methods of cure mentioned above, as well as of all others not mentioned, the consumptive immediately discovers that one fundamental principle underlies them all, to wit, *the making of the body as strong as possible by food, drink, air, and physical development.* It is to this indeed that all the recommendations of the physicians converge, namely, *that consumption is an unknown blood-poison, the only known method of counteracting which is to use such generous diet, fresh air, ameliorative appliances, and muscular and respiratory expansions as will bring the system to its highest state of resistive capacity.* This may be considered the eleventh commandment in consumption, including all the rest.

The problem is, therefore, for the consumptive to find out how best to practically apply this general rule to his own particular idiosyncrasies, habits, environment, and ability. In this connection it may be of use to mention two details of treatment.

(*a*) There is but one beneficial method of using stimulants. That is, *first to ascertain the proper dose (which varies indefinitely with different individuals), by experimenting until you have found such a quantity as neither quickens the pulse nor produces any sensation in the eyes, this quantity being usually very small; and then to take this ascertained dose at intervals of not less than one hour and a half, with the greatest regularity*; the theory being, that as the stimulus of the first dose decreases, its reaction will be met by the new stimulus of the second dose, the reaction of that by the action of the third, and so on, thus maintaining the system at its highest stage of resistance for such periods of time as enable it to throw off the disease. The kind of stimulant to be used is simply such as is found upon experiment to be most easily digested. In most cases, pure whisky (which should always be taken without sugar or any other mixture save its own quantity of water) has been found to be the best possible form of stimulant. Most wines available to persons of ordinary means are probably hurtful. Feeble and nervous patients, who find headache produced by stimulants, should diminish the dose, even to ten drops, and take it more frequently, say every hour. Perseverance for three or four days has been found to remove the tendency to headache and give full play to the beneficial effects of the stimulant.

This treatment—by regular doses of whisky administered at intervals of from an hour to an hour and a half through each entire day from sleep to sleep—has been known to effect marvels, unaided by any other remedies save generous food and proper exercise.

(*b*) *The physical expansion of the lungs is of the greatest importance in removing congestion and preventing hemorrhage.* It can be constantly practiced without any cumbrous appliances whatever. Whether you are standing, sitting, walking, riding, or lying in bed, at any time, whenever you think of it, *draw in*

your breath slowly until the chest is tolerably full—or, if you
have a cough, until you feel that the inspiration is about to pro-
voke it—and hold the breath so for a considerable time, then
gently release it. If not painful to do so, straighten the body
and put out the arms during the process. A habit of this sort
once acquired will soon develop a comfortable feeling in the
chest and a freedom from oppression quite astonishing in view
of the simplicity of the means used. The process itself is a better
expectorant than any known to the pharmacopœia, and often
has more efficacy in relieving the dreadful hack of the consumptive than all the drugs that can be administered, without
any of their injurious accompaniments. This gentle and constant expansion of the vesicles of the lung cannot be over-
estimated; every means should be devised to remind oneself of
it, and even to make it pleasant. The latter has been accomplished with great efficacy by playing the Boehm flute. The
operation of playing the flute — so far as it depends on the
breath — involves the precise motion of the lungs which is of
benefit to the consumptive, to wit, a full inspiration (always
take care, not *too* full, not straining in the least) succeeded by
a slow and gentle delivery of the breath. Of course an inex-
perienced player wastes breath at first; but with increasing skill
this disappears, and the operation of playing becomes so gentle
as to involve scarcely more violent inspirations and expirations
than those which a fully healthy man makes in ordinary breathing while asleep. It is hardly necessary to add that practicing
should never be carried to excess; the least sign of fatigue
should be the signal for stopping until the next day.

The recommendation of flute-playing to consumptives will
seem strange to some, and possibly there may be physicians who
would oppose it. It has, however, been long known as beneficial; Quantz, the flute-player to Friedrich, speaks particularly
of its value in this behalf.* Perhaps it may be proper to add
that this author knows positively and personally of most signal
benefits resulting therefrom.

In regard to the stimulant treatment marked (*a*) above, one
finds it necessary to say that no person entertaining the least
doubt as to the possibility of the stimulant habit so fastening

* [Johann J. Quantz (1697-1773) in his *Autobiography* (in Marpurg's
Beitrage).—ED.]

upon him or her as to become itself a controlling disease should meddle with it. As between dying a drunkard and dying a consumptive no one in his senses could hesitate a moment in favor of the latter alternative. And in this instance the dilemma is not so hard as that; for there are many other methods of treatment not involving this form of stimulant.

Thirdly. *Never get in the slightest degree wet, cold, or tired.*

One feels like saying, after Jean Paul, that herefrom many inferences are to be drawn, and I advise the reader to draw them. If, for example, you are a consumptive bent upon the open-air cure, and are going to the Indian River country in Florida to hunt and fish and camp out, you should provide yourself with a perfect suit of light India-rubber for head, neck, body, and feet, and a plentiful supply of thick flannel huntsman's-shirts to wear next the skin, no matter if it *is* warm; and your party should obey your slightest whim, with the instant devotion of slaves to a tyrant, in stopping and pitching camp as soon as you announce that you are tired. If, on the other hand, you are a feeble invalid, you should beware of long journeys by rail or otherwise in cold weather, where you may be subjected to sudden changes from hot cars to cold air; and should visit Florida (*e. g.*) while the weather is pleasant, remaining, then, over the whole winter, until the spring is nearly become summer. The same principle will lead you to avoid, after you have reached Florida, any long journey which might involve exposure. A single half-hour in the night air, a drenching from a five-minutes' shower, a walk of half a mile beyond your strength, may undo fatally the work of long and well-employed months. Often, in traveling, one's mere delicate reluctance to ask the person in the seat ahead to close his window may cause one to sit in the draught until the terrible chill comes on which bears its result in weeks of fever and of cough. In such case either change your seat, or, if that be impossible, make the request which seems so dreadful as long as you sit and brood over it and so simple as soon as made.

Finally, carry the supportive treatment herein recommended beyond the material into the moral. Be brave with your consumption: do not discuss it with bated breath. It is not necessary to go to the irreverent point of a certain jolly sufferer at San Antonio, Texas, who used to burst into one's room with

"Halloo, ——, how're your tube's [1] this morning?" Yet he was conducting an active business, and was faring along with considerable comfort upon something like half a legitimate allowance of lung. Probably he would not have done so if he had puled about it. Endeavor, therefore, in pursuance of this policy, to have some occupation consistent with your disease's requirements. Brooding kills. If you are near a Florida farm (*e. g.*), interest yourself in something that is going on there, the orange-culture, the grape-culture, the early vegetables, the banana-culture, the fig-culture, the fine tobacco culture, and the like. The field of Florida in these matters is yet so new, so untried by the resources of modern agricultural improvement, as to be full as fascinating, if one should once get one's interest aroused in it, as it was in the old days when the Spaniards believed it to be full of gold and pearls. Or you may, if you like that sort of woods-life, kill alligators and sell their teeth, as mentioned in the Jacksonville chapter of this book; or shoot herons, and collect their plumes for market — an occupation by which at least one invalid, of whom I have heard, has managed to support himself; or you might get a contract with some of the numerous colleges in the country to supply their cabinets with stuffed birds, or fish, or botanical specimens, from Florida. Of course, if you have means which preclude the necessity of doing these things for support, you can do them for pleasure, and in applying yourself to the study of science you will soon cease to wither under that true consumptive sense that life is done with you and that you have nothing left but to die. The flute-practicing above recommended is also valuable as affording some definite occupation for each day.

The ingenuity of every patient will indefinitely improve upon all these mere hints. If there were but any words in which to speak those devout and fervent hopes for the mitigation of any least pang which go with these meagre suggestions as they are hastily offered to you who are beyond all measure the keenest sufferers of all the stricken of this world!

---

[1] Short for *tubercles.*

CHAPTER XV

OTHER WINTER-RESORTS ON THE ROUTE TO FLORIDA

MANY INVALIDS, consumptive, rheumatic, or asthmatic, have varied their Florida experiences by spending a part of their winter in Charleston, Augusta, Savannah, or Aiken; and there are others who, in obedience to that difference of temperament which I have before referred to as making it impossible to predict with certainty the precise shade of climate best suitable for any given individual, have found complete or partial restoration in one or other of those places without going farther South. Besides this, the attractions which they present in the way of comfortable lodgment, of good company, of mild climate, of various diversions, and of the facilities of established cities draw many tourists and pleasure-seekers and tired people, who without being sick nevertheless desire to flee from the rigors of the Northern climate.

CHARLESTON

As one stands upon the steeple of old St. Michael's Church, a sheer hundred feet above any roofs in the neighborhood (where every visitor *should* stand, at his first sallying-forth into the city after arrival, for from here one may gain a complete idea of the entire environment almost at a glance), and looks over the general face of the city, perhaps no impression is more prominent than the thorough gentlemanliness of it. There is nothing " loud " in sight. This gentlemanly aspect is all the more striking, in that it exhibits itself under the disadvantage of at least two very unfavorable circumstances. One is, that the houses are all turned to a dingy color—even those newly-painted —by the unusually strong quality of the sea-air which here sweeps freshly in from the near ocean. The other is, that the physiognomy of the city is so peculiar as to render it absolutely unlike that of any other city in the world within my knowledge. The houses, with their long three-storied stretches of piazzas, do not front the street, they front the sea-breeze; they are all

147

arranged with their ends up the street, precisely like pews in a church.

I have called these disadvantageous circumstances, because it is certainly a severe test of a man's gentlemanly bearing, when he preserves it intact in spite of being dressed at once rustily and unlike everybody else.

But Charleston does: its air, as it stands there under the steeple of St. Michael's, is distinctly full of affable decorum; and no visitor with the least perception of the fitness of things can stay in the pleasant old city for a day or two without imbibing this sense of genial old-time dignity, to the extent of wishing that Charleston might always be, as it is, at once sober-suited and queer and delightful.

Going round the balcony of the steeple of St. Michael's to the battery-side, and facing seaward: the river sweeping down on your right is the Cooper; that on the left is the Ashley; as the glance runs down the farther bank of Cooper River seaward, the points of land which last meet the eye represent James and Morris Islands, whose batteries were so famous during the war; inclosing the harbor on the left is Sullivan's Island, on which one perceives the town of Moultrieville and Fort Moultrie. In the centre-view one sees Fort Sumter, and, more inland, Castle Pinckney. On the right appears Fort Johnson.

Yonder low banks of the Cooper and Ashley Rivers up which one's eye roves for a long distance from this elevated station, seem to be really in the strange Micawberness of things about to pour even as much wealth into Charleston as the friendly currents which run between them, or as the tributary sea itself. It is from them that the celebrated phosphate ores are being dug in great quantities; and now that the world—not only the American world, but England, France, Germany, Spain, Scotland, Ireland—has quite convinced itself of the enormous substantial value of these singular deposits as fertilizing material, no reasonable-sounding prophecy can be made concerning the ultimate extent of the trade in them from this point.

The " phosphate rocks" of this region occur in the form of nodules, which are of a yellowish-gray color, emit a fetid odor when broken, and vary in size from an inch in diameter to masses weighing two hundred pounds. The deposit along the peninsula between the Ashley and Cooper Rivers near Charleston lies below the surface at a depth of from four to five feet, cropping out immediately at the banks of the rivers. It is but a short time ago that the farmers along the river-banks piled up these outcropping rocks in pyramidal heaps to get them out of the way, their value being unknown. The deposit here is often from eighteen to twenty inches thick. It sometimes reaches a thickness of three feet; and is sometimes found in "pockets" several feet in width and depth. A uniform deposit of fifteen inches in depth yields six hundred tons to the acre; there are some now yielding a thousand tons to the acre. It is not confined to the Charleston peninsula, but is found—though not in a continuous stratum—all the way from the Wando and Cooper Rivers, fifteen miles above Charleston, running parallel with the coast as far as to St. Helena Sound, near Port Royal. It is often exposed in the beds of streams at low tide; and one of the numerous mining companies is devoted exclusively to collecting these river-bed riches.

The nodules constituting the ore are mainly composed of phosphate of lime. Their geological history is strange and intensely interesting.

[The Eocene Marl] is the foundation of the whole seaboard country of South Carolina, and . . . is composed of the Santee, Cooper, and Ashley River Marls, which in the aggregate are seven hundred feet thick, and extend from North Carolina into Georgia. Before the low country of South Carolina was raised above the level of the ocean, the waves of the Atlantic beat upon the granitic hills of Edgefield, Lexington, and Richland.

The shallow water of the coast with its submarine formation of undulating sand-banks was then, as now, resting upon this surface of the great Marl formation, of Eocene age; both were below the level of the ocean, exposed to the degrading influence of its waves, and bored by Mollusca and other marine animals.

The Eocene Marl is here represented as we have found it, with its surface washed into deep cavities and holes, bored by animals just named, and honey-combed to the depth of five or six feet. This is its condition off Charleston harbor at the present time; and wherever the surface of the bed inland has been uncovered, it is found irregular and broken, and the phosphate rocks show this plainly. From the coarsely honey-combed surface of this mother-bed, fragments were being continually broken off by the waves, rolled over the sand-beds, which wore off their angular edges, and finally deposited them in extensive masses in the great hollows or basins below the ocean-level. . . .

We apprehend it did not require a very long time nor much friction to reduce these comparatively soft lumps of Marl rock to the rounded or nodular forms they now have. Every gale drove them farther and farther upon the submarine beach, until at last they were deposited in the lagoons or basins formed within the sand-reach of the coast. . . .

Professor Ansted, describing the phosphate-beds near Cambridge, England, writes—and we quote him in corroboration of our own views on this subject: "Many years ago a discovery of phosphate of lime was made in the so-called Crag-beds of Suffolk, and afterwards in the Green-sands of many parts of the southeast of England." (This corresponds with the Eocene or Green-sand of South Carolina.) "The former contain beds consisting of nodules of exceedingly hard material, which, when ground, are soluble in sulphuric acid, and then form a most valuable manure. . . . The nodules themselves are believed to have been washed out of older rocks, also of Tertiary age." It was, undoubtedly, so with the South Carolina phosphate-rocks.

The next great change was the upheaval of the whole seaboard country by some geological agency, and the elevation of the coast above the level of the ocean. When the sand hills and the submarine lagoons were raised, the basins contained sea or salt water, and must have been so many small salt lakes along the sea-coast, having their bottoms covered or paved with a thin layer of the nodular fragments of Marl rock. As the evaporation of the salt water progressed, what was left became day after day a stronger brine, until at last a deposit of salt ultimately formed as a crust upon the pavement of Marl rocks. And here we must remind the reader, that these nodular fragments of Eocene rocks are composed (like the mother-rock from which they had been broken off) entirely of the dead shells of marine animals, which age after age were deposited at the bottom of the ocean or Eocene sea, and finally became an immense bed or formation of Marl inclosing throughout its great depth not only the *Polythalamous* [1] shells, corals and corallines, but the teeth and bones of sharks and other fish, and of whale-like and alligator-like animals; such alone as live in the sea; but no remains of any land animal *have ever yet been found in it*. All the remains of land animals obtained in such vast numbers are *mingled* with, and not *imbedded in*, the nodules found in the Phosphate basins; and this mingling of bones and teeth occurred in the POST-PLEIOCENE AGE, after the elevation of the basins above the ocean level. It was in this Post-Pleiocene age [that] the American Elephant, or Mammoth, the Mastodon, Rhinoceros, Megatherium, Hadrosaurus, and other gigantic quadrupeds roamed the Carolina forests, and repaired periodically to these Salt-lakes or Lagoons, or as they are called in

[1] Many-chambered.

Kentucky, *Salt-licks*; and during a series of indefinite ages, . . . they were first sipping brine, then licking salt, and depositing their fecal remains, and ultimately their bones and teeth, in fact their dead bodies, in these great open *crawls* or pens.[1]

The marl-nodules, over which these land animals thus herded for ages, were mainly composed of carbonate of lime. Now carbonate of lime may be dissolved away and replaced by silicious matter, as in the case of these same Santee marls which are exposed near Aiken, South Carolina, as Buhrstone or Millstone-rock; or it may, when subject to the action of the phosphoric fecal discharges of animals, become changed into phosphate of lime. Many persons have even confounded these phosphate rocks with bones, and some have imagined that the phosphatic qualities of the rock were solely derived from the great numbers of bones found associated with them. But the rock is, as has been said before, the transformed lime of shells, corals and corallines; and so far from owing its phosphatic nature to bones, it has been found that while fresh bones contain only about fifty-two per cent. of phosphate of lime, the bones dug up with the phosphate deposit yield ninety-two per cent. of phosphate of lime, thus showing that the bones have gained from the rock, rather than the rock from the bones. What is known as the great " Charleston Fish-bed " is not the phosphate-bed; it is the Ashley marl and sands underlying the phosphate deposit, and contains more carbonate than phosphate.

Such is the hypothesis of Professor Francis S. Holmes, of Charleston, South Carolina, a gentleman whose name is intimately connected not only with the first knowledge of these great deposits, but with the utilization which was made of them much later. It appears that in the year 1837 Professor Holmes, then a young student of geology, found

in an old rice-field, about a mile from the west bank of the Ashley, in St. Andrews Parish, . . . a number of rolled or water-worn nodules, of a rocky material filled with the impressions or casts of marine shells. These . . . were scattered over the surface of the land, and in some places had been gathered into heaps, so that they could not interfere materially with the cultivation of the field.*

[1] *The Phosphate Rocks of South Carolina*: By Francis S. Holmes. Holmes' Book House, Charleston, 1870.

* [This quotation and the one following are also from F. S. Holmes, *The Phosphate Rocks of South Carolina.*—ED.]

He soon gathered for his own cabinet " thousands of remark-able specimens; " and some six years afterwards showed them to Mr. Ruffin, who, as State Geologist, was actively searching out localities where marls could be obtained. At that time, how-ever, the value of phosphate of lime does not seem to have been known even to the agricultural geologist. Mr. Ruffin was looking for *carbonates* of lime, or marl, which were then being earnestly recommended to farmers for fertilizing purposes; and the phosphatic nodules were dismissed as valueless. Several years afterwards Professor Tuomey made a crude analysis of similar nodules, but found only sixteen per cent. of phosphate of lime in them.

In the year 1867, however, one of these specimens fell into the hands of Dr. N. A. Pratt, who was then residing in Charles-ton. He discovered upon analysis that it contained sixty per cent. of phosphate of lime; and on consulting Professor Holmes and finding that he had long been acquainted with the nodules, though unaware of their great proportion of phosphatic mat-ter, he resolved to ascertain the extent of the deposits.

Dr. Pratt left the next day with Mr. Lucas for Ashley Ferry, saw the rock *in situ,* and admitted " it surpassed his anticipation." On the very day the doctor and Mr. Lucas were visiting the Ashley we received Ansted's book from London, on the Geology of the Cambridge Beds of Phosphates, giving in detail the analysis of a rock similar to that of the Ashley, and discovered some time during our Confederate War. . . . On the doctor's return from the Ashley (with Mr. Lucas) we had the pleasure of placing the book in his hands and directing his attention to the article. Several persons were present at the time, and all expressed their surprise. . . . After SIX WEEKS OF UNAVAILING EXERTIONS in obtaining means to develop these treasures of the Ashley River, and to convince the good people of Charleston of the value of the discovery, we were obliged to resort to Northern cities for aid. Mr. James T. Welsman, of Charleston, one of the few who fully appreciated the dis-covery, furnished the necessary funds. Geo. T. Lewis and Fredk. Klett, Esqs., two gentlemen of Philadelphia, immediately took the matter in hand, rewarded us both for our discovery, and furnished the capital for the first Phosphate Mining Association—The Charleston, South Carolina, Mining and Manufacturing Company.

The beginning thus made was soon followed up, and com-pany after company organized. These organizations are of two sorts: those which merely dig up and wash the ore, shipping it to various parts of the world in its crude state,and those which manufacture the ore into commercial fertilizers. Of the former sort are the Charleston, Coosaw, Pacific Guano, Marine and River Phosphate, and Oak Point mining companies, and the mines of Pinckney & Gregg, and of William L. Bradley; of the latter sort are the Wando, Etiwan, Atlantic, Soluble Pacific, and Stono companies, and the works of J. B. Sardy. There are several other smaller mines and works besides those mentioned. Very large amounts of money are invested in the acid-chambers for the manufacture of sulphuric acid, and in the crushing and washing machinery and the like appliances of these works. The process is simple. The ore is dug by the pick, or, when taken from the beds of the streams, by powerful dredges. It is then dried, washed by machinery and shipped crude, or crushed, treated with sulphuric acid and manipulated into various forms of commercial fertilizers.

This ore is rendered additionally interesting by its association with the age of pre-historic man. In the year 1844 Professor Holmes in opening a marl-pit found among these nodules, directly under the roots of a large oak, a stone hatchet and some stone arrow-heads whose forms seemed to separate them from those usually found in the Indian mounds. Soon afterwards he found a human bone projecting from a bluff and touching the phosphate stratum; but not supposing it to belong to that age he threw it away. About a year afterwards, however, he found a lower jaw-bone with teeth in the same bed and preserved it; and in 1867 Dr. Pratt and Professor Kerr discovered near the same spot parts of a human femur and tibia. There seems now to be no doubt that these remains all point to the same age with that so richly illustrated by the discoveries in the Somme valley in France, and in Switzerland, known as the Stone Age.

During Professor Holmes's investigation into this subject, the circumstances revealed itself that Charleston is situated on the same geological formation with that over which London is built.[1]

[1] The author desires to acknowledge his obligation to the courtesy of Mr. Thomas D. Dotterer, superintendent of the Wando Company's works, for many of the facts embodied in this brief account of the Charleston phosphate deposits.

In the year 1662 his Majesty Charles II granted a charter to Edward, Earl of Clarendon, George, Duke of Albemarle, William, Lord Craven, John, Lord Berkeley, Antony, Lord Ashley, Sir George Carteret, Sir William Berkeley, and Sir John Colleton, conveying to them a certain vast domain lying between the thirty-first and thirty-sixth parallels of north latitude, and running west to the Pacific Ocean, to be held in free and common socage. A second charter afterwards enlarged the grant so as to make it embrace all the territory lying between 29° and 36° 30' of north latitude.

For the colony which was to inaugurate a civilization in this new region the Lords Proprietors procured John Locke to draw up that famous Constitution which was the first attempt to construct a clock-work society, warranted, when once set going, to run till the Day of Judgment. Perhaps one could scarcely engage in a more fruitful inquiry than a search for the principles underlying those prodigious contrasts which have revealed themselves between the moral excellences of some of the best men who have ever lived and the practical absurdities of their ideal projections for the benefit of society. The Republic which Plato devised, the Palatinate of John Locke,[1] and the Utopia of John Ruskin completely invert the qualities of their inventors and seem vicious in the precise degree that those were virtuous. As for Locke's Constitution, it quickly proved itself wholly unsuited to the needs of its people, and was virtually disused long before it was formally abandoned.

The Proprietors located a settlement at Port Royal in 1670. In 1671 the colonists removed to the west bank of the Ashley, not far above its mouth, and instituted " Old Charlestown." In 1679 the project was agitated, and in 1680 carried out, of moving to the present site of Charleston, then Oyster Point—a spot which on account of its situation between the Cooper and Ashley Rivers afforded better facilities and deeper water for shipping.

At our being there, [says T. A.,[2] writing in 1682 (supposed to have

[1] See the Constitution itself: probably easiest accessible to most readers in Vol. II of [B. R.] Carroll's *Hist. Coll. of South Carolina.* Harper & Bros., 1836.

[2] In "The Complete Discovery," by T. A., "clerk on board his Majestie's ship *The Richmond.*" [Quoted in B. R. Carroll, *Historical Collections of South Carolina.*—ED.]

been Thomas Ashe)] was judged in the country a 1000 or 1200 souls; but the great number of families from England, Ireland, Barbadoes, Jamaica, and the Caribbees have more than doubled that number.

The extravagant descriptions of the beauty of the climate, the fertility of the soil, the grandeur of the forests, and the like, were indeed enough to draw adventurers from many regions. T. A. wrote seductive accounts of even the medicinal productions of Carolina.

They have, [says he, *e. g.*,] three sorts of the Rattle Snake Root which I have seen: the Comous, or Hairy, the Smooth, the Nodous, or Knotted Root; and if I do not very much in my Observations err, the Leaves of all these roots of a Heart had the exact Resemblance; they are all sovereign against the mortal Bites of that Snake too frequent in the West Indies. In all pestilential Distempers, as Plague, Small Pox, and malignant Fevers, it's a noble Specifick; when stung they eat the Root, applying it to the Venemous Wound: or they boyl the Roots in Water, which drunk, fortifies and corroborates the Heart, exciting strong and generous Sweats; by which endangered Nature is relieved; and the Poyson carried off and expelled.

He writes similar accounts of the virtues of the ambergris found on the shores; and, along with some sprightly tales of the Carolinian Turtles,[1] declares that " the Flesh is commended for a good antiscorbutique Diet, . . . and some that have been far gone in consumption, with the constant use of this Diet have been thoroughly recovered and cured in 3 or 4 months."

And so, through ups and downs far too complicated for narration in this place; through harassments from the Stono and Westo Indians, who would possibly have quite eaten up the young colony save for the diversions created by the private wars between the Westoes and the Serannas; through civil seditions; through internal troubles betwixt Cavaliers and Puritans, who along with their goods and household gods had brought also their old quarrels with them over the sea; through prosperities drawn from diverse sources—now from West Indian pirates who would come into town and scatter their gold and silver about with lavish hand, the king permitting them so to do and even knighting one of them (Henry Morgan)—and

[1] See the account hereinbefore quoted from him in the " Gulf Coast " chapter of this book.

now from accessions of Huguenots driven here by the revocation of the Edict of Nantes; through wars with the Yemassee
and wars with the Spaniard; the Charleston colony fared along.
Says Oldmixon (mostly redacting Archdale), describing it in
1708:

> Charles Town, the capital of this province, lies in 30° 40″ north
> latitude, two leagues from the sea. . . . [It] is a market town, and
> thither the whole product of the province is brought for sale. Neither
> is its trade inconsiderable; for it deals near one thousand miles into the
> continent; however, 'tis unhappy in a bar that admits no ships above
> two hundred tons. Its situation is very inviting, and the country about it
> agreeable and fruitful; the highways extremely inviting, especially
> that called Broadway,[1] which for three or four miles make a road and
> walk " so pleasantly green that," says my author, " I believe no prince
> in Europe by all his art can make so pleasant a sight for the whole year.
> There are several fair streets in the town, and some handsome buildings.
> As for public edifices, the church is most remarkable; 'tis large and
> stately enough; . . . but the auditory begins to want room and another
> church.[2] This is dedicated to St. Philip." *

A later writer, in 1763, describes some lighter matters in
Charleston; and appears particularly to have fallen, perhaps on
some enchanted Charleston night by the water-side, into the
sweet hands of certain slender and lissome ladies whom every
visitor to modern Charleston will easily recognize as true an-
cestral types of the lithe and graceful girls that still abound
there.

> [The inhabitants of the Carolina province, he says,] are generally of
> a good stature and well made, with lively and agreeable countenances,
> sensible, spirited, and exceed most people in acts of benevolence, hospi-
> tality, and charity. . . . The personal qualities of the ladies are
> much to their credit and advantage; they are generally of a middling
> stature, genteel and slender; they have fair complexions— without the
> help of art—and regular features; their air is easy and natural; . . .
> their eyes sparkling, penetrating and inchantingly sweet; they are fond
> of dancing, an exercise they perform very gracefully; and many sing
> well, and play upon the harpsichord and guitar with great skill. . . .

[1] Meeting Street.

[2] The parish of St. Michael's was afterwards established.

* [Lanier's source was probably Carroll, *Historical Collections of South
Carolina.*—Ed.]

In summer . . . riding on horseback or in chaises (which few are without) in the evenings and mornings . . . is much practiced. In the autumn, winter and spring there is variety and plenty of game for the gun or dogs; the gentlemen are not backward in the chase. During the season there is once in two weeks a dancing assembly in Charleston, where is always a brilliant appearance of lovely and well-dressed women; we have likewise a genteel play-house, where a very tolerable set of actors, called the American Company of Comedians, exhibit; and often concerts of instrumental and vocal music, generally performed by gentlemen. Madeira wine and punch are the common drinks of the inhabitants; yet few gentlemen are without claret, port, Lisbon, and other wines of the French, Spanish, or Portugal vintages. The ladies, I mention it to their credit, are extremely temperate, and generally drink water, which, in Charleston, . . . is very unwholesome. . . . The cotton-tree likewise grows naturally in this province, and might be of great use in clothing the poor sort of white inhabitants and the negroes [what *would* this gentleman think of the degenerate cotton-clothed people of this day who are neither the poor sort of white inhabitants nor negroes?] if any pains were taken to cultivate it. . . . There are about eleven hundred dwelling houses in the town, built with wood or brick; many of them have a genteel appearance, though generally incumbered with balconies or piazzas, and are always decently and often elegantly furnished; the apartments are contrived for coolness, a very necessary consideration.*

These old glimpses of ancient Charleston reveal many features which the modern visitor will not fail to recognize. Through all its reverses, British occupations as well as terrible disasters of Confederate struggles, it seems to have preserved its individuality in a marvelous degree. One observes with pleasure many signs indicating a return of the commercial importance which the city had gained before the late war. Its old West India trade, which acquired such a lucrative momentum during the Anglo-French wars, is not now so great; but it is being replaced in other ways, notably by increased shipments of lumber and naval stores, due to the new activities in these directions recently inaugurated in South Carolina by the southward movement of lumbermen and distillers who have begun to abandon the worn-out pine-forests of North Carolina

---

* [George Milligan, " A Short Description of the Province of South Carolina," printed in Carroll, *Historical Collections of South Carolina.*—ED.]

for the new and comparatively untouched districts of South Carolina, Georgia and Florida.

Perhaps no city of equal size with Charleston has accumulated so long and brilliant a list of names eminent in diverse departments of activity. Pringle, Legare, Hayne, Simons, Langdon Cheves, Crafts, Petigru, Grimke, Brevard, Johnson, Desaussure, Parker, Lowndes, Gadsden, among the lawyers; Dickson, Ravenel, Geddings, Bruns, Ramsay, Prioleau, Frost, Bellinger, Gaillard, Miles, among the physicians; Yeadon, Pinckney, Morford, Rhett, among the editors; Bachman, Elliott; are names which occur to the hasty recollection of even a stranger, and could be largely supplemented by one familiar with the town's inner history from residence in it. As for the fine old merchants, and the fine old planters, who are associated with this city, the enumeration of them would fill a volume. Nothing can be pleasanter — in these days which one would feel strongly inclined to call degenerate did not one have unconquerable faith in the necessary continued bettering of times—than to dwell upon the confident and trustful relations existing between these old planters and merchants, the one producing, the other product-handling, and to trace their roots in the honesties of reputable dealings of many unimpeachable years of trade; and nothing can be more pitiable than that at the time when this amiable outcome of the old Southern civilization became known to the world at large, it became so through being laid bare by the sharp spasm of civil war. That was a time when all our eyes and faces were distorted with passion; none of us either saw, or showed, true. Thrice-pitiable, one says again, that the fairer aspects of a social state which though neither perfect as its violent friends preached nor satanic as its violent enemies denounced yet gave rise to so many beautiful relations of honor and fidelity should have now gone into the past, to remain illuminated only by the unfavorable glare of accidentally-associated emotions in which no man can see clearly.

The sojourner in Charleston will find several places of interest to visit. A steamer makes excursions in the winter to the celebrated Middleton Place, where one can see the capacities of this region in the matter of large and brilliant flowers. On Sullivan's Island, the beautiful beach, Fort Moultrie and the grave of heart-broken Osceola are the objective-points. One must drive or stroll through Rutledge Avenue, which is the Fifth Avenue of Charleston; and Magnolia Cemetery must be seen. The quaint interior of St. Michael's, with its high box-pews and antique suggestions; the old French Protestant Church; the Charleston College museum, an extensive collection, owing its origin to the suggestions of the lamented Agassiz, and intimately associated with the names of Bachman, Audubon, James Hamilton Couper, the Misses Annelly, and Mitchell King; the Charleston Library, a large collection of books which has been maintained by the Charleston Library Society since the year 1748; the antique and often renowned tombs of the old cemeteries of St. Philip's, St. Michael's, the Independent Congregationalist, Unitarian, First and Second Presbyterian, Baptist, German Lutheran, Roman Catholic, Trinity, and Hebrew churches; all offer inducements for the bestowal of one's mornings. Besides these, the historic battle-grounds of Fort Sumter and of James and Morris Islands may be made the objective-points of sailing-excursions; though there is really no reason why a sailing-excursion should have an objective-point, and *me judice* the aimless sort is your only perfect sail. A pleasant strolling-ground and meeting-place is the Battery, which is laid out in walks and adorned with trees, and commands ample water-prospects; where, if you meet a Charleston friend, you should get him to tell you the history of the beautiful chime of bells in the belfry of St. Michael's, as you pace up and down the white walks in the gentle air that comes off the near Gulf Stream.

One fares well in the matter of hostelry at Charleston; the Charleston Hotel has long had a delightful reputation among travelers. There are smaller hotels, such as the Victoria, Pavilion, and others. The Mills House appears to have been closed for some reason; though I believe rooms are still rented in a portion of the building.

There are two well-arranged street-railways. That called the Enterprise Railway is specially notable. Its tracks, which the visitor will frequently observe curving off towards the water-front, connect the principal wharves directly with the railroad depots, so affording extraordinary facilities for the shipment of cotton, rice, naval stores, and the like. Besides these more purely commercial tracks, it has a street-line proper, running *via* Meeting, John, Chapel, Washington, and East Bay Streets.

The other street-railway is known as The City Railway, and runs two lines of cars—the Rutledge Avenue line and King Street line—the former *via* Rutledge Avenue, Wentworth, and Meeting Streets, the latter *via* King, Calhoun, and Meeting Streets.

Charleston is connected with Savannah by The Savannah and Charleston Railway; with Florence, South Carolina—and at that point with the Wilmington, Columbia, and Augusta Railroad, and its northern system of connections—by The Northeastern Railway; with Columbia, Augusta (Georgia), and Camden, South Carolina, by The South Carolina Railway, which is notable as the first important railroad built in America.

The city has an admirable graded system of public schools, with a curriculum extending from the primary studies through an entire course terminating in the Charleston High School and Charleston College. There is also here an old and well-known medical college. The St. Andrew Society, dating back to 1731; the South Carolina Society, founded in 1737, and originating in the *Two Bit Club,* which used to hold meetings in a house known as *The Old Corner,* on Broad and Church Streets; the St. George, Fellowship, German Friendly, St. Patrick, Hebrew Benevolent, and Société Française organizations; are all charitable associations of great efficiency in the relief of distress.

One of the very sweetest names connected with Charleston is that of Henry Timrod, its poet, now dead.* Few more spontaneous or delicate songs have been sung in these later days

* [The first edition (1875) reads:—

" Perhaps the very sweetest name connected with Charleston is that of Henry Timrod, its poet, now dead. Few more spontaneous or delicate songs have been sung in these days than some of the almost perfect lyrics which appear in the published volumes of his poems. It is certainly evident from these that he had not reached the full height to which his genius would have borne him. Doubtless wider association with other poets, and more of that wine of success and of praise without which no man ever does the very best he might do (though many have done amazing things who never tasted it), would have been of inestimable service to his poetic faculty. But he had a poet's genuine art withal; as witness, *e. g.,* his deservedly popular poem of . . . " For further details concerning Lanier's critique of Timrod (1828-1867) see the Introduction, pp. xix-xx, above.—ED.]

than one or two of the briefer lyrics which appear in the published volumes of his poems. It is thoroughly evident from these that he had never had time to learn the mere craft of the poet—the technique of verse; and that a broader association with other poets, and a little of the wine of success and of praise without which no man ever does the very best he might do though many have done amazing things who never tasted it, would have been of inestimable service to his poetic faculty. But he had a dainty artless art withal; as witness, *e. g.,* particularly the last four lines of

BABY'S AGE

She came with April blooms and showers;
We count her little life by flowers;
As buds the rose upon her cheek
We choose a flower for every week.
A week of hyacinths, we say,
And one of heart's-ease ushered May.
And then because two wishes met
Upon the rose and violet,
—I liked the Beauty, Kate, the Nun—
The violet and the rose count one.
A week the apple marked with white;
A week the lily scored in light;
Red poppies closed May's happy noon
And tulips this blue week in June.
Here end as yet the flowery links;
To-day begins the week of pinks;
But soon—so grave and deep and wise
The meaning grows in Baby's eyes,
So *very* deep for Baby's age—
We think to date a week with sage!

SAVANNAH

On the first day of February in the year 1733 the city of Savannah, being then but a few hours old, consisted of four tents, which were sufficient for all its inhabitants and were pitched under four pine-trees near the edge of the bluff between Bull and Whitaker Streets.

It appears that for a year or two previous to this date the attention of certain good and charitable gentlemen of England had been called to the fact that many unfortunate persons were languishing in the debtors' prisons of that country, and that some radical means should be adopted in order to afford new avenues of fortune to poor men and younger sons of families. The interest of these gentlemen finally took the direction of procuring a charter from King George II, granted to them as trustees, authorizing the colonization of a tract lying between the Savannah and Altamaha Rivers; and in pursuance thereof James Oglethorpe set sail from Gravesend on the 17th of November, 1732, with thirty-five families, reaching Charleston, South Carolina, on the 13th of February * thereafter. Receiving the most cordial assistance from the South Carolinians, the party proceeded to Beaufort, where Oglethorpe left them and went ahead with Colonel William Bull of South Carolina (whose name is perpetuated in Bull Street, one of the most beautiful streets in America, and the present fashionable *promenade of Savannah*) to select a site for the city, which it had been previously determined to locate on the Savannah River.

I fixed, [says Oglethorpe, writing back to the Trustees in England on the 10th February, 1733,] upon a healthy situation, about ten miles from the sea. The river here forms a half-moon, along the south side of which the banks are about forty foot high, and on the top flat, which they call a bluff. . . . Upon the river-side in the centre of this plain I have laid out the town. Opposite to it is an island of very rich pasturage, which I think should be kept for the Trustees' cattle. The river is pretty wide, the water fresh, and from the key [quay] of the town you see its whole course to the sea, with the Island of Tybee, which forms the mouth of the river; and the other way you see the river for about six miles up into the country. . . . The whole people arrived here on the first of February. At night their tents were got up. . . . I marked out the town and common; half of the former is already cleared, and the first house was begun yesterday in the fore-noon.**

It was not without some difficulty that the site was obtained. The Indian chief Tomochichi had here his village of Yama-

---

* [Lanier should have written " on the 13th of January "—not February. —Ed.]

** [Lanier's source was probably F. D. Lee and J. L. Agnew, *Historical Record of Savannah*, a copy of which he owned—Ed.]

craw; and it was only by the intercession of a woman with the Indians that their consent was obtained. This woman was Mary Musgrove, the half breed wife of a white trader then residing at Yamacraw. She afterwards acted as interpreter, and played a romantic and varied part in the early history of Savannah.[1]

The account of the state of Savannah in 1736, by Francis Moore, existing in the collections of the Georgia Historical Society, gives so vivid an idea of the singularly far-seeing and statesman-like principles which appear to have controlled the whole plan of laying out and governing the city, that a brief extract from it cannot be uninteresting. One may fairly call this a unique beginning of a town, as here depicted:

> The town of Savannah is built of wood; all the houses of the first forty freeholders are of the same size with that Mr. Oglethorpe lives in. . . . The houses stand on large lots sixty foot in front by ninety foot in depth; each lot has a fore and back street to it. . . .
>
> There are several people of good substance in the town who came at their own expense, and also several of those who came over on the Charity are in a very thriving way; but this is observed, that the most substantial people are the most frugal, and make the least show, and live at the least expense. . . . The industrious ones have throve beyond expectation; most of them that have been there three years, and many others, have houses in the town, which those that let have for the worst ten pounds per annum, and the best for thirty pounds. . . . Those who have cleared their five-acre-lots have made a great profit out of them by greens, roots and corn.

From this last item it would appear that the charming market-gardens of Savannah, whose products have such reputation in New York, may claim an antique origin, in these " greens, roots and corn " which brought so much thrift to the early settlers.

> . . . All matters, civil and criminal [continues Francis Moore], are decided by grand and petit jurors, as in England; but there are no lawyers allowed to plead for him [sic]: nor no attorneys to take money, but (as in old times in England) every man pleads his own cause. In

---

[1] Those desirous of pursuing the history of Savannah in its details will find a well-written *Historical Record of Savannah*, published by J. H. Estill, of that city, for sale at the book-stores. [This volume, by F. D. Lee and J. L. Agnew, was apparently the source of Lanier's account of the early history of Savannah and of the three quotations immediately following.—Ed.]

case it should be an orphan, or one that cannot speak for themselves, there are persons of the best substance in the town appointed by the Trustees to take care of the orphans and to defend the helpless, and that without fee or reward, it being a service that each that is capable must perform in his turn.

They have some laws and customs that are peculiar to Georgia: *one is, that all brandies and distilled liquors are prohibited under severe penalties; another is, that no slavery is allowed, nor negroes; a third, that all persons who go among the Indians must give security for their good behavior, because the Indians, if any injury is done to them and they cannot kill the man that does it, expect satisfaction from the Government, which if not procured, they break out into war by killing the first white man they conveniently can. No victualler or alehouse-keeper can give any credit, so consequently cannot recover any debt.*

But the wise foresight does not stop here. To prevent the town lots from concentrating disadvantageously by inheritance, or by the designing buyings-in of rich speculators,

The Trustees grant the land in tail-male, that on the expiring of a male line they may regrant it to such man, having no other lot, as shall be married to the next female heir of the deceased as is of good character. . . . Each freeholder has a lot in town sixty foot by ninety foot, besides which he has a lot beyond the common of five acres, for a garden. Every ten houses make a tithing, and to every tithing there is a mile square, which is divided into twelve lots, besides roads; each freeholder of the tithing has a lot or farm of forty-five acres there, and two lots are reserved by the Trustees in order to defray the charge of the public. The town is laid out for two hundred and forty freeholds; the quantity of land necessary for that number is twenty-four square miles; every forty houses in town make a ward, to which four square miles in the country belong; each ward has a constable, and under him four tithing-men.

Where the town land ends the villages begin; four villages make a ward out, which depends upon one of the wards within the town. The use of this is, in case a war should happen, the villages without may have places in the town to bring their cattles and families into for refuge, and for that purpose there is a square left in every ward big enough for the outwards to encamp in. There is a ground also kept around about the town ungranted, in order for the fortifications whenever occasion shall require. Beyond the villages commences lots of five hundred acres; these are granted upon terms of keeping the servants, etc. There is near the town to the east a garden belonging to the Trustees consisting of ten acres; the situation is delightful, one-half of it upon the top of the hill, the foot of which the Savannah River washes, and from it you see the woody islands in the sea. The remainder of the garden is the side and some plain low ground at the foot of the hill, where several fine springs break out.

Truly an Arcadian city! It would really seem that these broad and noble ideas which thus came like good fairies to the birth of Savannah and contributed their gifts to it have never withdrawn themselves from watching over the further growth of the city. Perhaps no town of equal age has more clearly preserved the general plans and spirit of its founders. Here the visitor of today still sees the wide symmetrical streets, the generous and frequent squares, the lavish adornment of grasses, flowers and magnificent trees, which appear to render into material form the liberal and manly tone of Oglethorpe's inaugural management; and every one acquainted with the modes of Savannah life among its best citizens will recognize the spirit of quiet refinement, the reserve, the absence of ostentation which Francis Moore has commemorated in the opening words of the extract above given. The residences, many of which are very beautiful, appear to withdraw themselves from observation, and to hide behind their wide piazzas and balconies which are inclosed with Venetian blinds; and one may stroll along the pleasant promenade of Bull Street, or through the alleys of Forsyth Park, for a whole afternoon without encountering a lady dressed " loudly."

Savannah is much frequented by Northern and Western people during the winter and spring. The hotel accommodations are excellent; the Pulaski House, the Screven House and the Pavilion are the largest; and there are cheaper establishments, such as McConnell's and Bresnan's, on the European plan.

There are many points of interest to visit. Sailboats are always to be obtained for excursions down the river; and there is a small railway, connecting at Bolton with the street-cars, upon which one can with facility reach Thunderbolt, a noted spot on the river five miles from town where in the warm afternoons the owners of fine teams cluster on the pleasant riverbank under the trees ere turning about for the drive back to the city. A shell-road reaches to Thunderbolt which forms The Drive of Savannah and is a gay enough thoroughfare on pleasant afternoons.

A road turns off to the left from this shell-road and leads to the famous old burying-place called Bonaventure, a spot about a mile from Thunderbolt which no one sojourning at Savannah should fail to visit. It was formerly the seat of the famous old Tatnall family, but passed from their hands, and was finally purchased and converted into a cemetery. It is but sparsely tenanted, however, by the dead; and one entering its noble avenues will scarcely see aught at first besides the arching glories of the oaks and the weird solemnities of the moss. The great boles of the trees lean and their long muscular arms bend in attitudes of profound mournfulness; the gray mosses hang, as beards hang; it is as if all the ancient prophets of the ages had assembled in solemn convocation to meditate silently together upon the passing of time and the piteousness of death.

On the road to Bonaventure one sees the Catholic Cemetery; the main cemetery of the city, Laurel Grove, lies to the northwest of the town, not far from Forsyth Park.

One of the pleasantest strolls in Savannah, particularly in the early spring—that is, in April—is to Forsyth Park, along Bull Street which leads directly to it; on the way (say, from the Pulaski House) one passes first through Johnson Square containing the Green Monument; then through Wright Square, Chippewa Square, Madison Square, and Monterey Square which contains the Pulaski Monument.

Or, beginning at Bay Street—the main business thoroughfare, parallel with the river and next to it—and walking westward along Barnard Street, one passes through Ellis, St. James, Orleans, Pulaski, and Chatham Squares.

Or, on the other (south) side of Bull Street, turning into Abercorn Street and walking westward, one passes through Reynolds, Oglethorpe, Lafayette, and Calhoun Squares.

A good road leads to White Bluff, which is a favorite summer resort of the Savannah people, some ten miles out. This road is also much used as a fashionable drive.

JASPER SPRING, on the Augusta road two miles from town, is a spot famous in history. Every one remembers how the brave Jasper and Sergeant Newton, in casting about for a plan to rescue a lot of unhappy patriot prisoners who were being carried by a British guard to Savannah to be hung, foresaw that the guard would likely stop at a certain spring for water, hid themselves in the bushes near the spring, waited until the guard arrived and stacked arms, shot the two sentinels, seized the stack of arms, compelled the discomfited regulars to assume the very manacles which they had placed upon the prisoners, and marched the whole party into the partisan camp.*

BETHESDA, about ten miles from Savannah, is a spot consecrated by the nobleness of man in quite a different way from the latter. Here the great George Whitfield procured a grant of five hundred acres from the Trustees for the purpose of founding an orphan-home which had been suggested to him by Charles Wesley, and, with the co-operation of James Habersham and the aid of the Countess of Huntingdon, erected an institution which through many disasters was maintained for a long time. The buildings were finally destroyed by wind and fire; but a hundred and twenty-five acres of the original grant have been bought by the Union Society, a noted benevolent institution of Savannah, and devoted to the original purposes of the founders of Bethesda.

Savannah is one of the most prosperous cities in the Union, and is a port of growing commercial importance. The great exports are cotton, lumber and rice; and the activities incident to the handling of the large quantities of these staples which are here annually received make it a busy city in the fall and winter. It is the terminus of several railways: the Georgia Central, leading to Macon, and, by a branch running in at Millen, to Augusta; the Atlantic and Gulf, running to Albany, with branch at Dupont Station running to Live Oak, Florida, along which the great bulk of the annual Florida travel is transported; the Savannah and Charleston, running to Charleston, South Carolina; the Port Royal, to Port Royal and Augusta; and the Savannah, Skidaway, and Seaboard, to White Bluff, Isle of Hope, and Skidaway Island. There are also several lines of steamships to New York, one to Philadelphia, and one to Baltimore; a coast-line to Charleston; one to Brunswick and the Satilla River; one to Pilatka, on the St. Johns, Florida; one to Augusta, on the Savannah River; and two to Darien, one of which goes on up the Altamaha and Ocmulgee Rivers as far as to Hawkinsville. An important feeder of the city is the Savan-

* [Lanier's source was probably Lee and Agnew, *Historical Record of Savannah.*—ED.]

nah and Ogeechee Canal, extending between the Savannah and Ogeechee Rivers.

The city has a notable number of benevolent institutions; an admirable public school system; a fine antiquarian association known as the Georgia Historical Society, which has just erected a very handsome library building, and has recently come into a large bequest from the late Miss Mary Telfair; and a number of well-built churches, particularly the Independent Presbyterian, with the lofty spire, fronting on Bull Street. The city is furnished with water-works, which supply water from the Savannah River.

And lastly, its police headquarters is precisely the police headquarters which one would expect in an Arcadian city: being a plain building in a cool and shady brick court, overhung by trees, covered with climbing vines, and, to the view of the passer-by at least, as clean as a Dutch parlor.

Savannah is the residence of Henry R. Jackson,* a poet whose verses have been much admired by those who appreciate the chaste simplicities of a style of poetry which is unfortunately too much obscured by the less substantial though more dazzling productions of later schools. A fair sample of his power is the poem

TO MY FATHER

As die the embers on the hearth,
    And o'er the floor the shadows fall,
And creeps the chirping cricket forth,
    And ticks the death-watch in the wall,
I see a form in yonder chair
    That grows beneath the waning light;
There are the wan, sad features—there
    The pallid brow and locks of white.

My father! when they laid thee down
    And heaped the clay upon thy breast,
And left thee sleeping all alone
    Upon thy narrow couch of rest,
I know not why I could not weep,
    The soothing drops refused to roll,
And oh! that grief is wild and deep
    Which settles tearless on the soul.

---

* [Henry Rootes Jackson (1820-1898), author of *Tallulah and Other Poems* (1850), and perhaps best known for his " Red Old Hills of Georgia."—ED.]

But when I saw thy vacant chair,
 Thine idle hat upon the wall,
Thy book—the penciled passage where
 Thine eye had rested last of all;
The tree beneath whose friendly shade
 Thy trembling feet had wandered forth,
The very prints those feet had made
 When last they feebly trod the earth;

And thought while countless ages fled
 Thy vacant seat would vacant stand,
Unworn thy hat, thy book unread,
 Effaced thy footprints from the sand;
And widowed in this cheerless world
 The heart that gave its love to thee—
Torn like the vine whose tendrils curled
 More closely round the falling tree;

Then, father! then for her and thee
 Gushed madly forth the scorching tears;
And oft, and long, and bitterly
 Those tears have gushed in later years;
For as the world grows cold around
 And things their real hue take on,
'Tis sad to learn that love is found
 With thee above the stars alone!

AUGUSTA

This beautiful city was laid out at the instance of the Trustees of Georgia in the year 1735, and received its name from General Oglethorpe in honor of the royal Princess Augusta, daughter of George II.

Large warehouses were erected here, and the place quickly became a considerable depot for the merchandise employed in the trade with the Creeks and Chickasaws. The country in which it is situated was originally known as the District of Augusta, until 1758 when it was made St. Paul's Parish; but in 1777 it was called Richmond County, after the Duke of Richmond.

Doubtless the proximity of the town to the Indians rendered it at first a somewhat uneasy place of residence. For example, one finds in 1756 such communications as these passing to the then Governor, John Reynolds, who had been recently appointed by the English Government, the Trustees having surrendered their charter in 1752.

AUGUSTA, Saturday, 10 of the
clock in the morning
12th September, 1756

MAY IT PLEASE YOUR EXCELLENCY,—We have, as in duty bound, sent this express on purpose, with the inclosed information, by which you will understand that Indian blood has been spilt, and consequently an Indian war is almost inevitable; the only thing in all probability that can prevent it is the having of the murderers secured for to make him satisfaction, for which reason we issued hue and crys everywhere to apprehend them; and in case they come by the way of Savannah, we hope care will be taken to secure them. We are afraid we cannot hold this place long without speedy assistance, which we hope your Excellency will take into serious consideration. All the settlements on the Ogeechee are abandoned. The fort cannot contain all the inhabitants, so that we shall be obliged to fortify some other places. We beg your Excellency would send us instructions how to act as you shall think proper. There are some head men of the Creeks, in Charlestown, or on their way thither, on whom we have had great dependence, as we designed to assure them that we will take and do justice on the murderers and give them all the satisfaction they required. We wish we could hear from your Excellency before they went from this place, for which reason we hope your Excellency will dispatch the express with all haste possible. There is no match in the fort. Mr. ——— begs if there is any such thing in Savannah that you will send him some. And we are, with the greatest respect, your Excellency's most humble, most obedient servants,

DA. DOUGLASS,
JOHN ROE,
MARTIN CAMPBELL. *

Perhaps one of the most spirited contests of the Revolutionary war occurred in the memorable siege of Augusta by General Henry Lee in May 1781 during its occupation by the British.

Having seized the powder, ball, small arms, blankets, etc., which had been recently sent to Fort Galphin as presents to the Indians from the English Government, General Lee sent Major

* [Quoted in George White, *Historical Collections of Georgia.*—ED.]

Eggleston to reconnoitre below the city and to summon it to surrender. This was done, but no reply was received.

Augusta was at this time in command of one of those curious personnages who float to the surface in times of war, named Thomas Browne. He is described in a *Georgia Gazette* of 1774 as one of "two young gentlemen lately from England." In that year he suffered great indignities at the hands of the patriots. A number of the "Sons of Liberty" had called upon him to clear himself of the charge of being hostile to the cause of American freedom, and upon being defiantly informed that he did not recognize their right to demand any such account of him had incontinently tarred and feathered him and exposed him to the public view "in a cart from the head of Augusta to Mr. Weatherford's"; insomuch that next day he "consented voluntarily" (as the *Georgia Gazette* naïvely terms it) to abjure his loyalty to the king and to support the cause of liberty.*

Perhaps the "voluntary" feature in this "consent" was not so apparent to Browne as to the hot patriots; at any rate we find him soon engaged in the British army. Already in 1779 he had signalized his desperate obstinacy, fertility of resource and personal bravery. Colonel Elijah Clarke, advancing upon Augusta in that year for the purpose of taking it, was met by Browne—though the attack was an entire surprise to the latter —at the White House, some mile and a half west of the town, and was held in check for several days through a continuous and destructive fire of artillery and small arms until the advance of Colonel Cruger to whom Browne had sent for assistance disheartened the patriots and caused Clarke to retire from the attempt. During these days Browne was shot through both thighs and his garrison's supply of water was entirely cut off; but he continued to lead his men in spite of his wounds, and devised a supply of water—from what source I will not here detail—in the actual use of which he also led his men, thus carrying them through the siege.

Colonel Clarke retired with the loss of sixty killed and wounded. Twenty-nine of these latter remained in the hands of the enemy and met a dreadful fate. Twelve of them were hung, it is recorded, on the staircase of the White House, while

* [Lanier's source for the incident was probably George White, *Historical Collections of Georgia*, which quotes the *Georgia Gazette*.—ED.]

others were either hung or delivered over to the Indians by whom they were roasted to death.

It was against such a commander that General Lee, upon finding that no reply was made to his summons of surrender, proceeded to make his dispositions for attack. The troops of Colonel Clarke (the same who had made the unsuccessful attack here the year before), Eggleston and Pickens had been concentrated to the west of the town.

The first assault was made upon Fort Grierson, which is said to have been located on the present site of the upper market in Broad Street. The fort was taken after a short struggle, and many of its garrison were killed and captured. Colonel Grierson, its commander, was murdered after his capture by some lawless persons among the Americans. Lee now advanced to a brick building on the bank of the river south of Fort Grierson, and proceeded to besiege Fort Cornwallis, of which Thomas Browne was in command. This fort was located very near the present site of St. Paul's Church. The besiegers immediately commenced to push forward works of offense. On the night of the 28th Browne fell upon them violently, but was repulsed after a hard struggle; and again, on the night of the 29th. Finding no eminence or other vantage-ground on which to place their artillery, the besiegers now commenced the erection of a tower to command Fort Cornwallis, and by the evening of the 31st had brought it nearly to the height of the ramparts. Early in the night Browne was again at work actively attacking. Repulsed at one end of the line, he renewed his assault at the other, and had driven the militia under Pickens from the trenches when Handy's infantry, which had been placed in supporting distance of Pickens, came up and compelled him to retire to his fort. In this engagement both sides suffered heavily.

Browne now endeavored to devise means for burning the tower, and to this end sent over a pretended deserter to Lee who by an artful proposition to aid in directing the fire of Lee's artillery upon the powder-magazine of the fort procured himself to be stationed for the night in the tower. The trick, however, did not succeed; Lee's suspicions became aroused, and he caused the deserter to be removed from the tower during the night. Meantime, Browne had fired several houses which lay within rifle-shot of his position, between the lines.

But his failure to burn the tower seems to have disheartened Browne. To a summons of surrender made on the 31st, calling his attention to the progress of the besieging works, he had pithily replied, "Gentlemen,—What progress you have made in your works I am no stranger to. It is my duty and inclination to defend this place to the last extremity." But to a second summons made on the 3d of June, after first replying as before, he allows twenty-four hours to elapse and then signifies his desire to surrender. He makes several propositions which the besiegers decline, and finally has to accede to their terms; and so the siege terminates with his formal capitulation on the 5th of June.

This Thomas Browne was afterwards convicted of forging an order from The Lords of the Treasury to Sir Charles Brisbane, Governor of St. Vincent's, requiring him to grant to Browne a large and valuable body of land in that island. The British Government had already rewarded him with thirty thousand pounds in consideration of his Revolutionary services; but, not content with this, he caused the forged order to be presented. It so happened that the lands named in the order had been granted to other parties, who had paid a large sum of money into the treasury for them. Sir Charles Brisbane asked further instructions of the Home Government; and the forgery was immediately detected.

In this same month of May, just ten years afterwards, Augusta exhibited a much more pleasing concourse of sights and sounds than the bloody incidents of Thomas Browne's desperate defense. These were the processions and ceremonies in honor of the arrival of George Washington, President of the United States, at that city. There are some features of these beautiful old testimonials of a people's hearty affection that richly merit frequent recital, for they cannot but present noble ideals to our young men and women. Jean Paul Richter has somewhere declared that the great advantage of Greek and Roman history to young people is that in studying it they enter life as it were through a vestibule set round with large and heroic forms that must of necessity influence the mould of their lives.* So much of the majesty of simple and chaste manners, so much of true

* [Paraphrased from Jean Paul Friedrich Richter, *Levana,* an English translation of which was published by Ticknor and Fields, Boston, 1863.—ED.]

knightly courtesy, reveals itself incidentally in the narration of the progress of George Washington among his people that one cannot help reproducing it, if even in briefest form.

The officers having assembled agreeably to the order of yesterday [yesterday was the 17th of May, 1791] at eleven o'clock set forward, accompanied by a numerous train of respectable citizens. At the distance of five miles from town the President of the United States appeared in sight, when the procession halted, at which time he alighted from his coach, mounted his horse, and advanced with Major Jackson and the federal marshal. His Excellency the Governor [Edward Telfair] at the same time attended by the Secretary of the State, moved forward, and, after being announced, congratulated the President on his near approach to the residence of Government. This ceremony being ended, the procession was resumed, and the President conducted to the house provided for his reception.*

Then there were balls, dinners, toasts, and many festivities. Observe the address of the citizens of Augusta: what beautiful English, what dovetailing clauses, what perfect sentences compose it! and more than this, what large sincerity, what grave manliness, what genuine yet decorous devotion shine out through the lucid fluencies of it, as it were sands of good gold compacted at the bottom of a clear running stream!

TO THE PRESIDENT OF THE UNITED STATES OF AMERICA:

SIR,—Your journey to the southward being extended to the frontier of the Union, affords a fresh proof of your indefatigable zeal in the service of your country, and equal attention and regard to all the people of the United States. With these impressions, the citizens of Augusta present their congratulations upon your arrival here in health, with the assurance that it will be their greatest pleasure, during your stay with them, to testify the sincere affection they have for your person, their sense of obligation for your merits and for your services, and their entire confidence in you as the Chief Magistrate of their country. On your return, and at all times, their best wishes will accompany you, while they retain the hope that a life of virtue, benevolence, and patriotism may be long preserved for the benefit of the age and the example of posterity.

* [Lanier's source for this and the following quotations was probably White, *Historical Collections of Georgia*, where the passages here quoted are reproduced from the *Augusta Chronicle* of May 21, 1791.—ED.]

To which the good President replies:

GENTLEMEN,—I receive your congratulations on my arrival in Augusta with great pleasure. I am much obliged by your assurances of regard, and thank you with unfeigned sincerity for the favorable sentiments you are pleased to express towards me.

Entreating you to be persuaded of my gratitude, I desire to assure you that it will afford me the most sensible satisfaction to learn the progression of your prosperity. My best wishes for your happiness, collectively and individually, are sincerely offered.

The "progression of your prosperity" advanced in time; until Augusta has at length come to be one of the most important cities of the South.

The visitor here is immediately struck with the breadth and beauty of the streets. Broad Street, the main business thorough-fare of the city, is one hunderd and sixty-five feet in width, and nearly two miles and a fifth in length. Both above and below the immediate centre of trade it is planted with rows of mag-nificent trees.

Greene Street, running parallel with Broad, is famed through-out the United States for its beauty. It is from one hundred and sixty to one hundred and sixty-eight feet wide. Down the centre of it runs a double row of large trees, and along each sidewalk a similar single row: the effect of which is to form a lovely greenwood aisle, passing along between two ample and high-arched avenues. Here in the middle of a cloudless summer-day one can promenade for more than a mile in cool and grateful shade; and the spacious flower-gardens and pleasant dwellings which border the street make it altogether a posses-sion any city might envy.

The granite monument in this street, in front of the City Hall, is about fifty feet in height, and was erected in 1849 to the memory of the signers of the Declaration of Independence in behalf of Georgia.

A pleasant drive at Augusta is to

SUMMERVILLE

a fair cluster of dwellings, some of them summer residences, others permanent, situated on the high sand-hills about three miles from town. The view from the brow of this eminence commands a wide scope of country in Carolina and Georgia; and the village itself presents many charming evidences of taste in noble trees, flower-gardens and gentle-looking homes.

On this drive to Summerville one crosses the Augusta Canal, an important element in the industrial prosperity of the city. It was begun in 1845, and is fed from the Savannah River. It has a total fall of about forty-one feet, divided into three levels. The large manufacturing buildings which attract one's attention in crossing the canal belong to the Augusta Cotton Factory Company, one of the most prosperous organizations of the sort in America. This factory has been recently much enlarged in capacity. The water-power of the canal is applied to sundry other industrial purposes, notably to a group of flour- and grist-mills, which grind more than four hundred thousand bushels of grain annually.

Some distance beyond the factory, on the Summerville road, one will observe the Augusta Orphan Asylum, a very beautiful structure built mainly upon the benefactions of Mr. Tuttle and of Dr. Newton.

One of the hills cut through by this canal, some four miles above the city, is referred to by Charles C. Jones in a monograph on Indian Mounds * as filled with evidences of having been once a much-frequented locality for the manufacture of flint arrow-heads and other stone weapons by the Indians. The same gentleman mentions a very interesting Indian mound on Stalling's Island, one of the "Thousand Islands" in the Savannah River a short distance above the city.

Augusta is now, and has been in times past, the residence of several persons eminent in letters. At Berzelia on the Georgia railroad a short distance from the city is the home of Paul H. Hayne,** the poet. The peculiar loveliness of the yellow jessamine which covers the spring woods of this region, as well as the grace and musical flow of Mr. Hayne's own poetry, are pleasantly formulated in this sonnet of his to

* [*Monumental Remains of Georgia.*—ED.]
** [Lanier's friendship with Hayne (1830-1886)—one of the first to encourage him in his literary career—began by correspondence in 1869 and continued through life, though they never met. His critique of Hayne's poetry appeared in the *Southern Magazine* in January, 1875, just a few months before *Florida* was published.—ED.]

THE MOCKING-BIRD

Of all the woodland flowers of early spring,
   These golden jasmines, each in air-hung bower
   Meet for the Queen of Faery's tiring-hour,
Seem loveliest and most fair in blossoming.
How yonder mock-bird thrills his fervid wing
   And long lithe throat, where twinkling flower on flower
   Rains the globed dew-drops down, a diamond shower,
O'er his brown head, poised as in act to sing!
Lo the swift sunshine floods the flowery urns
Girding their delicate gold with matchless light
Till the blent life of bough, leaf, blossom, burns;
Then, then outbursts the mock-bird clear and loud,
Half-drunk with perfume, veiled by radiance bright,
A star of music in a fiery cloud!

Augusta is also the residence of the poet James R. Randall,* at present editor of the *Augusta Constitutionalist*. Perhaps the fervent spirit of his poems has never found better expression than in

EIDOLON

Ah, sweet-eyed Christ! Thy image smiles
   In its Cathedral cell,
Shrined in the Heaven-enamored arms
   Of her who never fell;
And if my phantom eyes implore
   A more benignant beam,
'Tis a nepenthe I would crave
   For a memorial dream!

Dear Leonie! here didst thou kneel
   That musky summer noon,
As the zephyrs kissed in ecstasy
   The dimpled cheeks of June—
As the sunlight drifted o'er thy brow
   A golden wave of grace,
Bright-blending with the miracles
   Of that angelic face.

---

* [James Ryder Randall (1839-1908), best known for his "Maryland, My Maryland."—ED.]

Adorably Madonna-like,
   By this communion rail,
Thy raptured face, though rich with youth
   Was spirit-lit and pale;
And oh, those opulent blue eyes,
   Those Meccas of despair—
They, they were glorious Eden-isles
   Lost in a lake of prayer!

Saint Leonie! I saw thee flit
   Gazelle-like to the street,
And pure, melodious angels led
   Thy dainty, tinkling feet.
My rebel thoughts were petrel-winged,
   Attendant upon thee,
Chasing thy loved and lissome shape
   As Arabs of the sea.

Long did I love thee, *belle Creole*,
   As Gebirs love the sun,
And in the temple of my soul
   Thou wast the eidolon;
Long did I love thee, *belle Creole*,
   Where corsair billows rise,
And where the silver planets soar
   In unfamiliar skies!

Dark Corcovado! did I not,
   With heart and soul aflame,
Carve on my broad, monarchal brow
   Her wildly-worshiped name—
Watching the homeward ships scud by
   Before the nimble breeze,
Till memory with them wept away
   Beyond the tropic seas!

Years, years had died and once again
   I saw the spires of home;
Then, armed with an undying hope,
   I stood beneath this dome.
But not within the pillared aisle,
   Nor by the sacred sign,
Could my bewildered eyes behold
   The loveliness of thine.

> The sad November days had come,
>   And eagerly I fled
> To find thee where the maidens deck
>   The kingdoms of the dead;
> I found thee—yes, I found thee, love,
>   Beneath the willow-tree—
> With marble cross and immortelle
>   And one word—" Leonie! "

Here lives also, engaged in the practice of law, Mr. Salem Dutcher,* a writer whose strong and brilliant articles in the columns of the New York *World* a few years ago were often admired and quoted by those to whom his name, lost in the anonymous oblivion of the current journalistic habit, was by no means so familiar as it deserved to be.

The Hon. Richard Henry Wilde, author of the celebrated poem " My Life is like the Summer Rose," and Judge Longstreet, author of *Georgia Scenes*, were once residents of Augusta. The " Gander-pulling," in *Georgia Scenes*, is said to have occurred at the spot where now stands that same upper market which was the site of Fort Grierson and the scene of the bloody events enacted there, as hereinbefore detailed.

The honorable and venerable Charles J. Jenkins, one of the fast-departing " old school " of statesmen and gentlemen, now lives here.

Augusta is the terminus of several important railway lines. The Charlotte, Columbia and Augusta, and Wilmington, Columbia and Augusta, belong to the great organization known as the Atlantic Coast Line, which, in co-operation with the Bay Line steamers from Baltimore to Portsmouth, and the fast railway line from Portsmouth to Weldon, as also with the all-rail routes north of Weldon, transports the crowds of Florida travelers every winter, *via* Wilmington, North Carolina, and Columbia, South Carolina, or *via* Charlotte, North Carolina, and Columbia, South Carolina, to Augusta, whence the route lies by either the Georgia Central or Port Royal roads to Savannah, and thence by rail or water to Jacksonville, Florida.

---

* [Lanier's friendship with Dutcher, beginning in 1867, was also influential in his early literary career (see VII, 260, n. 1, of the present edition). The two authors mentioned in the following paragraph—Wilde (1789-1847) and Longstreet (1790-1870)—he was not acquainted with.—Ed.]

The Georgia Central connects Augusta with Macon, and with Savannah, the Augusta branch uniting with the main line from Macon to Savannah at Millen.

The Macon and Augusta offers direct connection with Macon.

The Georgia railroad is a trunk line from Augusta to Atlanta, with branches to Washington, Warrenton, and Athens.

The South Carolina railroad runs to Columbia, Charleston, and Camden, South Carolina. At Graniteville, South Carolina, ten miles from Augusta—where every traveler's attention will be attracted by the romantic nature of the surrounding country, the fine water-power, and the prosperous manufacturing appearances—the tracks of the South Carolina railroad and of the Wilmington, Columbia and Augusta come together, and run nearly side by side until they diverge just before reaching their respective bridges across the Savannah River immediately at Augusta.

The street railway, which one notices running along Broad Street, extends to the village of Summerville, named above, and affords a pleasant and cheap method of transportation to that point.

The city has excellent hotel accommodations at the Planters', the Augusta, the Globe, and the Central Hotels; and there are numerous private boarding houses.

Sixteen miles from Augusta, on the line of the South Carolina Railway, is

AIKEN, SOUTH CAROLINA

This is a town of about two thousand inhabitants, situated on a high plateau of fine sand, at an elevation of near seven hundred feet above the sea. It is noted for the dryness and purity of its atmosphere. Probably this arises in great measure from the peculiar soils of the vicinity. Hereabouts are found, besides the sand, exceedingly fine qualities of kaolin (or porcelain clay), and these pulverized soils appear to absorb both the moisture and the impurities of the atmosphere, rendering it wholesome much in the same way that wounds are cured and foul gases absorbed by the " dry earth " process. These fine clays are of infinitely various hues, some of which are very brilliant; and quite a little industry is carried on by the small " darkies " of the region, who collect them in glass tubes and sell them to the visitors.

The air of Aiken is also filled with balsamic exhalations from the great pine-forests of that region, and many are disposed to attribute much value to the effect of this atmospheric constituent upon the lungs.

There can be no doubt of the happy results which have been secured by consumptives from visits to Aiken. A considerable number of persons from the North have found the climate so grateful that they have purchased lands here and fitted up charming residences for permanent occupation.

The process of change which goes on in the minds as well as bodies of visitors to this singular spot is at once uniform and remarkable. At first one is greatly disappointed. Except to the west of the town—a locality whose beauties one does not learn till several days after one's arrival—nothing is to be seen except vague aspects of a main street two hundred and fifty feet wide, a great hotel all piazza and windows, a flat surface of whitish soil, pleasant-looking Southern homes with flower-gardens, some oaks, and many pines. Most persons, particularly those who come from romantic hill-regions, are strongly inclined to pack up their traps and flee out of the flat lands.

But presently the vast tranquillities which here brood about the world (for one hears no sounds of vehicle in this soft earth); the delicious balms which come on the air out of the pines, or out of the heavens; the perfect strolls along the aimless paths that wander whitely about among unending aisles of the pines; the reverie-places and dreamy haunts in among the trickling rivulets and glens of the broken country to the west of the town; the charming gallops over level roads; the rose-gardens; the light-wood fires on cool evenings; the sense of superiority over those unhappy persons whom one has left in the Northern winter and of whom one reads in the morning telegrams as shivering in fabulous depressions of the thermometer; the healing of the lungs, the casing away of the cough, the returning elasticity of the limbs, the new brightness of countenance; — presently all these things have their influence, and the spots which to an invalid's first impatience were disgusting become even dear and hard to part with.

Rheumatics and gouty patients resort to Aiken, as well as consumptives, and probably the number of people visiting here in the winter who are not invalids exceeds considerably that of the sick, many persons fleeing to this milder climate merely to escape the rigors of the Northern winter. The hotel accommodations are excellent; the Highland Park Hotel is under the management of the same parties who keep the Planters' Hotel in Augusta; and there are numerous opportunities for private board.

A story called "Spring Days in Aiken," by Mr. Albert F. Webster, which recently appeared in *Appletons' Journal*,* is so evidently based upon the actual experiences of an invalid, and is withal so captivating a piece of writing, by virtue of a certain gracious, bright, tender, and graceful spirit which pervades it, that, in closing this brief notice of Aiken, one cannot help extracting a dainty bit from "Helena's diary." Helena is the invalid who has been brought to Aiken to win back her roses; and she is recording a journey to the home of one of the invalids who have settled near Aiken.

Day bright. No clouds. Sunlight everywhere, even in the shadows. Long, winding sand-road through forest. Mighty trees. Horse goes with what they call down here the Mexican lope. Modification of gallop. Jack abreast filling his mighty lungs with the piny air.

Came to B——'s place very unexpectedly. Turn in road. Saw the house before us on the right. Land quite high, because all the surrounding land is quite low. Grove of pines outside of paling. Very cool and very like a Moorish court-yard. Green gate with bell-pull. Terrible clang that started up some dogs. Cream-colored house, two wings, Doric façade, pillars, long windows, piazzas, etc. Oaks, pines, rose-bushes, Spanish bayonet, and so on. Clouds of leaves of splendid green rise everywhere.

Pretty mulatto-girl comes in a leisurely way around the corner, and lets us into the garden. B—— and wife at door. Rapturous meeting. Biscuit and Scuppernong wine in cool, lofty parlor, and then plenty of talk. Then into garden proper. A rose-garden. Fifty kinds of roses. Circles, terraces, and bowers of roses, of all shapes, colors, and perfumes—though the perfume is not as rich as I could have wished. We look upon a red-and-yellow valley. Brown reds and pale yellows. All sand. Beyond are masses of trees, and yet they are so massed as to be dense. The sunlight creeps down behind each one, and throws it in relief. Thus the whole wood is light and brilliant. How shall I speak of the air? How shall I describe its effect upon me? I neither laughed nor cried, yet I willingly would have done both at the same

* [XIII, 781-782 (June 19, 1875).—ED.]

time. It was cool, and yet it was warm. It came from the west, and yet it seemed to come from the east and from overhead and from either hand. And yet it did not seem to come at all. Still, the flowers moved, and turned upon their stems, and now and then a handful of leaves tossed upward with a rustle, and showed their white nether sides. The air seemed to be the sunlight, and the sunlight the air. Everything appeared to pause, and to say, half awake, "God be praised for this happy moment!" I stood still for quite half an hour. Jack was down below me in the distance looking at the vegetables. I fear Jack has very little soul—very little! He went and looked over a fence with B——, and then he called up to me, " Six acres in asparagus—think of that!" We had to pay fifty cents a bunch for some the other day. My appetite is capital.

B—— lives here in safety. He has searched all over the world—at Isle of Pines, Santa Barbara, Nice, Cannes, Mentone—and has finally settled in Aiken after some fifteen years of travel. He keeps a cellar of wine, some capital horses, and he has become an agriculturist. He has a half-dozen neighbors who are conducting their lives in the same way, and altogether they make a very queer neighborhood of it. I don't think there is a pair of sound lungs among them. They seem to be barons, all ill, to be sure, but still barons. I carried back quite a *ton* of buds in a sort of saddle-bag. Roses bloom eleven months in the year. Home, through the pine-woods at sunset. Glorious!

MISCELLANEOUS PROSE

LETTERS FROM TEXAS *

I. THE TEXAS TRAIL IN THE '70's

S AN ANTONIO, Texas, December 9 [1872].—The morning
was brilliant, the air was full of a certain dry balm which I
think is not known elsewhere in the world and of which I shall
have more to say anon, and as I stood on the hotel pavement,
after a breakfast which I shall endeavor to forget just as soon
as I *can* forget it, the stage—four-horses to the fore—came
merrily tooling down the street and rounded to, with a rare
tilt, up, down, sideways, and askew, followed by a general
tremulous settling down of things, such as can be accomplished by nothing in this world but a stage,—unless it be a
dromedary, perhaps, or a channel steamer. Baggage and self
are aboard in a trice, and we dash up the Main Street of
Austin. In a moment we draw to the sidewalk and stop. So:
we are not off? No, but my trunk is; for this is the stage office,
and they've whipped the baggage out of the boot to weigh it.
They weigh it. Presently the official calls my name, which is
on my trunk.

"Well," I say: "I'm the man."

"*Three dollars and a quarter for extra baggage!*" says he.
"We don't allow but fifty pounds."

"How much does she weigh, Captain?" I asked, with a
melancholy effort to be jocular.

"Ninety pounds. Three dollars and a quarter, *if* you please,"
he replies, with a slight tinge of impatience: for he knows it is
mean and he does not like to be long about it.

* [Title supplied by editor. The last section of Letter I (under the title, "The
Mesquit in Texas") and all of Letters II and III (under the titles here printed)
appeared in the New York *World* for Dec. 27, 1872, Feb. 6, 1873, and March
13, 1873, respectively. The last section of Letter I was reprinted in the San
Antonio *Herald*, Jan. 14, 1873; the entire letter appeared, with slight verbal
differences, in the *Outlook*, CV, 582-5 (Nov. 15, 1913). The MS for only
Letter I is known to exist (Huntington Library), here used as the text. The
World furnishes the text for Letters II and III.

All three letters are signed "Otfall," with a note penciled in Mary Day
Lanier's hand on the MS of Letter I: "Pen name, for newspaper publication, in
Texas."—ED.]

187

For the moment, a wild, vague idea of expostulation occurs to me: but on glancing around at the faces of my fellow-passengers,—two of whom have just been similarly phlebotomized before I got aboard, but now, base, dastardly wretches! are looking on at me with that half-smile which I think is the most abandoned expression of the human countenance, to-wit, the smile with which the man who has been sold regards the man who is being sold—I perceive that I have no moral support, I faint, I hand the Captain a five-dollar bill. He returns me a dollar and a quarter.

"How?" I say. "Three twenty-five from five leaves one seventy-five: you've only given me one *twenty*-five."

"Rates are in gold," he replies. "Knock off ten per cent from green backs: ten per cent on five dollars, fifty cents. Baggage on thar, Bill? All abode!" And I am whirled on, a moralizing, reflective, mute passenger, even like Thomas Carlyle's savage, with all thoughts in the wild heart of me, but with no speech for any thought.*

In a quarter of a mile, we stop. Looking out of the window, I perceive we are at the head of a steep roadway which has been cut through the precipitous bluffs walling the river, down to the water's edge. This, then, is the Colorado. The guard dismounts, comes to the window, and announces that he would prefer for the passengers to get out, as the bridge is not considered safe. Purely in order to humor this preference of the guard's, we come forth, descend the hill in advance of the stage, and cross the bridge.

It is such a bridge as I have not seen since the Confederate army laid pontoons during the war. It is a pontoon bridge, rigged of ropes, pegs and boxes of the very rudest description. Regarded horizontally, the bridge is in the shape of a bewildered S: and as the horses come with careful hoof across, the vertical undulation combines with the horizontal wriggle to serve me even as the world served Mr. Tulliver.** It is too many for me: and I turn to look at the strange appearance of the river.

We are in its dry bed. The bank we have left is a steep bluff:

* [The allusion is to *Sartor Resartus*.—ED.]
** [A character in George Eliot, *The Mill on the Floss*.—ED.]

this is a gradual ascent, like an enormously wide strip of sea-beach, winding on alongside the flowing stream—which is not more than forty or fifty yards wide—in a far-stretching series of riband-loops and curves. Strewed over this great, shelving, dry bed, are myriads of white limestone rocks, shapen marvel-lously like skulls and bones: it is, to all appearance, a broad exaggeration of that mournful *Jornada del Muerte* (Path of Death) across the plains.* The similitude heats one's imagi-nation all the more, in that this mock death-road is accom-panied by a plentiful stream of that life-giving water, the lack of which has produced the real *Jornada del Muerte.*

It is a River of Life, side by side with a River of Death.

Re-embarking, we quickly emerge upon the great expanse of the rolling-prairie. Occasionally there are trees, scattered singly, or in small groups. These are mostly a sort of oaks, squat-trunked, round-topped: and, what with the sere grass, the scene from the stage-window is so much like an old field, with ancient apple-trees here and there, that one is always looking for the old farm-house which should stand in some thicker clump, memorial of a time when these seeming fields were tilled and these seeming apple-trees were tended. At long intervals, one finds a thin belt of forest: and once, for a mile or two, the road winds through a bottom, between trees bearded with trailing moss. But mostly, on each hand, stretch the lonesome undulations of the prairie. Far, far, the eye strains; it is a kind of warm pursuit to look on farther, it is as if one hunted the distance; one grows eager, then sated, then tired, with one's acquisitions of spaces. The earth seems larger than the heavens: one feels that yonder horizon cannot circum-scribe this vastness. The prairie with its miles of space, like Keats's Grecian Urn with its years of time, does

> . . . Tease us out of thought
> As doth eternity: cold pastoral!

* [The Jornada del Muerte is that section of the Santa Fé trail in New Mexico where it leaves the Rio Grande River (now Rincon), passes around an obstructing mountain, and then returns to the river (now San Marcial),—in all about 80 miles. In Lanier's time it was known as one of the most dan-gerous passes of the West because of its lack of water. See Susan S. Magoffin, *Down the Santa Fé Trail* . . . (New Haven, 1926), 196.—ED.]

But presently, I am teased enough: and I turn, to regard my fellow-passengers more closely. We are seven in stage. An old miner (as I afterwards pick up), from Chico, California, in a cap with let-down flaps, a quiet man, a simple, good soul, whom, if you *can* imagine Captain Cuttle * with two sound arms and without his iron hook, you have before you; an editor, from Indiana, a fat man, with a pair of legs which might be very effective *on* the stage, but, *in* one, are very poor legs indeed, with no sort of capacity at all for folding, or crossing, or pressing together splint-wise, or " splitting " with a *vis-a-vis*—all of which made me conceive a violent admiration for this gentleman, for although he sat three-on-a-seat nearly the whole ride (of sixteen hours) he was nevertheless a marvel of good humor and cheerfulness all the time, *malgré* the nether torment he must have endured; a poor consumptive, from Arkansas, whom may God take heed of; a lieutenant of cavalry, from Pennsylvania, who has been home on leave, and is now returning to the frontier; a Michigoose, or female Michigander, with her daughter, a very sprightly little gosling indeed, going to San Antonio to set up in the millinery line; and your correspondent, who is travelling as valet to his right lung,—a service in which he has been engaged some years: these are the people whom I find that the four winds have blown into this little eddy.

Truly, I say to myself, all the world *is* a stage: ** and I begin to listen to the other players who seem to have their parts well conned. The lieutenant is talking:

I was out once [he is saying] on a scout after a party of Indians that had been committing some depredations. We had nearly caught up with them: in fact we were right *on* them. Everybody was so tired, however, that Major ————, who was in command, finally allowed the party to rest.

The orders were strict that no man should speak loudly, and no fire should be lighted; and particularly, that no gun should be fired on any account. Well, the command stopped, a line of sentinels was formed around, and the men threw themselves on the ground to rest. Presently, —after we'd all been lying about for a while—I happened to look up,

* [A charatcer in Dickens, *Dombey and Son.*—ED.]
** [The allusion is to Shakespeare, *As You Like It.*—ED.]

and, by Jupiter, there was a tremendous grisly bear, deliberately walking right on to the line of sentinels. *Nobody spoke a word*: the bear kept on. Presently he reached the line. The sentinels nearest him stood with their guns cocked, looking uneasily at the Major. (The men were all as ' fraid of him as death.) The Major was standing up amongst the men, looking down on the ground. The men by this time had all seen the grisly, and were all lying or sitting, with their guns cocked, glancing from the bear to the Major, in the greatest uneasiness. *The Major didn't say a word.* The bear deliberately walked between two of the sentinels, and came slowly on till he was nearly in the very midst of the party. The excitement was *too* intense. You could almost hear the men's hearts beating. Still they wouldn't fire: they were more scared of the Major than the bear, I suppose. The bear started towards the Major. Still he looked down, *and didn't say a word.* He waited a little while: the bear kept on, slowly. Suddenly, the Major threw up his head and bawled out, " *Why in the h-ll don't you shoot?* " I suppose forty bullets went into that bear's body at the same instant: at any rate, he never kicked.

We stop to dine, at a house on the bank of a large creek whose bed, now dry, meanders with its dreadful white stones far away; we change horses; we cross San Marcos River, a beautiful clear stream which is born full-grown of a few bold springs a mile or two above the crossing, and which would turn no end of mill-wheels, yea, which seems fairly to yearn for mill-wheels; a trot of a few hundred yards brings us into San Marcos, a smart and thriving town, where we take up a lady who tells us a world of things about matters in this land, and who becomes quite upset with surprise and pleasure at discovering accidentally that she has once met a lady who is known to the gentleman from Indiana; we prick forward and reach New Braunfels just at night-fall, finding a large clean German town, with all manner of evidences of German thrift on every hand, through which we pass, to the hotel, where mine host, a large-framed and seeming large-souled German, is ready with a chair for the ladies to step out on; we file between the seats on the hotel-porch, in which sit German giants —the people are all so large, splendid, healthy, that my lung fairly curdles with envious spite!—smoking, and take our honest German supper, brown bread, sausage, great collops of juicy venison, and coffee; we receive ourselves again into the stage, light our segars, *nem. mulierum con.*, * and fare merrily forward through the night, what time the miner, who never had courage enough to say much while the light was, does now in the dark proceed to tell us the story of Jack, the Indian,— how that one day, in camp, Jack got a dollar apiece from a lot of Chinese to hide them in a certain cave he wot of, away from the tax-collector, and how Jack, having hid them away snugly, did then and there get fifty dollars from the tax-collector to show him where "them Chinee was," which Jack did, and which (quoth my Ed'ard Cuttle) "Jack was the only one o' them Digger Indians with any sense that ever I see."

Presently I observe that the stage-lamps continually light up a curious sort of bare straggling-twigged shrub that seems to line the road and to cover the prairie. It [is] as if the apparitions of all the leafless peach-orchards in Georgia were lawlessly dancing past us and about us.

"That," says the Lieutenant, "is the mesquit."

The mesquit is a bush,—sometimes reaching to be a small tree—which has been extending eastward, it seems, for some time. Many have told me that it has covered this part of the country only within the last thirty years: and there is a popular belief that its spread on the prairies in the neighborhood of San Antonio has caused a marked increase in the rain-fall of this section within the last few years and has converted what was formerly a purely grazing district into an agricultural one. I fancy, however, that Dr. Draper ** would not admit this conclusion, even granting that the rain-fall *is* greater: and from meteorological facts which have been furnished me by Dr. V. Pettersen,—an accomplished Swedish physician resident here, who has for four years past been collecting these data with the aid of improved instruments—I think the inference is safe that the assumption of an increased rain-fall is incorrect, as based upon the mere concurrence of two years somewhat wetter than the average, but whose moisture is more than counterbalanced by the unusual dryness of the two contiguous years. Whether, however, the singular spread of the mesquit

* [Probably, *nemine mulierum contradicente* (none of the ladies objecting). —Ed.]

** [John William Draper (1811-1882), whose textbooks on chemistry (1846) and natural philosophy (1847) were the best known of Lanier's day.—Ed.]

(which *is* certainly true) may, or not, have increased the rain-fall, it has unquestionably been of vast benefit in otherwise.* Its roots do not penetrate downward, but grow horizontally, just beneath the surface of the ground. They are easily dug: and they are the principal fuel of the country. This root is of the color of black walnut, is exceedingly hard, and is said never to decay. It burns well; by token, at this writing a stove-full of it is merrily blazing here in my apartment.

But the mesquit has uses other than as firewood. It is a species of acacia. At certain times, a gum plentifully exudes from it, which, when the tannin which it contains is extracted, is equal to the best gum arabic for all the purposes to which the latter can be applied. This property of the mesquit has, I am told, begun to furnish employment to a considerable number of persons in this section and will likely create a new branch of industry.   OTFALL.

II. AN INDIAN RAID IN TEXAS

San Antonio de Bexar, January 23 [1873].—This is the land of slow travelling, and we have just received the particulars of an Indian raid which commenced more than a week ago, and which, for the impudence of the raiding party, for the long-displayed fortitude and cool bravery of one of the white men who encountered the raiders, and for the happy (from the Texan point of view) termination of the raid in the killing of one entire detachment of eleven Indians, has not been paralleled in this region for a long time.

On the 11th of this month, at a point near the Medina River about fifty miles from this place, Mr. Henry Hartman and four companions were suddenly set upon by a party of Indians, supposed to be Comanches, numbering between fifteen and twenty.** The Indians were well mounted, many of them had army overcoats, and all were armed with navy revolvers in addition to their usual weapons. The Indians fired immediately and killed Hartman's horse, without striking any of his party. His four companions escaped, and he saw nothing more

* [The *Outlook* (CV, 585) prints " in other ways."—ED.]
** [Lanier's account follows very closely news-stories appearing in the San Antonio *Herald*, Jan. 22, Jan. 17, and Jan. 15, 1873.—ED.]

of them. Whilst Hartman was writhing and twisting beneath his horse, which had fallen on him, the Indians, exulting in the near prospect of a scalp, were approaching him, and before they had quite reached him Hartman succeeded in extricating himself, and presented at them a Winchester rifle with which he was armed. Taken aback at this sudden demonstration, the Indians scattered and sought cover. Hartman also sheltered himself as best he could. Thus they confronted one another, each lying as close as possible. Presently Hartman discovered an Indian who had managed to approach within five paces of him. Both fired about simultaneously. The Indian's ball passed through Hartman's hat; the latter's bullet killed his opponent instantly. Perceiving this, Hartman thought the opportunity a good one to seek more secure cover, and made a dash towards a thicker chaparral. It was literally running the gauntlet. About fifteen shots were fired at him as he passed, one of which pierced entirely through his foot, inflicting a painful wound. He gained his thicket, however. The Indians now charged. Another shot from his faithful rifle killed one and wounded another of the assailants. Hereupon the red men seem to have determined that the game was not worth the candle. They fled, carrying off their dead and wounded on horseback. Meantime a negro who had been with Hartman made his way to his friends and informed them that Hartman had been killed by Indians. His friends started out to look for him with an ambulance; and in the morning of the next day, after he had passed a most painful night alone and wounded in the thicket, they discovered him and relieved him from his fearful situation.

The cool bravery of Hartman is said by frontiersmen never to have been surpassed on this frontier, and they regard his undaunted intrepidity, under circumstances which were enough to paralyze the energies of any man, as well meriting his miraculous escape.

The Indians appear to have abandoned Hartman upon the principle of business before pleasure, which, in the Comanche moralities, is interpreted, horse-stealing before scalping; for as soon as they left him they went vigorously to work, moving rapidly down the Medina, above Castroville, stealing as they moved, taking some horses from the very suburbs of the town.

They chased Mr. Wurzboch into his house, then took his horses, and were gone before he could get a shot. They next entered the field of Mr. Montel, and added to their drove all the horses he had except one, which they killed. During the Saturday night the rogues increased their *caballada* with eight horses belonging to Mr. Larreau; also with a lot of fine animals from the ranch of Judge Noonan. They killed two of the mares at this latter place, and shot one fine horse, which was found next day running about with an arrow sticking in its side.

They seem now to have divided their forces. Early on Sunday morning a Mexican, in the camp of Messrs. John and Oliver Brown, at the head of Block Creek, discovered five of the raiders approaching. He seized his gun and made off. Oliver Brown then saw the Indians. Concluding that the most desperate alternative was at once the most prudent, he started to meet them, calling out to his brother. The latter, perceiving that the Indians were about to cut him off, shouted for help; his brother stopped and began to fire at the Indians; while these, under cover of a return-fire, coolly herded all the Brown's horses before their eyes, and finally drove them off and went on their way rejoicing.

But business had now been brisk enough to authorize a little recreation. After proceeding a few miles the red scoundrels came upon two white men, Mr. Elijah Whitley and Mr. McRae. They shot both, killing Mr. Whitley immediately. Poor McRae was not dead when the Indians turned to leave, and, apparently for the purpose of writing a farewell message, he made a movement to get out his pencil and note-book. His movement was seen, unfortunately, by the Indians, one of whom immediately rode back and shot him through the head. It was but a few moments afterwards that the sons of Mr. Whitley rode up and found their father and his companion dead.

But it was now the white man's turn. The Indians having reunited to the number of eleven, proceeded towards the Hondo.* Near that stream they found a Mexican, and shot him through the lower part of the body. The Mexican instantly adopted that policy which is said to be the last resource for him who finds himself in the power of the most ferocious

* [The *World* incorrectly prints " Hindo."—ED.]

wild beasts. He fell over, and lay as if dead. So well did he feign, that the Indians stripped him of his clothes and rode off, ignorant of aught but that he had gone to their enemies' hell. As soon as they were out of sight the Mexican made his way to a camp of cow-hunters not far off, and gave information of what had occurred. The cow-hunters immediately took the trail and gave chase. The pursuit lasted five days. On Friday last the cow-hunters overhauled the raiders in the Sabinal canyon, and opened the fight. After a short contest the Indians proposed to surrender.

No surrender!

With this terrible reply the cow-hunters continued the conflict until every one of the eleven Indians lay dead.

And let him who thinks this a needlessly bloody resentment come to this land and listen to the tales that are told of children, of women and of men who have fallen into the hands of the Indian. Indeed, it is now just 160 years since Father Marest, in despair of these Indians, exclaimed, " It is necessary first to transform them into men, and afterward to labor to make them Christians! " *

OTFALL.

III. THE MEXICAN BORDER TROUBLES

San Antonio de Bexar, Texas, February 17 [1873].—What is the Mexican border? It is as broad as a Pharisee's phylactery and as long as his prayer. I say "broad" as well as long, because the Mexican border within the sense of the heading of this letter—i. e., the locality of Mexican depredations and outrages—is not a mere line of mathematical thinness, but a vast reach of country, whose length is something like 800 miles and whose breadth approaches 100.

Commencing at its northern extremity, one finds the Texan County of El Paso with a population of 3,671 souls; passing down the Rio Grande one finds next the great unorganized Texan County, or rather territory, of Presidio with 1,636 inhabitants; next the two enormous unorganized territorial counties of Pecos and Bexar, which are almost uninhabited. If now

* [Lanier's source was apparently H. Yoakum, *History of Texas*, the authority on which he drew for " San Antonio de Bexar," where this same quotation appears (see p. 214 of the present volume).—Ed.]

one will place on the map the point [of] a pair of dividers
at the western boundary of Kinney County, on the Rio Grande,
and stretching the other point eastward over a space equivalent
to 100 miles, will move the dividers southward, keeping the
western point upon the sinuosities of the river until the two
points rest at the coast of the Gulf of Mexico, one will describe
with tolerable accuracy the belt of country in which the greater
part of the Mexican border troubles have arisen. The three-
fold tier of counties nearly comprised within this belt present
a total area of 23,802 square miles and an aggregate population of 30,205. About 11,000 of these inhabitants live in the
city of Brownsville, so that, deducting them from the total,
one discovers that the Mexican border averages considerably
less than one inhabitant to the square mile of territory.

But, although so lonesome *quoad* humanity, this zone of
land supports a large number of living beings, for it is the
great stock-raising portion of Texas, and is devoted exclusively
to that business. Horse-ranches, sheep-ranches, and cattle-
ranches—mostly the latter—constitute the settlements on these
vast plains, increasing in thickness to the southward, in the
neighborhood of Brownsville and Corpus Christi. The extent
of the cattle-raising business here may be inferred from the
fact that during the year 1872 there were recorded 349,275
head of Texas cattle passing the single point of Caldwell, Kan.
Many were driven in other directions. In addition to this the
city of Galveston received, during the year 1872, 412,833 hides.

Now, the stock-raiser in Texas may be said to be absolutely
dependent upon the honesty of his neighbors; for the nature of
his business, as it is here carried on, requires him to live in just
that section of the country which offers perhaps greater facilities for unmitigated stealing than any other portion of this
world. For here the land is so lonesome that the robber need
scarcely fash his thumb to conceal himself; again he can maintain himself indefinitely upon these bullock-covered plains,
and so is relieved from that fatal necessity of resorting to trade-
centres for the purpose of procuring supplies, which most frequently cuts short the thief's career; and lastly, when pursued
he can quickly place the Rio Grande River betwixt himself and
his pursuer. In this last event the pursuer has two equally

worthless and unsatisfactory courses of procedure open to him. He can either cross the river and wage his war—and so render himself liable to the pains and penalties of levying battle against citizens of a country with which his own is at peace— or he can go over peaceably and apply to the Alcalde of the municipality for redress—and have his trouble for his pains, as the saying is.

One has only to think of these facts, in connection with the general *modus operandi* of the stock-raising business (which is, simply, to buy a lot of "stock-cattle"; to brand them with your particular device; to turn them loose upon the plains; to spend months of your time in hunting them up again, in order to brand whatever new calves may be found running with your cows; to hunt them up again periodically in order to pick out cattle for driving off to Kansas; to skin those who have died; and so on till calf-breeding time), in order to picture a veritable thieves' paradise. Shade this picture with great thickets of cactus whose thorny terrors can be braved by none save the Mexican in his cowhide pants, and with the scarcely less impenetrable chapparal; intensify it with the thought of the wild life of these stock-raisers, who, midst of the lusty cattle and the lawless plains are not apt to remember either government or social restraints, and redden it with the old hatreds left by the Mexican war; nay, with older mutual contempts— contempt, on the one hand, of the Mexican, who has not forgotten certain very suspicious coincidences between the movements of the United States and those of Texas about the time the latter was annexed—coincidences which the Mexican has interpreted to the credit of neither party; contempt, on the other hand, of the Texan, who has a thousand scornful antipathies of the assassins of Travis, of Bowie, and of Crockett— shade and color the picture thus, I say, and one is at no loss to understand why there should be Mexican border troubles.

These may be divided into three classes: First, outrages and depredations committed during the "Cortina war"; second, miscellaneous and unorganized thefts of stock; third, imprisonment and other outrages.

The recollection of the singular campaign of the Cortina war was so quickly swallowed up by the baleful brilliance of the war of secession that there are probably few persons other

than those immediately concerned who remember that there
was ever such an affair. Yet it was no insignificant business,
either in the numbers engaged or in the blood that fell. In
the latter part of the year 1858 Cortina, whose mother resided
at a fine hacienda on this side the Rio Grande, not far from
Brownsville, suddenly appeared in that city in command of a
body of men and proceeded to shoot down in the streets several persons who were well known in the community as
desperate characters. It is said by some that Cortina was acting
in the capacity of head of a vigilance committee, with the concurrence of many of the most orderly citizens of Brownsville,
who were tired of the reign of certain lawless men of that
neighborhood and were driven by long suffering into this
method of riddance. Others add a darker tale of foul wrong
perpetrated by these desperadoes against some female members
of Cortina's family, for which he was thus avenging himself.
Whatever may have been the true origin of the movement, it
at any rate quickly assumed more threatening proportions, and
Brownsville presently sent a petition for assistance. Meantime
the men of the town sallied forth in force, with two pieces of
artillery, and met Cortina in battle, with no other result than
that of leaving in the hands of the enemy their two pieces of
artillery. Presently, a party of Texans, under the command
of Major W. G. Tobin, arrived for the relief of the town.
These were soon reinforced till they numbered about three
hundred, and, under the command of Major Heintzelman, who
added a party of United States infantry, of cavalry, and of
artillery, moved in force against Cortina, who had by this
time assembled a force of some eight hundred men. The
campaign lasted about three months, in the course of which
three battles were fought, several lives were lost, and much
painful chasing done among the cactus thickets. It was in the
course of this campaign that the depredations were committed,
mentioned in the first class above enumerated. They are claimed
to amount in value to $1,806,619. I have found no evidence
whatever in support of the stories which have been circulated,
of the complicity of the Mexican Government with Cortina's
movements.*

* [Lanier was probably reminded of the Cortina incident by accounts of later

I cannot better illustrate the second class of "troubles" than by the following account of an actual one which happened about a month ago. I quote it from the sworn statement, forwarded to the Governor of Texas, made by Manuel Ban, the officer in charge of the Maverick County Minute Men. He says:

On January 23 [1873] I struck, between the Hermana Hills and the Rio Grande, large trails of cattle running towards the Rio Grande, as well as large trails of horses. . . . Following these trails, as large and plain as any main road in this State, I got down in the range of the river. On January 24 I continued to watch these trails, but was finally forced by want of water to make for the river, where I found a very much used crossing, where, by the signs and trails left, at least 1,500 head of cattle had passed within the last twenty days. . . . I hid my horses in the river-bottom so that they could not be seen on the other side, right in front of me, on the Mexican side, being a rancho called Los Arroyitos, about 110 miles below Eagle Pass. About two o'clock P. M., while my company was preparing for dinner, my spy reported a Mexican on horseback, coming on our back-track from the water. I made the men mount at once, and when nearly ready to start there came five more Mexicans and joined the first one. . . . When I with my command got to the river and in shooting range they had passed what I considered the United States boundary line, more than middle of the river, and no shot was fired at them. I formed my men on the bare shore of the river; meantime the party mentioned had dismounted on the other side, tied their horses in the bushes and came down to the river on foot, and entirely unexpected [sic] opened a rapid fire on us. They were armed with repeating guns. Whereupon I had my bugle sounded to inform them that we constituted a legal force, and they not ceasing to fire I ordered my men to fire so that we might drive them off out of their position and make a safe retreat from the river, where we were entirely exposed to their fire. After exchanging about 150 shots we drove them away, out of range to do us any harm, and I retreated to my camp, not having any authority to cross the United States boundary line. During this fight more men came down on foot to the assistance of the first party; said men came out the before-mentioned rancho called the Arroyitos.*

troubles with him and his band described in the San Antonio *Herald,* Jan. 18-26, 1873. For details of the earlier incidents he followed closely a "Letter from the Secretary of War, Communicating . . . Information in Relation to the Troubles on the Texas Frontier, May 5, 1860." *Ex. Doc. No. 81, 36th Congress, 1st Session,* a copy of which he probably had before him.—ED.]

* [The passage appeared in the San Antonio *Herald,* Feb. 9, 1873. All of the

From this naïve recital, there are (as Jean Paul Richter remarks of one of his chapters) many important inferences to be drawn, and I advise the reader to draw them. It is quite impossible, now, to estimate the total amount of damage done by the promiscuous thieving embraced in this class. Some idea of it may be gathered from the fact that the partial labor of our Mexican Border commissioners have [sic] already developed claims amounting to $25,049,722 in this especial particular; and these claims do not include transactions on the Upper Rio Grande, nor do they exhaust those on the Lower Rio Grande. I could give you some illustrative types of the third class of " troubles," but perhaps enough wise saws can be constructed out of the modern instances already detailed. The amount of damage under this head, already proven before the commissioners, is $903,022.97.

The Mexicans on the other side of the river have vigorously counter-accused the Texans of outrages, and the like, committed upon Mexican citizens. Doubtless these accusations are in many instances well founded. Certainly, reasoning *a priori*, one would expect to find them true; for the Texan " cow-boys " have been sorely and long provoked, and it is not among free men, living the wild life of these " cow-boys " that one would expect to find that patience under great provocation which, to restrain a man from retaliation, would require him to be as Dan Chaucer hath it, " stronger than Sampson, or holier than David, or wiser than Solomon! " *

OTFALL.

editing is Lanier's: the date supplied in brackets, the omissions, and " [sic]."
—ED.]
* [Chaucer, " Parson's Tale," slightly garbled.—ED.]

SAN ANTONIO DE BEXAR *

IF PECULIARITIES were quills, San Antonio de Bexar would be a rare porcupine. Over all the round of aspects in which a thoughtful mind may view a city, it bristles with striking idiosyncrasies and *bizarre* contrasts. Its history, population, climate, location, architecture, soil, water, customs, costumes, horses, cattle, all attract the stranger's attention, either by force of intrinsic singularity or of odd juxtapositions. It was a puling infant for a century and a quarter, yet has grown to a pretty vigorous youth in a quarter of a century; its inhabitants are so varied that the "go slow" directions over its bridges are printed in three languages, and the religious services in its churches held in four; the thermometer, the barometer, the vane, the hygrometer, oscillate so rapidly, so frequently, so lawlessly, and through so wide a meteorological range, that the climate is simply indescribable, yet it is a growing resort for consumptives; it stands with all its gay prosperity just in the edge of a lonesome, untilled belt of land one hundred and fifty miles wide, like *Mardi Gras* on the austere brink of Lent; it has no Sunday laws, and that day finds its bar-rooms and billiard-saloons as freely open and as fully attended as its churches; its buildings, ranging from the Mexican *jacal* to the San Fernando Cathedral, represent all the progressive stages of man's architectural progress in edifices of mud, of wood, of stone, of iron, and of sundry combinations of those materials; its soil is in wet weather an inky-black cement, but in dry a floury-white powder; it is built along both banks of two limpid streams, yet it drinks rain-water collected in cisterns; its horses and mules are from Lilliput, while its oxen are from Brobdingnag.**

* [Written in February, 1873, at San Antonio; published in the *Southern Magazine*, XIII, 83-99, 138-152 (July, Aug., 1873), the text here used. Reprinted, slightly condensed, in *San Antonio de Bexar: A Guide and History*, compiled and edited by William Corner (San Antonio, 1890), pp. 68-91. Reprinted in Lanier's *Retrospects and Prospects* (New York, 1899), pp. 34-93. Selections printed in Mary Burt's *The Lanier Book* (New York, 1904), pp. 67-97, and in Henry W. Lanier's *Selections From Sidney Lanier* (New York, 1916), pp. 107-116. No MS is known to exist.—ED.]

** [The allusion is to Swift, *Gulliver's Travels*.—ED.]

San Antonio de Bexar, Texas, had its birth in 1715. It was, indeed, born before its time, in consequence of a sudden fright into which its mother-Spain was thrown by the menacing activities of certain Frenchmen, who, upon other occasions besides this one, were in those days very much what immortal Mrs. Gamp has declared to Mrs. Harris * " these steam-ingines is in our business,"—a frequent cause of the premature development of projects. For Spain had not intended to allow any settlements, as yet, in that part of her province of the New Philippines which embraced what is now called Texas. In the then situation of her affairs, this policy was not without some reasons to support it. She had valuable possessions in New Mexico: between these possessions and the French settlements to the eastward, intervened an enormous breadth of country, whose obstacles against intruders, appalling enough in themselves, were yet magnified by the shadowy terrors that haunt an unknown land. Why not fortify her New Mexican silvermines with these sextuple barriers, droughts, deserts, mountains, rivers, savages, and nameless fears? Surely, if inclosure could be made impregnable, this would seem to be so; and accordingly the Spanish Government had finally determined, in 1694, not to revive the feeble posts and missions which had been established four years previously with a view to make head against the expedition of La Salle, but which had been abandoned already by soldier and friar, in consequence of the want of food and the ferocity of the savages.

But in 1712, Anthony Crozat, an enterprising French merchant, obtained from Louis XIV a conditional grant to the whole of the French province of Louisiana. Crozat believed that a lucrative trade might be established with the northeastern provinces of Mexico, and that mines might exist in his territory. To test these beliefs, young Huchereau St. Denis, acting under instructions from Cadillac, who had been appointed Governor of Louisiana by Crozat's influence, started westward, left a nucleus of a settlement at Natchitoches, and proceeded across the country to the Rio Grande, where his explorations, after romantic adventures too numerous to be related here, came to an inglorious suspension with his seizure

---

* [Characters in Dickens, *Martin Chuzzlewit.*—Ed.]

and imprisonment by the Spanish vice-regal authorities in Mexico.*

It was this expedition which produced the premature result hereinbefore alluded to. Spain saw that instead of surrounding New Mexico with inhospitable wastes and ferocious savages, she was in reality but leaving France free to occupy whatever coigns of vantage might be found in that prodigious Debatable Land, which was claimed by both and was held by neither.

Perhaps this consideration was heightened by Spain's consciousness that the flimsiness of her title to that part of the " New Philippines " which lay east of the Rio Grande really required an actual occupation in order to bolster it up. Pretty much all that she could prove in support of her claim was, that in 1494 Pope Alexander VI, acting as arbitrator between Portugal and Spain, had assigned to the latter all of the American possessions that lay west of a meridian running three hundred and seventy miles west of the Azores; that De Leon, De Ayllon, De Narvaez, and De Soto, in voyages made between the years 1512 and 1538, had sailed from Cape Florida to Cape Catorce; and that Philip II had denounced the penalty of extermination against any foreigner who should enter the Gulf of Mexico or any of the lands bordering thereupon.

These were, to say the least, but indefinite muniments of title; and to them France could oppose the unquestionable fact that La Salle had coasted the shore of Texas westward to Corpus Christi inlet, had returned along the same route, had explored bays and rivers and named them, and had finally built Fort St. Louis on the Lavaca River in 1685. Here now, in 1714, to crown all, was the daring young Lord Huchereau St. Denis traversing the whole land from Natchitoches to the Rio Grande, and thrusting in his audacious face like an apparition of energy upon the sleepy routines of post-life and mission-life at San Juan Bautista.

This was alarming; and in 1715 the Duke of Linares, Viceroy of Mexico, despatched Don Domingo Ramon to Texas with a party of troops and some Franciscan friars, to take steps for

* [For his historical sketch of San Antonio Lanier draws most of his information from H. Yoakum, *History of Texas.*—Ed.]

the permanent occupation of the country. Ramon established several forts and missions; among others he located a fort, or *presidio* (Spanish, " a garrison "), on the western bank of the San Pedro River, a small stream flowing through the western suburbs of the present city of San Antonio de Bexar, about three-fourths of a mile from the present Main Plaza. This *presidio* was called San Antonio de Valero. In May, 1718, certain Alcantarine Franciscans, of the College of Queretaro, established a mission under the protection of the *presidio,* calling it by the same invocation, San Antonio de Valero. It was this mission whose Church of the Alamo afterwards shed so red a glory upon the Texan revolution. It had been founded fifteen years before, in the valley of the Rio Grande, under the invocation of San Francisco Solano; had been removed to San Ildefonso in 1708, and again removed back to the Rio Grande in 1710 under the new invocation of San José. It had not indeed yet reached the end of its wanderings. In 1722, both the *presidio* and mission of San Antonio de Valero were removed to what is now known as the Military Plaza, and a permanent system of improvements begun.

Here then, with sword and crozier, Spain set to work at once to reduce her wild claim into possession, and to fulfill the condition upon which Pope Alexander had granted her the country—of christianizing its natives. One cannot but lean one's head on one's hand to dream out, for a moment, this old Military Plaza—most singular spot on the wide expanse of the lonesome Texan prairies—as it was a hundred and fifty years ago. The rude buildings, the church, the hospital, the soldiers' dwellings, the brethren's lodgings, the huts for the converted Indians (*Yndios Reducidos*) stand ranged about the large level quadrangle, so placed upon the same theory of protection which " parks " the wagon-train that will camp this night on the plains. Ah, here they come, the inhabitants of San Antonio, from the church-door; vespers is over; the big-thighed, bow-legged, horse-riding Apache steps forth, slowly, for he is yet in a maze—the burning candles, the shrine, the genuflexions, the chants, are all yet whirling in his memory; the lazy soldier slouches by, leering at him, yet observing a certain care not to be seen therein, for Señor Soldado is not wholly free from fear of this great-thewed Señor Apache; the soldiers' wives, the squaws, the catechumens, the children, all wend their ways across the plaza. Here advances Brother Juan, bare-footed, in a gown of serge, with his knotted scourge a-dangle from his girdle; he accosts the Indian, he draws him on to talk of Manitou, his grave pale face grows intense and his forehead wrinkles as he spurs his brain on to the devising of arguments that will convince this wild soul before him of the fact of the God of Adam, of Peter, and of Francis. Yonder is a crowd: alas, it is stout Brother Antonio, laying shrewd stripes with unsparing arm upon the back of a young Indian—so hard to convince these dusky youths and maidens of the wide range and ramifications of that commandment which they seem most prone to break. Ha! there behind the church, if you look, goes on another flagellation: Brother Francis has crept back there, slipped his woollen gown from his shoulders, and fallen to with his knotted scourge upon his own bare back, for that a quick vision did, by instigation of the devil, cross his mind even in the very midst of vespers,—a vision of a certain señorita as his wife, of a warm all-day sunned *hacienda,* of children playing, of fruits, of friends, of laughter—" O blessed St. Francis of Assisi, fend off Sathanas!" he cries, and raises a heavier welt.

Presently, as evening draws on, the Indians hold meetings, males in one place, females in another; reciting prayers, singing canticles; finally it is bed-time, honest Brother Antonio goes round and locks the unmarried young male Indians into their sleeping apartments on one side, the maidens on the other side into theirs, casts a glance mayhap towards Mexico, breathes a prayer, gets him to his pallet, and the Plaza of San Antonio de Valero is left in company of the still sentinel, the stream of the San Pedro purling on one side, that of the San Antonio whispering on the other, under the quiet stars, midst of the solemn prairie, in whose long grass yonder (by all odds) crouches some keen-eyed Apache *bravo,*[1] who has taken a fancy that he will ride Don Ramon's charger.

The infant settlement soon begins to serve in that capacity which gives it a "bad eminence" among the other Texan

---

[1] Sp. *Yndios Bravos*: unconverted Indians.

settlements for the next hundred years: to-wit, as the point to which, or from which, armies are retreating or advancing, or in which armies are fighting. Already, in 1719, before the removal to the Military Plaza, the scenes of war have been transacting themselves in the young San Antonio de Valero. On a certain day in the spring of that year, the peaceful people are astonished to behold all their Spanish brethren who belong to the settlements eastward of theirs, come crowding into the town: monks, soldiers, women, and all. In the confusion they quickly learn that in the latter part of the year before, France has declared war against Spain; that the Frenchmen at Natchitoches, as soon as they have heard the news, have rushed to arms with Gallic impetuosity, and led by La Harpe and St. Denis, have advanced westward, have put to flight all the Spanish at Adaes, at Orquizaco, at Aes, and at Nacogdoches; and that these are they who are here now, disturbing the peaceful mission with unwonted sights and sounds, and stretching its slender hospitalities to repletion. The French do not attack, however, but return towards Natchitoches. In a short time enter from the opposite side of the stage, that is to say from Mexico, the Marquis de Aguayo, Governor-General of New Estremadura and the New Philippines, with five hundred mounted men. These march through, take with them the men of Orquizaco, Adaes and Aes, re-establish those settlements, and pursue the French until they hear that the latter are in Natchitoches; De Aguayo then returns to San Antonio and sets on foot plans for its permanent improvement.

About this time occurs a short and spicy correspondence, which for the first time probably announces the name of the State of Texas, and which explicitly broaches a dispute that is to last for many a year. The Spanish Viceroy in Mexico appoints Don Martin D'Alarconne Governor of Texas. Soon afterwards La Harpe leaves the French post of Natchitoches and busies himself in advancing the French interests among the Nassonite [1] Indians. In beginning this enterprise La Harpe sends " a polite message " to the Spanish Governor, who thereupon writes:—

---

[1] A tribe, or set of tribes, whose seat of government seems to have been a village called *Texas*, on the east bank of the Neches River.

MONSIEUR, — I am very sensible of the politeness that M. de Bienville and yourself have had the goodness to show to me. The orders I have received from the King my master are to maintain a good understanding with the French of Louisiana; my own inclinations lead me equally to afford them all the services that depend upon me. But I am compelled to say that your arrival at the Nassonite village surprises me much. Your Governor could not be ignorant that the post you occupy belongs to my government, and that all the lands west of the Nassonites depend upon New Mexico. I counsel you to inform M. Bienville of this, or you will force me to oblige you to abandon lands that the French have no right to occupy. I have the honor, etc.

D'ALARCONNE.

TRINITY RIVER, May 20, 1719.

To this La Harpe makes reply:—

MONSIEUR,—The order from his Catholic Majesty to maintain a good understanding with the French of Louisiana, and the kind intentions you have yourself expressed towards them, accord but little with your proceedings. Permit me to apprise you that M. de Bienville is perfectly informed of the limits of his government, and is very certain that the post of Nassonite does not depend upon the dominions of his Catholic Majesty. He knows also that the Province of Lastekas,[1] of which you say you are Governor, is a part of Louisiana. M. de la Salle took possession in 1685, in the name of his Most Christian Majesty, and since the above epoch possession has been renewed from time to time. Respecting the post of Nassonite, I cannot comprehend by what right you pretend that it forms a part of New Mexico. I beg leave to represent to you that Don Antonio de Minoir, who discovered New Mexico in 1683, never penetrated east of that province or the Rio Bravo. It was the French who first made alliances with the savage tribes in this region, and it is natural to conclude that a river that flows into the Mississippi and the lands it waters belong to the King my master. If you will do me the pleasure to come into this quarter I will convince you I hold a post I know how to defend.

I have the honor, etc.,

DE LA HARPE.*

NASSONITE, July 8th, 1719.

[1] Lastekas, *i. e.* Las Tekas: *Texas.* The Frenchmen in those days appear to have great difficulty in inventing orthographies for these odious Indian names. The Choctaws, for instance, appear in the documents of the time as " Tchactas," the Chickasaws as " Chicachats," the Cherokees as " Cheraquis," and they can get no nearer to " Camanches " than " Choumans," or " Cannensis!"

* [The entire correspondence appears in Yoakum, *History of Texas.*—ED.]

For several years after the permanent location round the Military Plaza, no important events seem to be recorded as happening in San Antonio; but the quiet work of post and mission goes on, and the probable talk on the Plaza is of the three new missions which De Aguayo establishes on the San Antonio River, below the town, under the protection of its garrison; or of the tales which come slowly floating from the northward concerning the dreadful fate of a Spanish expedition which has been sent to attack the French settlements on the Upper Mississippi, and which, mistaking the hostile Missouris on the way for friendly Asages, distributes fifteen hundred muskets, together with sabres and pistols, to the said Missouris to be used against the French, whereupon the Missouris next morning at day-break fall upon the unsuspecting Spaniards, butcher them all (save the priest, whom they keep for a " magpie," as they call him, to laugh at), and march off into the French fort arrayed in great spoils, their chief wearing the chasuble and bearing the paten before him for a breastpiece; or of Governor De Aguayo's recommendation to the home government to send colonists instead of soldiers if it would help the friars to win the Indians; or of the appointment of a separate governor for Texas in 1727; or of the withdrawal of ten soldiers in 1729, leaving only forty-three in garrison at San Antonio. About 1731, however, an important addition is made to the town. Under the auspices of the home government—which seems to have accepted De Aguayo's ideas—thirteen families and two single men arrive, pure Spaniards from the Canary Islands, also some Tlascalans, and a party from Monterey. These set to work around a Plaza (the " Plaza of the Constitution," or " Main Plaza ") just eastward of and adjoining the Military Plaza, and commence a town which they call San Fernando. They are led, it seems, to this location by the same facility of irrigation which had recommended the Military Plaza to their neighbors. The new colonists impart vigor to affairs. The missions prosper, Indians are captured and brought in to be civilized whether or no, and on the 5th of March, 1731, the foundation is laid of the Mission of *La Purísima Concepcion de Acuña,* on the San Antonio River, a mile or so below the town.

Meantime a serious conspiracy against the welfare of San

Antonio and San Fernando is hatched in the northeast. The
Natchez Indians wish to revenge themselves upon the French,
who have driven them from their home on the Mississippi.
They resolve to attack St. Denis at Natchitoches, and to prevent
the Spaniards from helping him (the French and Spanish are
now friends, having united against England), they procure the
Apaches to assail San Antonio. St. Denis, however, surprises
and defeats the Natchez; and the Apaches appear to have made
no organized attack, but to have confined themselves to murdering and thieving in parties. These Apaches, indeed, were
dreadful scourges in these days to San Antonio and its environs.
The people of the *presidio* of San Fernando and of the missions
on the river complained repeatedly (says the *Testimonio de un
Parecer* [1] in the archives of Bexar) that they cannot expand (*sin
poder estenderse*) on account of "*las frequienttes hosttilidades
que experimenttan de los Yndios Apaches*." This great tribe
had headquarters about the Pass of Bandera, some fifty miles
to the northwestward, from which they forayed, not only up to
Antonio, but even as far as to Coahuila. Moreover, they
manage (says the *Testimonio*) horses, firearms, and arrows,
con mucha desttreza y agilidad. Finally the men of San Antonio
and San Fernando get tired of it, and after some minor counter-
forays, they organize an expedition in 1732 which conquers
comparative peace from the Apaches for a few years.

Nothing of special interest is recorded as happening in San
Antonio from this time until 1736. In September of that year
arrives Don Carlos de Franquis, who immediately proceeds to
throw the town into a very pretty ferment. Franquis had come
out from Spain to Mexico to be Governor of Tlascala. On
arriving, he finds that some one else is already Governor of
Tlascala. Vizarron, Archbishop of Mexico, and acting Viceroy
since Casa Fuerte's death, disposes of him—it is likely he made
trouble enough till that was done—by sending him off to Texas
to supersede Governor Sandoval, a fine old veteran, who has
been for two years governing the Province with such soldierly
fidelity as has won him great favor among the inhabitants.
Franquis begins by insulting the priests, and follows this up

---

[1] Testimony of a witness: this document is hereinafter described. [The document is printed by Yoakum, *History of Texas*.—ED.]

with breaking open people's letters. Presently he arrests Sandoval, has him chained, and causes criminal proceedings to be
commenced against him, charging him with treacherous complicity in certain movements of St. Denis at Natchitoches. It
seems that St. Denis, having found a higher and drier location,
has removed his garrison and the French Mission of St. John
the Baptist some miles further from Red River towards the
Texas territory, and built a new fort and settlements; that
Sandoval, hearing of it, has promptly called him to account
as an intruder on Spanish ground; and that a correspondence
has ensued between St. Denis and Sandoval, urging the rights
of their respective governments in the premises, which has
just been brought to the point of a flat issue upon which to go
to the jury of war when Sandoval is ousted by Franquis. The
Viceroy sends the Governor of New Leon to investigate the
trouble; and the famous lawsuit of Franquis *versus* Sandoval
is fairly commenced.* The Governor of New Leon seems to
find against Franquis, who is sent back to the *presidio* on the
Rio Grande. He gets away, however, and off to the Viceroy.
But Sandoval is not satisfied, naturally, for he has been mulcted
in some three thousand four hundred dollars, costs of the
investigating commission. He pays, and in 1738 files his petition against Franquis for redress of his injuries. Franquis,
thus attacked in turn, strengthens his position with a new line
of accusations. He now, besides the French business, charges
Sandoval with living at San Antonio instead of at Adaes, the
official residence; with being irregular in his accounts with the
San Antonio garrison; and with peculation in the matter of
the salaries of certain paid missionaries, whom Sandoval is
alleged to have discharged and then pocketed their stipends.
The papers go to the Viceroy, and from the Viceroy to Attorney-
General Vedoya. In 1740 Vedoya decides Sandoval guilty of
living at San Antonio, though it was his duty to be there to
defend it against the Apaches; guilty of irregular book-keep-
ing, though through memoranda it is found that there is a
balance in his favor of thirteen hundred dollars; not guilty of
stealing the missionary money. Upon the French matter Vedoya

* [Lanier's source for the entire account is again Yoakum, *History of Texas*,
which he closely paraphrases in many paragraphs.—Ed.]

will not decide without further evidence. With poor Sandoval it is pay again; he is fined five hundred dollars for his "guilt." Meantime, some months afterward, an order is made that testimony be taken in Texas with regard to the French affair, said testimony to embrace an account of pretty much everything in, about, and concerning Texas. The testimony being taken and returned, the Attorney-General, in November, 1741, entirely acquits Sandoval. But alas for the stout old soldier! this is in Mexico, where from of old, if one is asked who rules now, one must reply with the circumspection of that Georgia judge, who, being asked the politics of his son, made answer that *he knew not, not having seen the creature since breakfast.* Vizarron has gone out; the Duke de la Conquista has come into the Viceroyalty; and Sandoval has hardly had time to taste his hard-earned triumph before, through machinations of Franquis, he finds himself in prison by order of the new Viceroy. Finally, however, the rule works the other way; in December, 1743, a new Viceroy, Count Fuenclara, gets hold of the papers in the case, acquits Sandoval, and enjoins Franquis from proceeding further in the matter.

It was in the course of this litigation—a copy of the proceedings in which, " filling thirty volumes of manuscript," was transmitted to Spain—that the old document hereinbefore referred to as the *Testimonio de un Parecer* had its origin. In this paper San Antonio is called *San Antonio de Vejar ó Valero*, Vejar being the Spanish orthography of the Mexican *Bexar* (pronounced Váy-har). This name, San Antonio de Bexar, seems to have attached itself particularly to the military post, or *presidio*; its origin is not known. The town of San Fernando was still so called at this time; and the town and mission of San Antonio de Valero bore that name. In 1744 this latter extended itself to the eastward, or rather the extension had probably gone on before that time and was only evidenced then. At any rate, on the 8th of May, 1744, the first stone of the present Church of the Alamo was laid and blessed. The site of this church is nearly a quarter of a mile to the eastward of the Military Plaza, where the mission to which it belonged had been located in 1722. From an old record-book purporting to contain the baptisms in " the Parish of the Pueblo of *San José del Alamo,*" it would seem that there must have been also a settlement of that name. San Antonio de Bexar, therefore— the modern city—seems to be a consolidation of the *presidio* of San Antonio de Bexar, the mission and *pueblo* (or villa) of San Antonio de Valero, and the *pueblos* of San Fernando and San José del Alamo.

For the next forty years after the foundation of the Alamo in 1744, the colonists and missionaries seem to have pursued the ordinary round of their labors without unusual events; in point of material prosperity San Antonio seems to have led but a struggling existence. Yoakum [1] estimates the whole European population of Texas in 1744 to have been fifteen hundred, which, together with about the same number of converted Indians, " was divided mostly between Adaes and San Antonio." The same author again [2] estimates the population of Adaes and San Antonio in 1765 to have been " hardly five hundred " Europeans, besides converted Indians, of whom he adds that there were only about seven hundred and fifty in the whole province of Texas. It was impossible indeed during these years that any legitimate prosperity could have been attained. Up to the year 1762, when France, to save Louisiana from the clutches of England, ceded it to Spain, trade had been prohibited by the latter between her Texan colonists and the French settlers in Louisiana, though some intercourse always went on in a smuggling way between the two, whenever they could get a Spanish official to wink his eye or turn his back; and even after the cession of Louisiana matters were little better in point of commercial activity. There were also restrictions even upon the agricultural energies of the colonists; they were, it is said, pro- hibited from cultivating the vine and the olive, and also from the manufacture of many articles. Indeed, the immediate neces- sity of settlements having passed away with the removal of the danger of French occupation, the old policy of Spain seems to have been resumed in full force,—that of keeping her prov- inces around New Mexico and Mexico impenetrable wastes, as barriers against enterprising neighbors.

Nor was the spiritual prosperity much greater. The arduous toils and sublime devotions of the Franciscan brethren bore

[1] *History of Texas,* vol. i., p. 87.　　　[2] Vol. i., p. 97.

but moderate fruit. Father Marest had declared in 1712 that
the conversion of the Indians was "a miracle of the Lord's
mercy," and that it was "necessary first to transform them into
men, and afterward to labor to make them Christians." * These
noble brothers too had reason to believe in the inhumanity of
the Indians. They could remember the San Saba Mission where,
in 1758, the Indians had fallen upon the people and massacred
every human being, lay and clerical; and here, in 1785, they
could see for themselves the company of San Carlos de Parras
driven by the fierce Comanches to place their quarters within
the enclosure of the Alamo.

In 1783-5 San Antonio de Valero ceased to be a mission.
For some reason it had become customary to send whatever
captive Indians were brought in to the missions below the town
for christianization. The town, however, which had been built
up about the mission buildings, remained, having a separate
alcalde, and an organization politically and religiously distinct
from that of San Antonio de Bexar and San Fernando for
some years longer. In 1790 the population around the Alamo
was increased by the addition of the people from the Presidio
de las Adaes; this post was abandoned, and its inhabitants were
provided with lands which had been the property of the mission
of San Antonio de Valero, lying in the neighborhood of the
Alamo, to the north. "The upper *labor* [1] of the Alamo," says
Mr. Giraud, the present mayor of the city, in an interesting
note which constitutes Appendix IV of Yoakum's *History of
Texas,* ". . . is still commonly called by the old inhabitants the
labor de los Adaeseños." These mission lands about the Alamo
seem to have ceased to be such about this time, and to have been
divided off to the mission-people, each of whom received a portion, with fee-simple title. In 1793 the distinct religious organization of the Mission of San Antonio de Valero terminated,
and it was aggregated to the curacy of the town of San Fernando and the *presidio* of San Antonio de Bexar; as appears by
the following note which is found on the last page of an old
record-book of baptisms in the archives of Bexar:—

* [Quoted from Yoakum, *History of Texas.*—ED.]
[1] *Labor*: a Spanish land-measure of about one hundred and seventy-seven
acres.

On the 22d day of August, 1793, I passed this book of the records of the *pueblo* of San Antonio de Valero to the archives of the curacy of the town of San Fernando and *presidio* of San Antonio de Bexar, by order of the most illustrious Señor Dr. Don Andres de Llanos y Valdez, most worthy bishop of this diocese, dated January 2d, of the same year, by reason of said *pueblo* having been aggregated to the curacy of Bexar; and that it may be known, I sign it.

FR. JOSÉ FRANCISCO LOPEZ, *Parroco.*

In the year 1800 San Antonio began to see a new sort of prisoners brought in. Instead of captive Indians, here arrived a party of eleven Americans [1] in irons, who were the remainder of a company with which Philip Nolan, a trader between Natchez and San Antonio, had started out, and who, after a sharp fight with one hundred and fifty Spanish soldiers, in which Nolan was killed, had been first induced to return to Nacogdoches, and there were treacherously manacled and sent to prison at San Antonio. Again, in 1805, three Americans are brought in under guard. In this year, too, matters begin to be a little more lively in the town. Spain's neighbor on the east is not now France; for in 1803 Louisiana has been formally transferred to the United States. There is already trouble with the latter about the boundary line betwixt Louisiana and Texas. Don Antonio Cordero, the new Governor of Texas, has brought on a lot of troops through the town, and fixed his official residence here; and troops continue to march through *en route* to Natchitoches, where the American General Wilkinson is menacing the border. Again, in 1807, Lieutenant Zebulon M. Pike, of the United States army, passes through town in charge of an escort. Lieutenant Pike has been sent to explore the Arkansas and Red rivers, and to treat with the Camanches, has been apprehended by the Spanish authorities in New Mexico, carried to Santa Fé, and is now being escorted home.

At this time there are four hundred troops in San Antonio, in quarters near the Alamo. Besides these, the town has about two thousand inhabitants, mostly Spaniards and Creoles, the

[1] Americans, *i. e.* United States people; in which sense, to avoid the awkwardness of the only other equivalent terms, I shall hereafter use the word. [This same note appears in Yoakum, *History of Texas*, which is also the source for the quotation immediately above.—ED.]

remainder Frenchmen, Americans, civilized Indians, and half-breeds. New settlers have come in; and what with army officers, the Governor's people, the clergy, and prominent citizens, society begins to form and to enjoy itself. The Governor, Father McGuire, Colonel Delgado, Captain Ugarte, Doctor Zerbin, dispense hospitalities and adorn social meetings. There are, in the evenings, levees at the Governor's; sometimes Mexican dances on the Plaza, at which all assist; and frequent and prolonged card-parties.

But these peaceful scenes do not last long. In 1811 the passers across the San Antonio River between the Alamo and the Main Plaza behold a strange sight; it is the head of a man stuck on a pole, there, in bloody menace against rebels. This head but yesterday was on the shoulders of Colonel Delgado, a flying adherent of Hidalgo in Mexico: Hidalgo, initiator of how long a train of Mexican revolutions! having been also put to death in Chihuahua. It was not long before this blood was (as from of old) washed out with other blood. Bernardo Gutierrez, a fellow-rebel of the unfortunate Delgado, escaped to Natchitoches, and met young Magee, an officer of the United States army. In a short time the two had assembled a mixed force of American adventurers and rebellious Mexican republicans, had driven the Spanish troops from Nacogdoches, marched into Texas, captured the fort and supplies at La Bahia, enlisted its garrison, and sustained a siege there which the enemy was finally compelled to abandon with loss. It was in March, 1813, that the Spanish besieging force set out on its retreat up the river to San Antonio. Gutierrez—Magee having committed suicide in consequence of mortification at the indignant refusal of the troops to accept a surrender which he had negotiated soon after the beginning of the siege—determined to pursue. On the 28th of March he crossed the Salado, *en route* to San Antonio, with a force consisting of eight hundred Americans under Colonel Kemper, one hundred and eighty Mexicans led by Manchaco,[1] under Colonel James Gaines, three hundred Lipan and Twowokana Indians, and twenty-five Cooshattie Indians. Marching along the bank of the San Antonio River, with the left flank protected by the stream, this

[1] A prominent Mexican, of Texas, of strong but uncultivated intellect.

motley army arrived within nine miles of San Antonio, when the riflemen on the right suddenly discovered the enemy ambushed in the chaparral on the side of a ridge. Here the whole force that Governor Salcedo could muster had been posted, consisting of about fifteen hundred regular troops and a thousand militia. To gain time to form, the Indians were ranged to receive the opening charge of the Spanish cavalry; the enemy meantime having immediately formed along the crest of the ridge, with twelve pieces of artillery in the centre. The Indians broke at the first shock; only the Cooshatties and a few others stood their ground. These received two other charges, in which they lost two killed and several wounded. The Americans had now made their dispositions, and proceeded to execute them with matchless coolness. They charged up the hill, stopped at thirty yards of the enemy's line, fired three rounds, loaded, then charged again, and straightway the slope towards San Antonio was dotted with Spanish fugitives, whom the Indians pursued and butchered regardless of quarter. The Spanish commander, who had pledged sword and head to Governor Salcedo that he would kill and capture the American army, could not endure the sting of his misfortune. He spurred his horse upon the American ranks, attacked Major Ross, then Colonel Kemper, and while in the act of striking the latter was shot by private William Owen. The Spanish loss is said to have been near a thousand killed and wounded.

Next day the Americans advanced to the outskirts of San Antonio and demanded a surrender. Governor Salcedo desired to parley, to delay. A second demand was made—peremptory. Governor Salcedo then marched out with his staff. He presented his sword to Captain Taylor; Taylor refused, and referred him to Colonel Kemper. Presenting to Colonel Kemper, he was in turn referred to Gutierrez. No, not to that rebel! Salcedo thrust his sword into the ground, whence Gutierrez drew it. The victors got stores, arms, and treasure. Seventeen American prisoners in the Alamo were released and armed. The troops were paid,—receiving a bonus of fifteen dollars each in addition to wages,—clothed and mounted out of the booty. The Indians were not forgotten in the distribution; they " were supplied," says Yoakum, " with two dollars' worth of vermilion, together with presents of the value of a hundred and thirty dollars, and sent away rejoicing." *

And now flowed the blood that must answer that which dripped down the pole from poor Colonel Delgado's head. Shortly after the victory, Captain Delgado, a son of the executed rebel, falls upon his knees before Gutierrez, and demands vengeance upon the prisoner, Governor Salcedo, who apprehended and executed his father. Gutierrez arrays his army, informs them that it would be safe to send Salcedo and staff to New Orleans, and that it so happens that vessels are about to sail for that port from Matagorda Bay. The army consents (we are so fearfully and wonderfully republican in these days: *the army* consents) that the prisoners be sent off as proposed. Captain Delgado, with a company of Mexicans, starts in charge, ostensibly *en route* for Matagorda Bay. There are fifteen of the distinguished captives: Governor Salcedo of Texas, Governor Herrera of New Leon, Ex-Governor Cordero, whom we last saw holding levees in San Antonio, several Spanish and Mexican officers, and one citizen. Delgado gets his prisoners a mile and a half from town, halts them on the bank of the river, strips them, ties them, and cuts the throat of every man: " some of the assassins," says Colonel Navarro, whetting " their knives upon the soles of their shoes in presence of their victims."

The town of San Antonio must have been anything but a pleasant place for peaceful citizens during the next two months. Colonel Kemper, who was really the commanding officer of the American army, refused further connection with those who could be guilty of such barbarity, and left, with other American officers. Their departure left in the town an uncontrolled body of troops who feared neither God nor man; and these immediately proceeded to avail themselves of the situation by indulging in all manner of riotous and lawless pleasures. With the month of June, however, came Don Elisondo from Mexico with an army of royalists, consisting of about three thousand men, half of whom were regular troops. His advance upon

* [Lanier's entire account of the republican-royalist struggles (1811-1813) in the ensuing pages is closely paraphrased from Yoakum, *History of Texas*; the quotations are from the same source, which in turn quotes from Henry Stuart Foote, *Texas and the Texans.*—ED.].

San Antonio seems to have been a complete surprise, and to have been only learned by the undisciplined republican army in the town together with the fact that he had captured their horses, which had been out grazing, and killed part of the guard which was protecting the *caballada*. If Elisondo had marched straight on into town, his task would probably have been an easy one. But he committed the fatal mistake of encamping a short distance from the suburbs, where he threw up two bastions with a curtain between, on a ridge near the river Alozon.

Meantime the republican army in the town recovered from the confusion into which they had been thrown by the first intelligence of Elisondo's proximity, and organized themselves under Gutierrez and Captain Perry. It was determined to anticipate the enemy's attack. Ingress and egress were prohibited, the sentinels doubled, and all the cannon spiked except four field pieces. In the darkness of the night of June 4th the Americans marched quietly out of town, by file, to within hearing of the enemy's pickets, and remained there until the enemy was heard at matins. The signal to charge being given—a cheer from the right of companies—the Americans advanced, surprised and captured the pickets in front, mounted the enemy's work, lowered his flag and hoisted their own, before they were fairly discovered through the dim dawn. The enemy struggled hard, however, and compelled the Americans to abandon the works. The latter charged again, and this time routed the enemy completely. The royalist loss is said to have been about a thousand in killed, wounded and prisoners; and that of the Americans, ninety-four killed and mortally wounded.

For some reason Gutierrez was now dismissed from the leadership of the army (we republican soldiers decapitate our commanders very quickly if they please us not!), and shortly afterwards troops and citizens went forth in grand procession to welcome Don José Alvarez Toledo, a distinguished republican Cuban who had been forwarding recruits from Louisiana to San Antonio; and having escorted him into town with much ceremony, elected him commander-in-chief of the Republican Army of the North. Toledo immediately organized a government; but the people of San Antonio enjoyed the unaccustomed blessing of civil law only a little while.

In a few days enter, from over the Mexican border, General Arredondo with the remnant of Elisondo's men and some fresh troops, about four thousand in all, *en route* for San Antonio. Toledo marches out to meet him with about twenty-five hundred men, one third of whom are Americans, the balance Mexicans under Manchaco; and on the 18th of August, 1813, they come together. Arredondo decoys him into an ingenious *cul de sac* which he has thrown up just south of the Medina River, and has concealed by cut bushes; and pours such a murderous fire of cannon and small arms upon him, that in spite of the gallantry of the right wing, where the Americans are, the retreat which Toledo has ordered too late becomes a mere rout, and the republican army is butchered without mercy. One batch of seventy or eighty fugitives is captured by the pursuing royalists, tied, set by tens upon a log laid across a great grave, and shot!

On the 20th Arredondo enters San Antonio in great triumph, and straightway proceeds to wreak fearful vengeance upon the unhappy town for the massacre of his brother governors. Seven hundred citizens are thrown into prison. During the night of the 20th eighteen die of suffocation out of three hundred who are confined in one house. These only anticipate the remainder, who are shot, without trial, in detachments. Five hundred republican women are imprisoned in a building on the present site of the post-office, derisively termed the *Quinta,* and compelled to make up twenty-four bushels of corn into *tortillas* every day for the royalist army. Having thus sent up a sweet savor of revenge to the spirits of the murdered Salcedo, Cordero, Herrera, and the others, Arredondo finally gathers their bones together and buries them. In all this blood the prosperity of San Antonio was drowned. To settlers it offered no inducements; to most of its former citizens it held out nothing but terror; and it is described as almost entirely abandoned in 1816.

In December, 1820, arrived a person in San Antonio who, though not then known as such, was really a harbinger of better times. This was Moses Austin, of Connecticut. He came to see Governor Martinez, with a view of bringing a colony to Texas. The two, with the Baron de Bastrof, put in train the preliminary application for permission to Arredondo, Commandant-General at Monterey. Austin, it is true, died soon afterwards; but he left his project to his son Stephen F., who afterwards carried it out with a patience that amounted to genius and a fortitude that was equivalent to the favor of Heaven.

On the 24th of August, 1821, Don Juan O'Donojú and Iturbide entered into the Treaty of Córdova, which substantially perfected the separation of Mexico from the mother-country. When the intelligence of this event had spread, the citizens of San Antonio returned. Moreover, about this time a tide of emigration began to set towards Texas. The Americans who had composed part of the army of Gutierrez had circulated fair reports of the country. In 1823 San Antonio is said to have had five thousand inhabitants; though the Camanches appear still to have had matters all their own way when they came into town, as they frequently did, to buy beads and other articles with skins of deer and buffalo. One would find this difficult to believe, but reasoning *a priori,* it is rendered probable by the fact that in the decree of the Federal Congress of Mexico of the 24th of August, 1826, to provide for raising troops to serve in Coahuila and Texas as frontier defenders, it is ordered that out of the gross levies there shall be first preferred for military service " *los vagos y mal entretenidos,*" vagrant and evil-disposed persons; and *a posteriori,* it is quite confirmed by the experience of Olmstead in San Fernando (a considerable town west of the Rio Grande) so late as 1854, where he found the Indians " lounging in and out of every house . . . with such an air as indicated they were masters of the town. They entered every door," adds Olmsted, " fell on every neck, patted the women on the cheek, helped themselves to whatever suited their fancy, and distributed their scowls or grunts of pleasure according to their sensations." *

In the year 1824 a lot of French merchants passed through San Antonio *en route* to Santa Fé on a trading expedition. Some distance from town their pack-animals were all stolen by Indians; but they managed to get carts and oxen from San Antonio, and so conveyed their goods finally to Santa Fé,

* [Frederick Law Olmsted, *A Journey through Texas.*—ED.]

where they sold them at an immense profit. In 1831 the Bowie brothers, Rezin P., and James, organized in San Antonio their expedition in search of the old reputed silver mines at San Saba Mission. In the course of this unlucky venture occurred their famous Indian fight, where the two Bowies, with nine others, fought a pitched battle with one hundred and sixty-four Indians who had attacked them with arrow, with rifle, and with fire from sundown to sunset, killing and wounding eighty-four. They then fortified their position during the night, maintained it for eight days afterwards, and finally returned to San Antonio with their horses and three wounded comrades, leaving one man killed.

It is related that in 1832 a Camanche Indian attempted to abduct a Shawnee woman in San Antonio. She escaped him, joined a party of her people who were staying some thirty-five miles from town, and informed them where the Camanches (of whom five hundred had been in town for some purpose) would probably camp. The Shawnees ambushed themselves at the spot indicated. The Camanches came on and stopped as expected: the Shawnees poured a fire into them, and repeated it as they continually rallied, until the Camanches abandoned the contest with a loss of one hundred and seventy-five dead.*

Early in 1833 (or perhaps late in December, 1832) arrives in San Antonio for the first time one who is to be called the father of his country. This is Sam Houston. He comes in company with the famous James Bowie, son-in-law of Vice-Governor Veramendi, and holds a consultation with the Camanche chiefs here to arrange a meeting at Cantonment Gibson with a view to a treaty of peace. Meantime trouble is brewing. Young Texas does not get on well with his mother. What seems to hurt most is the late union of Texas with Coahuila. This we cannot stand. Stephen F. Austin goes to the City of Mexico with a memorial on the subject to the federal government. He writes from there to the municipality of San Antonio, Oct. 2d, 1833, informing the people that their request is likely

---

* [Lanier's source for this episode is Yoakum, *History of Texas*, which he likewise quotes from or closely paraphrases in the following pages for his entire account of the struggle for Texan independence, except where otherwise noted.—ED.]

to be refused, and advising them to make themselves ready for that emergency. The municipality hand this letter over to Vice-President Farias, who, already angry with Austin on an old account, arrests him on his way home and throws him into prison, back in the City of Mexico.

In October, 1834, certain people in San Antonio hold what Yoakum calls "the first strictly revolutionary meeting in Texas;" for Santa Ana has *pronounced,* and got to be at the head of affairs, and he refuses to separate Texas from Coahuila. So, through meetings all over the State; through conferences of citizen deputations with Colonel Ugartochea, Mexican Commandant at San Antonio, for the purpose of explaining matters; through confused arguments and resolutions of the peace party and the war party; through confused rumors of the advance of Mexican General Cos with an army; through squabbling and wrangling and final fighting over the cannon that had been lent by the Post of Bexar to the people of Gonzalez; through all manner of civic trouble consequent upon the imprisonment of Governor Viesca of Texas by Santa Ana, and the suspension of the progress of the civil law machine,—we come to the time when the committee of San Felipe boldly cry: "*Let us take Bexar and drive the Mexican soldiery out of Texas!*" and presently here, on the 28th of October, 1835, is General Cos with his army in San Antonio, fortifying for dear life, while yonder is Austin with a thousand Texans, at Mission Concepcion, a mile and a half down the river below town, where Fannin and Bowie with ninety men in advance have a few hours before waged a brilliant battle with four hundred Mexicans, capturing their field-piece, killing and wounding a hundred or more, and driving the rest back to town.

General Austin believes, it seems, that Cos will surrender without a battle; and so remains at Concepcion till November 2d, then marches up past the town on the east side, encamps four or five days, marches down on the west side, displays his forces on a hillside *in terrorem*, sends in a demand for surrender—and is flatly answered *no.* He resolves to lay siege. The days pass slowly; the enemy will not come out, though allured with all manner of military enticements, and the army has no "fun," with the exception of one small skirmish, until the 26th, when " Deaf " Smith [1] discovers a party of a hundred Mexican troops, who have been sent out to cut prairie-grass for the horses in town, and reporting them in camp, brings on what is known as the " grass-fight." Col. James Bowie attacks with a hundred mounted men; both sides are quickly reinforced, and a sharp running fight is kept up until the enemy get back to town; the Texans capturing seventy horses and killing some fifty of the enemy, with a loss of but two wounded and one missing. Meantime discontents arise. On the day before the " grass-fight " Austin resigns, having been appointed Commissioner to the United States, and Edward Burleson is elected by the army to the command. General Burleson, for some reason, seems loth to storm. Moreover, one Dr. James Grant seduces a large party with a wild project to leave San Antonio and attack Matamoros, when he declares that the whole of Mexico will rise and overwhelm Santa Ana; and on the 29th of November it is actually announced that two hundred and twenty-five men are determined to start the next morning.

But they do not start. It is whispered the town will be stormed. On the 3d of December, Smith, Holmes, and Maverick escape from San Antonio, and give the Texan commander such information as apparently determines him to storm. Volunteers are called for to attack early next morning; all day and all night of that December 3d the men make themselves ready, and long for the moment to advance: when here comes word from the General's quarters that the attack is put off! Chagrin and indignation prevail on all sides. On the morning of the 4th there is open disobedience of orders; whole companies refuse to parade. Finally, when on the same afternoon orders are issued to abandon camp and march for La Bahia at seven o'clock, the tumult is terrible, and it seems likely that these wild energetic souls, failing the Mexicans, will end by exterminating each other.

Midst of the confusion here arrives Mexican Lieutenant Vuavis, a deserter, and declares that the projected attack is *not* known (as had been assigned for reason of postponing), and that the garrison in town is in as bad order and discontent as

[1] One of the most celebrated and efficient scouts of the revolution. [Erastus Smith, 1787-1837.—ED.]

the besiegers. At this critical moment a brave man suddenly crystallizes the loose mass of discordant men and opinions into one compact force and one keen purpose. It is late in the morning, Col. Benjamin R. Milam steps forth among the men, and cries aloud: "Who will go with old Ben Milam into San Antonio?" Three hundred and one men will go.

A little before daylight on the 5th they " go," General Burleson agreeing to hold his position until he hears from them. Milam marches into and along Acequia Street with his party; Johnson with his along Soledad Street. Where these debouch into the Main Plaza, Cos has thrown up breastworks and placed raking batteries. The columns march parallel along the quiet streets. Presently, as Johnson gets near the Veramendi House (which he is to occupy, while Milam is to gain De la Ganza's house), a Mexican sentinel fires. Deaf Smith shoots the sentinel. The Mexicans prick up their ears, prick into their cannon-cartridges; the Plaza batteries open, the Alamo batteries join in; spade, crowbar, rifle, escopet, all are plied, and the storming of Bexar is begun.

But it would take many such papers as this to give even meagre details of all the battles that have been fought in and around San Antonio, and one must pass over the four days of this thrilling conflict with briefest mention. It is novel fighting; warfare intramural, one might say. The Texans advance inch by inch by piercing through the stone walls of the houses, pecking loopholes with crowbars for their rifles as they gain each room, picking off the enemy from his house-tops, from around his cannon, even from behind his own loopholes. On the night of the 5th with great trouble and risk the two columns succeed in opening communication with each other. On the 6th they advance a little beyond the Ganza house. On the 7th brave Karnes steps forth with a crowbar and breaks into a house midway between the Ganza house and the Plaza; brave Milam is stricken by a rifle ball just as he is entering the yard of the Veramendi house and falls instantly dead; and the Navarro house, one block from the Main Plaza, is gained. On the 8th they take the " Zambrano Row " of buildings, driving the enemy from it room by room; the enemy endeavor to produce a diversion with fifty men, and do, in a sense, for Burleson finds some diversion in driving them back precipitately with a six-pounder; at night those in the Zambrano Row are reinforced, and the " Priest's House " is gained amid heavy fighting.

This last is the stroke of grace. The Priest's House commands the Plaza. Early on the morning of the 9th General Cos sends a flag of truce, asking to surrender, and on the 10th agrees with General Burleson upon formal and honorable articles of capitulation.

The poor citizens of San Antonio de Bexar, however, do not yet enjoy the blessings of life in quiet; these wild soldiers who have stormed the town cannot remain long without excitement. Presently Dr. Grant revives his old Matamoros project, and soon departs, carrying with him most of the troops that had been left at Bexar for its defence, together with great part of the garrison's winter supply of clothing, ammunition, and provisions, and in addition " pressing " such property of the citizens as he needs, insomuch that Colonel Neill, at that time in command at Bexar, writes to the Governor of Texas that the place is left destitute and defenceless. Soon afterward Colonel Neill is ordered to destroy the Alamo walls and other fortifications, and bring off the artillery, since no head can be made there in the present crisis against the enemy, who is reported marching in force upon San Antonio. Having no teams Colonel Neill is unable to obey the order, and presently retires, his unpaid men having dropped off until but eighty remain, of whom Col. Wm. B. Travis assumes command. Colonel Travis promptly calls for more troops, but gets none as yet, for the Governor and Council are at deadly quarrel, and the soldiers are all pressing towards Matamoros. Travis has brought thirty men with him; about the middle of February he is joined by Colonel Bowie with thirty others, and these, with the eighty already in garrison, constitute the defenders of San Antonio de Bexar. On the 23d of February appears General Santa Ana at the head of a well-appointed army of some four thousand men, and marches straight on into town. The Texans retire before him slowly, and finally shut themselves up in the Alamo; here straightway begins that bloodiest, smokiest, grimiest tragedy of this century. William B. Travis, James Bowie, and

David Crockett, with their hundred and forty-five effective men, are enclosed within a stone rectangle one hundred and ninety feet long and one hundred and twenty-two feet wide, having the old church of the Alamo in the southeast corner, in which are their quarters and magazine. They have a supply of water from the ditches that run alongside the walls, and by way of provision they have about ninety bushels of corn and thirty beef-cattle, their entire stock, all collected since the enemy came in sight. The walls are unbroken, with no angles from which to command besieging lines. They have fourteen pieces of artillery mounted, with but little ammunition.

Santa Ana demands unconditional surrender. Travis replies with a cannon-shot, and the attack commences, the enemy running up a blood-red flag in town. Travis dispatches a messenger with a call to his countrymen for reinforcements, which concludes: " Though this call may be neglected, I am determined to sustain myself as long as possible, and die like a soldier who never forgets what is due to his own honor and that of his country. Victory or death! " Meantime the enemy is active. On the 25th Travis has a sharp fight to prevent him from erecting a battery raking the gate of the Alamo. At night it is erected, with another a half-mile off at the *Garita,* or powder-house, on a sharp eminence at the extremity of the present main street of the town. On the 26th there is skirmishing with the Mexican cavalry. In the cold—for a norther has commenced to blow and the thermometer is down to thirty-nine—the Texans make a sally successfully for wood and water, and that night they burn some old houses on the northeast that might afford cover for the enemy. So amid the enemy's constant rain of shells and balls, which miraculously hurt no one, the Texans strengthen their works and the siege goes on. On the 28th Fannin starts from Goliad with three hundred troops and four pieces of artillery, but for lack of teams and provisions quickly returns, and the little garrison is left to its fate. On the morning of the 1st of March there is doubtless a wild shout of welcome in the Alamo; Capt. John W. Smith has managed to convey thirty-two men from Gonzales into the fort. These join the heroes, and the attack and defence go on. On the 3d a single man, Moses Rose, escapes from the fort. His account of that day [1] must entitle it to consecration as one of the most pathetic days of time.

About two hours before sunset on the 3d of March, 1836, the bombardment suddenly ceased, and the enemy withdrew an unusual distance. . . . Colonel Travis paraded all his effective men in a single file, and taking his position in front of the centre, he stood for some moments apparently speechless from emotion; then nerving himself for the occasion, he addressed them substantially as follows:—

" My brave companions: stern necessity compels me to employ the few moments afforded by this probably brief cessation of conflict, in making known to you the most interesting, yet the most solemn, melancholy, and unwelcome fact that humanity can realize. . . . Our fate is sealed. Within a very few days, perhaps a very few hours, we must all be in eternity! I have deceived you long by the promise of help; but I crave your pardon, hoping that after hearing my explanation you will not only regard my conduct as pardonable, but heartily sympathize with me in my extreme necessity. . . . I have continually received the strongest assurances of help from home. Every letter from the Council, and every one that I have seen from individuals at home, has teemed with assurances that our people were ready, willing, and anxious to come to our relief. . . . These assurances I received as facts. . . . In the honest and simple confidence of my heart I have transmitted to you these promises of help and my confident hope of success. But the promised help has not come, and our hopes are not to be realized. I have evidently confided too much in the promises of our friends; but let us not be in haste to censure them. . . . Our friends were evidently not informed of our perilous condition in time to save us. Doubtless they would have been here by this time had they expected any considerable force of the enemy. . . . My calls on Colonel Fannin remain unanswered, and my messengers have not returned. The probabilities are that his whole command has fallen into the hands of the enemy, or been cut to pieces, and that our couriers have been cut off. [So does the brave simple soul refuse to feel any bitterness in the hour of death.] . . . Then we must die. . . . Our business is not to make a fruitless effort to save our lives, but to choose the manner of our death. But three modes are presented to us; let us

---

[1] As transmitted by the Zuber family, whose residence was the first place at which poor Rose had dared to stop, and with whom he remained some weeks, healing the festered wounds made on his legs by the cactus-thorns during the days of his fearful journey. The account from which these extracts are taken, is contributed to the *Texas Almanac* for 1873, by W. P. Zuber, and his mother, Mary Ann Zuber. [The editorial omissions and brackets in the following quotation are Lanier's.—ED.]

choose that by which we may best serve our country. Shall we surrender and be deliberately shot without taking the life of a single enemy? Shall we try to cut our way out through the Mexican ranks and be butchered before we can kill twenty of our adversaries? I am opposed to either method. . . . Let us resolve to withstand our adversaries to the last, and at each advance to kill as many of them as possible. And when at last they shall storm our fortress, let us kill them as they come! kill them as they scale our wall! kill them as they leap within! kill them as they raise their weapons and as they use them! kill them as they kill our companions! and continue to kill them as long as one of us shall remain alive! . . . But I leave every man to his own choice. Should any man prefer to surrender . . . or to attempt an escape . . . he is at liberty to do so. My own choice is to stay in the fort and die for my country, fighting as long as breath shall remain in my body. This will I do, even if you leave me alone. Do as you think best; but no man can die with me without affording me comfort in the hour of death!'"

Colonel Travis then drew his sword, and with its point traced a line upon the ground extending from the right to the left of the file. Then resuming his position in front of the centre, he said, "I now want every man who is determined to stay here and die with me to come across this line. Who will be first? March!" The first respondent was Tapley Holland, who leaped the line at a bound, exclaiming, "I am ready to die for my country!" His example was instantly followed by every man in the file with the exception of Rose. . . . Every sick man that could walk, arose from his bunk and tottered across the line. Colonel Bowie, who could not leave his bed, said, "Boys, I am not able to come to you, but I wish some of you would be so kind as to remove my cot over there." Four men instantly ran to the cot, and each lifting a corner, carried it across the line. Then every sick man that could not walk made the same request, and had his bunk removed in the same way.

Rose too was deeply affected, but differently from his companions. He stood till every man but himself had crossed the line. . . . He sank upon the ground, covered his face, and yielded to his own reflections. . . . A bright idea came to his relief; he spoke the Mexican dialect very fluently, and could he once get safely out of the fort, he might easily pass for a Mexican and effect an escape. . . . He directed a searching glance at the cot of Colonel Bowie. . . . Col. David Crockett was leaning over the cot, conversing with its occupant in an undertone. After a few seconds Bowie looked at Rose and said, "You seem not to be willing to die with us, Rose." "No," said Rose; "I am not prepared to die, and shall not do so if I can avoid it." Then Crockett also looked at him, and said, "You may as well conclude to die with us, old man, for escape is impossible." Rose made no reply, but looked at the top of the wall. "I have often done worse than to climb that wall," thought he. Suiting the action to the thought, he sprang up, seized his wallet of unwashed clothes, and ascended the wall. Standing on its top, he looked down within to take a last view of his dying friends. They were all now in motion, but what they were doing he heeded not; overpowered by his feelings, he looked away and saw them no more. . . . He threw down his wallet and leaped after it. . . . He took the road which led down the river around a bend to the ford, and through the town by the church. He waded the river at the ford and passed through the town. He saw no person . . . but the doors were all closed, and San Antonio appeared as a deserted city.

After passing through the town he turned down the river. A stillness as of death prevailed. When he had gone about a quarter of a mile below the town, his ears were saluted by the thunder of the bombardment, which was then renewed. That thunder continued to remind him that his friends were true to their cause, by a continual roar with but slight intervals until a little before sunrise on the morning of the 6th, when it ceased and he heard it no more.[1]

And well may it "cease" on that morning of that 6th; for after that thrilling 3d the siege goes on, the enemy furious, the Texans replying calmly and slowly. Finally Santa Ana determines to storm. Some hours before daylight on the morning of the 6th the Mexican infantry, provided with scaling-ladders, and backed by the cavalry to keep them up to the work, surround the doomed fort. At daylight they advance and plant their ladders, but give back under a deadly fire from the Texans. They advance again, and again retreat. A third time— Santa Ana threatening and coaxing by turns—they plant their ladders. Now they mount the walls. The Texans are overwhelmed by sheer weight of numbers and exhaustion of continued watching and fighting. The Mexicans swarm into the fort. The Texans club their guns; one by one they fall fighting—now Travis yonder by the western wall, now Crockett

[1] Rose succeeded in making his escape, and reached the house of the Zubers, as before stated, in fearful condition. After remaining here some weeks, he started for his home in Nacogdoches, but on the way his thorn-wounds became inflamed anew, and when he reached home "his friends thought that he could not live many months." This was "the last" that the Zubers "heard of him." [From this point Lanier returns to Yoakum, *History of Texas*, as his authority.—Ed.]

here in the angle of the church-wall, now Bowie butchered and mutilated in his sick-cot, breathe quick and pass away; and presently every Texan lies dead, while there in horrid heaps are stretched five hundred and twenty-one dead Mexicans and as many more wounded! Of the human beings that were in the fort five remain alive: Mrs. Dickinson and her child, Colonel Travis' negro-servant, and two Mexican women. The conquerors endeavored to get some more revenge out of the dead, and close the scene with raking together the bodies of the Texans, amid insults, and burning them.

The town did not long remain in the hands of the Mexicans. Events followed each other rapidly until the battle of San Jacinto, after which the dejected Santa Ana wrote his famous letter of captivity under the tree, which for a time relieved the soil of Texas from hostile footsteps. San Antonio was nevertheless not free from bloodshed, though beginning to drive a sharp trade with Mexico and to make those approaches towards the peaceful arts which necessarily accompany trade. The Indians kept life from stagnating, and in the year 1840 occurred a bloody battle with them in the very midst of the town. Certain Camanche chiefs, pending negotiations for a treaty of peace, had promised to bring in all the captives they had; and on the 19th of March, 1840, met the Texan Commissioners in the Council-house in San Antonio to redeem their promise. Leaving twenty warriors and thirty-two women and children outside, twelve chiefs entered the council-room and presented the only captive they had brought—a little white girl—declaring that they had no others. This statement the little girl pronounced false, asserting that it was made solely for the purpose of extorting greater ransoms, and that she had but recently seen other captives in their camp. An awkward pause followed. Presently one of the chiefs inquired, How the Commissioners liked it. By way of reply, the company of Captain Howard, who had been sent for, filed into the room, and the Indians were told that they would be held prisoners until they should send some of their party outside after the rest of the captives. The Commissioners then rose and left the room. As they were in the act of leaving, however, one of the Indian chiefs attempted to rush through the door, and being confronted by the sentinel, stabbed him. Seeing the sentinel hurt, and Captain Howard also stabbed, the other chiefs sprang forward with knives and bows and arrows, and the fight raged until they were all killed. Meantime the warriors outside began to fight, and engaged the company of Captain Read; but, taking shelther in a stone-house, were surrounded and killed. Still another detachment of the Indians managed to continue the fight until they had reached the other side of the river, when they were finally despatched. Thirty-two Indian warriors and five Indian women and children were slain, and the rest of the women and children were made prisoners. The savages fought desperately, for seven Texans were killed and eight wounded.

The war between Texas and Mexico had now languished for some years. The project of annexation was much discussed in the United States; one great objection to it was that the United States would embroil itself with a nation with which it was at peace—Mexico—by annexing Texas, then at war. The war, however, seemed likely to die away; and to prevent the removal of the obstacle to annexation in that way, Mexico made feeble efforts to keep up such hostilities as might at least give color to the assertion that the war had not ended. Accordingly in the year 1842 a Mexican army again invested San Antonio. After a short parley, Colonel Hays withdrew with his small force, and the Mexicans, numbering about seven hundred men under General Vasquez, took possession of the place and formally reorganized it as a Mexican town. They remained, however, only two days, and conducted themselves, officially, with great propriety, though the citizens are said to have lost a great deal of valuable property by unauthorized depredations of private soldiers and of Mexican citizens who accompanied the army on its departure.

Again on the 11th of September, 1842, a Mexican army of twelve hundred men under General Woll, sent probably by the same policy which had despatched the other, surprised the town of San Antonio, and after having a few killed and wounded, took possession, the citizens having capitulated. General Woll captured the entire bar of lawyers in attendance on the District Court, then in session, and held them as prisoners of war.

He did not escape, however, so easily as General Vasquez. The Texans gathered rapidly, and by the 17th had assembled two hundred and twenty men on the Salado, some six miles from town. Captain Hays with fifty men decoyed General Woll forth, and a battle ensued from which the enemy withdrew at sunset with a loss of sixty killed and about the same number wounded, the Texans 'losing one killed and nine wounded. It is easy to believe that the honest citizens of San Antonio got little sleep on that night of the 17th of September, 1842. General Woll was busy making preparations for retreat; and the Mexican citizens who intended to accompany him were also busy gathering up plunder right and left to take with them. At daylight they all departed. This was the last time that San Antonio de Bexar was ever in Mexican hands.

After annexation, in 1845, the town began to improve. The trade from certain portions of Mexico—Chihuahua and the neighboring States—seems always to have eagerly sought San Antonio as a point of supplies whenever peace gave it the opportunity. Presently, too, the United States government selected San Antonio as the base for the frontier army below El Paso, and the large quantities of money expended in connection with the supply and transportation of all *matériel* for so long a line of forts have contributed very materially to the prosperity of the town. From a population of about 3,500 in 1850, it increased to 10,000 in 1856, and has now about 15,000.

Abandoning now this meagre historical sketch, and pursuing the order indicated in the enumeration of contrast and eccentricities given in the early part of this paper: one finds in San Antonio the queerest juxtaposition of civilizations, white, yellow (Mexican), red (Indian), black (negro), and all possible permutations of these significant colors. The Germans, the Americans, and the Mexicans are not greatly unequal in numbers; besides these there are probably representatives from all European nationalities. At the Commerce Street bridge over the San Antonio River, stands a post supporting a large sign-board, upon which appear the following three legends:

Walk your horse over this bridge, or you will be fined.
Schnelles Reiten über diese Brücke ist verboten.
Anda despacio con su caballo, ó teme la ley.

To the meditative stroller across this bridge—and on a soft day when the Gulf breeze and the sunshine are king and queen, any stranger may be safely defied to cross this bridge without becoming meditative—there is a fine satire in the varying tone of these inscriptions—for they are by no means faithful translations of each other; a satire all the keener in that it must have been wholly unconscious. For mark: "Walk your horse, etc, *or you will be fined!*" This is the American's warning: the alternative is a money consideration, and the appeal is solely to the pocket. But now the German is simply informed that *schnelles Reiten* over this bridge *ist verboten—is forbidden;* as who should say: "So, thou quiet, law-abiding Teuton, enough for thee to know that it is forbidden, simply." And lastly, the Mexican direction takes wholly a different turn from either: Slow there with your horse, Mexicano, " *ó teme la ley,*" —or " *fear the law!*"

Religious services are regularly conducted in four languages, German, Spanish, English, and Polish.

Perhaps the variety of the population cannot be better illustrated than by the following " commodity of good names," occurring in a slip cut from a daily paper of the town a day or two ago:

MATRIMONIAL.—The matrimonial market for a couple of weeks past has been unusually lively, as evidenced by the following list of marriage licenses issued during that time: Cruz de la Cruz and Manuela Sauseda; Felipe Sallani and Maria del R. Lopez; G. Isabolo and Rafaela Urvana; Anto. P. Rivas and Maria Quintana; Garmel Hernandez and Seferina Rodriguez; T. B. Leighton and Franceska E. Schmidt; Rafael Diaz and Michaela Chavez; Levy Taylor and Anna Simpson, colored; Ignacio Andrada and Juliana Baltasar; August Dubiell and Philomena Muschell; James Callaghan and Mary Grenet; Albert Anz and Ida Pollock; Stephen Hoog and Mina Schneider; Wm. King and Sarah Wilson, colored; Joseph McCoy and Jessie Brown; Valentine Heck and Clara Hirsch; John F. Dunn and E. Annie Dunn.*

These various nationalities appear to take great pains in pre-

* [San Antonio *Herald*, Jan. 18, 1873.—ED.]

serving their peculiar tongues. In all the large stores the clerks must understand at least English, German, and Mexican; and one medical gentleman adds to his professional card in the newspaper that he will hold " consultations in English, French, Italian, and Spanish."

Much interest has attached, of late years, to the climate of San Antonio, in consequence of its alleged happy influence upon consumption. One of the recognized " institutions" of the town is the consumptives, who are sent here from remote parts of the United States and from Europe and who may be seen on fine days, in various stages of decrepitude, strolling about the streets. This present writer has the honor to be one of those strolling individuals; but he does not intend to attempt to *describe* the climate, for three reasons: first, because it is simply indescribable; second, if it were not so, his experience has been such as to convince him that the needs of consumptives in point of climate depend upon two variable elements, to wit, the stage which the patient has reached, and the peculiar temperament of each individual, and that therefore any general recommendation of any particular climate is often erroneous and sometimes fatally deceptive; and third, because he fortunately is able to present some of the *facts* of the climate, which may be relied upon as scientifically accurate, and from the proper study of which each intelligent consumptive can make up his mind as to the suitableness of the climate to his individual case. For the past five years, Dr. F. v. Pettersén, a Swedish physician and ardent lover of science, resident in San Antonio, has conducted a series of meteorological observations with accurate apparatus; and the results which follow have been compiled from his records:

MEAN THERMOMETER

		Spring	*Summer*	*Autumn*	*Winter*
Seasons of 1868	. . .	74.33	84.33	71.33	54.66
" 1869	. . .	66.43	83.10	67.53	52.93
" 1870	. . .	68.70	83.43	70.66	51.30
" 1871	. . .	71.28	87.45	68.38	54.31
" 1872	. . .	70.58	83.13	68.96	49.75

MEAN HYGROMETER

Seasons of 1868	. . .	65[1]	78	64	49
" 1869	. . .	62	77	62	49
" 1870	. . .	60	77	65	46
" 1871	. . .	64	73	63	50
" 1872	. . .	64	76	61	46

TOTAL RAINFALL

For the year 1868	. . . .	46.60 inches
" 1869	. . . .	49.03 "
" 1870	. . . .	35.12 "
" 1871	. . . .	24.86 "
" 1872	. . . .	31.62 "

These are averages, but the view which they present of the climate, although strictly accurate as far as it goes, is by no means complete. For the consumptive is specially interested in the uniformity and equableness of temperatures, and it remains therefore to supplement the above table with some account of the nature, extent, and suddenness of the *changes* of the thermometer in the climate under consideration. These at San Antonio are very peculiar, very great and very rapid. They mostly occur under the influence of those remarkable meteorological phenomena called "northers," which are peculiar to a belt of country that may be roughly defined as bounded on the east by the second tier of Texan counties from Red River, on the west by the Sierra Madre in Mexico, and on the north by a line drawn through the Indian Territory not far above the northern boundary of Texas. The northers are known as of two sorts: the wet and the dry. To know what a norther is, let one fancy himself riding along the undulating prairie about San Antonio on a splendid day in April, when the flowers, the birds, and the sunshine seem to be playing at a wild game of which can be maddest with delight, and the tender spring-sky looks on like a young mother laughing at the antics of her darlings. Presently you observe that it is very warm. An hour later you cannot endure your coat; you throw it off and hang it about the saddle, and soon the heat is stifling, thermometer

[1] Fractions omitted.

at ninety degrees, which on a windless prairie with the Gulf moisture in the air, is greatly relaxing. Standing on an elevation in the hope of getting some breath of air, suddenly you observe a bluish haze in the north, which has come no one knows when or whence. In a few moments a great roar advances; then you observe the mesquit grow tremulous, and presently the wind strikes you, blows your moist garment against your skin with a mortal chill; and if you are prudent at all you make for a house as fast as your horse can carry you, or in default of that for some thicket of mesquit in a ravine under the lee of a hill. In an hour the thermometer may have sunken to forty degrees from ninety degrees; this range of fifty degrees in an hour was noted by Dr. Pettersén during the observations before alluded to. This is the "dry norther;" for the wet norther, add a furious storm of rain, of hail, or of snow, to the phenomena just described. The norther may last but twelve hours; it may also last nine days, the usual duration being probably about three days. Dr. Pettersén's records show that in the year 1868 there were at San Antonio twelve northers, of which nine were dry, two wet, and one with hail; in 1869 twenty northers—eighteen dry and two wet; in 1870 twenty-four northers—seventeen dry, seven wet; in 1871 twenty-six northers—twenty-two dry, three wet, one with hailstorm; in 1872 thirty northers—twenty dry, nine wet, and one with hail. These occurred during all months of the year except June, July, and August; less frequently in May than during the other months. There is also, besides the genuine norther, a wind which the inhabitants call a " gentle norther." This is rather a northwesterly, or sometimes westerly wind, and its prevalence creates what, in this present writer's experience, is by far the finest winter weather in Texas. One came up two days ago. The night had been sultry, though in February; a nameless oppression was in the air, and a heavy mist rolled along over the river. After an uneasy half-slumber I woke at dawn, and immediately heard a pleasant *drawing* sound in the air, greatly like the noise made by the water against the prow of one's boat when after a calm the sail has caught the steady breeze and she begins to cut swiftly and smoothly along. In a few moments the wind was howling about the house, but when I came out for breakfast I found that its bark was worse than its bite; for this was a typic " gentle norther," the air crystalline, brittle, and dry, the sun shining brightly, the sky clear, the wind strong but balmy, the temperature soft yet bracing. In about three months of residence, commencing near the middle of November, 1872, there have occurred not more than three of these, lasting about two days each. I have no authentic data upon which to base a conclusion as to their average frequency. Any one who discovers a land where such weather prevails for two or three months at a time, will have found the place where consumption can be cured.

It is proper to add that the city of San Antonio is situated in the valley of the San Antonio River, and that malarious mists creep down this stream, when not blown away by contrary winds, which subject the stranger to liability to those diseases which require quinine, such as remittent fevers, fever and ague, epidemic colds, etc. These are, however, of mild form, and can probably be prevented by taking small quantities of quinine each day in anticipation.[1]

While the thermometer cuts such capers as leaping over 50° in an hour, the hygrometer, in whose motions invalids are no less interested, often seems to behave with equal want of dignity. During one of the " gentle northers " above alluded to, the hygrometer has shown the relative moisture of the atmosphere to be as low as 18, full saturation being 100; but again the same instrument has shown, during the month of August, 1872, a state of moisture represented by 101; a period when rain must have been actually exuding from the air like water from a sponge. Frequently the writer has seen remarkable examples of complete saturation of the air in the strange aspect of the river which runs a few yards from his window. All day long a great cloud of mist sometimes goes steaming up from the surface of the stream to such an extent that its milky-green water will be completely obscured, and standing at a short distance one seems to have arrived at some long rift in the earth from which the smoke of the nether fires is continually pouring

---

[1] Perhaps it may be mentioned here for the benefit of consumptives that the climates of Boerne (30 miles above) and of Fredericksburg (80 miles above) are said to be better in this particular than that of San Antonio, and also cooler.

up. I have seen this uprising of thick mist go on day and night for several days together. The water of the stream is said to be at 72° the year round. This high temperature must keep up a rapid evaporation; and when the vapor-capacity of the superincumbent air has been surcharged, with at the same time sufficiently cold air to condense the vaporous mist, the evaporation becomes visible and produces the effect described.

The following table, which will conclude this account of the San Antonio climate, will give to the invalid a very important, and at the same time authoritative and accurate series of facts upon which to project his preparations for weather-defence in the way of clothing, etc. This table is calculated from the records for the four years beginning with 1868 and ending with 1871. The plain interpretation of it is, taking the month of February for instance, that on this present 10th day of that month neither I nor any other man can tell whether the temperature tomorrow may be 84°, when we shall yearn to throw away our coats and to burn all our flannel goods, or whether it may be 26°, when we shall desire to stand all day with our arms clasped affectionately round our respective stove-pipes.

MAXIMUM AND MINIMUM OF THERMOMETER DURING THE FOUR
YEARS ABOVE-MENTIONED FOR EACH MONTH

	Jan.	Feb.	Mar.	Apr.	May	June	July	Aug.	Sept.	Oct.	Nov.	Dec.
Maximum	75	84	82	87	95	106	102	104	99	90	89	79
Minimum	27	26	29	46	63	71	75	75	57	43	22	14

San Antonio is at an altitude of 564 feet above the level of the sea, in latitude 29° 28', longitude 98° 24'. It is placed just in the edge of a belt of country one hundred and fifty miles wide, reaching to the Rio Grande, and principally devoted to cattle-raising. One can sit on one's horse, in the western suburbs of the city and mark where the line of the rude Mexican *jacals* (huts) abruptly breaks off, and yields place to the vast mesquit-covered plain, over which the eye ranges for great lonely distances without detecting any traces of the occupancy of man. No gardens, pastures, scattered houses, or the like are there to break the sudden transition: it is the city, then the plain; it is home cheek by jowl with desert. Inside, the location of the city is no less picturesque. Two streams, the San Antonio and San Pedro rivers, run in a direction generally parallel, though specially as far from parallelism as capricious crookedness can make itself, through the entire town. The San Antonio is about sixty feet wide; its water is usually of a lovely milky-green. The stranger strolling on a mild sunny day through the streets often finds himself suddenly on a bridge, and is half startled with the winding vista of sweet lawns running down to the water, of weeping-willows kissing its surface, of summer-houses on its banks, and of the swift yet smooth-shining stream meandering this way and that, actually combing the long sea-green locks of a trailing water-grass which sends its waving tresses down the centre of the current for hundreds of feet, and murmuring the while with a palpable Spanish lisping which floats up among the rude noises of traffic along the rock-paved street, as it were some dove-voiced Spanish nun out of the convent yonder, praying heaven's mitigation of the wild battle of trade. Leaving this bridge, walking down the main (Commerce) street, across the Main Plaza, then past the San Fernando Cathedral, then across the Military Plaza, one comes presently to the San Pedro, a small stream ten or fifteen feet in width, up which the gazing stroller finds no romance but mostly strict use; for there squat the Mexican women on their haunches, by their flat stones, washing the family garments, in a position the very recollection of which gives one simultaneous stitches of lumbago and sciatica, yet which they appear to maintain for hours without detriment. If it had been summer-time we would most likely have seen, before we left the bridge over the San Antonio, the black-locked heads of these same ladies bobbing up and down the surface of the river; for they love to lave themselves in this tepid water, these sleek, plump, black-eyed, olive-cheeked *Mexicanas*.

Crossing the San Pedro we are among the *jacals*. Here is surely the very first step Architecture made when she came out of the cave. A row of stakes is driven into the ground, in and out between these mesquit-twigs are wattled, a roof of twigs and straw is fastened on somehow, anyhow, and there you are. Not only you, but your family of astonishing numbers are there, all huddled into this kennel whose door has to be crawled into. Of course typhus-fevers and small-pox are to be found among such layers of humanity. People are not sardines.

Now we come to a step in advance in the matter of houses. A row of stakes is put down, this is enclosed by another row, leaving a space between of about a foot's width, which is filled in with stones and mud, a thatched roof of straw is then put on, and the house is complete. Still more pretentious dwellings are built of *adobes,* or sun-dried brick. The majority of the substantial houses of the town are constructed of a whitish limestone, so soft when first quarried that it can be cut with a knife, but quickly hardening by exposure into a very durable building material. The prevailing style of dwelling houses is low, windows are few and balconies scarce, though in the more pretentious two-storied dwellings there are some very good Moorish effects of projecting stone and lattice-work.

By far the finest and largest architectural example in the town is the San Fernando Cathedral, which presents a broad, varied, and imposing façade upon the western side of the Main Plaza. Entering this building, one's pleasure in its exterior gives way to curious surprise; for one finds inside the old stone church built here more than a century ago, standing, a church within a church, almost untouched save that parts of some projecting pediments have been knocked away by the builders. In this inner church services are still regularly held, the outer one not being yet quite completed. The curious dome, surrounded by a high wall over which its topmost slit-windows just peer—an evident relic of ancient Moorish architecture, which one finds in the rear of most of the old Spanish religious edifices in Texas—has been preserved, and still adjoins the queer priests' dormitories, which constitute the rear end of the cathedral building.

There are other notable religious edifices in town. Going back to Commerce Street, one can see a fine large church just being completed for the German Catholics (San Fernando Cathedral is Mexican Catholic). Crossing a graceful iron foot-bridge, down an alley that turns off to the north from Commerce Street, one glances up and down the stream, which here flows between heavy and costly abutments of stone to protect the rear of the large stores whose fronts are on the Main

Street, and whose rear doors open almost immediately over the water. Across the bridge the alley widens into a street, and here in this odd nook of the stream is St. Mary's, the American Catholic Church, its rear adjoining a long three-storied stone convent building, and its yard sloping down to the water. Strolling up the river a quarter of a mile, one comes upon a long white stone building which has evidently had much trouble to accommodate itself to the site upon which it is built, and whose line is broken into four or five abrupt angles, while its roof is varied with dormer-windows and sharp projections and spires and quaint clock-faces, and its rear is mysterious with lattice-covered balconies and half-hidden corners and corridors. This is the Ursuline Convent; and standing as it does on a rocky and steep (steep for Texas plains) bank of the river, whose course its broken line follows, and down to which its long stern-looking wall descends, it is an edifice at once piquant and sombre, and one cannot resist figuring Mr. James' horseman * spurring his charger up the white limestone road that winds alongside the wall, in the early twilight, when dreams come whispering down the current among the willow-sprays.

There are notable places about the town which the stranger must visit. He may ride two miles along a level road between market gardens which are vitalized by a long *acequia,* or ditch, fed from the river, and come presently upon the quaint gray towers of the old Mission Concepcion [1] whose early location has been incidentally mentioned in the foregoing history. The old church, with its high-walled dome in the rear, is in a good state of preservation, and traces of the singular many-colored frescoing on its front are still plainly visible. Climbing a very shaky ladder, one gets upon the roof of a long stone corridor running off from the church building, and, taking good heed of the sharp-thorned cactus which abounds up there, looks over upon a quaint complication of wall-angles, nooks, and small-windowed rooms. The place ceased to be used for religious purposes some years ago, and is now occupied by a German with his family, his Mexican laborers, and his farm

* [A rider under the conditions described here was one of G. P. R. James' most frequently recurring characters. Lanier was probably familiar with Thackeray's parody " Barbazure," in *Novels by Eminent Hands.*—ED.]

[1] The Mission of Our Lady of the Concepcion de Acuña.

animals. This German tills the fertile mission lands. Heaven send him better luck with his crops than he had with his English!

Further down the river a couple of miles one comes to the Mission San José de Aguayo. This is more elaborate and on a larger scale than the buildings of the first Mission, and is still very beautiful. Religious services are regularly conducted here; and one can do worse things than to steal out here from town on some wonderfully calm Sunday morning, and hear a mass, and dream back the century and a half of strange, lonesome, devout, hymn-haunted and Indian-haunted years that have trailed past these walls. Five or six miles further down the river are the ruins of the Mission San Juan, in much dilapidation.

Or the visitor may stroll off to the eastward, climb the hill, wander about among the graves of heroes in the large cemetery on the crest of the ridge, and please himself with the noble reaches of country east and west and with the perfect view of the city, which from here seems " sown," like Tennyson's, " in a monstrous wrinkle of the " prairie.* Or, being in search of lions, one may see the actual animal by a stroll to the " San Pedro Springs Park," a mile or so to the northward. Here, from under a white-ledged rocky hill, burst forth three crystalline springs, which quickly unite and form the San Pedro. Herr Dürler, in charge, has taken admirable advantage of the ground, and what with spreading water-oaks, rustic pleasure buildings, promenades along smooth shaded avenues between concentric artificial lakes, a race-course, an aviary, a fine Mexican lion whom burly Herr Dürler scratches on the head, but who does not seem to appreciate similar advances from other persons, a bear-pit in which are an emerald-eyed blind cinnamon-bear, a large black bear, a wolf and a *coyote,* and other attractions, this is a very green spot indeed in the waste prairies. Or one may drive five miles to northward and see the romantic spot where the San Antonio River is forever being born, leaping forth from the mountain, complete, *totus,* even as Minerva from the head of Jove. Or one may take one's stand on the Commerce Street bridge and involve oneself in the life that

* [Quoted, inaccurately, from Tennyson, " Will."—ED.]

goes by this way and that. Yonder comes a long train of enormous blue-bodied, canvas-covered wagons, built high and square in the stern, much like a fleet of Dutch galleons, and lumbering in a ponderous way that suggests cargoes of silver and gold. These are drawn by fourteen mules each, who are harnessed in four tiers, the three front tiers of four mules each, and that next to the wagon of two. The " lead " mules are wee fellows, veritable mulekins; the next tier larger, and so on to the two wheel-mules, who are always as large as can be procured. Yonder fares slowly another train of wagons, drawn by great wide-horned oxen, whose evident tendency to run to hump and fore-shoulder irresistibly persuades one of their cousinship to the buffalo.

Here, now, comes somewhat that shows as if Birnam Wood had been cut into fagots and was advancing with tipsy swagger upon Dunsinane.* Presently one's gazing eye receives a sensation of hair, then of enormous ears, and then the legs appear, of the little roan-gray *bourras,* or asses, upon whose backs that Mexican walking behind has managed to pile a mass of mesquit firewood that is simply astonishing. This mesquit is a species of acacia, whose roots and body form the principal fuel here. It yields, by exudation, a gum which is quite equal to gum arabic, when the tannin in it is extracted. It appears to have spread over this portion of Texas within the last twenty-five years, perhaps less time. The old settlers account for its appearance by the theory that the Indians—and after them the stock-raisers—were formerly in the habit of burning off the prairie-grass annually, and that these great fires rendered it impossible for the mesquit shrub to obtain a foothold; but that now the departure of the Indians, and the transfer of most of the large cattle-raising business to points further westward, have resulted in leaving the soil free for the occupation of the mesquit. It has certainly taken advantage of the opportunity. It covers the prairie thickly, in many directions, as far as the eye can reach, growing to a pretty uniform height of four or five feet—though occasionally much larger—and presenting, with its tough branches and innumerable formidable thorns, a singular appearance. The wood when dry is exceedingly hard

* [The allusion is to Shakespeare, *Macbeth.*—ED.]

and durable, and of a rich walnut color. This recent over-spread of foliage on the plains is supposed by many persons to be the cause of the quite remarkable increase of moisture in the climate of San Antonio which has been observed of late years. The phenomena—of the coincident increase of moisture and of mesquit—are unquestionable; but whether they bear the relation of cause and effect, is a question upon which the unscientific lingerers on this bridge may be permitted to hold themselves in reserve.*

But while we are discussing the mesquit, do but notice yonder Mexican in gorgeous array, promenading, intent upon instant subjugation of all his countrywomen in eye-shot! His black trowsers with silver buttons down the seams; his jaunty hussar-jacket; his six-inch brimmed felt *sombrero,* with marvellous silver filigree upon all available spaces of it, save those occupied by the hat-band, which is like two silver snakes tied parallel round the crown; his red sash, serving at once to support the trowsers and to inflate the full white shirt-bosom—what *Mexicana* can resist these things? And—if it happen to be Sunday afternoon—yonder comes the German *Turnverein,* marching in from the San Pedro Springs Park, where they have been twisting themselves among the bars, and playing leap-frog and other honest games what time they emptied a cask of beer. Walking too, as tired men will walk, one sees sundry sportsmen returning from the prairies, where they have been popping away at quail and donkey-rabbits all this blessed Sunday. In especial notice that old German walking lustily in the middle of the street. He has a rusty gun on his shoulder; his game-bag is bloody and full; his long white beard and white moustache float about a face determined, strong, yet jovial. It is Rip Van Winkle in person. " But where is Schneider? " said one, the day we saw this man—" what a pity he hasn't Schneider with him! " " By Jove, there *is* Schneider! " in a moment cried another of the party; and veritably there he was. He came dashing round the corner, and ran and trotted behind his grizzled master, bearing an enormous donkey-rabbit tied by its legs around his neck.

---

* [For a similar account of the mesquit see Lanier's " Letters from Texas," pp. 192, 193, above.—ED.]

And now as we leave the bridge in the gathering twilight and loiter down the street, we pass all manner of odd personages and " characters." Here hobbles an old Mexican who looks like old Father Time in reduced circumstances, his feet, his body, his head all swathed in rags, his face a blur of wrinkles, his beard gray-grizzled—a picture of eld such as one will rarely find. There goes a little German boy who was captured a year or two ago by Indians within three miles of San Antonio, and has just been retaken and sent home a few days ago. Do you see that poor Mexican without any hands? A few months ago a wagon-train was captured by Indians at Howard's Wells; the teamsters, of whom he was one, were tied to the wagons and these set on fire, and this poor fellow was released by the flames burning off his hands, the rest all perishing save two. Here is a great Indian-fighter who will show you what he calls his " vouchers," being scalps of the red braves he has slain; there is a gentleman who blew up his store here in '42 to keep the incoming Mexicans from benefiting by his goods, and who afterwards spent a weary imprisonment in that stern castle of Perote away down in Mexico, where the Mier prisoners (and who ever thinks now-a-days of that strange, bloody Mier Expedition?) were confined; there a portly, handsome, buccaneer-looking captain who led the Texans against Cortina in '59; there a small, intelligent-looking gentleman * who at twenty was first Secretary of War of the young Texan Republic, and who is said to know the history of everything that has been done in Texas from that time to this minutely; and so on through a perfect gauntlet of people who have odd histories, odd natures, or odd appearances, we reach our hotel. It is time, for the dogs—there are far more dogs here than in Constantinople—have begun to howl, and night has closed in upon San Antonio de Bexar.

* [This was most likely Henry P. Brewster (1816-1884), who fits Lanier's description in every detail except one—he was the third, not the first, Secretary of War of the Republic of Texas, the first (Thomas J. Rusk, 1802-1856) and the second (Mirabeau Lamar, 1798-1859) having resigned. Brewster was appointed in August, 1836, when he was twenty. He practiced law in San Antonio from 1866 to 1883. The year of his death, on account of his reputation for knowledge of Texas men and events, he was appointed Commissioner of Insurance, Statistics, and History.—Ed.]

PEACE *

MY SON is two years, one month and five days old. My nephew is older; he is two years, one month and six days of age.

This disparity is a source of prodigious consolation to my wife. Whenever the multitudinous events of each day (for with these two young men the plot of life already begins to thicken) reveal particulars in which Eddy, our nephew, is indisputably superior to Charley, our son, my wife accounts for this superiority with entire motherly satisfaction, by remarking that of course Eddy ought to know, or to be or to do, as the case may be, more than Charley, because he is older.

I was just going into my study yesterday to resume work upon my great essay entitled *Peace*. In this essay I was demonstrating that it was very wrong indeed to make war; and I will not conceal the satisfaction with which I was reflecting that if Prince Bismarck (*e. g.*) should become convinced that it *is* wrong to make war, he would never again send his armies into the sweet fields of France. Nor will I deny certain secret yet benign hopes regarding the effect of my essay in tranquillising the disposition of Spotted Tail.**

" My love," says my wife, as I was going into my study as aforesaid, " Charley's nurse is sick to-day and can't mind him. He'll be obliged to stay in the house, and I don't see how you'll ever write."

" More by token," says my sister, " Eddy's nurse has gone to see her mother, and he'll have to stay in; so you might as well give it up."

" Pooh, pooh! " said I. " Give 'em to *me*; I'll take 'em with

* [Written on Oct. 17, 1870, the day when his second son Sidney Lanier, Jr., was born. (Date arrived at from the evidence of the opening sentence, which refers to his oldest son, Charles, born on Sept. 12, 1868.) Published in the *Southern Magazine*, XV, 406-410 (Oct., 1874), the text here followed. Not subsequently reprinted. No MS is known to exist.—ED.]

** [Lanier probably had in mind Tiger-Tail, a Seminole chief whose exploits against the whites furnished some of the most dramatic episodes in the Indian wars. See John Lee Williams, *The Territory of Florida* (N. Y., 1837).—ED.]

me. I'll write in the bosom of my family, like Jean Paul among
the pots and kettles in the kitchen.* Do you remember Jean
Paul, my dear, writing his immortal works among the pots and
kettles—Fight? Scratch? Squall? Oh no, *my* boys won't
fight; nor scratch, nor squall either. It's all a mistake. Nothing
surprises me more," I continued, warming with my subject,
" than the ignorance of mothers upon this point. A child will
not fight, if properly managed. I tell you it's abnormal—to
fight. Just keep the child entertained; that's all. The child
doesn't *want* to fight. He does it reluctantly always. He fights
under protest invariably. No child will fight his playmate
unless he's driven to it. The childish soul is loving, it is confid-
ing; it is a tendril, it desires to twine around necks; opposition
and combat are alien to it. War," I continued, insensibly gliding into my essay, " war is *not* the natural condition of man.
That is a libel on the race. Love and hunger—which indeed
are two words for the same thing in different phases, love being
the soul's hunger, and hunger the body's love—these are the
natural operations of the normal man, spiritual and bodily, and
not war. Dash the philosophers who have declared battle to
be the earliest occupation of man! I will confound these
slanderers! "

" Well," says my wife, with a curious expression in her gray
eyes.

" Well," says my sister, with a very curious twinkle in her
blue ones. " Go along, children, with him, and let him write
in the bosom of his family."

I marched, with my two innocents trotting on either hand,
to my study. I was in a fine glow of enthusiasm for the cause
of peace and harmony. I was ablaze with philosophy, which
I proposed to put into practical operation. My deep design
was this. I am a keen observer. I have observed that it is utterly
futile to attempt to entertain a boy-child with anything with
which he cannot hurt himself and make himself cry; and my
selection of articles for the amusement of my two charges was
made wholly with a view to this somewhat paradoxical principle in the young male nature. I set my son down carefully

---

* [Lanier's immediate source was probably Thomas Carlyle's essay, " Jean
Paul Frederich Richter."—Ed.]

on the floor in one corner of the apartment, and furnished him with the following articles, to-wit:—

One bear, tin, with a very sharp-edged tail, with which he could scratch his finger and make himself cry;

One turkey, tin, mounted on a spiral spring, which when agitated gave a very life-like imitation of pecking, and with which, by pecking it in his eye—which he always did—he could always make himself cry;

One box, containing a farm-house and barn-yard, together with all the cattle, fowls, laborers, rights, members and appurtenances thereunto belonging or in anywise appertaining, the same being painted in divers strong colors, which he could always suck, and by reason of the diabolical taste thereof so make himself cry;

One large chair, to sit under and get his head between the rounds, and make himself cry;

One small ditto to fall over or out of, as he should see proper, and make himself cry;

One silk hat, of which he is always careful, not sitting on it very hard, nor putting anything in it except small billets of wood—either of which is good, as he invariably sits down too suddenly or mashes his finger with the wood, and so makes himself cry;

One pair of tongs, to tweak his own nose with, of which he is very fond, and make himself cry;

One box, to hold his left leg when he plays circus, or to hurt his head against, as he should see proper, and make himself cry;

One pillow, for him to kick, which I laid beside him with some hesitation, fearing that it would not suit him, inasmuch as he could not well hurt his shins against it and make himself cry;

One knife, to compensate for the pillow, since he could easily cut his finger with it and make himself cry;

One wire mouse-trap, with which he could always catch his finger and make himself cry.

To these I added a promiscuous assortment of articles, with which he could hurt himself in any miscellaneous way he should see proper, including his whistle, against which he always bites his tongue when he blows it, and makes himself cry; and his dear little wicker-chair with one bent leg, which always tumbles him over on the back of his head when he wishes to make himself cry.

I deposited my nephew in the opposite corner of the apartment, and seated him in the midst of a collection of articles not differing widely from those which I had furnished my son. I designed to illustrate the progress of civilization. I said to myself: " Presently each will grow tired of solitary amusement, however many resources he may have for making himself cry. Then the gregarious instinct will assert itself, as in the youth of humanity, and they will rise from their corners and go toward each other. This will represent the lonesome Aborigine seeking society. Then they will meet, and the commercial instinct will assert itself. Each will recognize the right of property which the other has in his toys, and this will lead to a proposition for amicable exchange. The manifest advantage of exchange, in which each acquires something he did not have before, will quickly lead to the idea of a partnership, in which each shall have a joint interest in all the other has. So I shall behold harmony, mutual accord and peace—both of them, for instance, drawing the same chair into the fire, &c.—which will finally result in their sitting in the same corner, i. e. building a city, &c. So we will have reached the age of civilization from the age of solitary barbarism."

Pleased with these thoughts, I addressed myself to my essay, keeping one eye upon the two young persons.

Whilst, therefore, my right eye occupied itself in superintending my powerful demonstration in behalf of peace, my left eye saw that my son instantly cut his finger with his knife, and as I had foreseen, made himself cry. He then rubbed his cut finger in a persistent manner into his eye, and smeared his eye with blood, which made him cry very satisfactorily indeed. He received considerable aid through the operation of a certain phenomenon, which, as I am a stern realist in matters of description, I will not omit: I mean the physiological effect of tears upon the nose of childhood. This physiological effect mingled with the blood and tears, and the three being vigorously triturated together into his eye, which he did not cease to rub with his cut finger, made him cry in a manner which was, I may say, truly gratifying.

Success so far had crowned my efforts, and I watched with great anxiety for the moment when the reign of civilization should commence, *i. e.* when the gregarious instinct and the intuitive respect for property should bring them together, and lead to amicable exchanges and partnerships. Nor did I have long to wait. Eddy, seeing that Charley was quite blinded in one eye by reason of the fourfold fact that he now had a large quantity of blood, of tears, of physiological effect and of finger in the eye aforesaid, arose from his corner, and approached Charley in a somewhat sidelong manner, surprisingly like the manner in which Mr. Mike McCoole is said to approach his antagonist when Mr. McC. enters the ring for a sparring-match.*

Having arrived within, I shall say, about one foot of Charley, Eddy paused.

" You old debble! " says Charley.

Now this, I will confess, gave me some surprise, and I read-justed my spectacles. For with all the pious and continued efforts of his mother and myself, we have never yet been able to instill any very clear religious ideas into his mind; yet his conception of the devil—a conception obtained, as well as the word itself, from some source wholly unknown to me—seemed quite distinct and well-defined.

" Gim my knife! " shouts Eddy, in a very peremptory manner indeed. And this, I further confess, surprised me still more. For Eddy actually dropped his own knife, which I had furnished him, out of his hands while he uttered the words; and why he should have wished to take by force a piece of property which did not belong to him, and which he could not possibly need, inasmuch as he already had one too many by his own showing— for, as I said, he dropped his own knife—is a question which I have postponed, to occupy my next summer's vacation.

Immediately subsequent to Eddy's peremptory demand, the following circumstances occurred in the order in which I mention them:

* [Mike McCoole (1837-1886), known as the Deck Hand Fistic Champion of America, held the bare-knuckle title, 1866-1869. His bout with Joe Coburn lasted sixty-seven rounds.—ED.]

1. Eddy makes a savage grab for Charley's knife.

2. Charley parries; and, in so doing, wipes his hand, tears, blood and all down the profile of Eddy's face, producing the appearance to me, who had a front view, of having suddenly divided the face aforesaid into two equal sections with a cleaver.

3. Eddy with his left hand makes a kind of reconnaissance of Charley's face, which terminates with the following position of the hand aforesaid, to-wit: the little finger of it lodges in Charley's mouth, where it is instantly seized by Charley's teeth, and held *in status quo*; the third finger rests firmly, nail downward upon Charley's cheek, the second finger presses threateningly upon the angle of Charley's eye, and the first finger and thumb clamp Charley's nose with wonderful tenacity.

4. Charley extends the hand with the knife in it at arm's length upward in avoidance of—

5. A very vigorous and well-planned, but unsuccessful lunge by Eddy in that direction.

6. A short pause, in the nature of an armistice on the basis of the *status quo,* succeeds. But the *status quo* is exceedingly oppressive upon Eddy, and he therefore breaks the brief truce and commences a lively series of skirmishes for the knife, which Charley causes to gyrate rapidly, at the same time making a combined movement of the left hand, involving a severe tug with the thumb and forefinger on Charley's nose, and a simultaneous desperate twist of the other fingers with a view to relieve the existing digital beleaguerment.

7. Which energetic strategy has at least the effect of producing serious apprehensions of the loss of his knife in Charley's mind, and he therefore drops it to the floor, and instantly covers the movement with his rear, *i. e.* sits down on the knife.

8. Not, however, before Eddy, who is very agile in his movements, has made an aquatic dive between Charley's legs after the knife, so that the situation now presents the spectacle of a small boy a-straddle of the neck of another small boy, and by no means confident in the security of that position.

9. This want of confidence in the security of his position instantly displays the soundness of the judgment upon which

it is founded; for Eddy, elevating the posterior portion of his anatomy to a surprising height, throws up his heels with such *élan* that the most prodigious consequences ensue.

10. One of the most important of which is a curious example of poetic retribution, in the fact that Eddy's right heel deals a furious avenging blow upon those very teeth of Charley's which had just been grinding Eddy's left little finger, whereby Charley is knocked backward as if from a catapult, and—

11. The grand denouement ensues, to-wit: the back of Charley's head strikes with tremendous impact against the legs of my writing-table and overturns it, my large inkstand falls off, lodges on Eddy's temple and quietly empties itself into his ear, which gets full and overflows into Charley's other eye, and thence over the scattered sheets of my essay on the floor. Eddy inserts his hand in Charley's hair, pulls the same, and yells as Charley inserts *his* hand into Eddy's hair and pulls the same and yells; at which instant my wife and my sister, attracted by the noise, appear together at the door, and I observe a curious expression in the gray eyes of the former, which is apparently answered by a singular twinkle in the blue eyes of the latter, what time both with uplifted hands exclaim: " Do look at his poor Essay on Peace! "

SKETCHES OF INDIA *

I

"Come," says my Hindu friend, "let us do Bombay."

THE NAME of my Hindu friend is Bhima Gandharva. At the same time his name is *not* Bhima Gandharva. But— for what is life worth if one may not have one's little riddle?— in respect that he is *not* so named let him be so called, for thus will a pretty contradiction be accomplished, thus shall I secure at once his privacy and his publicity, and reveal and conceal him in a breath.

It is eight o'clock in the morning. We have met—Bhima Gandharva and I—in "The Fort." The Fort is to Bombay much as the Levee, with its adjacent quarters, is to New Orleans; only it is—one may say *Hibernice*—a great deal more so. It is on the inner or harbor side of the island of Bombay. Instead of the low-banked Mississippi, the waters of a tranquil and charming haven smile welcome out yonder from between wooded island-peaks. Here Bombay has its counting-houses, its warehouses, its exchange, its "Cotton Green," its docks. But not its dwellings. This part of the Fort where we have met is, one may say, only inhabited for six hours in the day— from ten in the morning until four in the afternoon. At the former hour Bombay is to be found here engaged at trade; at the latter it rushes back into the various quarters outside the Fort which go to make up this many-citied city. So that at this particular hour of eight in the morning one must expect to

* [Written during the fall of 1875, and published anonymously, with illustrations, in *Lippincott's Magazine*, XVII, 37-51, 172-183, 283-301, 409-427 (Jan.-Apr., 1876), the text here followed (except that the use of italics for foreign words has been regularized); reprinted, with slight changes, in *Retrospects and Prospects* (New York, 1899), 136-228. No manuscript is known to exist. Lanier explained to Gibson Peacock in a letter of Dec. 16, 1875: " Bhima Gandharva (*Bhima* was the name of the ancient Sanscrit hero, *The Son of the Air*, and *Gandharva* means *a heavenly musician*) is only another name for Imagination— which is certainly the only Hindu friend I have." Lanier never visited India.—ED.]

find little here that is alive, except either a philosopher, a stranger, a policeman, or a rat.

" Well, then," I said as Bhima Gandharva finished communicating this information to me, " we are all here."

" How? "

" There stand you, a philosopher; here I, a stranger; yonder, the policeman; and, heavens and earth! what a rat! " I accompanied this exclamation by shooing a big musky fellow from behind a bale of cotton whither I had just seen him run.

Bhima Gandharva smiled in a large, tranquil way he has, which is like an Indian plain full of ripe corn. " I find it curious," he said, " to compare the process which goes on here in the daily humdrum of trade about this place with that which one would see if one were far up yonder at the northward, in the appalling solitudes of the mountains, where trade has never been and will never be. Have you visited the Himalaya? "

I shook my head.

" Among those prodigious planes of snow," continued the Hindu, " which when level nevertheless frighten you as if they were horizontal precipices, and which when perpendicular nevertheless lull you with a smooth deadly half-sense of confusion as to whether you should refer your ideas of space to the slope or the plain, there reigns at this moment a quietude more profound than the Fort's. But presently, as the sun beats with more fervor, rivulets begin to trickle from exposed points; these grow to cataracts and roar down the precipices; masses of undermined snow plunge into the abysses; the great winds of the Himalaya rise and howl, and every silence of the morning becomes a noise at noon. A little longer, and the sun again decreases; the cataracts draw their heads back into the ice as tortoises into their shells; the winds creep into their hollows, and the snows rest. So here. At ten the tumult of trade will begin; at four it will quickly freeze again into stillness. One might even carry this parallelism into more fanciful extremes. For, as the vapors which lie on the Himalaya in the form of snow have in time come from all parts of the earth, so the tide of men that will presently pour in here is made up of people from the four quarters of the globe. The Hindu, the African, the Arabian, the Chinese, the Tartar, the European, the American, the Parsee, will in a little while be trading or working here."

"What a complete *bouleversement*," I said, seating myself on a bale of cotton and looking toward the fleets of steamers and vessels collected off the great cotton-presses awaiting their cargoes, " this particular scene effects in the mind of a traveller just from America! India has been to me, as to the average American, a dream of terraced *ghâts*, of banyans and bunga-lows, of Taj Mahals and tigers, of sacred rivers and subter-ranean temples, and—and that sort of thing. I come here and land in a big cotton-yard. I ask myself, ' Have I left Jonesville —dear Jonesville!—on the other side of the world in order to sit on an antipodal cotton-bale? ' "

"There is some more of India," said Bhima Gandharva, gently. " Let us look at it a little."

One may construct a good-enough outline map of this won-derful land in one's mind by referring its main features to the first letter of the alphabet. Take a capital A ; turn it up side down, ∀ ; imagine that the inverted triangle forming the lower half of the letter is the Deccan, the left side representing the Western *Ghâts*, the right side representing the Eastern *Ghâts*, and the cross-stroke standing for the Vindhya Moun-tains; imagine further that a line from right to left across the upper ends of the letter, trending upward as it is drawn, repre-sents the Himalaya, and that enclosed between them and the Vindhyas is Hindustan proper. Behind—*i. e.* to the north of— the centre of this last line rises the Indus, flowing first north-westward through the Vale of Cashmere, then cutting sharply to the south and flowing by the way of the Punjab and Scinde to where it empties at Kurrachee. Near the same spot where the Indus originates rises also the Brahmaputra, but the latter empties its waters far from the former, flowing first southeast-ward, then cutting southward and emptying into the Gulf of Bengal. Fixing, now, in the mind the sacred Ganges and Jumna, coming down out of the Gangetic and Jumnatic peaks in a general southeasterly direction, uniting at Allahabad and emptying into the Bay of Bengal, and the Nerbudda River flow-ing over from the east to the west, along the southern bases of the Vindhyas, until it empties at the important city of

Brooch, a short distance north of Bombay, one will have thus located a number of convenient points and lines sufficient for general references.

This **A** of ours is a very capital A indeed, being some nineteen hundred miles in length and fifteen hundred in width. Lying on the western edge of this peninsula is Bombay Island. It is crossed by the line of 19° north latitude, and is, roughly speaking, halfway between the Punjab on the north and Ceylon on the south. Its shape is that of a lobster, with his claws extended southward and his body trending a little to the west of north. The larger island of Salsette lies immediately north, and the two, connected by a causeway, enclose the noble harbor of Bombay. Salsette approaches near to the mainland at its northern end, and is connected with it by the railway structure. These causeways act as breakwaters, and complete the protection of the port. The outer claw, next to the Indian Ocean, of the lobster-shaped Bombay Island is the famous Malabar Hill; the inner claw is the promontory of Calaba; in the curved space between the two is the body of shallow water known as the Back Bay, along whose strand so many strange things are done daily. As one turns into the harbor around the promontory of Calaba—which is one of the European quarters of the manifold city of Bombay, and is occupied by magnificent residences and flower-gardens—one finds just north of it the great docks and commercial establishments of the Fort; then an enormous esplanade farther north; across which, a distance of about a mile, going still northward, is the great Indian city called Black Town, with its motley peoples and strange bazars; and still farther north is the Portuguese quarter, known as Mazagon.

As we crossed the great esplanade to the north of the Fort—Bhima Gandharva and I—and strolled along the noisy streets, I began to withdraw my complaint. It was not like Jonesville. It was not like any one place or thing, but like a hundred, and all the hundred *outré* to the last degree. Hindu beggars, so dirty that they seemed to have returned to dust before death; three fakirs, armed with round-bladed daggers with which they were wounding themselves apparently in the most reckless manner, so as to send streams of blood flowing to the ground, and redly tattooing the ashes with which their naked bodies were covered; Parsees with their long noses curving over their moustaches, clothed in white, sending one's thoughts back to Ormuz, to Persia, to Zoroaster, to fire-worship and to the strangeness of the fate which drove them out of Persia more than a thousand years ago, and which has turned them into the most industrious traders and most influential citizens of a land in which they are still exiles; Chinese, Afghans—the Highlanders of the East—Arabs, Africans, Bahrattas, Malays, Persians, Portuguese half-bloods; men that called upon Mohammed, men that called upon Confucius, upon Krishna, upon Christ, upon Gotama the Buddha, upon Rama and Sita, upon Brahma, upon Zoroaster; strange carriages shaded by red domes that compressed a whole dream of the East in small, and drawn by humped oxen, alternating with palanquins, with stylish turnouts of the latest mode, with cavaliers upon Arabian horses; half-naked workmen, crouched in uncomfortable workshops and ornamenting sandal-wood boxes; dusky curb-stone shopkeepers, rushing at me with strenuous offerings of their wares; lines of low shop-counters along the street, backed by houses rising in many stories, whose black-pillared verandahs were curiously carved and painted; cries, chafferings, bickerings, Mussulman prayers, Arab oaths extending from " Praise God that you exist " to " Praise God *although* you exist; "—all these things appealed to the confused senses.

The tall spire of a Hindu temple revealed itself.

" It seems to me," I said to Bhima Gandharva, " that your steeples—as we would call them in Jonesville—represent, in a sort of way, your cardinal doctrine: they seem to be composed of a multitude of little steeples, all like the big one, just as you might figure your Supreme Being in the act of absorbing a large number of the faithful who had just arrived from the dismal existence below. And then, again, your steeple looks as if it might be the central figure of your theistic scheme, surrounded by the three hundred millions of your lesser deities. How do you get on, Bhima Gandharva, with so many claims on your worshipping faculties? I should think you would be well lost in such a jungle of gods."

" My friend," said Bhima Gandharva, " a short time ago a

play was performed in this city which purported to be a translation into the Mahratta language of the *Romeo and Juliet*
which Shakspere wrote.* It was indeed a very great departure
from that miraculous work, which I know well, but among its
many deviations from the original was one which for the
mournful and yet humorous truth of it was really worthy of the
Master. Somehow, the translator had managed to get a modern Englishman into the play, who, every time that one of my
countrymen happened to be found in leg-reach, would give him
a lusty kick and cry out, ' Damn fool! ' Why is the whole
world like this Englishman?—upon what does it found its
opinion that the Hindu is a fool? Is it upon our religion?
Listen! I will recite you some matters out of our scriptures: **
Once upon a time Arjuna stood in his chariot betwixt his army
and the army of his foes. These foes were his kinsmen. Krishna
—even that great god Krishna—moved by pity for Arjuna, had
voluntarily placed himself in Arjuna's chariot and made himself the charioteer thereof. Then—so saith Sanjaya—in order
to encourage him, the ardent old ancestor of the Kurus blew
his conch-shell, sounding loud as the roar of a lion. Then on
a sudden trumpets, cymbals, drums, and horns were sounded.
That noise grew to an uproar. And, standing on a huge car
drawn by white horses, the slayer of Madhu and the son of
Pandu blew their celestial trumpets. Krishna blew his horn
called Panchajanya; the Despiser of Wealth blew his horn
called the Gift of the Gods; he of dreadful deeds and wolfish
entrails blew a great trumpet called Paundra; King Yudish-
thira, the son of Kunti, blew the Eternal Victory; Nakula and
Sahadeva blew the Sweet-toned and the Blooming-with-Jewels.
The King of Kashi, renowned for the excellence of his bow,
and Shikandin in his huge chariot, Dhrishtyadumna, and
Virata, and Satyaki, unconquered by his foes, and Drupada and

---

* [The anecdote that follows is told by Charles W. Dilke, *Greater Britain*,
undoubtedly Lanier's source.—ED.]
** [Lanier is paraphrasing from the *Bhagavad-Gita*, a metrical dialogue in
which the divine Krishna expounds to the human being, Arjuna, certain philosophical doctrines; the poem is interpolated in the *Mahabharata*, an Indian epic.
Lanier seems to be using Charlotte Speir [Manning] (1807-1871), *Life in
Ancient India* and Samuel Johnson (1822-1882), *Oriental Religions* as second-
ary sources. The editorial omissions and brackets in the following quoted
passages are Lanier's.—ED.]

the sons of Drupadi all together, and the strong-armed son of
Subhadrá, each severally blew their trumpets. That noise lacer-
ated the hearts of the sons of Dhartarashtra, and uproar re-
sounded both through heaven and earth. Now when Arjuna
beheld the Dhartarashtras drawn up, and that the flying of
arrows had commenced, he raised his bow, and then addressed
these words to Krishna:

"Now that I have beheld this kindred standing here near together
for the purpose of fighting, my limbs give way and my face is blood-
less, and tremor is produced throughout my body, and my hair stands
on end. My bow Gandiva slips from my hand, and my skin burns.
Nor am I able to remain upright, and my mind is as it were whirling
round. Nor do I perceive anything better even when I shall have slain
these relations in battle. I seek not victory, Krishna, nor a kingdom,
nor pleasures. What should we do with a kingdom, Govinda? What
with enjoyments, or with life itself? Those very men on whose
account we might desire a kingdom, enjoyments, or pleasures are
assembled for battle. Teachers, fathers, and even sons, and grand-
fathers, uncles, fathers-in-law, grandsons, brothers-in-law, with connections also,—these I would not wish to slay, though I were slain
myself, O Killer of Madhu! not even for the sake of the sovereignty
of the triple world—how much less for that of this earth! When we
had killed the Dhartarashtras, what pleasure should we have, O thou
who art prayed to by mortals? How could we be happy after killing
our own kindred, O Slayer of Madhu? Even if they whose reason is
obscured by covetousness do not perceive the crime committed in
destroying their own tribe, should we not know how to recoil from
such a sin? In the destruction of a tribe the eternal institutions of
the tribe are destroyed. These laws being destroyed, lawlessness prevails. From the existence of lawlessness the women of the tribe become corrupted; and when the women are corrupted, O son of Vrishni!
confusion of caste takes place. Confusion of caste is a gate to hell.
Alas! we have determined to commit a great crime, since from the
desire of sovereignty and pleasures we are prepared to slay our own
kin. Better were it for me if the Dhartarashtras, being armed, would
slay me, harmless and unresisting in the fight.

"Having thus spoken in the midst of the battle, Arjuna,
whose heart was troubled with grief, let fall his bow and arrow
and sat down on the bench of the chariot."

"Well," I asked after a short pause, during which the Hindu
kept his eyes fixed in contemplation on the spire of the temple,
"what did Krishna have to say to that?"

" He instructed Arjuna, and said many wise things. I will tell you some of them, here and there, as they are scattered through the holy *Bhagavad-Gítá*: Then between the two armies, Krishna, smiling, addressed these words to him, thus downcast:

" Thou hast grieved for those who need not be grieved for, yet thou utterest words of wisdom. The wise grieve not for dead or living. But never at any period did I or thou or these kings of men not exist, nor shall any of us at any time henceforward cease to exist. There is no existence for what does not exist, nor is there any non-existence for what exists. . . . These finite bodies have been said to belong to an eternal, indestructible, and infinite spirit. . . . He who believes that this spirit can kill, and he who thinks that it can be killed—both of these are mistaken. It neither kills nor is killed. It is born, and it does not die. . . . Unborn, changeless, eternal both as to future and past time, it is not slain when the body is killed. . . . As the soul in this body undergoes the changes of childhood, prime, and age, so it obtains a new body hereafter. . . . As a man abandons worn-out clothes and takes other new ones, so does the soul quit worn-out bodies and enter other new ones. Weapons cannot cleave it, fire cannot burn it, nor can water wet it, nor can wind dry it. It is impenetrable, incombustible, incapable of moistening and of drying. It is constant; it can go everywhere; it is firm, immovable, and eternal. And even if thou deem it born with the body and dying with the body, still, O great-armed one! thou art not right to grieve for it. For to everything generated death is certain; to everything dead regeneration is certain. . . . One looks on the soul as a miracle; another speaks of it as a miracle; another hears of it as a miracle; but even when he has heard of it, not one comprehends it. . . . When a man's heart is disposed in accordance with his roaming senses, it snatches away his spiritual knowledge as the wind does a ship on the waves. . . . He who does not practise devotion has neither intelligence nor reflection. And he who does not practise reflection has no calm. How can a man without calm obtain happiness? The self-governed man is awake in that which is night to all other beings; that in which other beings are awake is night to the self-governed. He into whom all desires enter in the same manner as rivers enter the ocean, which is always full, yet does not change its bed, can obtain tranquillity. . . . Love or hate exists toward the object of each sense. One should not fall into the power of these two passions, for they are one's adversaries. . . . Know that passion is hostile to man in this world. As fire is surrounded by smoke and a mirror by rust, and a child by the womb,

so is this universe surrounded by passion. . . . They say that the
senses are great. The heart is greater than the senses. But the intellect
is greater than the heart, and passion is greater than the intellect. . . .

" I and thou, O Arjuna! have passed through many transmigrations.
I know all these. Thou dost not know them. . . . For whenever there
is a relaxation of duty, O son of Bharata! and an increase of impiety,
I then reproduce myself for the protection of the good and the destruction of evil-doers. I am produced in every age for the purpose
of establishing duty. . . . Some sacrifice the sense of hearing and the
other senses in the fire of restraint. Others, by abstaining from food,
sacrifice life in their life. [But] the sacrifice of spiritual knowledge
is better than a material sacrifice. . . . By this knowledge thou wilt
recognize all things whatever in thyself, and then in me. He who
possesses faith acquires spiritual knowledge. He who is devoid of
faith and of doubtful mind perishes. The man of doubtful mind
enjoys neither this world nor the other nor final beatitude. Therefore,
sever this doubt which exists in thy heart, and springs from ignorance,
with thy sword of knowledge: turn to devotion and arise, O son of
Bharata! . . .

"Learn my superior nature, O hero! by means of which this world
is sustained. I am the cause of the production and dissolution of the
whole universe. There exists no other thing superior to me. On me
are all the worlds suspended, as numbers of pearls on a string. I
am the savor of waters, and the principle of light in the moon and
sun, the mystic syllable *Om* in the Vedas, the sound in the ether, the
essence of man in men, the sweet smell in the earth; and I am the
brightness in flame, the vitality in all beings, and the power of mortification in ascetics. Know, O son of Prithá! that I am the eternal seed
of all things which exist. I am the intellect of those who have intellect; I am the strength of the strong. . . . And know that all dispositions, whether good, bad, or indifferent, proceed also from me. I do
not exist in them, but they in me. . . . I am dear to the spiritually
wise beyond possessions, and he is dear to me. A great-minded man
who is convinced that *Vasudevu* [Krishna] *is everything* is difficult to
find. . . . If one worships any inferior personage with faith, I make
his faith constant. Gifted with such faith, he seeks the propitiation
of this personage, and from him receives the pleasant objects of his
desires, which [however] were sent by me alone. But the reward of
these little-minded men is finite. They who sacrifice to the gods go
to the gods; they who worship me come to me. I am the immolation.
I am the whole sacrificial rite. I am the libation to ancestors. I am
the drug. I am the incantation. I am the fire. I am the incense. I
am the father, the mother, the sustainer, the grandfather of this uni-

verse—the path, the supporter, the master, the witness, the habitation, the refuge, the friend, the origin, the dissolution, the place, the receptacle, the inexhaustible seed. I heat. I withhold and give the rain. I am ambrosia and death, the existing and the non-existing. Even those who devoutly worship other gods with the gift of faith, worship me, but only improperly. I am the same to all beings. I have neither foe nor friend. I am the beginning and the middle and the end of existing things. Among bodies I am the beaming sun. Among senses I am the heart. Among waters I am the ocean. Among mountains I am Himalaya. Among trees I am the banyan; among men, the king; among weapons, the thunderbolt; among things which count, time; among animals, the lion; among purifiers, the wind. I am Death who seizes all; I am the birth of those who are to be. I am Fame, Fortune, Speech, Memory, Meditation, Perseverance, and Patience among feminine words. I am the game of dice among things which deceive; I am splendor among things which are shining. Among tamers I am the rod; among means of victory I am polity; among mysteries I am silence, the knowledge of the wise. . . .

" They who know me to be the God of this universe, the God of gods and the God of worship—they who know me to be the God of this universe, the God of gods and the God of worship—yea, they who know me to be these things in the hour of death, they know me indeed."

When my friend finished these words there did not seem to be anything particular left in heaven or earth to talk about. At any rate, there was a dead pause for several minutes. Finally I asked—and I protest that in contrast with the large matters whereof Bhima Gandharva had discoursed my voice (which is American and slightly nasal) sounded like nothing in the world so much as the squeak of a sick rat, " When were these things written? "

" At least nineteen hundred and seventy-five years ago, we feel sure. How much earlier we do not know."

We now directed our course toward the hospital for sick and disabled animals which has been established here in the most crowded portion of Black Town by that singular sect called the Jains, and which is only one of a number of such institutions to be found in the large cities of India. This sect is now important more by influence than by numbers in India, many of the richest merchants of the great Indian cities being among its adherents, though by the last census of British India there appears to be but a little over nine millions of Jains and Buddhists together, out of the one hundred and ninety millions of Hindus in British India. The tenets of the Jains are too complicated for description here, but it may be said that much doubt exists as to whether it is an old religion of which Brahmanism and Buddhism are varieties, or whether it is itself a variety of Buddhism. Indeed, it does not seem well settled whether the pure Jain doctrine was atheistical or theistical. At any rate, it is sufficiently differentiated from Brahmanism by its opposite notion of castes, and from Buddhism by its cultus of nakedness, which the Buddhists abhor. The Jains are split into two sects—the *Digambaras*, or nude Jains, and the *Svetambaras*, or clothed Jains, which latter sect seem to be Buddhists, who, besides the Tirthankars (*i. e.*, mortals who have acquired the rank of gods by devout lives, in whom all the Jains believe), worship also the various divinities of the Vishnu system. The Jains themselves declare this system to date from a period ten thousand years before Christ, and they practically support this traditional antiquity by persistently regarding and treating the Buddhists as heretics from their system. At any event, their religion is an old one. They seem to be the gymnosophists, or naked philosophers, described by Clitarchos as living in India at the time of the expedition of Alexander, and their history crops out in various accounts,—that of Clement of Alexandria, then of the Chinese Fu-Hian in the fourth and fifth centuries, and of the celebrated Chinese Hiouen-Tsang in the seventh century, at which last period they appear to have been the prevailing sect in India, and to have increased in favor until in the twelfth century the Rajpoots, who had become converts to Jainism, were schismatized into Brahmanism and deprived the naked philosophers of their prestige.

The great distinguishing feature of the Jains is the extreme to which they push the characteristic tenderness felt by the Hindus for animals of all descriptions. Jaina is, distinctly, *the purified*. The priests eat no animal food; indeed, they are said not to eat at all after noon, lest the insects then abounding should fly into their mouths and be crushed unwittingly. They go with a piece of muslin bound over their mouths, in order to avoid the same catastrophe, and carry a soft brush wherewith to remove carefully from any spot upon which they are about to sit such insects as might be killed thereby.

" Ah, how my countryman Bergh * would luxuriate in this scene!" I said as we stood looking upon the various dumb exhibitions of so many phases of sickness, of decrepitude and of mishap—quaint, grotesque, yet pathetic withal—in the precincts of the Jain hospital. Here were quadrupeds and bipeds, feathered creatures and hairy creatures, large animals and small, shy and tame, friendly and predatory—horses, horned cattle, rats, cats, dogs, jackals, crows, chickens; what not. An attendant was tenderly bandaging the blinking lids of a sore-eyed duck: another was feeding a blind crow, who, it must be confessed, looked here very much like some fat member of the New York Ring cunningly availing himself of the more toothsome rations in the sick ward of the penitentiary.** My friend pointed out to me a heron with a wooden leg.

" Suppose a gnat should break his shoulder-blade," I said, " would they put his wing in a sling?"

Bhima Gandharva looked me full in the face, and, smiling gently, said, " They would if they could."

The Jains are considered to have been the architects *par excellence* of India, and there are many monuments, in all styles, of their skill in this kind. The strange statues of the Tirthankars in the gorge called the Ourwhaï of Gwalior were (until injured by the " march of improvement ") among the most notable of the forms of rock-cutting. These vary in size from statuettes of a foot in height to colossal figures of sixty feet, and nothing can be more striking than these great forms, hewn from solid rock, represented entirely nude, with their impassive countenances, which remind every traveller of the Sphinx, their grotesque ears hanging down to their shoulders, and their heads, about which plays a ring of serpents for a halo, or out of which grows the mystical three-branched *Kalpa Vrich*, or Tree of Knowledge.

* [Henry Bergh (1823-1888) was the founder (1866) and first president of the American Society for the Prevention of Cruelty to Animals.—ED.]

** [The " Tweed Ring," composed of William Marcy Tweed (Boss), Mayor A. Oakley Hall, Peter Sweeny, and Richard Connolly, ruled New York City from 1869 to 1871, when it was dramatically exposed by the New York *Times*. It had robbed the City of more than forty-five million dollars.—ED.]

The sacred hill of Sunaghur, lying a few miles to the south of Gwalior, is one of the Meccas of the Jains, and is covered with temples in many styles, which display the fertility of their architectural invention: there are over eighty of these structures in all.

" And now," said Bhima Gandharva next day, " while you are thinking upon temples, and wondering if the Hindus have all been fools, you should complete your collection of mental materials by adding to the sight you have had of a Hindu temple proper, and to the description you have had of Jain temples proper, a sight of those marvellous subterranean works of the Buddhists proper which remain to us. We might select our examples of these either at Ellora or at Ajunta (which are on the mainland a short distance to the northeast of Bombay), the latter of which contains the most complete series of purely Buddhistic caves known in the country; or, indeed, we could find Buddhistic caves just yonder on Salsette. But let us go and see Karli at once: it is the largest *shaîtya* (or cave-temple) in India."

Accordingly, we took railway at Bombay, sped along the isle, over the bridge to the island of Salsette, along Salsette to Tannah, then over the bridge which connects Salsette with the mainland, across the narrow head of Bombay harbor, and so on to the station of Khandalla, about halfway between Bombay and Poona, where we disembarked. The caves of Karli are situated but a few miles from Khandalla, and in a short time we were standing in front of a talus at the foot of a sloping hill whose summit was probably five to six hundred feet high. A flight of steps cut in the hillside led up to a ledge running out from an escarpment which was something above sixty feet high before giving off into the slope of the mountain. From the narrow and picturesque valley a flight of steps cut in the hillside led up to the platform. We could not see the façade of the *shaîtya* on account of the concealing boscage of trees. On ascending the steps, however, and passing a small square Brahmanic chapel, where we paid a trifling fee to the priests who reside there for the purpose of protecting the place, the entire front of the excavation revealed itself and with every moment of gazing grew in strangeness and solemn mystery.

The *shaîtya* is hewn in the solid rock of the mountain. Just to the left of the entrance stands a heavy pillar (*Silasthamba*) completely detached from the temple, with a capital upon whose top stand four lions back to back. On this pillar is an inscription in Pâli, which has been deciphered, and which is now considered to fix the date of the excavation conclusively at not later than the second century before the Christian era. The eye took in at first only the vague confusion of windows and pillars cut in the rock. It is supposed that originally a music-gallery stood here in front, consisting of a balcony supported out from the two octagonal pillars, and probably roofed or having a second balcony above. But the woodwork is now gone. One soon felt one's attention becoming concentrated, however, upon a great arched window cut in the form of a horseshoe, through which one could look down what was very much like the nave of a church running straight back into the depths of the hill. Certainly at first, as one passes into the strange vestibule which intervenes still between the front and the interior of the *shaîtya*, one does not think at all—one only feels the dim sense of mildness raying out from the great faces of the elephants, and of mysterious farawayness conveyed by the bizarre postures of the sculptured figures on the walls.

Entering the interior, a central nave stretches back between two lines of pillars, each of whose capitals supports upon its abacus two kneeling elephants: upon each elephant are seated two figures, most of which are male and female pairs. The nave extends eighty-one feet three inches back, the whole length of the temple being one hundred and two feet three inches. There are fifteen pillars on each side the nave, which thus enclose between themselves and the wall two side-aisles, each about half the width of the nave, the latter being twenty-five feet and seven inches in width, while the whole width from wall to wall is forty-five feet and seven inches. At the rear, in a sort of apse, are seven plain octagonal pillars—the other thirty are sculptured. Just in front of these seven pillars is the *Daghaba*—a domed structure covered by a wooden parasol. The *Daghaba* is the reliquary in which or under which some relic of Gotama Buddha is enshrined. The roof of the *shaîtya* is vaulted, and ribs of teak-wood—which could serve no possible architectural purpose—reveal themselves, strangely enough, running down the sides.*

As I took in all these details, pacing round the dark aisles and finally resuming my stand near the entrance from which I perceived the aisles, dark between the close pillars and the wall, while the light streamed through the great horseshoe window full upon the *Daghaba* at the other end, I exclaimed to Bhima Gandharva, "Why, it is the very copy of a Gothic church—the aisles, the nave, the vaulted roof and all—and yet you tell me it was excavated two thousand years ago!"

"The resemblance has struck every traveler," he replied. "And, strange to say, all the Buddhist cave-temples are designed upon the same general plan. There is always the organ-loft, as you see there; always the three doors, the largest one opening on the nave, the smaller ones each on its side-aisle; always the window throwing its light directly on the *Daghaba* at the other end; always, in short, the general arrangement of the choir of a Gothic round or polygonal apse cathedral. It is supposed that the devotees were confined to the front part of the temple, and that the great window through which the light comes was hidden from view, both outside by the music-galleries and screens, and inside through the disposition of the worshippers in front. The gloom of the interior was thus available to the priests for the production of effects which may be imagined."

Emerging from the temple, we saw the Buddhist monastery (*Vihara*), which is a series of halls and cells rising one above the other in stories connected by flights of steps, all hewn in the face of the hill at the side of the temple. We sat down on a fragment of rock near a stream of water with which a spring in the hillside fills a little pool at the entrance of the *Vihara*. "Tell me something of Gotama Buddha," I said. "Recite some of his deliverances, O Bhima Gandharva!—you who know everything."

"I will recite to you from the *Sutta Nipata*,** which is supposed by many pundits of Ceylon to contain several of the old-

* [Lanier borrows generously from Bayard Taylor, *India*, for this description.—ED.]

** [A collection of seventy didactic poems constituting one of the fifteen parts of the Indian *Khuddaka-Nikaya*.—ED.]

est examples of the Pâli language. It professes to give the conversation of Buddha, who died five hundred and forty-three years before Christ lived on earth; and these utterances are believed by scholars to have been brought together at least more than two hundred years before the Christian era. The *Mahámangala Sutta,* of the *Nipata Sutta,* says for example:

Thus it was heard by me. At a certain time Bhagavá [Gotama Buddha] lived at Sávatthi in Jetavana, in the garden of Anáthupindika. Then, the night being far advanced, a certain god, endowed with a radiant color illuminating Jetavana completely, came to where Bhagavá was, [and] making obeisance to him, stood on one side. And, standing on one side, the god addressed Bhagavá in [these] verses:

1. Many gods and men, longing after what is good, have considered many things as blessings. Tell us what is the greatest blessing.
2. Buddha said: Not serving fools, but serving the wise, and honoring those worthy of being honored: this is the greatest blessing.
3. The living in a fit country, meritorious deeds done in a former existence, the righteous establishment of one's self: this is the greatest blessing.
4. Extensive knowledge and science, well-regulated discipline and well-spoken speech: this is the greatest blessing.
5. The helping of father and mother, the cherishing of child and wife, and the following of a lawful calling: this is the greatest blessing.
6. The giving alms, a religious life, aid rendered to relatives, blameless acts: this is the greatest blessing.
7. The abstaining from sins and the avoiding them, the eschewing of intoxicating drink, diligence in good deeds: this is the greatest blessing.
8. Reverence and humility, contentment and gratefulness, the hearing of the law in the right time: this is the greatest blessing.
9. Patience and mild speech, the association with those who have subdued their passions, the holding of religious discourse in the right time: this is the greatest blessing.
10. Temperance and charity, the discernment of holy truth, the perception of Nibbána: this is the greatest blessing.
11. The mind of any one unshaken by the ways of the world, exemption from sorrow, freedom from passion, and security: this is the greatest blessing.
12. Those who having done these things become invincible on all sides, attain happiness on all sides: this is the greatest blessing.

" At another time also Gotama Buddha was discoursing on caste. You know that the Hindus are divided into the Brahmans, or the priestly caste, which is the highest; next the Kshatriyas, or the warrior and statesman caste; next the Vaishyas, or the herdsman and farmer caste; lastly, the Sudras, or the menial caste. Now, once upon a time the two youths Vásettha and Bháradvaja had a discussion as to what constitutes a Brahman. Thus, Vásettha and Bháradvaja went to the place where Bhagavá was, and having approached him were well pleased with him; and having finished a pleasing and complimentary conversation, they sat down on one side. Vásettha, who sat down on one side, addressed Buddha in verse: . . .

3. O Gotama! we have a controversy regarding [the distinctions of] birth. Thus know, O wise one! the point of difference between us: Bháradvaja says that a Brahman is such by reason of his birth.

4. But I affirm that he is such by reason of his conduct. . . .

7. Bhagavá replied: . . .

53. I call him alone a Brahman who is fearless, eminent, heroic, a great sage, a conqueror, freed from attachments—one who has bathed in the waters of wisdom, and is a Buddha.

54. I call him alone a Brahman who knows his former abode, who sees both heaven and hell, and has reached the extinction of births.

55. What is called ' name ' or ' tribe ' in the world arises from usage only. It is adopted here and there by common consent.

56. It comes from long and uninterrupted usage, and from the false belief of the ignorant. Hence the ignorant assert that a Brahman is such from birth.

57. One is not a Brahman nor a non-Brahman by birth: by his conduct alone is he a non-Brahman.

58. By his conduct he is a husbandman, an artisan, a merchant, a servant;

59. By his conduct he is a thief, a warrior, a sacrificer, a king. . . .

62. One is a Brahman from penance, charity, observance of the moral precepts and the subjugation of the passions. Such is the best kind of Brahmanism."

" That would pass for very good republican doctrine in Jonesville," I said. " What a pity you have all so backslidden from your orthodoxies here in India, Bhima Gandharva! In my native land there is a region where many orange-trees grow.

Sometimes, when a tree is too heavily fertilized it suddenly shoots out in great luxuriance and looks as if it were going to make oranges enough for the whole world, so to speak. But somehow, no fruit comes: it proves to be all wood and no oranges, and presently the whole tree changes and gets sick and good for nothing. It is a disease which the natives call 'the dieback.' * Now, it seems to me that when you old Aryans came from—from—well, from wherever you did come from— you branched out at first into a superb magnificence of religions and sentiments and imaginations and other boscage. But it looks now as if you were really bad off with the dieback."

It was, however, impossible to perceive that Bhima Gandharva's smile was like anything other than the same plain full of ripe corn.

II

I had now learned to place myself unreservedly in the hands of Bhima Gandharva. When, therefore, on regaining the station at Khandalla he said, " The route by which I intend to show you India will immediately take us quite away from this part of it; first, however, let us go and see Poona, the old Maharatta capital, which lies but a little more than thirty miles farther to the southeastward by rail,"—I accepted the proposition as a matter of course, and we were soon steaming down the eastern declivity of the *ghâts*. As we moved smoothly down into the treeless plains which surround Poona I could not resist a certain feeling of depression.

" Yes," said Bhima Gandharva, when I mentioned it to him, " I understand exactly what you mean. On reaching an unbroken expanse of level country after leaving the tops of mountains, I always feel as if my soul had come bump against a solid wall of rock in the dark. I seem to hear a dull *thud* of discouragement somewhere back in my soul, as when a man's body falls dead on the earth. Nothing, indeed, could more heighten such a sensation than the contrast between this and the Bombay side of the *ghâts*. There we had the undulating waters, the lovely harbor with its wooded and hilly islands,

---

* [In the appendix of *Florida* (1876) Lanier included "On the Dieback in Orange-Trees," by J. H. Fowler.—ED.]

the ascending terraces of the *ghâts*: everything was energetic, the whole invitation of Nature was toward air, light, freedom, heaven. But here one spot is like another spot; this level ground is just the same level ground there was a mile back; this corn stands like that corn; there is an oppressive sense of bread-and-butter about; one somehow finds one's self thinking of ventilation and economics. It is the sausage-grinding school of poetry—of which modern art, by the way, presents several examples—as compared with that general school represented by the geniuses who arise and fly their own flight and sing at a great distance above the heads of men and of wheat."

Having arrived and refreshed ourselves at our hotel, whose proprietor was, as usual, a Parsee, we sallied forth for a stroll about Poona. On one side of us lay the English quarter, consisting of the houses and gardens of the officers and government employes and of the two or three hundred other Englishmen residing here. On the other was the town, extending itself along the banks of the little river Moota. We dreamed ourselves along in the lovely weather through such of the seven quarters of the town as happened to strike the fancy of my companion. Occasionally we were compelled to turn out of our way for the sacred cattle, which, in the enjoyment of their divine prerogatives, would remain serenely lying across our path; but we respected the antiquity if not the reasonableness of their privileges, and murmured not.

Each of the seven quarters of Poona is named after a day of the week. As we strolled from Monday to Tuesday, or passed with bold anachronism from Saturday back to Wednesday, I could not help observing how these interweavings and reversals of time appeared to take an actual embodiment in the scenes through which we slowly moved, particularly in respect of the houses and the costumes which went to make up our general view. From the modern-built European houses to the mediæval-looking buildings of the Bhoodwar quarter, with their massive walls and loop-holes and crenellations, was a matter of four or five centuries back in a mere turn of the eye; and from these latter to the Hindu temples here and there, which, whether or not of actual age, always carry one straight into antiquity, was a further retrogression to the obscure depths of time. So, too, one's glance would often sweep in a twinkling from a European clothed in garments of the latest mode to a Hindu whose sole covering was his *dhotee,* or clout about the loins, taking in between these two extremes a number of distinct s*t*ages in the process of evolution through which our clothes have gone. In the evening we visited the *Sangam,* where the small streams of the Moola and the Moota come together. It is filled with cenotaphs, but, so far from being a place of weeping, the pleasant air was full of laughter and of gay conversation from the Hindus, who delight to repair here for the purpose of enjoying the cool breath of the evening as well as the pleasures of social intercourse.

But I did not care to linger in Poona. The atmosphere always had to me a certain tang of the assassinations, the intrigues, the treacheries which marked the reign of that singular line of usurping ministers whose capital was here. In the days when the Peishwas were in the height of their glory Poona was a city of a hundred and fifty thousand inhabitants, and great traffic was here carried on in jewelry and such luxuries among the Mahratta nobles. The Mahrattas once, indeed, possessed the whole of India practically; and their name is composed of *Mahu,* a word meaning " great," and often to be met with in the designations of this land, where so many things really are great, and *Rachtra,* " kingdom," the propriety of the appellation seeming to be justified by the bravery and military character of the people. They have been called the Cossacks of India from these qualities combined with their horsemanship. But the dynasty of the usurping ministers had its origin in iniquity; and the corruption of its birth quickly broke out again under the stimulus of excess and luxury, until it culminated in the destruction of the Mahratta empire in 1818. So, when we had seen the palace of the Peishwa, from one of whose balconies the young Peishwa Mahadeo committed suicide by leaping to the earth in the year 1797 through shame at having been reproved by his minister Nana Farnavese in presence of his court, and when we had visited the Hira-Bâgh, or Garden of Diamonds, the summer retreat of the Peishwas, with its elegant pavilion, its balconies jutting into the masses of foliage, its cool tank of water, reposing under the protection of the temple-studded Hill of Pararati, we took train again for Bombay.

The Great Indian Peninsula Railway's main line leads out of Bombay over the *ghâts* to Jabalpúr, six hundred miles; thence a railway of some two hundred and twenty miles runs to Allahabad, connecting them with the great line known as the East Indian Railway, which extends for more than a thousand miles northwestward from Calcutta *via* Patna, Benares, Allahabad, Cawnpore, Lucknow, Agra, and Delhi. Our journey, as marked out by Bhima Gandharva, was to be from Bombay to Jabalpúr by rail; thence by some slow and easy conveyance across country to Bhopal, and from Bhopal northward through Jhansi to Delhi and the northern country, thence returning by rail to Calcutta.

As one ascends the Western *Ghâts* shortly after leaving Bombay one has continual occasion to remark the extraordinary resources of modern railway engineering. Perhaps the mechanical skill of our time has not achieved any more brilliant illustrations of itself than here occur. For many miles one is literally going up a flight of steps by rail. The word *ghât* indeed means the steps leading up from pools or rivers, whose frequent occurrence in India attests the need of easy access to water, arising from the important part which it plays both in the civil and religious economies of the Hindu. The *ghâts* are so called from their terraced ledges, rising one above another from the shores of the ocean like the stairs leading up from a pool. In achieving the ascent of these gigantic stairs all the expedients of road-makers have been resorted to: the zigzag, the trestle, the tunnel, the curve, have been pushed to their utmost applications; for five continuous miles on the Thull Ghát Incline there is a grade of one in thirty-seven, involving many trying curves, and on nineteen miles of the Bhore Ghát Incline there are thirty tunnels.

That which gives tone and character to a general view of the interior of a railway-car in traveling is, from the nature of things, the head-covering of the occupants, for it is this which mostly meets the eye; and no one who has travelled in the United States, for example, can have failed to observe the striking difference between the aspect of a car in the South, where the felt slouch prevails, and of one in the North, where the silk hat is more affected. But cars full of turbans! There were turbans of silk, of muslin, of woollen; white turbans, red, green, and yellow turbans; turbans with knots, turbans with ends hanging; neat turbans, baggy turbans, preternatural turbans, and that curious spotted silk inexpressible mitre which the Parsee wears.

Bhima Gandharva was good enough to explain to me the turban; and really, when within bounds, it is not so nonsensical a headdress as one is apt at first to imagine. It is a strip of cloth from nine to twelve inches wide, and from fifteen to twenty-five yards long. They are known, however, of larger dimensions, reaching to a yard in width and sixty yards in length. The most common color is white; next, perhaps, red, and next yellow; though green, blue, purple, and black are worn, as are also buff, shot colors, and gray, these latter being usually of silk; but this does not exhaust the varieties, for there are many turbans made of cotton cloth printed in various devices to suit the fancies of the wearers.

"The *puttee-dar* (*pugri*, or turban)," continued my companion, "is a neat compact turban, in general use by Hindus and Mohammedans; the *joore-dar* is like the *puttee-dar*, except that it has the addition of a knot on the crown; the *khirkee-dar* is the full-dress turban of gentlemen attached to native courts; the *nustalik* is a small turban which fits closely to the head, and is worn for full dress at the Mohammedan *durbars*, or royal receptions; the *mundeel* is the military turban, with stripes of gold and ends; the *séthi* is like the *nustalik*, and is worn by bankers; the *shumla* is a shawl-turban; and I fear you do not care to know the other varieties—the *morassa, the umamu*, the *dustar*, the—"

"Thank you," I said, "life is short, my dear Bhima, and I shall know nothing but turbans if this goes on, which will be inconvenient, particularly when I return to my home and my neighbor Smith asks me that ghastly question, 'What do I think of India?'"

"It is a more 'ghastly' question as to India than as to any other country in the world," said the Hindu. "Some years ago, when Mr. Dilke * was travelling in this country, a witty

* [Charles W. Dilke, author of *Greater Britain*, a volume published in 1869, which Lanier used as a source here and elsewhere in the sketches.—ED.]

officer of one of the hill-stations remarked to him that *all general observations about India were absurd.* This is quite true. How could it be otherwise? Only consider, for example, the languages of India,—the Assamese, with its two branches of the Deccan-göl and the Uttar-göl; the Bengalee; the Maithilee, Tirhutiya, or Tirabhuchti, spoken between the Coosy and the Gunduck; the Orissan, of the regions around Cuttack; the Nepalese; the Kosalese, about Almora; the Dogusee, between Almora and Cashmere; the Cashmiran; the Panjabee; the Mooltanee, or Vuchee, on the middle Indus; the two dialects of Sindhi, or Tatto, on the lower Indus; the Cutché, on the west coast of the peninsula; the Guseraté, spoken on the islands of Salsette and Bombay and the opposite coast of the Coucan, as well as by the Parsees in the cities, where it is corrupted with many words of other languages through the influence of commercial relations; the Coucané, from Bombay to Goa and along the parallel Gháts, where it is called Ballagate; the Bikaneeré, the Marvareé, the Jeyporé, the Udayaporé, of Rajpootana; the Vrajabhasha (the cow-pen language) of the Doab, between the Ganges and the Jumna, which is probably the parent of Hindí (or Oordú); the Malooé, of the tableland of Malwa; the Bundelakhandé, of the Bundelkhand; the Mogadhé, of Behar; the Maharachtré, of the country south of the Vindhyas; the—"

"It gives me pain to interrupt you, Bhima Gandharva," I said (fervently hoping that this portion of my remark might escape the attention of the recording angel), "but I think we are at Jabalpúr."

Apropos of Jubbulpoor, it is well enough to remark that by the rules of Indian orthography which are now to be considered authentic, the letter " a " without an accent has a sound equivalent to short " u," and a vowel with an acute accent has what is usually called its long sound in English. Accordingly, the word written " Jabalpúr " should be pronounced as if retaining the " u " and the " oo " with which it was formerly written, " Jubbulpoor." The termination *púr*, so common in the designation of Indian places, is equivalent to that of *ville* in English, and means the same. The other common termination, *abad*, means " dwelling " or " residence ": *e. g.*, Ahmedabad, the residence of Ahmed.

Jabalpúr is but about a mile from the right bank of the
Nerbadá ("Nerbudda") River; and as I wished to see the
famous Marble Rocks of that stream, which are found a short
distance from Jabalpúr, my companion and I here left the railway, intending to see a little of the valley of the Nerbadá and
then to strike across the Vindhyas, along the valley of the
Tonsa, to Bhopal, making our journey by such slow, irregular
and easy stages as should be compatible with that serene and
philosophic disposition into which the Hindu's beautiful gravity
had by this time quite converted my American tendencies
toward rushing through life at the killing pace.

It was a little past midday when we made our first journey
along the river between the Marble Rocks. Although the
weather was as nearly perfect as weather could be, the mornings being deliciously cool and bracing and the nights cold
enough to produce often a thin layer of ice over a pan of water
left exposed till daybreak, yet the midday sun was warm
enough, especially after a walk, to make one long for leaves
and shade and the like. It would be difficult, therefore, to
convey the sensations with which we reclined at our ease in a
flat-bottomed punt while an attendant poled us up toward
the "Fall of Smoke," where the Nerbadá leaps out eagerly
toward the low lands he is to fertilize, like a young poet anxious
to begin his work of grace in the world. On each side of us
rose walls of marble a hundred feet in height, whose pure
white was here and there striped with dark green or black: all
the colors which met the eye—the marmoreal whites, the bluish grays of the recesses among the ledges, the green and black
seams, the limpid blue of the stream—were grateful, calm-
toned, refreshing; we inhaled the coolness as if it had been a
mild aroma out of a distant flower. This pleasant fragrance,
which seemed to come up out of all things, was presently
intensified by a sort of spiritual counterpart—a gentle breath
that blew upon us from the mysterious regions of death; for
on a Ghát we saw a small company of Hindus just launching
the body of a pious relative into the waters of Mother Nerbadá
in all that freedom from grief, and even pleasant contemplation, with which this singular people regard the transition from
present to future existence. These corpses, however, which are

thus committed to the wave, do not always chime so happily in with the reveries of boating-parties on the Nerbadá. The Marble Rocks are often resorted to by pic-nic parties in the moonlit evenings; and one can easily fancy that to have a dusky dead body float against one's boat and sway slowly round alongside in the midst of a gay jest or of a light song of serenade, as is said to have happened not unfrequently here, is not an occurrence likely to heighten the spirits of revellers. Occasionally, also, the black, ugly double snout of the *magar* (or Nerbadá crocodile) may pop up from the surface, which may here serve as a warning to the young lady who trails her hand in the water—and I have yet to be in a boating-party where the young lady did not trail her hand in the water— that on the Nerbadá it is perhaps as well to resign an absent-minded hand to the young officer who sits by her in the boat lest *magar* should snap it off.

Leaving the Nerbadá we now struck off northward toward the Tonsa, intending to pass round by way of Dumoh, Sangor, Bhilsa, and Sanchi to Bhopal. We might have pursued a route somewhat more direct by following directly down the valley of the Nerbadá to Hoshangabad, and thence straight across to Bhopal, but my companion preferred the circuitous route indicated, as embracing a greater variety of interesting objects. He had procured for our conveyance a vehicle which was in all respects suitable to the placidity of his temper; and I make bold to confess that, American as I am—born on the railroad, so to speak—I have never enjoyed travelling as I did in this novel carriage. It was what is called a *chapaya*. It consists of a body nearly ten feet in length by more than five in breadth, and was canopied by a top supported upon sculptured pillars of wood. The wheels were massive and low. There were no springs; but this deficiency was atoned for by the thick cushion-ment of the rear portion of the vehicle, which allowed us to lie at full length in luxurious ease as we rolled along. Four white bullocks, with humps and horns running nearly straight back on the prolongation of the forehead line, drew us along in a very stately manner at the rate of something like a mile and a half an hour.

We were now in the Góndwana, in some particulars one of

the most interesting portions of the country. Here are the Highlands of Central India; here rise the Nerbadá and the Tapti—which flow to the westward in a generally parallel direction, and empty into the Gulf of Cambaye, the one at Broode and the other at Surat—as well as the Sôn, the Keyn (or Cane) and the Tonsa, which flow northward into the Jumna. The valley of the Keyn and that of the Tonsa here run across the Vindhyas, which are known to the eastward of this as the Kyrmores, and afford communication between Northern and Southern India. It is along the depression of the latter stream that the railway has been built from Jabalpúr to Allahabad.

The eight hundred thousand Gónds of the Góndwana are supposed to be members of the great autochthonal family of ancient India. These hills of the Góndwana country appear to have been considered by the incoming Aryans for a long time as a sort of uncanny land, whose savage recesses were filled with demons and snakes; indeed in the epics of the *Máhábhárata* and *Rámáyana* this evil character is attributed to that portion of India lying south of the Vindhyas. The forest of Spenser's *Faerie Queene,* in which wandering knights meet with manifold beasts and maleficent giants and do valorous battles against them in the rescue of damsels and the like—such seem to have been the Góndwana woods to the ancient Hindu imagination. It was not distressed damsels, however, whom they figured as being assisted by the arms of the errant protectors, but religious devotees who dwelt in the seclusion of the forest, and who were protected from the pranks and machinations of the savage denizens by opportune heroes of the northern race. It appears, however, that the native demons of the Góndwana had fascinating daughters; for presently we find the rajahs from the north coming down and marrying them; and finally, in the fourteenth and fifteenth centuries, the keen urgency of the conquering Mohammedans sends great numbers of Rajpúts down into the Góndwana, and a considerable mixture of the two bloods takes place. With this incursion of Hindu peoples come also the Hindu gods and tenets; and Mahadeo, the " great god," whose home had been the Kailas of the Himalayas, now finds himself domesticated in the moun-

tains of Central India. In the Mahadeo mountain is still
a shrine of Siva, which is much visited by pilgrims and
worshippers.

The Gónd—he who lives back in the hills far off from
the neighborhood of the extensive planting districts, which
have attracted many of those living near them to become at
least half-civilized laborers in harvest-time—is a primitive being
enough.

"Only look," said Bhima Gandharva, "at that hut if you
desire to see what is perhaps one of the most primitive houses
since ever the banyan tree gave to man (as is fabled) the idea
of sheltering himself from the elements artificially." It was
simply made of stakes driven into the ground, between which
were wattled branches. This structure was thatched with grass,
and plastered with mud.

The Gónd, like the American Indian, has his little patch of
grain, which he cultivates, however, in a fashion wholly his
own. His sole instrument of agriculture seems to be the axe.
Selecting a piece of ground which presents a growth of small
and easily-cut saplings—and perhaps, by the way, thus destroying in a few hours a whole cargo of teak trees worth more
than all the crops of his agricultural lifetime—he hews down
the growth, and in the dry season sets fire to the fallen timber.
The result is a bed of ashes over a space of two or three acres.
His soil is now ready. If the patch thus prepared happens to
be level, he simply flings out a few handfuls of grain, coarse
rice, *kútki* (*ponicum*) or *kódon* (*paspalum*), and the thing
is done. The rest is in the hands of the god who sends the
rains. If the patch be on a declivity, he places the grain at the
upper part, where it will be washed down by the rains over
the balance of the field. Next year he will burn some more
wood—the first burning will have left many charred stumps
and trunks, which he supplements with a little wood dragged
from other parts of the forest—on the same spot, and so the
next year, by which time it will become necessary to begin a
new clearing, or *dhya*. The *dhya* thus abandoned does not
renew the original growth which clothed it, like the pinelands
of the Southern United States, which, if allowed to run waste
after having been cleared and cultivated, clothe themselves

either with oaks or with a wholly different species of pine from the original growth. The waste *dhya*, which may have perhaps nourished a splendid growth of teak, becomes now only a dense jungle.

The Gónd also raises pumpkins and beans; and this vegetable diet he supplements with game ensnared in the *dhyas*, to which peafowl, partridges, hares, and the like resort. Many of the villages, however, have a professional huntsman, who will display the most incredible patience in waiting with his matchlock for the game to appear.

Besides these articles of diet the aborigines of the Góndwana have their *mhowa* tree, which stands them in much the same multifarious stead as the palm does to its beneficiaries. The flowers of the *mhowa* fall and are eaten, or are dried and pressed, being much like raisins: they also produce a wine by fermentation and the strong liquor of the hill-people by distillation. Of the seed, cakes are made and an oil is expressed from them which is an article of commerce.

In addition, the poor Gónd appears to have a periodical godsend resulting from a singular habit of one of the great Indian plants. The bamboo is said to undergo a general seeding every thirty years: at this period, although, in the mean time, many individual bamboos may have passed through the process of reproduction, it is said that the whole bamboo growth of a section will simultaneously drop its leaves and put forth large panicles of flowers, after which come great quantities of seeds much like rice. These are gathered for food by the inhabitants with all the greater diligence in consequence of a tradition—which, however, does not seem to be at all supported by facts—that the general seeding of the bamboo portends a failure of the regular crops. The liberal forests of the Góndwana furnish still other edibles to their denizens. The ebony plums, the wild mango, the seeds of the *sál* tree, the beans of the giant *bauhinia* creeper, a species of arrowroot, and a wild yam, are here found and eaten.

It is not long since the Gónds had arrived at a melancholy condition under the baleful influences of the *kulars*, or liquordealers, who resided among them and created an extraordinary demand for their intoxicating wares by paying for service and for produce in liquor. The *kulars* have, however, been thrown into the background by wise efforts toward their suppression, and matters have improved for the poor autochthones.

We spent our first night in our *chapaya*, my companion having so arranged matters that we were quite independent of the bungalows which the Englishmen have erected at suitable distances along the great roads for the convenience of travellers. The night was clear; betwixt the corner pillars which upheld our canopy a thousand friendly salutations from the stars streamed in upon us; the tranquil countenance of my friend seemed, as he lay beside me, like the face of the Past purified of old errors and calm with great wisdom got through great tribulation, insomuch that betwixt the Hindu and the stars I felt myself to be at once in communication with antiquity and with eternity.

Thus we pursued out ambulatory meditations through the Góndwana. If we had been sportsmen, we should have found full as varied a field for the bagging of game as for that more spiritual hunt after new ideas and sensations in which we were engaged. Gray quail, gray partridges, painted partridges (*Francolinus pictus*), snipe, and many varieties of water-fowl, the *sambor,* the black antelope, the Indian gazelle or ravine deer, the *gaur* or Indian bison, chewing the cud in the midday shade or drinking from a clear stream, troops of *nilgaé* springing out from the long grass and dwarf growth of *polás* and *jujube* trees which covered the sites of abandoned villages and fields,—all these revealed themselves to us in the most tempting situations. But although I had been an ardent devotee of the double-barrel, the large and manly tenderness which Bhima Gandharva invariably displayed toward all animals, whether wild or tame, had wrought marvels upon me, and I had grown fairly ashamed—nay, horrified—at the idea that anything which a generous and brave man could call *sport* should consist wholly in the most keen and savage cruelties inflicted upon creatures whom we fight at the most unknightly odds, we armed, they unarmed. While I knew that our pleasures are by the divine order mostly distillations from pain, I could not now help recognizing at the same time that this circumstance was part of an enormous plan which the slaughter of innocent creatures in the way of "sport" did in no wise help to carry out.

The truth is, although I had been for some days wavering upon the brink of these conclusions in a quiet way, I found the old keen ardor of the sportsman still burning too strongly, and I had started out with a breech-loader, intent upon doing much of the Góndwana route gun in hand. It was not long before a thoughtless shot operated to bring my growing convictions sharply face to face with my decreasing practice, and thus to quite frown the latter out of existence. It happened in this wise: One day, not far from sunset, I was walking idly along behind the *chapaya*, in which Bhima Gandharva was dreamily reclining, when suddenly a pair of great *sáras* cranes rose from the low banks of a small stream and sailed directly across the road. Quick as thought—indeed, quicker than thought; for if I had thought, I would not have done it—I fired, and brought down one of the monstrous birds. As I started to approach it, Bhima Gandharva said, in a tone just a trifle graver than usual, "Stop! wait a moment," and at the same time halted the *chapaya*. The mate of the bird I had shot, seeing him fall, alighted on the same spot, then flew up, then returned, flew up again, returned again, with an exhibition of sad and lingering affection of which I had not dreamed, and which penetrated me beyond expression; so I stood half stolid outwardly and wholly ashamed and grieved inwardly. "The *sáras*," said my friend, "is the type of conjugal affection among the Hindus. The birds nearly always go in pairs; and when one is killed, the other invariably makes those demonstrations of tenderness which you have just seen."

As we journeyed along in the dusk came notes from another pair of feathered lovers, "chukwa, chukwi," "chukwa, chukwi," in a sort of mournful alternation. They were the branning ducks, he on one side, she on the other side of the stream, as is their habit, whence they are fabled to be a pair of lovers who must yearn unavailingly through the long nights from opposite banks of the river.

That night, when Bhima Gandharva was asleep, I gently arose, took my double-barrel—thou dear Manton! * how often

* [A name given to fowling pieces made by Joseph Manton (1766-1835), a London gunsmith.—Ed.]

has not Jonesville admired thee returning from the field at late evening slanting at a jaunty angle high above my bagful of snipe or of quail as the case might be!—yes, I took this love of a gun, together with the cartridges, accoutrements, and all other rights, members, and appurtenances thereunto belonging or in any wise appertaining, and slid the whole lot softly into a deep green pool of the very stream from which had flown my *sáras*.

The taste of gypsy life which I was now enjoying contributed to add a sort of personal element to that general interest which hangs about the curious Banjaris, whom we met constantly, with their families and their bullocks, along our road. *Banjara* is literally "forest-wanderer." The women were especially notable for their tall stature, shapely figures, and erect carriage; which circumstances are all the more wonderful from the life of hardship which they lead, attending as they do at once to the foraging of the cattle, the culinary preparations for the men, and the cares of the children. From the profusion of ornaments which they wore one may imagine, however, that they were well cared for by their lords in return for their affectionate labors; and the general bearing of the tall Banjara who bore a long two-handed sword gave evidence of a certain inward sense of protection over his belongings which probably found vent in many an affectionate gift of rings and bracelets to his graceful partner. It must be confessed that the gypsying of these Eastern Bohemians is not so free a life as is popularly supposed. The *naik*, or sovereign, of each *tanda*, or camp, seems to be possessed of absolute power, and in this connection the long two-handed sword suggested much less gentle reflections. The Banjara, however, though a nomad, is a serviceable one, for he is engaged in trade. With his bullocks he is the carrier of Central India, and is to be met with all over that section bringing salt and other commodities and returning with interior produce.

III

Thus we fared leisurely along. We passed Cabul merchants peddling their dried fruit on shaggy-haired camels; to these succeeded in more lonesome portions of the road small groups of Korkas, wretched remnants of one of the autochthonal families of Central India—even lower in the scale of civilization than the Gónds among whom they are found; and to these the richly-caparisoned elephants of some wealthy Bhopal gentleman making a journey. We lingered long among the marvellous old Buddhistic *topes* or tumuli of Sanchi, and I interested my companion greatly in describing the mounds of the United States, with which I was familiar, and whose resemblance to these richly-sculptured and variously orna- mented ruins, though rude and far off, was quite enough to set his active fancy to evolving all manner of curious hypotheses going to explain such similarity. The whole way, by Sangor, Gharispore, Bhilsa, Sanchi, Sonori, presented us with the most interesting relics of the past, and the frequent recurrence of the works of the once prevalent Buddhistic faith continually incited us to new discussions of the yet unsolved question, Why has Buddha's religion, which once had such entire pos- session of this people's hearts, so entirely disappeared from the land?

And, as nothing could be more completely contrasted with the desert asceticism which Buddha's tenets inculcated than the luxury into which Mohammed's creed has flowered, so nothing could have more strikingly broken in upon our discussions of the Buddhistic monuments than the view which we at last obtained of the lovely Mohammedan city of Bhopal. To the south and east ran a strip of country as barren and heartacheish as if the very rocks and earth had turned Buddhist, beyond which a range of low rounded hills, not unlike *topes,* com- pleted the ascetic suggestion. But, turning from this, we saw Mohammedanism at its very loveliest. Minarets, domes, pal- aces, gardens, the towers of the citadel, waters of lovely lakes, all mingled themselves together in the voluptuous light of the low sun: there was a sense of music, of things that sparkled, of pearly lustres, of shimmering jewels, of softness, of delight, of luxury. Bhopal looked over the ragged valley like a sultan from the window of his *zenana* regarding afar off an unkempt hermit in his solitude.

My companion had arranged for permission to enter the town, and it was not long ere we were installed in the house of a friend of Bhima Gandharva's, whose guests we remained during our stay in Bhopal.

On a rock at the summit of a hill commanding this interesting city stands the fort of Fatehgarh, built by a certain Afghan
adventurer, Dost Mohammed Khan, who, in a time when this
part of India must have been a perfect paradise for all the free
lances of the East, was so fortunate as to win the favor of
Aurungzebe, and to receive as evidence thereof a certain district in Malwa. The Afghan seems to have lost no time in
improving the foothold thus gained, and he thus founded the
modern district of Bhopal, which was formerly divided between
Malwa and Góndwana, one gate of the town standing in the
former and one in the latter country. Dost Mohammed Khan
appears, indeed, to have been not the only adventurer who bet-
tered his fortunes in Bhopal. It is a curious fact, and one well
illustrating the liberality which has characterized much of the
more modern history of the Bhopal government, that no long
time ago it was administered by a regency consisting of three
persons,—one a Hindu, one a Mohammedan, and the other a
Christian. This Christian is mentioned by Sir John Malcolm *
as "Shahzed Musseah, or Belthazzar Bourbona" (by which
Sir John means *Shahzahad Messiah*—a native appellation signi-
fying " the Christian prince "), or *Balthazar of Bourbon*, and is
described by that officer, to whom he was well known, as a
brave soldier and an able man. He traced his lineage to a certain Frenchman calling himself John of Bourbon, who in the
time of Akbar was high in favor and position at Delhi. His
widow, the princess Elizabeth of Bourbon, still resides at
Bhopal in great state, being possessed of abundant wealth and
ranking second only to the Begum. She is the acknowledged
head of a large number of descendants of John of Bourbon,
amounting to five or six hundred, who remain at Bhopal and
preserve their faith—having a church and Catholic priest of
their own—as well as the traditions of their ancestry, which,
according to their claim, allies them to the royal blood of
France.

No mention of Bhopal can fail to pay at least a hasty tribute
in commemoration of the forcible character and liberal politics
of the Begum, who has but of late gone to her account after

* [Lanier's account of Dost Mohammed is paraphrased from John Malcolm,
Memoir of Central India.—ED.]

a long and sometimes trying connection with the administration of her country's affairs. After the death of her husband—who was accidentally killed by a pistol in the hands of a child not long after the treaty with the English in 1818—their nephew, then in his minority, was considered as the future nawab, and was betrothed to their daughter, the Begum being regent during his minority. When the time came, with his majority, for the nuptials, the Begum refused to allow the marriage to take place, for reasons which need not here be detailed. After much dispute a younger brother of the nephew was declared more eligible, but the Begum still managed in one way or another to postpone matters, much to his dissatisfaction. An arbitration finally resulted in placing him on the throne, but his reign was short and he died after a few years, leaving the Begum again in practical charge of affairs,—a position which she improved by instituting many wise and salutary reforms and bringing the state of Bhopal to a condition of great prosperity. The Pearl Mosque (*Monti Masjid*), which stands immediately in front of the palace, was built at her instance in imitation of the great cathedral-mosque of Delhi, and presents a charming evidence of her taste, as well as of the architectural powers still existing in this remarkable race.

The town proper of Bhopal is inclosed by a much-decayed wall of masonry some two miles in circuit, within which is a fort similar both in its condition and material to the wall. Outside these limits is a large commercial quarter (*gunge*). The beautiful lake running off past the town to the south is said to be artificial in its origin, and to. have been produced at the instance of Bho Pal, the minister of King Bohoje, as long ago as the sixth century, by damming up the waters of the Bess (or Besali) River, for the purpose of converting an arid section into fertile land. It is still called the Bhopal Tal.

If this were a ponderous folio of travel, one could detail the pleasures and polite attentions of one's Bhopalese host; of the social *utter-pán*; of the sprinklings with rose-water; of the dreamy talks over fragrant hookahs; of the wanderings among bazaars filled with moving crowds of people hailing from all the ports that lie between Persia and the Góndwana; of the *fêtes* where the *nautch*-girl of Baroda contended in graceful emulation with the *nautch*-girl of Ulwur, and the *cathacks* (or male dancers) with both; of elegantly-perfumed Bhopalese young men; of the palaces of nobles guarded by soldiers whose accoutrements ranged from the musket to the morion; of the Moharum, when the Mohammedan celebrates the New Year. But what would you have? A sketch is a sketch. We have got only to the heart of India: the head and the whole prodigious eastern side are not yet reached. It is time one were off for Jhansi.

At Bioura we encountered modern civilization again in the shape of the southwest branch of the Grand Trunk road, which leads off from the main stem at Agra. The Grand Trunk is not a railroad but a firm and smooth highway with which the English have united Calcutta to the Northwest Provinces and to the west of India. Much of this great roadway is metalled with *kunkur,* an oölitic limestone found near the surface of the soil in Hindustan; and all Anglo-India laughed at the joke of an irreverent punster, who, *apropos* of the fact that this application of *kunkur* to the road-bed was made under the orders of Lord William Bentinck, then governor-general, dubbed that gentleman William the Kunkurer.*

We had abandoned our *chapaya*—which, we may add for the benefit of future travelers, we had greatly improved as against jolting by causing it to be suspended upon a pair of old springs which we found, a relic of some antique break-down, in a village on the route—and after a short journey on elephants were traveling *dâk,* that is, by post. The *dâk-gharri* is a comfortable-enough long carriage on four wheels, and constitutes the principal mode of conveyance for travelers in India besides the railway. It contains a mattress inside, for it goes night and day, and one's baggage is strapped on top, much as in an American stage-coach after the "boot" is full. Frequent relays of horses along the route enable the driver to urge his animals from one station to the other with great speed, and the only other stoppages are at the *dâk*-bungalows.

"I have discovered," I said to Bhima Gandharva, after a

* [Lanier's source for this anecdote was Charles W. Dilke, *Greater Britain.* —ED.]

short experience of the *dâk-gharri* and the *dâk*-bungalows—" I have discovered a general remark about India which is *not* absurd: all the horses are devils and all the *dâk*-bungalow servants are patriarchs."

" If you judge by the heels of the former and the beards of the latter, it is true," he said.

This little passage was based on the experience of the last relay, which was, however, little more than a repetition of many previous ones. My friend and I having arranged ourselves comfortably in the *dâk-gharri* as soon as it was announced ready to start, the long and marvellously lean Indian who was our driver signified to his team by the usual horse-language that we should be glad to go. The horse did not even agitate his left ear—a phenomenon which I associate with a horse in that moment when he is quietly making up his mind to be fractious. " Go, my brother," said the driver, in a melli-fluous and really fraternal tone of voice. The horse disdained to acknowledge the tie: he stood still.

Then the driver changed the relationship, with an access of tenderness in voice and in adjuration. " Go, my son," he entreated. But the son stood as immovable as if he were going to remain a monument of filial impiety to all time.

" Go, my grandson, my love." This seemed entirely too much for the animal, and produced apparently a sense of abasement in him which was in the highest degree uncompli-mentary to his human kinsman and lover. He lay down. In so doing he broke several portions of the ragged harness, and then proceeded with the most deliberate absurdity to get himself thoroughly tangled in the remainder.

" I think I should be willing," I said to my companion, " to carry that horse to Jhansi on my own shoulders if I could have the pleasure of seeing him blown from one of the rajah's cannon in the fort."

But the driver without the least appearance of discomposure had dismounted, and with his long deft Hindu fingers soon released the animal, patched up his gear, replaced him between the shafts, and resumed his place.

Another round of consanguinities: the animal still remained immovable, till presently he lunged out with a wicked kick which had nearly obliterated at one blow the whole line of his ancestry and collateral relatives as represented in the driver. At this the latter became as furious as he had before been patient: he belabored the horse, assistants ran from the stable, the whole party yelled and gesticulated at the little beast simultaneously, and he finally broke down the road at a pace which the driver did not suffer him to relax until we arrived at the bungalow where we intended to stop for supper.*

A venerable old Mohammedan in a white beard that gave him the majesty of Moses advanced for the purpose of ascertaining our wants.

" Had he any mutton-chops? " asked Bhima Gandharva in Hindustani, the *lingua franca* of the country.

" Cherisher of the humble! no."

" Any beefsteak?"

" Nourisher of the poor! no."

" Well, then, I *hear* a chicken," said my friend, conclusively.

" O great king," said the Mohammedan, turning to me, " there *is* a chicken."

In a twinkling the cook caught the chicken; its head was turned toward Mecca. Bismillah! O God the Compassionate, the Merciful! the poor fowl's head flew off, and by the time we had made our ablutions supper was ready.

Turning across the ridges to the northeastward from Sipri, we were soon making our way among the tanks and groves which lie about the walls of Jhansi. Here, as at Poona, there was ever present to me a sense of evil destinies, of blood, of treacheries, which seemed to linger about the trees and the tanks like exhalations from the old crimes which have stained the soil of the country. For Jhansi is in the Bundelcund, and the Bundelcund was born in a great iniquity. The very name—which properly is *Bundelakhand*, or " the country of the Bundelas "—has a history thickly set about with the terrors of caste, of murder and of usurpation. Some five hundred years ago a certain Rajpút prince, Hurdeo Sing, committed the unpardonable sin of marrying a slave (*bundi*), and was in consequence expelled from the Kshatriya caste to

---

* [Similar anecdotes concerning horse-starting appear in Charles W. Dilke, *Greater Britain*, and Bayard Taylor, *India*—Lanier's probable sources.—ED.]

which he belonged. He fled with his disgrace into this region, and after some years found opportunity at least to salve his wounds with blood and power. The son of the king into whose land he had escaped conceived a passion for the daughter of the slave wife. It must needs have been a mighty sentiment, for the conditions which Hurdeo Sing exacted were of a nature to try the strongest love. These were, that the nuptial banquet should be prepared by the unmentionable hands of the slave wife herself, and that the king and his court should partake of it,—a proceeding which would involve the loss of their caste also. But the prince loved, and his love must have lent him extraordinary eloquence, for he prevailed on his royal father to accept the disgrace. If one could only stop here and record that he won his bride, succeeded his magnanimous old parent on the throne, lived a long and happy life with his queen, and finally died regretted by his loving people! But this is in the Bundelcund, and the facts are, that the treacherous Hurdeo Sing caused opium to be secretly put into all the dishes of the wedding-feast, and when the unsuspecting revellers were completely stupefied by the drug, had the whole party assassinated, after which he possessed himself of the throne and founded the Bundelcund.

One does not wonder that the hills and forests of such a land became the hiding-places of the strangling Thugs, the home of the poisoning Dacoits, the refuge of conspirators and insurgents, and the terror of Central India.

As for Jhansi, the district in whose capital we were now sojourning, its people must have tasted many of the sorrows of anarchy and of despotism even in recent times. It was appurtenant no long time ago to the Bundela rajah of Ourcha; from him it passed by conquest into the possession of the Peishwa. These small districts were all too handy for being tossed over as presents to favorites: one finds them falling about among the greedy subordinates of conquerors like nuts thrown out to school-boys. The Peishwa gave Jhansi to a *soubahdar*; the British government then appeared, and effected an arrangement by which the *soubahdar* should retain it as hereditary rajah on the annual payment of twenty-four thousand rupees. This so-called rajah, Ramchund Rao, died without issue in 1835. Amid great disputes as to the succession the British arbitrators finally decided in favor of Rugonath Rao; but new quarrels straightway arose, a great cry being made that Rugonath Rao was a leper, and that a leper ought not to be a rajah. His death in some three years settled that difficulty, only to open fresh ones among the conflicting claimants. These perplexing questions the British finally concluded quite effec-tually by assuming charge of the government themselves, though this was attended with trouble, for the stout old mother of Ramchund Rao made armed resistance from the fort or castellated residence of the rajahs, which stands on its great rock overlooking the town of Jhansi. A commission finally decreed the succession to Baba Gunghadar Rao, but retained the substantial power until the revenues had recovered from the depression consequent upon these anarchic disturbances.

" At any rate," I said, as Bhima Gandharva finished this narrative while we were walking about the burial-place of the rajahs of Jhansi, and occupying ourselves with tracing the curious admixture of Moslem with Hindu architecture pre-sented by the tombs, " these rajahs, if they loved each other but little in life, appear to have buried each other with proper enough observances: the cenotaphs are worthy of tenderer remembrances."

" Yes," he said: " this part of India is everywhere a land of beautiful tombs which enclose ugly memories. I recall one tomb, however, near which I have spent many hours of tranquil meditation, and which is at once lovely without and within: it is the tomb of the Moslem saint Allum Sayed at Baroda. It was built of stones taken from an old Jain temple, whose ruins are still visible near by; and with a singular fitness, in view of its material, the Moslem architect has mingled his own style with the Hindu, so that an elegant union of the keen and naked Jain asceticism with the mellower and richer fancy of the luxu-rious Mohammedan has resulted in a perfect work of that art which makes death lovely by recalling its spiritual significance. Besides, a holy silence broods about the cactus and the euphor-bian foliage, so that a word will send the paroquets, accus-tomed to such unbroken stillness, into hasty flights. The tomb proper is in the chamber at the centre, enclosed by delicatelytrellised walls of stone. I can easily fancy that the soul of Allum Sayed is sitting by his grave, like a faithful dog loath to quit his dead master."

Jhansi was once in the enjoyment of a considerable trade. The caravans from the Deccan to Furruckabad and other places in the Douab were in the habit of stopping here, and there was much trafficking in the cloths of Chanderi and in bows, arrows, and spears—the weapons of the Bundela tribes—which were here manufactured. Remnants of the wealth then acquired remain; and on the evening of the same day when we were wandering among the rajahs' tombs, we proceeded to the house of a rich friend of Bhima Gandharva's where we were to witness a *nautch,* or dance, executed by a wandering troop of Mewati *bayadères.* We arrived about nine o'clock. A servant sprinkled us with rose-water, and we were ushered into a large saloon, where the *bayadères* were seated with a couple of musicians, one of whom played the tam-tam and another a sort of violin. When the family of our host, together with a few friends, were seated at the end of the room opposite the *bayadères,* the signal was given and the music commenced with a soft and indescribably languorous air. One of the *bayadères* rose with a lithe and supple movement of the body not comparable to anything save the slow separating of a white scud from the main cloud which one sees on a summer's day high up in the cirrus regions. She was attired in a short jacket, a scarf, and a profusion of floating stuff that seemed at once to hide and expose. Presently I observed that her jewelry was glittering as it does not glitter when one is still, yet her feet were not moving. I also heard a gentle tinkling from her anklets and bracelets. On regarding her more steadily, I saw that her whole body was trembling in gentle and yet seemingly intense vibrations, and she maintained this singular agitation while she assumed an attitude of much grace, extending her arms and spreading out her scarf in gracefully-waving curves. In these slow and languid changes of posture which accommodated themselves to the music like undulations in running water to undulations in the sand of its bed, and in the strange trembling of her body, which seemed to be an inner miniature dance of the nerves, consisted her entire performance. She intensified the languid nature of her movements by the languishing coquetries of her enormous black eyes, from which she sent piercing glances between half-closed lids. It was a dance which only southern peoples understand. Any one who has ever beheld the *slow juba* of the negro in the Southern United States will recognize its affinity to these movements, which, apparently deliberate, are yet surcharged with intense energy and fire.

Her performance being finished, the *bayadère* was succeeded by others, each of whom appeared to have her specialty,—one imitating by her postures a serpent-charmer; another quite unequivocally representing a man-charmer; another rapidly executing what seemed an interminable *pirouette*. Finally, all joined in a song and a closing round, adding the sound of clapping hands to the more energetic measures of the music.

" I can now understand," I said when the *nautch* was finished, " the remark of the shah of Persia which set everybody laughing not long ago in England. During his visit to that country, being present at a ball where ladies and gentlemen were enjoying themselves in a somewhat laborious way in dancing, he finally asked, ' Why do you not make your servants do this for you? ' It is at least entertaining to see a *nautch*, but to wade through the English interpretation of a waltz, *hic labor hoc opus est*, and the servants ought to perform it." *

" Do you know," said Bhima Gandharva, " that much the same national mode of thought which prompts the Hindu to have his dancing done by the *nautch*-girls also prompts him to have his tax-gathering and general governing done by the English? We are often asked why the spectacle has so often been seen of our native princes quietly yielding up their kingdoms to strangers, and even why we do not now rise and expel the foreigner from power over us. The truth is, most Hindus are only glad to get some one else to do the very hard work of governing. The Englishman is always glad to get a French cook, because the French can cook better than the English. Why should not we be also glad to get English governors, when the English govern so much better than the Hindus? In truth, governing and cooking are very like—the successful

* [Again Lanier's sources were apparently Charles W. Dilke, *Greater Britain*, and Bayard Taylor, *India*.—ED.]

ruler, like the successful cook, has only to consult the tastes
of his employers; and upon any proper theory of politics government becomes just as purely an economic business as cooking. You do not cook your own dinner: why? Because you
desire to devote your time to something better and higher.
So we do not collect taxes and lay them out for the public
convenience, because there are other things we prefer to do.
I am amazed at the modern ideas of government: it is looked
upon as an end, as an objective result in itself, whereas it is
really only the merest of means toward leaving a man at leisure
to attend to his private affairs. The time will come "—and here
the Hindu betrayed more energy than I had hitherto ever seen
him display—" when the world will have its whole governing
work done upon contract by those best fitted for it, and when
such affairs will be looked upon as belonging simply to
the police function of existence, which negatively secures
us from harm without at all positively touching the substantial
advancement of man's life."

The next day we fared northward toward Agra, by Duttiah,
Gwailor, and Dholepore. Learning at Agra that the north-
ward-bound train—for here we had come upon complete civilization again in the East Indian Railway—would pass in an
hour, we determined to reserve the Taj Mahal (the lovely
Pearl Mosque of Agra) until we should be returning from
Delhi to Calcutta. Bhima Gandharva desired me, however, to
see the Douab country and the old sacred city of Mattra; and
so when we had reached Hatras Station, a few miles north of
Agra, we abandoned the railway and struck across to the
southwestward toward Mattra, in a hired carriage.

We were now veritably in ancient Hindustan. It was among
these level plains through which we were rolling that the
antique Brahmans came and propounded that marvellous system which afterward took the whole heart of the land. Nothing could have been more striking than to cast one's eye thus
over the wide cotton-fields—for one associates cotton with
the New—and find them cultivated by these bare-legged and
breech-clouted peasants of the Douab, with ploughs which
consisted substantially of a crooked stick shod with iron at the
end, and with other such farming-implements out of the time

that one thinks of as forty centuries back. Yet in spite of this primitive rudeness of culture, and an aridity of soil necessitating troublesome irrigation, these plains have for a prodigious period of time supported a teeming population; and I could not help crying out to Bhima Gandharva that if we had a few millions of these gentle and patient peasants among the cottonfields of the United States, the South would quickly become a Garden of Delight, and the planters could build Jammah Masjids with rupees for marble.

The conservatism which has preserved for so long a time the ancient rude methods of industry begins to grow on one as one passes between these villages of people who seem to be living as if they were perfectly sure that God never intended them to live any other way.

"It is not long," said my friend, "since a British officer of engineers, on some expedition or other, was encamped for the night at no great distance from here. His tent had been pitched near one of those Persian water-wheels such as you have seen, which, although of great antiquity, are perhaps as ingeniously adapted to the purpose of lifting water as any machine ever invented. The creaking of the wheel annoyed him very much, and after a restless night owing to that cause, he rose and went out of his tent and inquired of the proprietor of the wheel (a native) why in the name of Heaven he never greased it. 'Because,' said the conservative Hindu, 'I have become so accustomed to the noise that I can only sleep soundly while it is going on; when it stops, then I wake, and knowing from the cessation of the sound that my bullock-driver is neglecting his duty, I go out and beat him.' Thus, even the conservation of the useless comes in time to create habits which are useful."

"It is true," I replied, "and it recalls to me a somewhat unusual illustration. A summer or two ago a legal friend of mine who is the possessor of a large family of children, came into the court-room one morning with very red eyes, and to my inquiry concerning the cause of the same he replied: 'To tell you the truth, I can't go to sleep unless a child is crying about the house somewhere; but my wife left town yesterday for the summer with all the children, and I haven't had a wink the whole night.'"

A drive of some five hours brought us to Mattra after dark, and as we crossed the bridge of boats over the sacred Jumna (the *Yamuna* of the Sanskrit poems) he seemed indeed thrice holy with his bosom full of stars. Mattra, which lies immediately on the western bank of the river, stands next to Benares among the holy cities of the Hindus; here both the soil and the river-water are consecrated, for this was the birthplace of Krishna, or, more properly speaking, the scene of that avatar of Vishnu which is known as Krishna. When we rose early in the morning and repaired to the river-bank, hundreds of the faithful were ascending and descending the numerous *ghâts* leading down the high bank to the water, while a still more animated crowd of both sexes were standing up to their middle in the stream, throwing the water in this direction and that, and mingling their personal ablutions with the rites of worship in such a way as might at once clean both souls and bodies. Evidences of the holy character of the town met us everywhere as we strolled back to our lodgings. Sacred monkeys, painted red over their hind quarters in consecration to the monkey-god Hanuman, capered and grinned about us, and sacred bulls obstructed our way along the narrow and dirty streets, while everywhere we saw pictures representing Krishna,—sometimes much like an Apollo in the guise of a youthful shepherd playing the flute to a group of young ladies who danced under a tree; sometimes as a Hercules strangling a serpent or performing other feats of physical strength.

Fabulous stories are told of the early wealth and glory of Mattra. Ferishta relates that when Mahmoud of Ghazni had arrived with his troops in the neighborhood in the year 1017, he heard of this rich city consecrated to Krishna Vasu-Deva, and straightway marching upon it captured it and gave it up to plunder. Writing of it afterward to the governor of Ghazni, he declared that such another city could not be built within two centuries; that it contained one thousand edifices " as firm as the faith of the faithful," and mostly built of marble; that in one of the temples had been found five golden idols in whose heads were ruby eyes worth fifty thousand *dinars*; that in another was a sapphire weighing four hundred *miskals* (the present *miskal* of Bosrah is seventy-two grains), the image itself producing after being melted ninety-eight thousand three hundred *miskals* of pure gold; and that besides these there were captured one hundred silver idols, each of which was a camel's load.

We spent a pleasant morning in wandering about the old ruined fort which was built here by Jey Singh (or Jaya Sinha), the famous astronomer, and we were particularly attracted, each in his own contemplative and quiet way, by the ruins of an observatory which we found on the roof of one of the buildings, where the remains of old dials, horizontal circles, and mural instruments lay scattered about. I think the only remark made by either of us was when Bhima Gandharva declared in a voice of much earnestness, from behind a broken gnomon where he had esconced himself, that he saw Time lying yonder on his back with his head on a broken dial, nearly asleep.

Returning to Hatras Station on the same day, we again took the train, and this time did not leave it until we had crossed the great tubular bridge over the Jumna and come to a standstill in the station at Delhi. Here we found one of the apparently innumerable friends of Bhima Gandharva, a banker of Delhi, awaiting us with a carriage, and we were quickly driven to his residence,—a circumstance, by the way, which I discovered next day to be a legitimate matter of felicitation to myself, for there is, strange to say, no hotel in Delhi for Europeans, travellers being dependent upon the accommodations of a *dák*-bungalow where one is lodged for a rupee a day.

In the morning we made an early start for the palace of the padishahs, which stands near the river and indeed may be said to constitute the eastern portion of the city, having a wall of a mile in extent on its three sides, while the other abuts along the offset of the Jumna upon which Delhi is built. Passing under a splendid Gothic arch in the centre of a tower, then along a vaulted aisle in the centre of which was an octagonal court of stone, the whole route being adorned with flowers carved in stone and inscriptions from the Koran, we finally gained the court of the palace in which is situated the Dewani Khas, the famous throne-room which contained the marvellous "peacock throne." I found it exteriorly a beautiful pavilion of white marble crowned by four domes of the same material,

opening on one side to the court, on the other to the garden
of the palace. On entering, my eye was at first conscious only
of a confused interweaving of traceries and incrustations of
stones, nor was it until after a few moments that I could bring
myself to any definite singling out of particular elements from
the general dream of flowing and intricate lines; but presently
I was enabled to trace with more discriminating pleasure the
flowers, the arabesques, the inscriptions which were carved
or designed in incrustations of smaller stones, or inlaid or gilt
on ceiling, arch, and pillar.

Yet what a sense of utter reverse of fortune comes upon one
after the first shock of the beauty of these delicate stone fantasies! Wherever we went—in the Dewani Aum, or hall of
audience; in the Akbari Hammun, or imperial baths; in the
Samman Burj, or private palace of the padishahs, that famous
and beautiful palace over whose gate the well-known inscription stands, " If there is a Paradise on earth, it is here; " in the
court, in the garden—everywhere was abandonment, everywhere the filthy occupations of birds, everywhere dirt, decay,
desolation.

It was therefore a prodigious change when, emerging from
the main gate of the palace, we found ourselves in the great
thoroughfare of Delhi, the Chandni Chowk (literally " Shining
street "), which runs straight to the Lahore gate of the city.
Here an immense number of daily affairs were transacting
themselves, and the Present eagerly jostled the Past out of the
road. The shops were of a size which would have seemed very
absurd to an enterprising American tradesman, and those dealing in the same commodities appeared to be mostly situated
together—here the shoemakers, there the bankers, and so on.

The gold-embroidered cloths—Delhi is famous for them—
made me think of those embroidered in stone which we had
just seen in the Dewani Khas. These people seem to dream in
curves and flowing lines, as the German dreams in chords and
meandering tones, the Italian in colors and ripe forms.

(" And as the Americans—? " said Bhima Gandharva, with
a little smile as we were walking down the Chandni Chowk.

" The American does not dream—yet," I answered.)

We saw much of the embroidered fabrics known as " kin-

cob " (properly, *kunkhwab*) and "*kalabatu*" ; and Bhima
Gandharva led me into an inner apartment where a *nakad* was
manufacturing the gold thread (called *kalabatoon*) for these
curious loom embroideries. The *kalabatoon* consists of gold
wire wound about a silk thread; and nothing could better illustrate the deftness of the Hindu fingers than the motions of the
workman whom we saw. Over a polished steel hook hung
from the ceiling the end of a reel of slightly twisted silk
thread was passed. This end was tied to a spindle with a long
bamboo shank, which was weighted and nearly reached the
floor. Giving the shank of the spindle a smart roll along his
thigh, the workman set it going with great velocity; then applying to the revolving thread the end of a quantity of gold wire
which was wound upon a different reel, the gold wire twisted
itself in with the silk thread and made a length of *kalabatoon*
about as long as the workman. The *kalabatoon* was then reeled
off on a separate reel, and the process continually repeated.

We stopped at the office of our banker for a moment on our
way along the Chandni Chowk in order to effect some changes
of money. As we were leaving, Bhima Gandharva inquired if
I had observed the young man in the red cotton turban who
had politely broken off in our favor a long negotiation with
our banker, which he resumed when we had finished our little
business.

"Of course I did," I replied. "What a beautiful young
man he was! His acquiline nose, his fair complexion, his
brilliant eyes, his lithe form, his intelligent and vivacious
expression,—all these irresistibly attracted me to hm."

"Ha!" sad Bhima Gandharva, as if he were clearing his
throat. He grasped my arm: "Come, I thought I saw the
young man's father standing near the door as we passed out.
I wonder if *he* will irresistibly attract you?" He made me
retrace my steps to the banker's office. "There he is."

He was the image of the son in feature, yet his face was as
repulsive as his son's was beautiful: the Devil after the fall,
compared with the angel he was before it, would have
presented just such a contrast.

"They are two *Vallàbhàchàryas*," said my companion, as we
walked away. "You know that the trading community of

India, comprehended under the general term of Baniahs, is divided into numerous castes which transmit their avocations from father to son and preserve themselves free from inter-mixture with others. The two men you saw are probably on some important business negotiation connected with Bombay or the west of India; for they are Bhattias, who are also fol-lowers of the most singular religion the world has ever known, —that of the Vallàbhàchàrya or Maharaja sect. These are Epicureans who have quite exceeded, as well in their formal creeds as in their actual practices, the wildest dreams of any of those mortals who have endeavored to make a religion of luxury. They are called Vallàbhàchàryas, from *Vallabha*, the name of their founder, who dates from 1479, and *àchàrya*, a " leader." Their *Pushti Marga,* or eat-and-drink doctrine, is briefly this: in the centre of heaven (*Gouloka*) sits Krishna, of the complexion of a dark cloud, clad in yellow, covered with unspeakable jewels, holding a flute. He is accompanied by Roaha, his wife, and also by three hundred millions of Gopis, or female attendants, each of whom has her own palace and three millions of private maids and waiting-women. It appears that once upon a time two over-loving Gopis quarrelled about the god, and, as might be expected in a place so given over to love, they fell from heaven as a consequence. Animated by love for them, Krishna descended from heaven, incarnated him-self in the form of Vallabha (founder of the sect), and finally redeemed them. Vallabha's descendants are therefore all gods, and reverence is paid them as such, the number of them being now sixty or seventy. To God belong all things—*Tan* (the body), *Man* (the mind) and *Dahn* (earthly possessions). The Vallàbhàchàryas therefore give up all first to be enjoyed by their god, together with his descendants (the Maharajas, as they royally term themselves) and his representatives, the *gosains* or priestly teachers. Apply these doctrines logically, and what a carnival of the senses results! A few years ago one Karsandas Mulji, a man of talent and education, was sued for libel in the court at Bombay by this sect, whose practices he had been exposing. On the trial the evidence revealed such a mass of iniquity, such a complete subversion of the natural proprietary feelings of manhood in the objects of its love, such systematic worship of beastly sin, as must forever give the Vallàbhácháryas pre-eminence among those who have manufactured authority for crime out of the laws of virtue. For the Vallàbhácháryas derive their scriptural sanction from the eighth book of the *Bhagavata Purana*, which they have completely falsified from its true meaning in their translation called the *Prem Sagar*, or *Ocean of Love*. You saw the son? In twenty years—for these people cannot last long—trade and cunning and the riot of all the senses will have made him what you saw the father."

On the next day we visited the Jammah Masjid, the " Great Mosque " of Shah Jehan the renowned, and the glory of Delhi. Ascending the flight of steps leading to the principal entrance, we passed under the lofty arch of the gateway and found ourselves in a great court four hundred and fifty feet square, paved with red stone, in the centre of which a large basin supplied by several fountains contained the water for ceremonial ablutions. On three sides ran light and graceful arcades, while the fourth was quite enclosed by the mass of the mosque proper. Crossing the court and ascending another magnificent flight of stone steps, our eyes were soon commanding the façade of the great structure, and revelling in those prodigious contrasts of forms and colors which it presents. No building could, for this very reason, suffer more from that lack of simultaneity which is involved in any description by words; for it is the vivid shock of seeing in one stroke of the eye these three ripe and luxuriant domes (each of which at the same time offers its own subsidiary opposition of white and black stripes), relieved by the keen heights of the two flanking minarets,—it is this, together with the noble admixtures of reds, whites and blacks in the stones, crowned by the shining of the gilded minaret-shafts, which fills the eye of the beholder with a large content of beautiful form and color.

As one's eye becomes cooler one begins to distinguish in the front, which is faced with slabs of pure white marble, the divisions adorned by inscriptions from the Koran inlaid in letters of black marble, and the singularly airy little pavilions which crown the minarets. We ascended one of the minarets by a winding staircase of one hundred and thirty steps, and here, while our gaze took flight over Delhi and beyond, traversing in a second the achievements of many centuries and races, Bhima Gandharva told me of the glories of old Delhi. Indra-nechta—as Delhi appears in the fabulous legends of old India, and as it is still called by the Hindus—dates its own birth as far back as three thousand years before our era. It was fifty-seven years before the time of Christ that the name of Delhi began to appear in history. Its successive destructions (which a sketch like this cannot even name) left enormous quantities of ruins, and as its successive rebuildings were accomplished by the side of (not upon) these remains, the result has been that from the garden of Shahlimar, the site of which is on the northwest of the town, to beyond the Kantab Minar whose tall column I could plainly distinguish rising up nine miles off to the south-west, the plain of Delhi presents an accumulation and variety of ruins not to be surpassed in the whole world.*

IV

The Koutab Minar, which I had first viewed nine miles off from one of the little kiosquelets crowning the minarets of the Jammah Masjid, improved upon closer acquaintance. One recognizes in the word "minaret" the diminutive of "minar," the latter being to the former as a tower to a turret. This minar of Koutab's—it was erected by the Mussulman general Koutab-Oudeen-Eibeg in the year 1200 to commemorate his success over the Rajpút emperor Pirthi-Raj—is two hundred and twenty feet high, and the cunning architect who designed it managed to greatly intensify its suggestion of loftiness by its peculiar shape. Instead of erecting a shaft with unbroken lines, he placed five truncated cones one upon another in such a way that the impression of their successively lessening diameters should be lengthened by the four balconies which result from the projection of each lower cone beyond the narrower base of the cone placed on it—thus borrowing, as it were, the perspective effects of five shafts and concentrating them upon one. The lower portion, too, shows the near color of red—it is built

* [Lanier's sources for this sketch of Delhi were apparently Charles W. Dilke, *Greater Britain*, and Bayard Taylor, *India.*—ED.]

of the universal red sandstone with which the traveller becomes
so familiar, while the upper part reveals the farther color of
white from its marble casing. Each cone, finally, is carved into
reeds, like a bundle of buttresses supporting a weight enormous
not by reason of massiveness, but of pure height.

The group of ruins about the Koutab Minar was also very
fascinating to me. The Gate of Aladdin, a veritable fairy
portal, with its bewildering wealth of arabesques and flowing
traceries in white marble inlaid upon red stones; the Tomb of
Altamsh; the Mosque of Koutab,—all these, lying in a singular
oasis of trees and greenery that forms a unique spot in the arid
and stony ruin-plain of Delhi, drew me with great power. I
declared to Bhima Gandharva that it was not often in a lifetime that we could get so many centuries together to talk with
at once, and wrought upon him to spend several days with
me, unattended by servants, in this tranquil society of the dead
ages which still live by sheer force of the beautiful that was in
them.

"Very pretty," said my companion, "but not by force of
the beautiful alone. Do you see that iron pillar?" We were
walking in the court of the Mosque of Koutab, and Bhima
pointed, as he spoke, to a plain iron shaft about a foot in
diameter rising in the centre of the enclosed space to a height
of something over twenty feet. "Its base is sunken deeper in
the ground than the upper part is high. It is in truth a gigantic
nail, which, according to popular tradition, was constructed by
an ancient king who desired to play Jael to a certain Sisera that
was in his way. It is related that King Anang Pal was not
satisfied with having conquered the whole of Northern India,
and that a certain Brahman, artfully seizing upon the moment
when his mind was foolish with the fumes of conquest, informed him there was but one obstacle to his acquisition of
eternal power. 'What is that?' said King Anang Pal.—'It is,'
said the Brahman, 'the serpent Sechnaga, who lies under the
earth and stops it, and who at the same time has charge of
Change and Revolution.'—'Well, and what then?' said King
Anang Pal.—'If the serpent were dead there would be no
change,' said the Brahman.—'Well, and what then?' said
King Anang Pal.—'If you should cause to be constructed a

great nail of iron, I will show you a spot where it shall be driven so as to pierce the head of the serpent.' It was done; and the nail—being this column which you now contemplate—was duly driven. Then the Brahman departed from the court. Soon the king's mind began to work, to question, to doubt, to harass itself with a thousand speculations, until his curiosity was inflamed to such a degree that he ordered the nail to be drawn out. With great trouble and outlay this was done; slowly the heavy mass rose, while the anxious king regarded it. At last the lower end came to his view. Rama! it was covered with blood. 'Down with it again!' cries the joyful king; 'perhaps the serpent is not yet dead, and is escaping even now.' But, alas! it would not remain stable in any position, pack and shove howsoever they might. Then the wise Brahman returned. 'O king,' said he, in reply to the monarch's interrogatories, 'your curiosity has cost you your kingdom: the serpent has escaped. Nothing in the world can again give stability to the pillar or to your reign.' And it was true. Change still lived, and King Anang Pal, being up, quickly went down. It is from this pillar that yon same city gets its name. In the tongue of these people *dilha* is, being interpreted, 'tottering'; and hence Dilhi or Delhi. It must be confessed, however, that this is not the account which the iron pillar gives of itself, for the inscription there declares it to have been erected as a monument of victory by King Dhara in the year 317, and it is known as the Lâth (or pillar) of Dhara."

Next day we took train for Agra, which might be called Shah Jehan's "other city," for it was only after building the lovely monument to his queen—the Taj Mahal—which has made Agra famous all over the world, that he removed to Delhi, or that part of it known as Shahjehanabad. Agra, in fact, first attained its grandeur under Akbar, and is still known among the natives as Akbarabad.

"But I am all for Shah Jehan," I said, as, after wandering about the great citadel and palace at the south of the city, we came out on the bank of the Jumna and started along the road which runs by the river to the Taj Mahal. "A prince in whose reign and under whose direct superintendence was fostered the style of architecture which produced that little Mouti Masjid

(Pearl Mosque) which we saw a moment ago—not to speak of the Jammah Masjid of Delhi which we saw there, or of the Taj which we are now going to see—must have been a spacious-souled man, with frank and pure elevations of temper within him, like that exquisite white marble superstructure of the Mouti Masjid which rises from a terrace of rose, as if the glow of crude passion had thus lifted itself into the pure white of tried virtue."

A walk of a mile—during which my companion reviewed the uglinesses as well as the beauties of the great Mogol reign with a wise and impartial calmness that amounted to an affectionate rebuke of my inconsiderate effusiveness—brought us to the main gate of the long red stone enclosure about the Taj. This is itself a work of art—in red stone banded with white marble, surmounted by kiosques, and ornamented with mosaics in onyx and agate. But I stayed not to look at these, nor at the long sweep of the enclosure, crenellated and pavilioned. Hastening through the gate, and moving down a noble alley paved with freestone, surrounded on both sides with trees, rare plants, and flowers, and having a basin running down its length studded with water-jets, I quickly found myself in front of that bewilderment of incrustations upon white marble which constitutes the vistor's first impression of this loveliest of Love's memorials.

I will not describe the Taj. This is not self-denial: the Taj cannot be described. One can, it is true, inform one's friends that the red stone platform upon which the white marble mausoleum stands runs some nine hundred and sixty feet east and west by three hundred and twenty north and south; that the dome is two hundred and seventy feet high; that the incrustations with which the whole superstructure is covered without and within are of rock-crystal, chalcedony, turquoise, lapis-lazuli, agate, carnaline, garnet, oynx, sapphire, coral, Pannah, diamonds, jasper, and conglomerates, brought respectively from Malwa, Asia minor, Thibet, Ceylon, Temen, Broach, Bundel-cund, Persia, Colombo, Arabia, Pannah, the Panjab, and Jes-salmir; that there are, besides the mausoleum, two exquisite mosques occupying angles of the enclosure, the one built be-cause it is the Moslem custom to have a house of prayer near the tomb, the other because the architect's passion for symmetry demanded another to answer to the first, whence it is called *Jawab* (" the answer "); that out of a great convention of all the architects of the East one Isa (Jesus) Mohammed was chosen to build this monument, and that its erection employed twenty thousand men from 1630 to 1647, at a total cost of twelve millions of dollars; and, finally, that the remains of the beautiful queen variously known as Mumtazi Mahal, Mumtazi Zemani, and Taj Bibi, as well as those of her royal husband Shah Jehan, who built this tomb to her memory, repose here.*

But this is not description. The only way to get an idea of the Taj Mahal is—to go and see it.

" But it is ten thousand miles! " you say.

" But it is the Taj Mahal," I reply with calmness. And no one who has seen the Taj will regard this answer as aught but conclusive.

But we had to leave it finally—it and Agra—and after a railway journey of some twelve hours, as we were nearing Allahabad, my companion began, in accordance with his custom, to give me a little preliminary view of the peculiarities of the town.

" We are now approaching," he said, " a city which distinguishes itself from those which you have seen by the fact that besides a very rich past it has also a very bright future. It is situated at the southern point of the Lower Douab, whose fertile and richly-cultivated plains you have been looking at to-day. These plains, with their wealth, converge to a point at Allahabad, narrowing with the approach of the two rivers— the Ganges and the Jumna—that enclose them. The Douab, in fact, derives its name from *do*, " two," and *ab*, " rivers." But Allahabad, besides being situated at the junction of the two great water-ways of India—for here the Jumna unites with the Ganges—is also equally distant from the great extremes of Bombay, Calcutta, and Lahore, and here centres the railway system which unites these widely-separated points. Add to this singular union of commercial advantages the circumstance—so important in an India controlled by Englishmen—that the cli-

* [Again Lanier's sources were apparently Charles W. Dilke, *Greater Britain*, and Bayard Taylor, *India.*—ED.]

mate, though warm, is perfectly wholesome, and you will see
that Allahabad must soon be a great emporium of trade."

" Provided," I suggested, " Benares yonder—Benares is too
close by to feel uninterested—will let it be so."

" Oh, Benares is the holy city. Benares is the blind Teiresias
of India; it has beheld the Divine Form, and in this eternal
grace its eyes have even lost the power of seeing those practical
advancements which usually allure the endeavors of large cities.
Allahabad, although antique and holy also, has never become
so wrapped up in religious absorption."

On the day after our arrival my companion and I were
driven by an English friend engaged in the cultivation of
indigo to an indigo-factory near the town, in compliance with
a desire I had expressed to witness the process of preparing
the dye for market.

" Not long ago," I said to our friend as we were rolling out
of the city, " I was wandering along the banks of that great
lagoon of Florida which is called the Indian River, and my
attention was often attracted to the evidences of extensive cultivation which everywhere abounded. Great ditches, growths of
young forests upon what had evidently been well-ploughed
fields within a century past, and various remains of settlements
constantly revealed themselves. On inquiry I learned that these
were the remains of those great proprietary indigo-plantations
which were cultivated here by English grantees soon after
Florida first came under English protection, and which were
afterward mournfully abandoned to ruin upon the sudden
recession of Florida by the English government." *

" They are ruins of interest to me," said our English friend,
" for one of them—perhaps some one that you beheld—repre-
sents the wreck of my great-great-grandfather's fortune. He
could not bear to stay among the dreadful Spaniards and
Indians; and so, there being nobody to sell to, he simply abandoned homestead, plantations and all, and returned to England,
and, finding soon afterward that the East India Company was
earnestly bent upon fostering the indigo-culture of India, he
came here and recommenced planting. Since then we've all
been indigo-planters—genuine ' blue blood,' we call ourselves."

* [Mentioned briefly in Lanier's *Florida*, see p. 85, above.—ED.]

Indigo itself had a very arduous series of toils to encounter before it could manage to assert itself in the world. The ardent advocates of its azure rival, woad, struggled long before they would allow its adoption. In 1577 the German government officially prohibited the use of indigo, denouncing it as that pernicious, deceitful, and corrosive substance, the Devil's dye. It had, indeed, a worse fate in England, where hard names were supplemented by harsh acts, for in 1581 it was not only pronounced *anathema maranatha* by act of Parliament, but the people were authorized to institute search for it in their neighbors' dye-houses, and were empowered to destroy it wherever found. Not more than two hundred years have passed since this law was still in force. It was only after a determined effort, which involved steady losses for many years, that the East India Company succeeded in re-establishing the culture of indigo in Bengal. The Spanish and French in Central America and the West Indies had come to be large growers, and the production of St. Domingo was very large. But the revolt in the latter island, the Florida disasters, and the continual unsettlement of Mexico, all worked favorably for the planters of India, who may now be called the indigo-producers of the world.

The seed is usually sown in the latter part of October in Bengal, as soon as the annual deposit of the streams has been reduced by drainage to a practicable consistency, though the sowing-season lasts quite on to the end of November. On dry ground the plough is used, the *ryots*, or native farm-laborers, usually planting under directions proceeding from the factory. There are two processes of extracting the dye, known as the method " from fresh leaves " and that " from dry leaves." I found them here manufacturing by the former process. The vats or cisterns of stone were in pairs, the bottom of the upper one of each couple being about on a level with the top of the lower, so as to allow the liquid contents of the former to run freely into the latter. The upper is the fermenting vat, or " steeper," and is about twenty feet square by three deep. The lower is the " beater," and is of much the same dimensions with the upper, except that its length is five or six feet greater. As the twigs and leaves of the plants are brought in from the fields the cuttings are placed in layers in the steeper, logs of wood secured by bamboo withes are placed upon the surface to prevent overswelling, and water is then pumped on or poured from buckets to within a few inches of the top. Fermentation now commences, and continues for fourteen or fifteen hours, varying with the temperature of the air, the wind, the nature of the water used, and the ripeness of the plants. When the agitation of the mass has begun to subside, the liquor is racked off into the lower vat, the "beater," and ten men set to work lustily beating it with paddles (*busquets*), though this is sometimes done by wheels armed with paddle-like appendages. Meanwhile the upper vat is cleaned out, and the refuse mass of cuttings stored up to be used as fuel or as fertilizing material. After an hour and a half's vigorous beating the liquor becomes flocculent. The precipitation is sometimes hastened by lime-water. The liquor is then drained off the dye by the use of filtering-cloths, heat being also employed to drain off the yellow matter and to deepen the color. Then the residuum is pressed in bags, cut into three-inch cubes, dried in the drying-house, and sent to market.

The dry-leaf process depends also upon maceration, the leaves being cropped from the ripe plant, and dried in the hot sunshine during two days, from nine in the morning until four in the afternoon.

On the next day, at an early hour in the morning, my companion and I betook us to the Plain of Alms. I have before mentioned that Allahabad, the ancient city of Prayaga, is doubly sanctified because it is at the junction of the Jumna and the Ganges, and these two streams are affluents of its sanctity as well as of its trade. The great plain of white sand which is enclosed between the blue lake-like expanses of the two meeting rivers is the Plain of Alms. In truth, there are three rivers which unite here—the Ganges, the Jumna and the Saravasti—and this thrice-hallowed spot is known in the Hindu mythologic system as the Triveni.*

"But where is the third?" I asked as we stood gazing across the unearthly-looking reaches of white sand far down the blue sweep of the mysterious waters.

* [Lanier's probable sources were Charles W. Dilke, *Greater Britain*, and Bayard Taylor, *India*.—ED.]

" Thereby hangs a tale," replied my companion. " It is invisible here, but I will show you what remains of it presently when we get into the fort. Here is a crowd of pilgrims coming to bathe in the purifying waters of the confluence: let us follow them."

As they reached the shore a Brahman left his position under a great parasol and placed himself in front of the troop of believers, who, without regard to sex, immediately divested themselves of all clothing except a narrow cloth about the loins, and followed him into the water. Here they proceeded to imitate his motions, just as pupils in a calisthenic class follow the movements of their teacher, until the ceremonies of purification were all accomplished.

" A most villainous-faced penitent!" I exclaimed as one of their number came out, and, as if wearied by his exertions, lay down near us on the sand.

Bhima Gandharva showed his teeth: " He is what your American soldiers called in the late war a substitute. Some rich Hindu, off somewhere in India, has found the burden of his sins pressing heavily upon him, while at the same time the cares of this world, or maybe bodily infirmities, prevent him from visiting the Triveni. Hence, by the most natural arrangement in the world, he has hired this man to come in his place and accomplish his absolution for him."

Striking off to the westward from the Plain of Alms, we soon entered the citadel of Akbar, which he built so as to command the junction of the two streams. Passing the Lâth (pillar) of Asoka, my companion led me down into the old subterranean Buddhistic temple of Patal Pouri and showed me the ancient Achaya Bat, or sacred tree-trunk, which its custodians declare to be still living, although more than two thousand years old. Presently we came to a spot under one of the citadel towers where a feeble ooze of water appeared.

" Behold," said my friend, " the third of the Triveni rivers! This is the river Saravasti. You must know that once upon a time, Saravasti, goddess of learning, was tripping along fresh from the hills to the west of Yamuna (the Jumna), bearing in her hand a book. Presently she entered the sandy country, when on a sudden a great press of frightful demons uprose, and so terrified her that in the absence of other refuge she sank into the earth. Here she reappears. So the Hindus fable."

On our return to our quarters we passed a verandah where an old pedagogue was teaching a lot of young Mussulmans the accidence of Oordoo, a process which he accomplished much as the " singing geography " man used to impart instruction in the olden days when I was a boy,—to wit, by causing the pupils to sing in unison the A, B, C. Occasionally, too, the little, queer-looking chaps squatted tailorwise on the floor would take a turn at writing the Arabic character on their slates. A friendly hookah in the midst of the group betrayed the manner in which the wise man solaced the labors of education.

On the next day, as our indigo-planter came to drive us to the gardens of Chusru, he said, " An English friend of mine who is living in the Moffussil—the Moffussil is anywhere *not* in Calcutta, Bombay, or Madras—not far from Patna has just written me that word has been brought from one of the Sontal villages concerning the depredations of a tiger from which the inhabitants have recently suffered, and that a grand hunt, elephant-back, has been organized through the combined con- tributions of the English and native elephant-owners. He presses me to come, and as an affair of this sort is by no means common—for it is no easy matter to get together and support a dozen elephants and the army of retainers considered neces- sary in a great hunt—I thought perhaps you would be glad to accompany me."

Of course I was; and Bhima Gandharva, though he would not take any active part in the hunt, insisted upon going along in order to see that no harm came to me.

On the next day, therefore, we all took train and fared southeastward toward Calcutta as far as to Bhagalpur, where we left the railway, sending our baggage on to Calcutta, and took private conveyance to a certain spot among the Rajmahal Mountains, where the camp had been fixed by retainers on the day before. It was near a village of the Sontals that we passed before reaching it,—a singular-enough spectacle this last, with its round-roofed huts and a platform at its entrance upon which and under which were ghastly heaps of the skulls of animals slain by the villagers. These Sontals reminded me of the

Gónds whom I had seen, though they seemed to be far manlier representatives of the autochthonal races of India than the former. They are said to number about a million, and inhabit a belt of country some four hundred miles long by one hundred broad, including the Rajmahal Mountains, and extending from near the Bay of Bengal to the edge of Behar. So little have they been known that when in the year 1855 word was brought to Calcutta that the Sontals had risen and were murdering the Europeans, many of the English are said to have asked not only *Who* are the Sontals? but *What* are the Sontals?

The more inaccessible tops of the same mountains, the Rajmahal, are occupied by a much ruder set of people, the Mâlers, who appear to have been pushed up here by the Sontals, as the Sontals were themselves pressed by the incoming Aryans.

As we arrived at the camp I realized the words of our English friend concerning the magnitude of the preparations for a tiger-hunt undertaken on the present scale. The tents of the sportsmen, among whom were several English army officers and civil officials, besides a native rajah, were pitched in a beautiful glade canopied by large trees, and near these were the cooking-tents and the lodging-places of the servants, of whom there was the liberal allowance which is customary in India. Through the great tree-trunks I could see elephants, camels, and horses tethered about the outskirts of the camp, while the carts, elephant-pads and other *impedimenta* lying about gave the whole the appearance of an army at bivouac. Indeed, it was not an inconsiderable force that we could have mustered. There were fifteen or twenty elephants in the party. Every elephant had two men, the *mahaut* and his assistant; every two camels, one man; every cart, two men; besides whom were the *kholassies* (tent-pitchers), the *chikarries* (native huntsmen to mark down and flush the tiger), letter-carriers for the official personages, and finally the personal servants of the party, amounting in all to something like a hundred and fifty souls. The commissary arrangements of such a body of men and beasts were no light matter, and had on this occasion been placed by contract in the hands of a flour-and-grain merchant from Patna. As night drew on the scene became striking in the extreme, and I do not think I felt the fact of India more keenly at any time than while Bhima Gandharva and I, slipping away from a party who were making merry over vast allowances of pale ale and cheroots, went wandering about under the stars and green leaves, picking our way among the huge forms of the mild-countenanced elephants and the bizarre figures of the camels.

On the next day, after a leisurely breakfast at eight—the hunt was to begin at midday—my kind host assigned me an elephant, and his servants proceeded to equip me for the hunt, placing in my howdah brandy, cold tea, cheroots, a rifle, a smooth-bore, ammunition, an umbrella, and finally a blanket.

" And what is the blanket for? " I asked.

" For the wild-bees; and if your elephant happens to stir up a nest of them, the very best thing in the world you can do is to throw it incontinently over your head," added my host, laughing.

The tiger had been marked down in a spot some three miles from camp, and when our battle-array, which had at first taken up the line of march in a very cozy and gentleman-militia sort of independence, had arrived within a mile of our destination, the leader who had been selected to direct our movements caused us all to assume more systematic dispositions, issued orders forbidding a shot to be fired at any sort of game, no matter how tempting, less than the royal object of our chase, and then led the way down the glade, which now began to spread out into lower and wetter ground covered by tall grasses and thickets. The hunt now began in earnest. Hot, flushed, scratched as to the face by the tall reeds, rolling on my ungainly animal's back as if I were hunting in an open boat on a chopping sea, I had the additional nervous distraction of seeing many sorts of game—deer, wild-hogs, pea-fowl, partridges— careering about in the most exasperating manner immediately under my gun-muzzle. To add to my dissatisfaction, presently I saw a wild-hog dash out of a thicket with her young litter immediately across our path, and as my elephant stepped excitedly along one of his big fore feet crunched directly down on a beautiful little pig, bringing a quickly-smothered squeak which made me quite cower before the eye of Bhima Gandharva as he stood looking calmly forward beside me. So we tramped on through the thickets and grasses. An hour passed; the deployed huntsmen had again drawn in together, somewhat bored; we were all red-faced and twig-tattooed; no tiger was to be found; we gathered into a sort of circle and were looking at each other with that half-foolish, half-mad disconsolateness which men's faces show when they are unsuccessfully engaged in a matter which does not amount to much even after it is successfully achieved,—when suddenly my elephant flourished his trunk, uttered a shrill trumpeting sound, and dashed violently to one side, just as I saw a grand tiger, whose coat seemed to be all alive with throbbing spots, flying through the air pass me to the haunches of the less wary elephant beside which mine had been walking. Instantly the whole party was in commotion. "*Bagh! bagh!*" yelled the *mahauts* and attendants; the elephants trumpeted and charged hither and thither. The tiger seemed to become fairly insane under the fusillade which greeted him; he leapt so desperately from one side to the other as to appear for a few moments almost ubiquitous, while at every discharge the frantic natives screamed "*Lugga! lugga!*" without in the least knowing whether he was hit (*lugga*) or not, till presently, when I supposed he must have received at least forty shots in his body, he fell back from a desperate attempt to scale the back of the rajah's elephant, and lay quite still.

"I thought that last shot of mine would finish him," said one of the English civil officials as we all crowded around the magnificent beast.

"Whether it did or not, I distinctly saw him cringe at *my* shot," hotly said another. "There's always a peculiar look a tiger has when he gets his death-wound: it's unmistakable when you once know it."

"And I'll engage to eat him," interjected a third, "if I didn't blow off the whole side of his face with my smooth-bore when he stuck his muzzle up into my howdah."

"Gentlemen," said our leader, a cool and model old hunter, "the shortest way to settle who is the owner of this tiger-skin is to examine the perforations in it."

Which we all accordingly fell to doing.

" B——, I'm afraid you've a heavy meal ahead of you: his muzzle is as guiltless of harm as a baby's," said one of the claimants.

" Well," retorted B——, " but I don't see any sign of that big bore of yours, either."

" By Jove! " said the leader, in some astonishment as our search proceeded unsuccessfully, " has *anybody* hit him? Maybe he died of fright."

At this moment Bhima Gandharva calmly advanced, lifted up the great fore leg of the tiger and showed us a small blue hole just underneath it: at the same time he felt along the tiger's skin on the opposite side to the hole, rolled the bullet about under the cuticle where it had lodged after passing through the animal, and deftly making an incision with his knife drew it forth betwixt his thumb and finger. He handed it to the gentleman whose guests we were, and to whom the rifle belonged which had been placed in our howdah, and then modestly withdrew from the circle.

" There isn't another rifle in camp that carries so small a bullet," said our host, holding up the ball, " and there can't be the least doubt that the Hindu is the man who killed him."

Not another bullet-hole was to be found.

" When *did* you do it? " I asked of Bhima. " I knew not that you had fired at all."

" When he made his first leap from the thicket," he said quietly. " I feared he was going to land directly on you. The shot turned him."

At this the three discomfited claimants of the tiger-skin (which belongs to him who kills) with the heartiest English good-nature burst into roars of laughter, each at himself as well as the others, and warmly shook Bhima's hand amid a general outbreak of applause from the whole company.

Then amid a thousand jokes the tiffin-baskets were brought out, and we had a royal lunch while the tiger was " padded "— *i. e.*, placed on one of the unoccupied elephants; and finally we got us back to camp, where the rest of the day was devoted to dinner and cheroots.

From the tiger to the town, from the cries of jackals to those of street-vendors—this is an easy transition in India; and it was only the late afternoon of the second day after the tiger-hunt when my companion and I were strolling along the magnificent Esplanade of Calcutta, having cut across the mountains, elephant-back, early in the morning to a station where we caught the down-train.

Solidity, wealth, trade, ponderous ledgers, capacious ships' bottoms, merchandise transformed to magnificence, an ample-stomached *bourgeoisie*,—this is what comes to one's mind as one faces the broad walk in front of Fort William and looks across the open space to the palaces, the domes, the columns of modern and English Calcutta; or again as one wanders along the strand in the evening when the aristocrats of commerce do congregate, and, as it were, gazette the lengths of their bank-balances in the glitter of their equipages and appointments; or again as one strolls about the great public gardens or the amplitudes of Tank Square, whose great tank of water suggests the luxury of the dwellers hereabout; or the numerous other paths of comfort which are kept so by constant lustrations from the skins of the water-bearers. The whole situation seems that of ease and indulgence. The very circular verandahs of the rich men's dwellings expand like the ample vests of trustees and directors after dinner. The city extends some four and a half miles along the left bank of the Hooghly, and its breadth between the " Circular Road " and the river is about a mile and a half. If one cuts off from this space that part which lies south of a line drawn eastward from the Beebee Ross Ghát to the Upper Circular Road—the northern portion thus segregated being the native town—one has a veritable city of palaces, and when to these one adds the magnificent suburbs lying beyond the old circumvallation of the " Mahratta Ditch "—Chitpore, Nundenbagh, Bobar, Simla, Sealdah, Entally, Ballygunge, Bhovaneepore, Allypore, Kidderpore—together with the riverward-sloping lawns and stately mansions of " Garden Reach " on the sea-side of town, and the great dockyards and warehouses of the right bank of the river opposite the city, one has enclosed a space which may probably vie with any similar one in the world for the appearances and the realities of wealth within it.

But if one should allow this first impression of Calcutta—

an impression in which good eating and the general pamper-
ing of the flesh seem to be the most prominent features—to
lead one into the belief that here is nothing but moneymaking
and grossness, one would commit a serious mistake. It is
among the rich *babous*, or commercial natives, of Calcutta that
the remarkable reformatory movement known as "Young
India" has had its origin, and it would really seem that the
very same qualities of patience, of prudence, of foresight, and
of good sense which have helped these *babous* to accumulate
their wealth are now about being applied to the nobler and far
more difficult work of lifting their countrymen out of the
degradations of old outworn customs and faiths upon some
higher plane of reasonable behavior.

"In truth," said Bhima Gandharva to me one day as we were
taking our customary stroll along the Esplanade, "you have
now been from the west of this country to the east of it. You
have seen the Past of India; I wish that you may have at least
a glimpse of its Future. Here comes a young *babou* of my
acquaintance to whom I will make you known. He is an
enthusiastic member of 'Young India'; he has received a
liberal education at one of the numerous schools which his
order has so liberally founded in modern years, and you will,
I am convinced, be pleased with the wisdom and moderation of
his sentiments."

Just as I was reaching out my hand to take that of the
babou, in compliance with Bhima's introduction, an enormous
adjutant—one of the great pouched cranes (*arghilahs*) that
stalk about Calcutta under protection of the law, and do much
of the scavenger-work of the city—walked directly between us,
eyeing each of us with his red round eyes in a manner so
ludicrous that we all broke forth in a fit of laughter that lasted
for several minutes, while the ungainly bird stalked away with
much the stolid air of one who has seen something whereof he
thinks but little.

The *babou* addressed me in excellent English, and after some
preliminary inquiries as to my stay in Calcutta, accompanied by
hospitable invitations, he gradually began, in response to my
evident desire, to talk of the hopes and fears of the new party.

"It is our great misfortune," said he, "that we have here

to do with that portion of my countrymen which is perhaps most deeply sunk in the mire of ancient custom. We have begun by unhesitatingly leading in the front ourselves whenever any disagreeable consequences are to be borne by reason of our infringement of the old customs. Take, for example, the problem of the peculiar position of women among the Hindus. Perhaps "—and here the *babou's* voice grew very grave and earnest—" the human imagination is incapable of conceiving a lot more wretched than that of the Hindu widow. By immemorial tradition she could escape it only through the flames of the *satti*, the funeral-pile upon which she could burn herself with the dead body of her husband. But the *satti* is now prohibited by the English law, and the poor woman who loses her husband is, according to custom, stripped of her clothing, arrayed in coarse garments, and doomed thenceforth to perform the most menial offices of the family for the remainder of her life, as one accursed beyond redemption. To marry again is impossible: the man who marries a widow suffers punishments which no one who has not lived under the traditions of caste can possibly comprehend. The wretched widow has not even the consolations which come from books: the decent Hindu woman does not know how to read or write. There was still one avenue of escape from this life. She might have become a *nautchni*. What wonder that there are so many of these? How, then, to deal with this fatal superstition, or rather conglomerate of superstitions, which seems to suffer no more from attack than a shadow? We have begun the revolution by marrying widows just as girls are married, and by showing that the loss of caste—which indeed we have quite abolished among ourselves—entails necessarily none of those miserable consequences which the priests have denounced; and we strike still more deeply at the root of the trouble by instituting schools where our own daughters, and all others' whom we can prevail upon to send, are educated with the utmost care. In our religion we retain Brahma—by whom we mean the one supreme God of all—and abolish all notions of the saving efficacy of merely ceremonial observances, holding that God has given to man the choice of right and wrong, and the dignity of exercising his powers in such accordance with his convictions as shall secure his eternal happiness. To these cardinal principles we subjoin the most unlimited toleration for other religions, recognizing in its fullest extent the law of the adaptation of the forms of belief to the varying moulds of character resulting from race, climate, and all those great conditions of existence which differentiate men one from another."

"How," I asked, "do the efforts of the Christian missionaries comport with your own sect's?"

"Substantially, we work together. With the sincerest good wishes for their success—for every sensible man must hail any influence which instils a single new idea into the wretched Bengalee of low condition—I am yet free to acknowledge that I do not expect the missionaries to make many converts satisfactory to themselves, for I am inclined to think them not fully aware of the fact that in importing Christianity among the Hindus they have not only brought the doctrine, but they have brought the *Western form* of it, and I fear that they do not recognize how much of the nature of substance this matter of form becomes when one is attempting to put new wine into old bottles. Nevertheless, God speed them! I say. We are all full of hope. Signs of the day meet us everywhere. It is true that still, if you put yourself on the route to Orissa, you will meet thousands of pilgrims who are going to the temple at Jaghernâth (what your Sunday-school books call Juggernaut) for the purpose of worshipping the hideous idols which it contains; and although the English policemen accompany the procession of the Rattjattra—when the idol is drawn on the monstrous car by the frenzied crowd of fanatics—and enforce the law which now forbids the poor insane devotees from casting themselves beneath the fatal wheels, still it cannot be denied that the devotees are there, nor that Jaghernâth is still the Mecca of millions of debased worshippers. It is also true that the pretended exhibitions of the tooth of Buddha can still inspire an ignorant multitude of people to place themselves in adoring procession and to debase themselves with the absurd rites of frenzy and unreason. Nor do I forget the fact that my countrymen are broken up into hundreds of sects, and their language frittered into hundreds of dialects. Yet, as I said, we are full of hope, and there can be no man so bold as to limit the capabilities of that blood which flows in English veins as well as in Hindu. Somehow or other, India is now not so gloomy a topic to read of or to talk of as it used to be. The recent investigations of Indian religion and philosophy have set many European minds upon trains of thought which are full of novelty and of promise. India is not the only land—you who are from America know it full well—where the current orthodoxy has become wholly unsatisfactory to many of the soberest and most practically earnest men; and I please myself with believing that it is now not wholly extravagant to speak of a time when these two hundred millions of industrious, patient, mild-hearted, yet mistaken Hindus may be found leaping joyfully forward out of their old shackles toward the larger purposes which reveal themselves in the light of progress."

At the close of our conversation, which was long and to me intensely interesting, the *babou* informed us that he had recently become interested with a company of Englishmen in reclaiming one of the numerous and hitherto wholly unused islands in the Sunderbunds for the purpose of devoting it to the culture of rice and sugar-cane, and that if we cared to penetrate some of the wildest and most picturesque portions of that strange region he would be glad to place at our disposal one of the boats of the company, which we would find lying at Port Canning. I eagerly accepted the proposition; and on the next day, taking the short railway which connects Calcutta and Port Canning, we quickly arrived at the latter point, and proceeded to bestow ourselves comfortably in the boat for a lazy voyage along the winding streams and canals which intersect the great marshes. It was not long after leaving Port Canning ere we were in the midst of the aquatic plants, the adjutants, the herons, the thousand sorts of water-birds, the crocodiles, which here abound.

The Sunderbunds—as the natives term that alluvial region which terminates the delta of the Ganges—can scarcely be considered either land or sea, but rather a multitudinous reticulation of streams, the meshes of which are represented by islands in all the various stages of consistency between water and dry land. Sometimes we floated along the lovely curves of canals which flowed underneath ravishing arches formed by the meeting overhead of great trees which leaned to each other from either bank; while again our course led us between shores which were mere plaits and interweavings of the long stems and broad leaves of gigantic water-plants. The islands were but little inhabited, and the few denizens we saw were engaged either in fishing or in the manufacture of salt from the brackish water. Once we landed at a collection of huts where were quartered the laborers of another company which had been successfully engaged in prosecuting the same experiment of rice-culture which our friend had just undertaken. It was just at the time when the laborers were coming in from the fields. The wife of the one to whose hut my curiosity led me had prepared his evening meal of rice and curry, and he was just sitting down to it as I approached. With incredible deftness he mingled the curry and the rice together— he had no knife, fork, or spoon—by using the end-joints of his thumb and fingers; then, when he had sufficiently amalgamated the mass, he rolled up a little ball of it, placed the ball upon his crooked thumb as a boy does a marble, and shot it into his mouth without losing a grain. Thus he despatched his meal, and I could not but marvel at the neatness and dexterity which he displayed, with scarcely more need of a finger-bowl at the end than the most delicate feeder you shall see at Delmonico's.

The crops raised upon the rich alluvium of these islands were enormous, and if the other difficulties attending cultivation in such a region could be surmounted, there seemed to be no doubt of our friend the *babou's* success in his venture. But it was a wild and lonesome region, and as we floated along, after leaving the island, up a canal which flamed in the sunset like a great illuminated baldric slanting across the enormous shoulder of the world, a little air came breathing over me as if it had just blown from the mysterious regions where space and time are not, or are in different forms from those we know. A sense of the crudity of these great expanses of sea-becoming-land took possession of me; the horizon stretched away like a mere endless continuation of marshes and streams; the face of my companion was turned off seaward with an expression of ineffably mellow tranquillity; a glamour came about as if the world were again formless and void, and as if the marshes were chaos. I shivered with a certain eager expectation of beholding the shadowy outline of a great and beautiful spirit moving over the face of the waters to create a new world. I drew my gaze with difficulty from the heavens and turned toward my companion.

He was gone. The sailors also had disappeared.

And there, as I sat in that open boat, midst of the Sunderbunds, at my domestic antipodes, happened to me the most wondrous transformation which the tricksy stage-carpenters and scene-shifters of the brain have ever devised. For this same far-stretching horizon which had just been alluring my soul into the depths of the creative period, suddenly contracted itself four-square into the somewhat yellowed walls of a certain apartment which I need not now further designate, and the sun and his flaming clouds became no more nor less than a certain half dozen of commonplace pictures upon these same yellowish walls; and the boat wherefrom I was about to view the birth of continents degraded itself into a certain—or, I had more accurately said, a very uncertain—cane chair, wherein I sit writing these lines and mourning for my lost Bhima Gandharva.

THE STORY OF A PROVERB *

I

ONCE UPON a time,—if my memory serves me correctly, it was in the year 6⅞,—His Intensely-Serene-and-Alto-gether-Perfectly-Astounding Highness the King of Nimporte was reclining in his royal palace. The casual observer (though it must be said that casual observers were as rigidly excluded from the palace of Nimporte as if they had been tramps) might easily have noticed that his majesty was displeased.

The fact is, if his majesty had been a little boy, he would have been whipped and sent to bed for the sulks; but even during this early period of which I am writing, the strangeness of things had reached such a pitch, that in the very moment at which this story opens the King of Nimporte arose from his couch, seized by the shoulders his grand vizier (who was not at all in the sulks, but was endeavoring, as best he could, to smile from the crown of his head to the soles of his feet), and kicked him down-stairs.

As the grand vizier reached the lowest step in the course of his tumble, a courier covered with dust was in the act of putting his foot upon the same. But the force of the grand vizier's fall was such as to knock both the courier's legs from under him; and as, in the meantime, the grand vizier had wildly clasped his arms around the courier's body, to arrest his own descent, the result was such a miscellaneous rolling of the two men, that for a moment no one was able to distinguish which legs belonged to the grand vizier and which to the courier.

"Has she arrived?" asked the grand vizier, as soon as his breath came.

* [Written at West Chester, Pa., during the summer of 1876; published, with illustrations by E. B. Bensell, in *St. Nicholas*, IV, 468-472 (May, 1877), the text here followed; reprinted in Mary Burt's *The Lanier Book* (New York, 1904), pp. 3-19, and in Henry W. Lanier's *Selections from Sidney Lanier* (New York, 1916), pp. 117-125. The MS, signed "Sidney Lanier, West Chester, Pa.," now at the Huntington Library, differs from the text here printed only in a few minor stylistic details.—ED.]

" Yes," said the courier, already hastening up the stairs.

At this magic word, the grand vizier again threw his arms around the courier, kissed him, released him, whirled himself about like a teetotum, leaped into the air and cracked his heels thrice before again touching the earth, and said:

" Allah be praised! Perhaps now we shall have some peace in the palace."

In truth, the King of Nimporte had been waiting two hours for his bride, whom he had never seen; for, according to custom, one of his great lords had been sent to the court for the bride's father, where he had married her by proxy for his royal master, and whence he was now conducting her to the palace. For two hours the King of Nimporte had been waiting for a courier to arrive and announce to him that the cavalcade was on its last day's march over the plain, and was fast approaching the city.

As soon as the courier had delivered his message, the king kicked him down-stairs (for not arriving sooner, his majesty incidentally remarked), and ordered the grand vizier to cause that a strip of velvet carpet should be laid from the front door of the grand palace, extending a half-mile down the street in the direction of the road by which the cavalcade was approaching; adding that it was his royal intention to walk this distance, for the purpose of giving his bride a more honorable reception than any bride of any king of Nimporte had ever before received.

The grand vizier lost no time in carrying out his instructions, and in a short time the king appeared stepping along the carpet in the stateliest manner, followed by a vast and glittering retinue of courtiers, and encompassed by multitudes of citizens who had crowded to see the pageant.

As the king, bareheaded and barefooted (for at this time everybody went barefoot in Nimporte), approached the end of the carpet, he caught sight of his bride, who was but a few yards distant on her milk-white palfrey.

Her appearance was so ravishingly beautiful, that the king seemed at first dazed, like a man who has looked at the sun; but, quickly recovering his wits, he threw himself forward, in the ardor of his admiration, with the intention of running to his bride and dropping on one knee at her stirrup, while he would gaze into her face with adoring humility. And as the king rushed forward with this impulse, the populace cheered with the wildest enthusiasm at finding him thus capable of the feelings of an ordinary man.

But in an instant a scene of the wildest commotion ensued. At the very first step which the king took beyond the end of the carpet, his face grew suddenly white, and, with a loud cry of pain, he fell fainting to the earth. He was immediately surrounded by the anxious courtiers; and the court physician, after feeling his pulse for several minutes, and inquiring very carefully of the grand vizier whether his majesty had on that day eaten any green fruit, was in the act of announcing that it was a violent attack of a very Greek disease indeed, when the bride (who had dismounted and run to her royal lord with wifely devotion) called the attention of the excited courtiers to his majesty's left great toe. It was immediately discovered that, in his first precipitate step from off the carpet to the bare ground, his majesty had set his foot upon a very rugged pebble, the effect of which upon tender feet accustomed to nothing but velvet, had caused him to swoon with pain.

As soon as the King of Nimporte opened his eyes in his own palace, where he had been quickly conveyed and ministered to by the bride, he called his trembling grand vizier and inquired to whom belonged the houses at that portion of the street where his unfortunate accident had occurred. Upon learning the names of these unhappy property-owners, he instantly ordered that they and their entire kindred should be beheaded, and the adjacent houses burned for the length of a quarter of a mile.

The king further instructed the grand vizier that he should instantly convene the cabinet of councilors and devise with them some means of covering the whole earth with leather, in order that all possibility of such accidents to the kings of Nimporte might be completely prevented,—adding that if the cabinet should fail, not only in devising the plan, but in actually carrying it out within the next three days, then the whole body of councilors should be executed on the very spot where the king's foot was bruised.

Then the king kissed his bride, and was very happy.

But the grand vizier, having communicated these instructions to his colleagues of the cabinet,—namely, the postmaster-general, the praetor, the sachem, and the three Scribes-and-Pharisees,—proceeded to his own home, and consulted his wife, whose advice he was accustomed to follow with the utmost faithfulness. After thinking steadily for two days and nights, on the morning of the third day the grand vizier's wife advised him to pluck out his beard, to tear up his garments, and to make his will; declaring that she could not, upon the most mature deliberation, conceive of any course more appropriate to the circumstances.

The grand vizier was in the act of separating his last pair of bag-trousers into very minute strips indeed, when a knocking at the door arrested his hand, and in a moment afterward the footman ushered in a young man of very sickly complexion, attired in the seediest possible manner. The grand vizier immediately recognized him as a person well known about Nimporte for a sort of loafer, given to mooning about the clover-fields, and to meditating upon things in general, but not commonly regarded as ever likely to set a river on fire.

"O grand vizier!" said this young person (the inhabitants of Nimporte usually pronounced this word much like the French *personne*, which means nobody), "I have come to say that if you will procure the attendance of the king and court to-morrow morning at eleven o'clock in front of the palace, I will cover the whole earth with leather for his majesty in five minutes."

Then the grand vizier arose in the quietest possible manner, and kicked the young person down the back-stairs; and when he had reached the bottom stair, the grand vizier tenderly lifted him in his arms and carried him back to the upper landing, and then kicked him down the front-stairs,—in fact, quite out of the front gate.

Having accomplished these matters satisfactorily, the grand vizier returned with a much lighter heart, and completed a draft of his last will and testament for his lawyer, who was to call at eleven.

Punctually at the appointed time—being exactly three days

from the hour when the grand vizier received his instructions—
the King of Nimporte and all his court, together with a great
mass of citizens, assembled at the scene of the accident to witness the decapitation of the entire cabinet. The headsman had
previously arranged his apparatus; and presently the six unfortunate wise men were seen standing with hands tied behind,
and with heads bent forward meekly over the six blocks in a
row.

The executioner advanced and lifted a long and glittering
sword. He was in the act of bringing it down with terrific force
upon the neck of the grand vizier, when a stir was observed in
the crowd, which quickly increased to a commotion so great
that the king raised his hand and bade the executioner wait
until he could ascertain the cause of the disturbance.

In a moment more, the young person appeared in the open
space which had been reserved for the court, and with a mingled air of proud self-confidence and of shrinking reserve,
made his obeisance before the king.

" O king of the whole earth! " he said, " if within the next
five minutes I shall have covered the whole earth with leather
for your majesty, will your gracious highness remit the sentence
which has been pronounced upon the wise men of the cabinet? "

It was impossible for the king to refuse.

" Will your majesty then be kind enough to advance your
right foot? "

The young person kneeled, and drawing a bundle from his
bosom, for a moment manipulated the king's right foot in a
manner which the courtiers could not very well understand.

" Will your majesty now advance your majesty's left foot? "
said the young person again; and again he manipulated.

" Will your majesty now walk forth upon the stones? " said
the young person; and his majesty walked forth upon the stones.

" Will your majesty now answer: If your majesty should
walk over the entire globe, would not your majesty's feet find
leather between them and the earth the whole way? "

" It is true," said his majesty.

" Will your majesty further answer: Is not the whole earth,
so far as your majesty is concerned, now covered with leather? "

" It is true," said his majesty.

" Oh king of the whole earth, what is it? " cried the whole court in one breath.

" In fact, my lords and gentlemen," said the king, " I have on, what has never been known in the whole, great kingdom of Nimporte until this moment, a pair of—of—"

And here the king looked inquiringly at the young person.

" Let us call them shoes," said the young person.

Then the king, walking to and fro over the pebbles with the greatest comfort and security, looked inquiringly at him. " Who are you? " asked his majesty.

" I belong," said the young person, " to the tribe of the poets —who make the earth tolerable for the feet of man."

Then the king turned to his cabinet, and pacing along in front of the six blocks, pointed to his feet, and inquired:

" What do you think of this invention? "

" I do not like it; I cannot understand it: I think the part of wisdom is always to reject the unintelligible; I therefore advise your majesty to refuse it," said the grand vizier, who was really so piqued, that he would much rather have been beheaded than live to see the triumph of the young person whom he had kicked down both pairs of stairs.

It is worthy of note, however, that when the grand vizier found himself in his own apartments, alive and safe, he gave a great leap into the air and whirled himself with joy, as on a former occasion.

The postmaster-general also signified his disapproval. " I do not like it," said he; " they are not rights and lefts; I therefore advise your majesty to refuse the invention."

The praetor was like minded. " It will not do," he said; " it is clearly obnoxious to the overwhelming objection that there is absolutely nothing objectionable about it; in my judgment, this should be sufficient to authorize your majesty's prompt refusal of the expedient and the decapitation of the inventor."

" Moreover," added the sachem, " if your majesty once wears them, then every man, woman and child, will desire to have his, her and its whole earth covered with leather; which will create such a demand for hides, that there will shortly be not a bullock or a cow in your majesty's dominions: if your majesty will but contemplate the state of this kingdom without beef and butter! —there seems no more room for argument! "

" But these objections," cried the three Scribes-and-Pharisees, " although powerful enough in themselves, O king of the whole earth, have not yet touched the most heinous fault of this inventor, and that is, that there is no reserved force about this invention; the young person has actually done the very best he could in the most candid manner; this is clearly in violation of the rules of art,—witness the artistic restraint of our own behavior in this matter! "

Then the King of Nimporte said: " O wise men of my former cabinet, your wisdom seems folly; I will rather betake me to the counsels of the poet, and he shall be my sole adviser for the future; as for you, live—but live in shame for the littleness of your souls! " And he dismissed them from his presence in disgrace.

It was then that the King of Nimporte uttered that proverb which has since become so famous among the Persians; for, turning away to his palace, with his bride on one arm and the young person on the other, he said:

" To him who wears a shoe, it is as if the whole earth was covered with leather."

THE STORY OF A PROVERB *

II

IT IS NECESSARY to recall how one of the kings of Nimporte, who lived at a time when all men went barefoot, had the misfortune to bruise his royal toe with a stone; how he thereupon ordered his grand vizier and the other members of the council to cause that the whole earth should be covered with leather in three days, upon pain of decapitation; how at the moment when the unhappy grand vizier and his colleagues were in the act of undergoing punishment for their failure to accomplish this behest, a young person appeared who described himself as one whose business was to make the earth tolerable for the feet of man, and who afterward turned out to be a poet; how the poet interceded for the grand vizier and his colleagues, undertaking to cover the whole earth with leather for the king in five minutes; how he thereupon fitted upon the king's feet a pair of shoes; and, finally, how His Majesty, dismissing his councilors in disgrace, embraced the poet, and uttered then and there that famous proverb: " To him who wears a shoe the whole earth is covered with leather."

On the next day the kingdom of Nimporte was electrified with the announcement that the poet had been installed in the office of grand vizier, and that the king would in future dispense with a cabinet.

" A poet for grand vizier! "

These words ran through the whole commonwealth amid a universal burst of apprehension and angry astonishment.

---

* [Written in the summer of 1877; published in *Lippincott's Magazine*, XXIII, 109-113 (Jan., 1879), the text here followed—except that the spelling of " councillors " has been altered to conform with " Proverb I." Not subsequently reprinted. An incomplete MS, lacking the sub-title, survives (Charles D. Lanier Collection, Johns Hopkins University), which contains approximately 460 words omitted from the printed version: principally a background of child-listeners, and a comic incident of the Cabinet Members' attempts to save their Nimporte securities.—ED.]

It must be confessed that the young functionary began to conduct the affairs of Nimporte in a manner surprisingly different from the course of any grand vizier who had ever before administered the affairs of that kingdom. For example, on the day after his elevation to office he was pacing with the king of Nimporte up and down a shaded alley in the garden of the royal palace, conversing upon the deplorable condition of society in certain particulars.

" Oh king of the whole earth," said the poet, " I have long cherished a plan which, if Your Majesty will deign to listen, I will now unfold, so that if Your Majesty shall think well of it, it may be immediately carried out."

" Proceed," said the king.

" Your Majesty is aware that two rays of light may be made to encounter each other in such a way as to produce darkness, and that two musical sounds may be caused to meet with such precisely opposing forces that silence will result. Now—"

" In truth, I was not aware of it," interrupted His Majesty.

" It will give me great pleasure to demonstrate it by a couple of very simple experiments whenever Your Majesty shall please to see them. But, as I was proceeding to remark, I wish to apply this principle in relieving certain very serious troubles which have long prevailed throughout this kingdom. Suppose, if Your Majesty pleases, that two armies stood ranged in line of battle opposite each other, with bows drawn and javelins poised; and suppose that I could arrange matters so that every javelin and arrow launched from one side should meet a corresponding missile from the other with such correctness that both would fall harmless to the earth exactly halfway between the two ranks; fancy, moreover, that this should happen in spite of all changes of position and manoeuvres whatsoever. The result would be that the battle would no sooner commence than it would degenerate from a tragedy into a farce; that the soldiers would become disgusted, and would presently return to the avocations of peace; and that there would not be a single widow or orphan to break our hearts after the fight."

" It would greatly shorten my pension list," said the king, remembering his treasury, and not clearly perceiving the drift of the poet's remarks. " If you can do it, you must surely be

one of those benevolent jins or genii of our old tales. I believe
you *are*: henceforth I will call you ' Genius.' "

" Now," continued Genius, without heeding His Majesty's
interruption, " I ask Your Majesty to hold these matters in
mind for a moment while I array another set of considerations
with which I wish to combine them. It is my belief that all
wars between states, all conflicts between guilds and all heart-
burnings between individuals are caused by the following
classes of persons: First, those who are born with a talent for
abuse, and who therefore engage in every current argument
not for the purpose of discussion, but of invective. Second,
those who come into this world with great yet perverse ingenui-
ties, whereby they can gather from the four quarters of learning very plausible arguments against any proposition whatever, so that they always place themselves in the opposition
for the greater display of their peculiar talent. Third, such
critics as exercise their noble calling not to help art or their
fellowmen, but to avenge certain injuries which they believe
themselves to have received from society. Fourth, such other
critics as, even with good intentions, have fallen fortuitously
into criticism after having failed in other avocations, under
the mistaken idea that this business, like life insurance, can
be carried on without any capital, forgetting that the very
first qualification of a critic is to know more than the criticised
about the matter in hand. Fifth, dyspeptic diplomatists, ad-
venturous Baker Pachas and bloodthirsty newspaper colonels.
Sixth, common scolds and all place-hunters out of office. It is
true, I can foresee a time when men may be allowed to exercise all these predilections without harm—nay, when even
benefit may arise therefrom—and when the waves of opinion
may wash ashore the pearl of truth, which still water would
have forever held concealed; but in the present age, if Your
Majesty please, the state of culture is not such as to permit
those beneficent results which in a higher civilization would
offset the immediate disadvantages of the free exercise of their
agitating powers by the persons I have named.

" As Your Majesty's prime minister I have before me, therefore, the task of at once keeping alive the talents of these disturbing classes—for the time will come when they will be

useful—and yet of practically suppressing them. The problem is, How shall we encourage them to quarrel while protecting society from the turmoil? It is in solving this problem that I propose to apply the principle of the obliteration of light— and heat-rays. For this purpose I ask, in the first place, that all persons in the kingdom of Nimporte falling under any of the six classes specified, together with their families, shall be immediately brought to a certain point of assemblage: I will there part them off into a tribe, which shall be called the Dia-tribe. They shall then be conducted to a certain corner of the territory of Nimporte, where I will have previously arranged habitations, printing-offices, pot-houses to talk politics in, and all other facilities for carrying on their avocations; and they shall then be left to themselves, measures being taken to prevent intercourse with the outer world. Now—"

" It will be a lively place of abode," said the king, with an expression as much like a grin as a royal mouth could possibly assume.

" On the contrary," replied Genius—" humbly begging your royal pardon—if my theory be not a total failure in logic, this will soon become the most tranquil spot in Your Majesty's dominions; for there will be nothing to criticise but criticisms, nothing to complain of but complaints, nothing to curse but curses. The effect will be that of a great many centres of disturbance having isochronous pulsations in a homogeneous fluid: each wave of agitation will be met, immediately at its beginning, by a similar wave from an opposite direction, and the result must be complete neutralization. Thus, as we make darkness out of two lights and silence out of two sounds, I propose to make peace out of several troubles."

The king of Nimporte was so delighted with this plan that he immediately put it in execution, and not more than three days had elapsed before the entire disturbing element of his kingdom, as classified by his young grand vizier, had been safely secluded in a distant portion of Nimporte.

At the outset, events did not appear likely to crown the young minister's experiment with success. Stirring things began to happen in this region. In spite of the prohibition of intercourse, rumors of certain other extradorinary proceedings of

the new grand vizier frequently found their way to the Diatribe. These proved particularly disgusting to the former councilors of the king, who, either under the class of " dyspeptic
diplomatists," or under that of " place-hunters," had all been
included in the Diatribe.

In no long time the news was of such a nature as to be completely beyond endurance. It was related, for example, how
the poet sent word to a certain nation, with whom Nimporte
had been at war for more than a hundred years about a
wretched corner of bog-land which bordered upon both their
territories, that he would be glad to submit their rival claims
to any respectable government which the opposing nation
might select; how the poet thereupon withdrew all the armies
of Nimporte from that theatre of war and set the soldiers to
ploughing; and how, on the same day, he devoted the entire
proceeds of the new bonds of Nimporte (which had been
negotiated for the express purpose of defraying the expenses
of this very war) to the erection of free schoolhouses all over
Nimporte, in which he employed teachers of whom the very
lowest grades received salaries of three thousand dollars a
year, the women-teachers being paid precisely the same amounts
as the men for the same work!

This was stinging enough to the dismissed functionaries of
the Diatribe, but other wild stories came which wrought up
their rage to white heat. It appeared that the new grand vizier
lived in the utmost simplicity as regards eating, drinking, dress,
retinue and the like, but that he was liberal of expenditure for
good music, books, pictures and statues; that he was in the
constant habit of paying the expenses of widows' sons at colleges, and that almost every young musician, poet, painter or
sculptor in Nimporte who revealed any fervent and devout
purpose in his art had found mysterious credits at his banker's,
enabling him to devote his whole time to the pursuit of his
beloved studies; that the new grand vizier had by some means
succeeded in separating the deserving poor from the lazy good-
for-naughts, and had established comfortable homes for the
former upon revenues derived from the compulsory labors
of the latter; and a hundred more such goings-on, which laid
the seal of condemnation upon the preceding ministry by precisely reversing all their modes of action.

So that one day the sachem—who by reason of his great superiority in biliousness was easily chief of the Diatribe—stirred up a great revolution among those exiles.

" My friends," he shouted to the excited throng, " ever since the first critics appeared in history they have been suffering from the acts of this same Genius and his predecessors. Genius has always been invading our territories just at the moment when we have been crying that he was dead for ever and that the world would never see him again; he has always been accomplishing the very things we have declared to be impossible; time and again he has erected works which we have proved conclusively to be gossamer, but which have turned out to be stone; and, to crown all these insults, he has committed his crimes against us under the hypocritical pretense of a desire to elevate the race of mankind. It is grown intolerable, and I now propose to you a method of protecting ourselves for the future against this smooth-faced monster who has been covering us with shame through ages of affliction. Come, let us build a great fort on the borders of Diatribeland, which shall command every approach to it: this we will garrison with the most dyspeptic of our sentinels, who cannot sleep by night, and with the most bilious of our soldiers, who thirst for blood insatiably; and thus, on the first approach of Genius—vile invader!—toward these territories, we shall discover him and avenge the insults of centuries! "

These words roused the whole Diatribe to a frenzy: every man, woman and child seized a spade, a shovel, a pick-axe, whatever came to hand, and all marched away, behind the sachem, to the borders of their territory. Here the sachem, after thoroughly inspecting the country, selected a certain hill as a site for their fort, and the entire body of the Diatribe with one will fell to throwing up breastworks around the crest of the elevation, which was approached by a long rounding ridge.

That you may understand the singular catastrophe which happened a few hours after these entrenchments were begun, it is now necessary to relate a certain adventure of the poet which happened on the night before. Among other curious habits, he was accustomed often to walk forth under the stars very late at night, while the world was asleep, far away into

the desert or the great forest. As soon as he would pass the
habitations of men the most wonderful transformation would
occur in his figure: in fact, he was a genuine jin or genius, and
would then assume his natural size, which was at least seven
thousand times that of an ordinary man. Having attained this
prodigious enlargement, he would wander about, often gazing
steadily at the stars, as if he were speaking to them and listen-
ing to their discourse; he would tremble with ecstacy in looking
at the trees, which he handled as a man handles the tiniest
flower; and sometimes would even burst into tears of strange
rapture while he listened to the communications which leaves,
rivers, mountains and all Nature continually poured into his
soul. He would then return toward his dwelling, resuming
his ordinary stature as soon as he was in sight of an inhabited
district.

Now, on the night in question Genius had wandered farther
than usual. Just as he had reached the boundaries of the Land
of the Diatribe on his way homeward, he felt a slight sense of
fatigue, and, intending only to rest for a few moments, he
stretched his vast and beautiful naked body (for on these solitary excursions he rejoiced in freeing himself from all those
conventionalities which he ordinarily observed with great care
for the sake of his fellow-men, who needed them) along a
valley which afforded a gentle slope at one end for his pillow.

Gradually, however, without even remembering to resume
his customary stature, he fell into a profound slumber, and
presently a light morning wind from the desert blew over him
and covered him, as he lay, with a light coating of dust.

Now, it was to this very spot where Genius lay asleep that
the unwitting sachem had led his tribe: it was the bulk of the
body of Genius which the sachem mistook for a mountain-
range; and, in fact, stepping upon the finger-nail, and thence
scrambling up the finger and wrist, the whole Diatribe had
marched along the outstretched right arm of Genius, which
they conceived to be a long ridge gradually increasing in height,
until they arrived at his right breast, where, as I have
already remarked, they all had set to work at raising a great
fortification.

In the meantime Genius slept profoundly.

It was not long before the enthusiastic labors of so many hands had raised a large entrenched work upon the supposed hill; and after the most accomplished engineers of the Diatribe had minutely inspected and approved the scarp, the counterscarp, the lunettes, the barbican, the salient and re-entering angles, and all the various devices of the sachem's defensive art, the whole company assembled around the flagstaff in the centre of the fort to listen to a congratulatory address from their leader.

" Friends and countrymen! " cried the delighted sachem, " the sufferings of millions are at an end! Tyranny is dead! In this hour of triumph I call upon you to mark the security of our impregnable fortification. Yonder narrow ridge or causeway, which stretches to the plain, will scarcely admit three abreast of any attacking force, and from the bastions and salient angles of the work we could mow down such a column with an enfilading fire of arrows, javelins and great stones which no army in the world could resist for a quarter of an hour. That ridge, my countrymen, is the only approach to this citadel. On every other side, explore as far as you will, this range of hills upon which we now stand terminates in precipices which are abrupt—yea, some of which even curve inward toward the base, frowning gloomily upon the puny mortal who ventures beneath. Genius, henceforth and for ever, we defy thee! Henceforth and for ever, we—"

At this moment Genius turned in his sleep.

" An earthquake! an earthquake! " shouted the terrified Diatribe as they rolled down the sides of their mountain.

Then Genius awoke, and feeling a slight irritation of his right breast, placed his finger thereupon, when he gathered into his palm a great many minute objects which he immediately recognized as human beings.

In a moment he knew—for Genius understands all things— what had happened.

But he had not the least thought of punishing the folly of the Diatribe. Instead of doing so, he took the whole population of that district into the hollow of his hand, and smiling tenderly, carried them into a far higher and more beautiful region than that which they had previously inhabited, together with all their flocks and herds, houses and goods, of every description.

Then with one stride he disappeared from that place.

The Diatribe appeared to be little astonished, and, it must be confessed, enjoyed the new beauties about them in a somewhat stolid way, though clearly they were gentler, and even larger in form, than before.

Genius now took on again the appearance of an ordinary man, and, presenting himself on the same day before the king, related all that had happened in explaining the change of residence of the Diatribe, whereof word had already been brought to His Majesty.

" And yet," said the king, gazing upon him with a steady regard full of affection and of reverence, " if you should go tomorrow, you would probably find the sachem still plotting against you and reviling you: it but fulfils the saying of the ancient Eastern poet: ' I visited them a hundred times, and they knew not my face.' "

" Nay," replied Genius, " if Your Majesty will pardon me, that is true, but it is not the whole matter. How can these poor ones know Genius when they see him? Their eyes are hurt with much work, with much error, with much wrangling, with little food, with ignorance. Unworthy, indeed, is that artist who allows himself to be long bitter against them." Then Genius crossed his hands upon his breast with modesty, raised his eyes devoutly upward, as if his words were to refer to some other than himself, and uttered that beautiful saying which is a proverb esteemed of all truly wise men:

> I was as a treasure concealed;
> But I loved, and I became known.

BOB: THE STORY OF OUR MOCKING BIRD *

NOT THAT his name *ought* to be Bob at all. In respect of his behavior during a certain trying period which I am presently to recount, he ought to be called Sir Philip Sidney: yet, by virtue of his conduct in another very troublesome business which I will relate, he has equal claim to be known as Don Quixote de la Mancha: while, in consideration that he is the Voice of his whole race, singing the passions of all his fellows better than anyone could sing his own, he is clearly entitled to be named William Shakspere.

For Bob is our mocking-bird. He fell to us out of the top of a certain great pine in a certain small city on the sea-coast of Georgia. In this tree and a host of his lordly fellows which tower over that little city, the mocking-birds abound in unusual numbers. They love the prodigious masses of the leaves, and the generous breezes from the neighboring Gulf-Stream, and, most of all, the infinite flood of the sunlight which is so rich and cordial that it will make even a man lift his head toward the sky, as a mocking-bird lifts his beak, and try to sing something or other.

About three years ago, in a sandy road which skirts a grove of such tall pines, a wayfarer found Bob lying in a lump. It could not have been more than a few days since he was no bird at all, only an egg with possibilities. The finder brought him to our fence and turned him over to a young man who had done us the honor to come out of a Strange Country and

---

* [Written shortly before May, 1878, the date of the bird's death, which Lanier commemorated in a poem ("To Our Mocking Bird," vol. I, present edition). Published in the *Independent*, XXIV, 1-3 (Aug. 3, 1882); reprinted as a book, with sixteen illustrations in color by A. R. Dugmore, by Scribner's (New York, 1899); reprinted in Mary Burt's *The Lanier Book* (New York, 1904), pp. 107-124, and in Henry W. Lanier's *Selections from Sidney Lanier* (New York, 1916), pp. 128-142.

The MS, signed "Sidney Lanier," which serves as the text here printed, is now in the Henry W. Lanier Collection of the Johns Hopkins University, its thirty-seven pages interleaved with a copy of the published *Bob* (Scribner's, 1899). The heretofore published versions exhibit a few variants in matters of punctuation and a few slight verbal differences.—ED.]

live at our house about six years before. Gladly received by
this last, Bob was brought within, and family discussions were
held. He could not be put back into a tree: the hawks would
have had him in an hour. The original nest was not to be
found. We struggled hard against committing the crime—as
we had always considered it—of caging a bird. But finally it
became plain that there was no other resource. In fact, we were
obliged to recognize that he had come to us from the hand of
Providence: and, though we are among the most steady-going
democrats of this Republic, we were yet sufficiently acquainted
with the etiquette of courts to know that one does not refuse
the gift of The King.

Dimly hoping, therefore, that we might see our way clear
to devise some means of giving Bob an education that would
fit him for a forester, we arranged suitable accommodations
for him, and he was tended with motherly care.

He repaid our attentions from the very beginning. He immediately began to pick up in flesh and to increase the volume
of his rudimentary feathers. Soon he commenced to call for
his food as lustily as any spoiled child. When it was brought
he would throw his head back and open his yellow-lined beak
to a width which no one would credit who did not see it. Into
this enormous cavity, which seemed almost larger than the bird,
his protectress would thrust—and the more vigorously the
better he seemed to like it—ball after ball of the yolk of hard-
boiled egg mashed up with Irish potato.

How, from this dry compound which was his only fare except an occasional worm off the rose-bushes, Bob could have
wrought the surprising nobleness of spirit which he dis-
placed about six weeks after he came to us—is a matter which
I do not believe the most expansive application of Mr. Herbert
Spencer's theory of the genesis of emotion could even remotely
account for.* I refer to the occasion when he fairly earned
the title of Sir Philip Sidney. A short time after he became
our guest a couple of other fledglings were brought and placed
in his cage. One of these soon died, but the other continued

* [Herbert Spencer, in *The Principles of Psychology*, emphasized the physical
basis of the nervous system and the emotions. Lanier's copy of this book is
preserved in the Johns Hopkins Library.—ED.]

for some time longer to drag out a drooping existence. One day, when Bob was about six weeks old, his usual ration had been delayed, owing to the pressure of other duties upon his attendant. He was not slow to make this circumstance known by all the language available to him. He was very hungry indeed, and was squealing with every appearance of entreaty and of indignation when at last the lady of the house was able to bring him his breakfast. He scrambled to the bars of the cage—which his feeble companion was unable to do—took the proffered ball of egg-and-potato fiercely in his beak, and then, instead of swallowing it, deliberately flapped back to his sick guest in the corner and gave *him* the whole of it without tasting a morsel.

Now when Sir Philip Sidney was being carried off the battle-field of Zutphen with a fearful wound in his thigh, he became very thirsty and begged for water. As the cup was handed him, a dying soldier who lay near cast upon it a look of great long-ing. This Sidney observed: refusing the cup, he ordered that it should be handed to the soldier, saying "his necessity is greater than mine."

A mocking-bird is called Bob just as a goat is called Billy or Nan, as a parrot is called Poll, as a squirrel is called Bunny, or as a cat is called Pussy or Tom. In spite of the suggestions forced upon us by the similarity of his behavior to that of the sweet young gentleman of Zutphen, our bird continued to bear the common appellation of his race, and no efforts on the part of those who believe in the fitness of things have availed to change the habits of Bob's friends in this particular. Bob he was, is, and will probably remain.

Perhaps under a weightier title he would not have thriven so prosperously. His growth was amazing in body and in mind. By the time he was two months old he clearly showed that he was going to be a singer. About this period certain little feeble trills and experimental whistles began to vary the monot-ony of his absurb squeals and chirrups. The musical business, and the marvellous work of feathering himself, occupied his thoughts continually. I cannot but suppose that he superin-tended the disposition of the black, white and gray markings on his wings and his tail as they successively appeared: he certainly manufactured the pigments with which those colors were laid on, somewhere within himself,—and all out of egg-and-potato. How he ever got the idea of arranging his feather-characteristics exactly as those of all other male mocking-birds are arranged—is more than I know. It is equally beyond me to conceive why he did not—while he was about it—exert his individuality to the extent of some little peculiar black dot or white stripe whereby he could at least tell himself from any other bird. His failure to attend to this last matter was after-ward the cause of a great battle from which Bob would have emerged in a plight as ludicrous as any of Don Quixote's,—considering the harmless and unsubstantial nature of his an-tagonist—had not this view of his behavior been changed by the courage and spirit with which he engaged his enemy, the gallantry with which he continued the fight, and the good faithful blood which he shed while it lasted. In all these particulars his battle fairly rivalled any encounter of the much-bruised Knight of la Mancha.

He was about a year old when it happened, and the fight took place a long way from his native heath. He was spend-ing the summer at a pleasant country home in Pennsylvania. He had appeared to take just as much delight in the clover-fields and mansion-studded hills of this lovely region as in the lonesome forests and sandy levels of his native land. He had sung, and sung: even in his dreams at night his sensitive little soul would often get quite too full and he would pour forth rapturous bursts of sentiment at any time between twelve o'clock and daybreak. If our health had been as little troubled by broken slumber as was his, these melodies in the late night would have been glorious: but there were some of us who had gone into the country specially to sleep: and we were finally driven to swing the sturdy songster high up in an outside porch at night, by an apparatus contrived with careful reference to cats. Several of these animals in the neighborhood had longed unspeakably for Bob ever since his arrival. We had seen them eyeing him from behind bushes and through windows, and had once rescued him from one who had thrust a paw between the very bars of his cage. That cat was going to eat him, art and all, with no compunction in the world. His music seemed to make no more impression on cats than Keats's made on critics. If only some really discriminating person had been by, with a shotgun, when *The Quarterly* thrust its paw into poor Endymion's cage! *

One day at this country-house Bob had been let out of his cage and allowed to fly about the room. He had cut many antics, to the amusement of the company, when presently we left him, to go down to dinner. What occurred afterward was very plainly told by circumstantial evidence when we returned. As soon as he was alone, he had availed himself of his unusual freedom, to go exploring about the room. In the course of investigation he suddenly found himself confronted by—it is impossible to say what he considered it. If he had been reared in the woods he would probably have regarded it as another mocking-bird,—for it was his own image in the looking-glass of a bureau. But he had never seen any member of his race, except the forlorn little unfledged specimen which he had fed at six weeks of age, and which bore no resemblance to this tall, gallant, bright-eyed figure in the mirror. He had thus had no opportunity to generalize his kind: and he knew nothing whatever of his own personal appearance except the partial hints he may have gained when he smoothed his feathers with his beak after his bath in the morning. It may therefore very well be that he took this sudden apparition for some Chimæra or dire monster which had taken advantage of the family's temporary absence to enter the room, with evil purpose. Bob immediately determined to defend the premises. He flew at the invader, literally beak and claw. But beak and claw taking no hold upon the smooth glass, with each attack he slid struggling down to the foot of the mirror. Now it so happened that a pin-cushion lay at this point, which bristled not only with pins but with needles which had been temporarily left in it and which were nearly as sharp at the eye-ends as at the points. Upon these, Bob's poor claws came down with fury: he felt the wounds, and saw the blood: both he attributed to the strokes of his enemy, and this roused him

* [Allusion to the popular tradition that the death of John Keats was hastened by a savage review of his poem *Endymion*, appearing in *The Quarterly Review* in April, 1818.—Ed.]

to new rage. In order to give additional momentum to his onset he would retire toward the other side of the room and thence fly at the foe. Again and again he charged; and as many times slid down the smooth surface of the mirror and wounded himself upon the perilous pin-cushion. As I entered, being first up from table, he was in the act of fluttering down against the glass. The counterplane on the bed, the white dimity cover of the bureau, the pin-cushion, all bore the bloody resemblances of his feet in various places, and showed how many times he had sought distant points in order to give himself a running start. His heart was beating violently, and his feathers were ludicrously tousled. And all against the mere shadow of himself! Never was there such a temptation for the head of a family to assemble his people and draw a prodigious moral. But better thoughts came: for, after all, was it not probable that the poor bird was defending—or at any rate believed he was defending—the rights and properties of his absent masters against a foe of unknown power? All the circumstances go to show that he made the attack with a faithful valor as reverent as that which steadied the lance of Don Quixote against the windmills. In after days, when his cage has been placed among the boughs of trees, he has not shown any warlike feelings against the robins and sparrows that passed about, but only a sincere friendly interest.

At this present writing, Bob is the most elegant, trim, electric, persuasive, cunning, tender, courageous, artistic little dandy of a bird that mind can imagine. He does not confine himself to imitating the songs of his tribe. He is a creative artist. I was witness not long ago to the selection and adoption by him of a rudimentary whistle-language. During an illness, it fell to my lot to sleep in a room alone with Bob. In the early morning, when a lady—to whom Bob is passionately attached—would make her appearance in the room, he would salute her with a certain joyful chirrup which appears to belong to him peculiarly. I have not heard it from any other bird. But sometime the lady would merely open the door, make inquiry, and then retire. It was now necessary for his artistic soul to find some form of expressing grief. For this purpose he selected a certain cry almost identical with that of the cow-bird—an indescribably plaintive, long-drawn, thin whistle. Day after day I heard him make use of these expressions. He had never done so before. The mournful one he would usually accompany, as soon as the door was shut, with a sidelong inquiring posture of the head, which was a clear repetition of the lover's *Is she gone? Is she really gone?*

There is one particular in which Bob's habits cannot be recommended to the young readers of the SUNDAY MAGAZINE.* He eats very often. In fact if Bob should hire a cook, it would be absolutely necessary for him to write down his hours for her guidance; and this writing would look very much like a Time-Table of the Pennsylvania, or the Hudson River, or the Old Colony Railroad. He would have to say: " Bridget will be kind enough to get me my breakfast at the following hours: 5, 5.20, 5.40, 6, 6.15, 6.30, 6.45, 7, 7.20, 7.40, 8, (and so on, every fifteen or twenty minutes, until 12 M.); my dinner at 12, 12.20, 12.40, 1, 1.15, 1.30, (and so on, every fifteen or twenty minutes until 6 P.M.); my supper is irregular, but I wish Bridget particularly to remember that I *always* eat whenever I awake in the night, and that I usually awake four or five times between bed-time and daybreak." With all this eating, Bob never neglects to wipe his beak after each meal. This he does by drawing it quickly, three or four times on each side, against his perch.

I never tire of watching his motions. There does not seem to be the least friction between any of the component parts of his system. They all work, give, play in and out, stretch, contract, and serve his desires generally with a smoothness and soft precision truly admirable. Merely to see him leap from his perch to the floor of his cage is to me a never-failing marvel. It is so instantaneous, and yet so quiet: *clip,* and he is down, with his head in the food-cup: I can compare it to nothing but the stroke of Fate. It is perhaps a strained association of the large with the small: but when he suddenly leaps down in this instantaneous way, I always feel as if, while looking upon the three large Forms of the Antique Sculpture lying in serene postures along the ground, I suddenly heard the *clip* of the fatal shears.

* [Apparently *Frank Leslie's Sunday Magazine,* the periodical to which Lanier intended submitting his story for publication.—ED.]

His repertory of songs is extensive. Perhaps it would have been much more so if his life had been in the woods where he would have had the opportunity to hear the endlessly-various calls of his race. So far as we can see, the stock of songs which he now sings must have been brought in his own mind out of the egg,—or from some further source whereof we know nothing. He certainly never *learned* these calls: many of the birds of whom he gives perfect imitations have been always beyond his reach. He does not apprehend readily a new set of tones. He has caught two or three musical phrases from hearing them whistled near him. No systematic attempt however has been made to teach him anything. His procedure in learning these few tones was peculiar. He would not, on first hearing them, make any sign that he desired to retain them, beyond a certain air of attention in his posture. Upon repetition on a different day, his behavior was the same: there was no *attempt* at imitation. But some time afterward, quite unexpectedly, in the hilarious flow of his bird songs would appear a perfect reproduction of the whistled tones. Like a great artist he was rather above futile and amateurish efforts. He took things into his mind, turned them over, and, when he was perfectly sure of it, brought it forth with perfection and with unconcern.

He has his little joke. His favorite response to the endearing terms of the lady whom he loves is to scold her. Of course he understands that she understands his wit. He uses for this purpose the angry warning cry which mocking-birds are in the habit of employing to drive away intruders from their nests. At the same time he expresses his delight by a peculiar gesture which he always uses when pleased. He extends his right wing and stretches his leg along the inner surface of it as far as he is able.

He has great capacities in the way of elongating and contracting himself. When he is curious or alarmed, he stretches his body until he seems incredibly tall and of the size of his neck all the way. When he is cold, he makes himself into a perfectly round ball of feathers.

I think I envy him most when he goes to sleep. He takes up one leg somewhere into his bosom, crooks the other a trifle, shortens his neck, closes his eyes,—and it is done. He does not appear to hover a moment in the border-land between sleeping and waking but hops over the line with the same superb decision with which he drops from his perch to the floor. I do not think he ever has anything on his mind, after he closes his eyes. It is my belief that he never committed a sin of any sort in his whole life. There is but one time when he ever looks sad. This is during the season when his feathers fall. He is then unspeakably dejected. Never a note do we get from him until it is over. Nor can he be blamed. Last summer not only the usual loss took place, but every feather dropped from his tail. His dejection during this period was so extreme that we could not but believe he had some idea of his personal appearance under the disadvantage of no tail. This was so ludicrous that his most ardent lovers could scarcely behold him without a smile: and it appeared to cut him to the soul that he should excite such sentiments.

But in a surprisingly short time his tail-feathers grew out again, the rest of his apparel reappeared fresh and new, and he lifted up his head: insomuch that whenever we wish to fill the house with a gay, confident, dashing, riotous, innocent, sparkling glory of jubilation, we have only to set Bob's cage where a spot of sunshine will fall on it. His beads of eyes glisten, his form grows intense, up goes his beak, and he is off.

Finally we have sometimes discussed the question: is it better, on the whole, that Bob shoud have lived in a cage than in the wildwood? There are conflicting opinions about it: but one of us is clear that it *is*. He argues that although there are many songs which are never heard, as there are many eggs which never hatch, yet the general end of a song is to *be* heard, as that of an egg is to be hatched. He further argues that Bob's life in his cage has been one long blessing to several people who stood in need of him; whereas in the woods, leaving aside the probability of hawks and bad boys, he would not have been likely to gain one appreciative listener for a single half-hour out of each year. And, as I have already mercifully released you from several morals (continues this disputant) which I might have drawn from Bob, I am resolved that no power on earth shall prevent me from drawing this final one.

We have heard much of " the privileges of genius," of " the right of the artist to live out his own existence free from the conventionalities of society," of " the un-morality of art," and the like. But I do protest that the greater the artist, and the more profound his piety toward the fellow-man for whom he passionately works, the readier will be his willingness to forego the privileges of genius and to cage himself in the conventionalities even as the mocking-bird is caged. His struggle against these will, I admit, be the greatest: he will feel the bitterest sense of their uselessness in restraining *him* from wrong-doing. But nevertheless one consideration will drive him to enter the door and get contentedly on his perch: his fellow-men, his fellow-men. These he can reach through the respectable bars of use and wont: in his wild thickets of lawlessness they would never hear him, or, hearing, would never listen. In truth, this is the sublimest of self-denials, and none but a very great artist can compass it: to abandon the sweet green forest of liberty, and live a whole life behind needless constraints, for the more perfect service of his fellow-man.

LANIER GENEALOGY *

I

July 6, 1877.

My Dear Sir:

IT HAS LONG been matter of common knowledge that ancestors transmit to their progeny those ingrained and radical peculiarities which constitute what might be called Family Individuality. The modern habit of scientific observation would seem to have established a much more extensive range of this process than had hitherto been suspected; and it may probably be considered fairly settled that not only the broader family traits are hereditarily transmissible, but that even the mental acquisitions of any individual parent do, to a certain extent, pass on to his children; so that if a man shall have made himself an expert in any particular branch of human activity, there will result the strong tendency that a peculiar aptitude towards the same branch will be found among some of his descendants.

The slight esteem, therefore, in which genealogical investigations are sometimes held can legitimately attach only to such as are pursued from unseemly motives of display. For, indeed, to the earnest man, the study of his ancestry must be regarded as the study of himself. Christian insight, no less than heathen wisdom, has sanctioned the ancient admonition, *Know thyself*; and if it be true that in order to know oneself one must know one's ancestors, then the practice of genealogic research must

* [The two " letters " that follow were addressed to J. F. D. Lanier, Sidney Lanier's New York cousin. The first letter was published as an appendix to the second edition (1877) of the autobiographical *Sketch of the Life of J. F. D. Lanier*; the second was published (1879) as a pamphlet, designed, as shown by the pagination, to be added to the *Sketch*, though it was never actually bound into the book. The Dallas *News* (Sept. 14, 1924) notes a fragment of a MS, which does not seem, on account of the handwriting, to be genuine. No other MS is known to survive, and no reprintings have appeared. A few typographical errors have been corrected in preparing the present text. For corrections of Lanier's genealogical researches see L. E. Jackson and A. H. Starke, " New Light on the Ancestry of Sidney Lanier," *Virginia Historical Magazine*, XLIII, 160-168 (April, 1935).—Ed.]

be regarded as a duty, and with a peculiar propriety the Family Tree is inscribed in the Family Bible.

It is therefore with pleasure that I communicate to you such items of family history as have come to my notice, regretting only that a laborious life has never allowed me the opportunity which I desired of making some special research into these matters. Perhaps it will not be amiss to add here, for the behoof of any member of the family who may hereafter have leisure and means to pursue this subject, that without doubt many interesting reminiscences of the Laniers might be obtained by intelligent inquiry prosecuted in the South of France, and in England and Wales, according to the migrations of the family hereinafter set forth. I was once disposed to think that our forefathers had been singularly careless in failing to preserve more ample written records of our descent and history; but a somewhat closer acquaintance with the nomadic habits of the Laniers inclines me to attribute the paucity of our genealogical remains to other causes. The main secret of it appears to have been their continual movements from place to place during the last two hundred years. The original breaking up of the Huguenot Laniers in France, and their flight into England; then their removal to Virginia in the sturdy days of the old colonists, when it must have been of great importance to be encumbered with as little luggage as possible; and, finally, the dispersion of the family throughout the East, West, and South of the United States; have all been circumstances unfavorable to the preservation of family archives. Indeed, I think a certain intolerance of restraint, and a powerful tendency among younger members to break off from the parental stem as soon as possible, may be very distinctly traced as a prominent family characteristic among us. I know of Laniers now existing in New York, Maryland, Virginia, North Carolina, South Carolina, Georgia, Florida, Alabama, Mississippi, Louisiana, Texas, Tennessee, and Indiana; and I do not recall a single instance where any considerable family have remained together continuously for a great while, but all appear to have early felt the hereditary tendency to leave the parental county or State and set up separate existences.

SIR JOHN LANIER

Perhaps the first authentic mention of our name in history is that which records the part borne by Sir John Lanier at the battle of the Boyne, July 1 (12), 1690, where he commanded the Queen's regiment of horse. In Macaulay's *History of England* (page 494, Vol. III, Harper & Bros.' edition, New York, 1856) occurs the following paragraph, among others detailing the array of King William's army on that eventful morning: " Sir John Lanier, an officer who had acquired military experience on the Continent, and whose prudence was held in high esteem, was at the head of the Queen's regiment of horse, now the First Dragoon Guards."

It is not an improbable conjecture that this Sir John, instead of flying with our other Huguenot ancestors to England, may have chosen to seek his asylum in Holland, and may have there made the acquaintance of the great Dutch Prince who so valiantly defended the Protestant cause. However this may be, he appears to have been a brave and faithful officer; for within the next two years we find him rising to the rank of General, and perishing along with the gallant Mackay and Douglas at the battle of Steinkirk. This fact is recorded on page 226, Vol. IV, of Macaulay's *History of England* (edition above cited), where Lanier is mentioned as a General " distinguished among the conquerors of Ireland."

Macaulay does not cite the documents from which he obtained these particular items, further than to give the authorities for his general history of the period. I have an impression, however, that somewhat minute regimental records have long been kept in the British Army: and it is very likely that many interesting details of the career of Sir John Lanier might be therein found.

It is a family tradition that he was one of our lineal ancestors. Indeed, putting together all the accounts which have ever come to me from many widely-scattered branches, I find that they all point in one direction, namely, to the existence of a single family of Laniers in the South of France, from whom all persons now bearing that name have descended: so that, in any given instance, I think the fact of the name alone may with perfect security be taken as evidence of kinship.

THOMAS LANIER

(The materials from which the facts in the following statement have been gathered are: (1) a MS. work entitled "History of the Harris Family," which was kindly sent to me by my friend Iverson Lanier Harris,* at the time one of the Justices of the Supreme Court of Georgia, having been compiled by him from documents furnished to his kinsman Henry Clay Harris, of Kentucky, by Benjamin Watkins Leigh, of Virginia: (2) a work called "The Old Churches and Families of Virginia," by Bishop William Meade, of that State, a copy of which is, I believe, now in your possession: (3) The Family Tree, hereinafter set forth, which, in its present form, first came (I think) to my grandfather, Sterling Lanier, from the papers of the late George Washington Parke Custis, of Virginia: (4) traditions of the Harris and Lanier families.)

Some time between the years 1691 and 1716 a party of colonists, consisting of the Laniers, the Maxwells, the Mayhews, the Bondurants, the Howells, the Harrises, and others whose names are frequently met with among the early families of Virginia, came to that colony from Great Britain, and settled upon a grant of land ten miles square which embraced the present site of the city of Richmond.

One of these Laniers appears to have been the Thomas Lanier hereinafter mentioned. The grant of land was made by William and Mary in 1691 to Henry Harris and John Jourdan, conveying to them a certain tract of Crown-lands lying along the James River, in the county of Powhatan, Virginia. The original of this grant was in the possession of Benjamin Watkins Leigh, of Virginia, in the year 1844. This Henry Harris (with whose family ours afterwards became intimately connected by intermarriage) belonged to an ancient house of Harrises whose seat was in Glamorgan, Wales. They were enthusiastic members of the "Welsh Baptist" Society; and during the fluctuating religious troubles of that period had been compelled to fly into France. Here they united with the Huguenots: and it is strongly probable that some acquaintance

---

* [Lanier's letter to Harris (see VII, 18, n. 1, of the present edition) shows that his interest in family history began as early as 1859, at which time he apparently borrowed this MS.—ED.]

may have been formed at this time between the French Laniers and the Welsh Harrises, which afterwards led to their joint emigration to America.

For, on the promulgation of the Edict of Nantes, the Welsh refugees in France had returned to Wales, where they lived until the Revocation of the Edict. After this event the Huguenot Laniers left their home in the South of France, and appear to have gone first to England or Wales. We find them emigrating thence soon afterward in company with the Harrises and others, as already mentioned, to America. Here they settled a town near the Falls of the James River, which was called Manakin town or Monacan town. This name (says Bishop Meade, page 466, Vol. I, of " Old Churches and Families of Virginia ") " was derived from the Indian *Monacan*— the name of a war-like tribe of Indians whom the great King Powhatan in vain attempted to subdue," and who " resided on James River from the Falls " (the present site of Richmond) " to Manakin."

Bishop Meade mentions the Laniers as early settlers in Manakin town, and refers to the mixture of French and Welsh elements in that colony.

It is therefore from Manakin town that our family derives its origin in the United States.

Both the Harrises and the Laniers now began to spread about the land. We find Thomas Lanier (according to the Family Tree hereinbefore mentioned) marrying Elizabeth Washington, the paternal aunt of George Washington. In this connection it will be of interest to remark that in the year 1747 Thomas Lanier obtained a grant of Crown-lands in Brunswick County, Virginia, as more fully appears by the following copy of the original instrument conveying the estate to him:

George the Second, by the Grace of God of Great Britain, France and Ireland King, Defender of the Faith, *etc.*: To all to whom these presents shall come Greeting: Know ye that for divers good causes and considerations but more especially for and in consideration of the sum of forty shillings of good and lawful money for our use paid to our Receiver General of our revenues in this our Colony and Dominion of Virginia, we have given, granted and confirmed, and by these presents for us, our heirs and successors do give, grant and confirm unto Thomas Lanier, one certain tract or parcel of land containing three hundred and eighty acres lying and being in the County of Brunswick on both sides of Mitchell's Creek, joining Shepard Lanier's line and his own, and bounded as followeth to wit: Beginning at Shepard Lanier's lower corner white oak on the creek, thence along his line south seventeen degrees west one hundred poles to a red oak on his line, thence along his line south seventy-one degrees east sixty poles to a red oak on the creek, thence down the said creek as it meanders to a white oak on the said creek, thence of [*sic*] north forty-three degrees east one hundred and eighteen poles to a white oak, thence north twenty-three degrees east one hundred and eighty-eight poles to his own corner sweet gum on a branch, thence north fourteen degrees west one hundred and sixty-six poles to a pine on William Hill's line, thence south seventy degrees west one hundred and sixty-six poles to Hill's corner dogwood on a branch, thence down the said branch as it meanders to the mouth of the same, thence down Mitchell's Creek aforesaid as it meanders to the Beginning, With all wood, under-woods, swamps, marshes, low grounds, meadows, feedings, and his due share of all veins, mines and quarries as well discovered as undis-covered within the bounds aforesaid and being part of the said quan-tity of three hundred and eighty acres of land, and the rivers, waters and water-courses therein contained, together with the privileges of Hunting, Hawking, Fishing, Fowling, and all other profits, commodi-ties and hereditaments whatsoever to the same or any part thereof belonging or in any wise appertaining: To Have, Hold, possess and enjoy the said tract or parcel of land and all other the before-granted premises and every part thereof with their and every of their appur-tenances unto the said Thomas Lanier and to his heirs and assigns forever: to the only use and behoof of him said Thomas Lanier his heirs and assigns forever: To be held of us, our heirs and successors, as of our manor of East Greenwich in the County of Kent in free and common socage and not *in capite* or by knight service, Yielding and paying unto us our heirs and successors for every fifty acres of land and so proportionately for a lesser or greater quantity than fifty acres the fee rent of one shilling yearly to be paid upon the feast of Saint Michael the Archangel, and also cultivating and improving three acres part of every fifty of the tract above-mentioned within three years after the date of these presents. Provided always that if three years of the said fee rent shall at any time be in arrear and unpaid, or if the said Thomas Lanier his heirs or assigns do not within the space of three years next coming after the date of these presents cultivate and improve three acres part of every fifty of the tract above-mentioned, then the

estate hereby granted shall cease and be utterly determined, and thereafter it shall and may be lawful to and for us, our heirs and successors
to grant the same lands and premises with the appurtenances unto
such other person or persons as we, our heirs and successors shall think
fit: In Witness Whereof we have caused these our Letters Patent to be
made. Witness our trusty and well-beloved Sir William Gooch Bar.,
our Lieutenant Governor and Commander in Chief of our said Colony
and Dominion at Williamsburg under the seal of our said Colony the
twelfth day of January one thousand seven hundred and forty-seven in
the twenty-first year of our reign.

(Signed) William Gooch

Information obtained from the Register of the Virginia Land
Office reveals that Thomas Lanier obtained other grants in
addition to this: namely, a grant dated August 5, 1751, conveying to him 318 acres of land lying in Lunenburg County,
Virginia; one dated March 3, 1760, conveying 400 acres in
the same county; and one dated September 20, 1768, conveying
838 acres in the same county.

Besides these conveyances to Thomas Lanier, I find that two
grants were issued to " Thomas Bird Lanier," one dated January 2, 1737, for 312 acres of land in Brunswick County, Virginia, and one dated January 12, 1747, for 374 acres in the
same county. It seems probable that this Thomas Bird Lanier
was a different person from Thomas Lanier: for I observe that
two of the grants mentioned above were issued on the same
day—January 12, 1747—and that one of them conveyed land
to " Thomas Lanier," while the other conveyed to " Thomas
Bird Lanier " : which renders it extremely unlikely that these
were names of the same individual, particularly as the instruments date from a time when legal technicalities were much
more rigorously observed than at present.

It is clear, however, from the deeds cited, that Thomas
Lanier was a considerable land-owner in the counties of Brunswick and Lunenburg; and it is to these counties, together with
the adjoining county of Rockingham in North Carolina (where
my grandfather Sterling Lanier was born), that we may trace
the original seat of our family after the initial settlement at
Monacan town.

It is proper to subjoin also, at this point, the Family Tree, to which I have already referred. The following is a copy from the Tree furnished by G. W. P. Custis, Esq., with the single addition of the names of the three grandchildren of Winifred Lanier, two of which are taken from the Tree furnished by Mrs. Hallowes, of Florida, and one—that of Mrs. Bryson—added upon information furnished by herself:

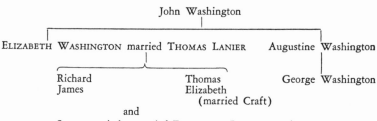

John Washington

ELIZABETH WASHINGTON married THOMAS LANIER   Augustine Washington

Richard   Thomas   George Washington
James   Elizabeth
            (married Craft)
      and
SAMPSON (who married ELIZABETH CHAMBERLIN)

Children of Sampson Lanier and Elizabeth Chamberlin:

LEWIS LANIER, of Screven County, Georgia;
Buckner   "   ;
Burwell   "   ;
WINIFRED (who married Col. Drury Ledbetter, of Virginia, and was grandmother of Judge John C. Nicoll, of Savannah, Georgia, and of Mrs. Caroline M. S. Hallowes, of Florida, and of Mrs. A. K. S. Bryson, of Kentucky;
Nancy (who married Major Vaughn, of Roanoke, North Carolina);
Rebecca (who married Walton Harris, of Virginia; she was grandmother of Judge Iverson L. Harris, of Georgia).

Rebecca Lanier—a granddaughter of Thomas Lanier—was united in marriage to Walton Harris, of Brunswick County, Virginia, a member of the original Harris family of Monacan town. This couple afterwards removed to North Carolina, where, according to the Harris History hereinbefore quoted, " they owned the great fishery at the narrows of the Yadkin River."

Rebecca was the daughter of " Sampson " Lanier. This has long been a family name, both in my own branch of the Lanier family and among the Harrises. My great-uncle Sampson Lanier recently died in Florida, and my father's given name is Robert Sampson.

It is in this same Rebecca Lanier's father, Sampson, that your lineage and mine come together. His two sons, Lewis and Buckner, were the heads of our respective families: Lewis of yours, and Buckner of mine. Lewis Lanier was your great-grandfather through your father Alexander Chalmers Lanier, and your grandfather James Lanier.

Winifred Lanier—a sister of your great-grandfather, Lewis —married Col. Drury Ledbetter, of Virginia. In a letter from their granddaughther, Mrs. A. K. S. Bryson (your " Aunt Bryson "), which I have had the pleasure of perusing, I find the following paragraph: " He " (meaning Lewis Lanier) " married an interesting woman in N. C.; if I mistake not she was a Miss Ball. I think she was a sister of Gen. Geo. Washington's mother, as my grandmother called Mrs. W. aunt." I understand this to be in accordance with the traditions of your own immediate family upon the same subject.

From Lewis Lanier's sister, Winifred, have descended many interesting persons. She was born in North Carolina, where she and her husband appear to have lived until the close of the Revolutionary war, when they moved to Georgia, and thenceforth resided in that State. One of their daughters, Susan W. Ledbetter (the mother of Mrs. Bryson, to whom reference has been made), was born in North Carolina, in the year 1773. After she moved with her father to Georgia, she married Major Thomas Martin, of the United States Army, who was then in command of a fort called Point Peter, a few miles from St. Mary's, Georgia. The marriage, however, occurred in Wilkes County, Georgia. Major Martin was born in Albemarle County, Virginia, in the year 1751. In 1801 he left Georgia and took command of a fort near Norfolk, Virginia: but did not remain there long, for I find that after having been successively ordered to Pittsburgh and Detroit, he finally came, in the year 1804, to Newport Barracks, Kentucky, and assumed command at that place. Major Martin's manners were genial; his wife, Mrs. Susan W. Martin, is described as an accomplished lady, of fine presence, and endowed with many virtues; while their daughters were also estimable and charming women; so that their house soon became a rendezvous for the best society of that region, and appears to have been a point of great social attraction for a long time.

The following are names of Major Martin's children:

Ann K. S. Bryson;

Eliza W. Oldham;

Susan L. Sanford;

Mary F. Winston (whose daughter, Sabella Winston, married Gov. Stevenson, of Kentucky);

Louisa W. Prather;

Harriet Joyce;

Thomas Martin;

James Martin.

It is to the remarkable memory of Mrs. Bryson—the last survivor of Major Martin's children, now residing at Covington, Kentucky—that most of the foregoing recitals concerning the Ledbetter family are due. Mrs. Bryson, now at the age of eighty-seven, retains all her faculties, writing long and intelligent letters, giving names and dates with great precision.

Col. Ledbetter's daughter, Caroline Agnes, married Col. A. Y. Nicoll, of the United States Army. Their only daughter, Mrs. Caroline M. S. Hallowes, is now residing near Remington Park, Florida, a beautiful point nearly opposite the famous winter-resort known as Green Cove Springs, across the St. John's River which is here about seven miles wide. Mrs. Hallowes—a lady of great piety and cultivation, and the mother of an accomplished family—is the wife of Col. Hallowes, an English officer, who, after having served the Queen for several years in India, retired on half-pay and came to this country.

Drury Ledbetter and Winifred Lanier had twelve children. Of these, Nancy married a Scotch gentleman, James Gardiner; and Mary married Francis Yates, son of the Spanish Consul at St. Augustine, Florida.

The following are the names of the living heads of families who represent widely distinct branches of the Laniers, but all of whom derive their lineage from our common Huguenot stock hereinbefore described. They will serve as useful clues to any member of the family who may hereafter desire to obtain some more complete account of it.

William L. Lanier, of Selma, Alabama, President of the Alabama Central Railway.

Sampson Lanier, of Greenville, Alabama.

Thomas Lanier, of Lake Griffin, Florida.

Joseph Lanier, of Quincy, Florida.

Lewis Lanier, of Fort Meade, Florida.

Robert Sampson Lanier (my father), of Macon, Georgia.

W. L. Lanier, of West Point, Georgia. (The town of Lanier, in Schley County, Georgia, owes its name to the Laniers who once lived in Screven County, and who are referred to in the Family Tree hereinbefore given.)

D. G. Lanier, of Flat Rock, North Carolina.

Lucius Lanier, of Baltimore, Maryland.

There are also distinct branches in Mississippi, Texas, Virginia, and North Carolina, the names of whose representatives I do not know. I am told that the Hon. Thomas Lanier Clingman, of the latter State, derives his lineage in part—as indicated by his name—from the Rockingham County ancestors to whom I have alluded.

The late Edmund Lanier, Commander in the United States Navy, was, I believe, the son of a Presbyterian clergyman living in Nashville, Tennessee, who is of a still different branch from any of those specified above.

There is also a group of Laniers in the island of Cuba. One family of this group attended the Centennial Exhibition last year, and I regret that I was unable to meet them. I remember to have heard you relate that you were once accosted by a young Cuban while on one of your voyages to Europe, who informed you that his mother's name was Lanier, and that she was a descendant of the Huguenot Laniers from the South of France.

Some of the branches above indicated by a single name consist of many members, who are spread over several Southern and Northern States.

It cannot be improper for me to close this sketch by adding that I have read with great interest and profit the account of your life which you were kind enough to send me, and that I sincerely wish you a long and peaceful enjoyment of the remarkable successes therein set forth.

Very truly yours,

SIDNEY LANIER

II

MY DEAR SIR:

In a letter addressed to you, July 6th, 1877, and printed as an Appendix to the Second Edition of your autobiography, I had occasion to remark (page 77, under the caption " Sir John Lanier,") that "perhaps the first authentic mention of our name in history is that which records the part borne by Sir John Lanier at the Battle of Boyne, July 1, 1690, where he commanded the Queen's Regiment of horse."

In some recent studies * connected with the state of art in Shakspere's time I have happened to come upon several references which extend our knowledge of our name over a hundred years further back than the date mentioned. I have found these allusions of great interest, and I think it worth while to put together, in some connected form, the items of information which they furnish. They bring to us, in one way and another, the names of ten Laniers who flourished in England between the years 1568 and 1666, namely, two Jerome Laniers, two Nicholas Laniers, Clement, William, Andrew and John Lanier; while they give us some interesting additional details of Sir John Lanier in the Irish wars.

THE FIRST JEROME LANIER

" Nicholas Lanier was *one of the sons of Jerome*, who emigrated with his family to England in the latter part of the reign of Queen Elizabeth," says a note in Walpole's *Anecdotes of Painting in England.*

This Jerome Lanier was employed in the household of Queen Elizabeth. It is notable that these early Laniers enjoyed the personal favor of four consecutive English monarchs who differed greatly in disposition. Jerome was, as just remarked, in the household service of Queen Elizabeth; Nicholas, his son, was employed and encouraged by James the First; the same Nicholas was the friend of Charles the First, held two offices

* [Lanier's Peabody Lectures, printed in the present edition as *Shakspere and His Forerunners* (see III, 3-310).—ED.]

in his household, and was many times engaged in his affairs; while a second Nicholas, probably son of the Nicholas just named, was in the favor of Charles the Second and received from him an important franchise.

Several circumstances, which will appear in detail as the narrative advances, lead me to believe that this Jerome Lanier was one of those early Huguenots who were often compelled to leave their homes suddenly and flee into foreign countries between the year 1572 (when the Massacre of St. Bartholomew occurred in France) and the close of the sixteenth century. For example, in the year 1601 Charles Emanuel decreed that all the Protestants in his states should abjure, or quit the country within two months, under penalty of death and confiscation of goods. Hoping that something might occur to alter his determination, many of them lay idle for the two months without either abjuring or preparing to depart. At the end of this time, however, they were ordered at once to do the one or the other. Thus many were compelled to flee into other lands at a moment's warning, without the chance to gather their goods together.

Now it is my belief that Jerome Lanier, in one of the numerous troubles of this sort which came to the French and Savoyard Huguenots during the last quarter of the sixteenth century —that is, " in the latter part of the reign of Queen Elizabeth," as the quotation from Walpole's book puts it—found himself obliged to seek an asylum in some foreign country; and that he fled without the opportunity of carrying property with him. I judge that he *had* property because the tastes and habits which he transmitted to his children, and which we find them exhibiting so prominently as to secure the very mention of their names to which I am indebted for these items of information, were the tastes and habits of an educated and well-to-do person. It is therefore probable that after a sudden flight such as I have described, he found himself in England, with his family to support, and that he availed himself of his accomplishments in music to secure a place in Queen Elizabeth's household where such qualifications were appreciated.

This seems to me the only way to account for (1) his name, (2) his sudden appearance with his family in England, (3) the refined tastes of his children, and (4) their subsequent history.

THE FIRST NICHOLAS LANIER

The most prominent of the sons of Jerome seems to have been Nicholas Lanier. To distinguish him from a younger Nicholas whom I find flourishing in the time of Charles the Second and in the prime of manhood as far on as 1666, I have called him the first Nicholas.

He was born in the year 1568, and lived until 1646, possibly until 1649. We first hear of him in favor at the court of King James II. I find a note in Granger's *Biographical History of England* (Vol. III, p. 192), which speaks of him as follows:

In the reign of James I he was employed both as a composer and as a performer in the grand masque exhibited in the Banqueting-house at Whitehall, at the Earl of Somerset's wedding. The masquers were of high rank, namely: the Duke of Lenox, the earls of Pembroke, Dorset, Salisbury and Montgomery; the lords Walden, Scroope, North and Hayes; Sir Thomas, Sir Henry and Sir Charles Howard; the queen herself bore a part in the performance . . . being addressed by the name of Bel Anna. There is a particular description of this masque in print.

In a note to this note the reader is referred, for the said " particular description," to a work published by James Howell in 1656, called " *Finetti Philoxenis*; some choice observations of Sir John Finett, Knight, &c." The words to this masque were written by Dr. Thomas Campion. It was given in 1614.

I find Nicholas Lanier again referred to in the same reign. In Vol. VII of Gifford's edition of Ben Jonson's works (London, 1816) a note to *The Masque of Lethe* says: " The whole masque was sung . . . *stylo recitativo* by master Nicholas Lanier, who ordered and made both the scene and the music." This *Masque of Lethe* was composed by Ben Jonson and Nicholas Lanier in collaboration, to be " presented " (as stated in its title in Ben Jonson's works) " in the house of the right honorable the lord Hay, by divers of noble quality his friends, for the entertainment of monsieur le Baron de Tour, extraordinary ambassador for the French king, on Saturday, February 22d, 1617." These festivities are stated to have been of an unwonted splendor, in return for the extraordinary magnificence with which the English ambassador had been recently entertained in France.

The favor extended to Nicholas Lanier by James I is a some-what remarkable circumstance, in view of the fact that other men of his profession who had been encouraged in the preced-ing reign were now neglected. "During the reign of James I" (says Sir John Hawkins) * "the household musicians, those of the chapel, and many others of eminence whom the patronage of Elizabeth had produced, were neglected, and very little of the royal favor was extended to any besides Laniere and Coperario." This "Coperario" was an Englishman named *Cooper*, who had been to Italy for purposes of study, and who was called by an Italianized form of his name after his return to England. The reason for this preference of Lanier and Cooper is guessed by Sir John Hawkins to be their Italian leanings, under the impression (produced by a single statement in Anthony a-Wood) that Lanier was an Italian. I think, however, the true reason is much easier to come at in Lanier's case. The queen of James I was Anne of Denmark, who had a passion for the gorgeous masques in which the talents of Nicholas were eminent, and nothing seems more likely than that she was glad to favor—and to induce her royal husband to favor—one whose tastes ran so well with her own.

It was, however, in the following reign—that of Charles the First—that Nicholas Lanier prospered most. "He was" (says Walpole) "one of those artists whose various talents were so happy, all, as to suit the state of Charles the First. He had great share" (continues Walpole) "in the purchases made for the royal collection, and probably was even employed in the treaty of Mantua. One picture is said expressly in the king's catalogue to have been changed with Mr. Lanier." In a note to this passage it is added that, according to the author of the *English School*,** Nicholas Lanier was in the habit of putting "a particular mark on the pictures bought by him for the king," and the mark is given as this,*** which seems to be a sort of triple involved *L*. "He marked his own etchings with

* [John Hawkins (1719-1789), *A General History of the Science and Practice of Music.*—ED.]

** [B. Buckeridge, "An Essay toward an English School of Painters," printed in De Piles (1635-1709), *The Art of Painting* . . . ; quoted in Wal-pole.—ED.]

*** [At this point Lanier left a blank in his text, but failed to reproduce the symbol, which Walpole prints as ▩.—ED.]

an L," says the same note. Another note records that " he was a complete courtier, and much associated with Vandyck, whose portrait of him was most excellent."

Nicholas Lanier was " Closet-keeper " to Charles the First, and also held the post of " Master of the King's Music " at a salary of two hundred pounds a year. I have found a copy of the grant appointing him to this latter position, taken from Rymer's *Fœdera*. It bears date July 11th, 1626—a short time after Charles ascended the throne—and runs as follows:

Charles, by the grace of God, &c. To the treasurer and under-treasurer of our exchequer nowe being, and that hereafter for the time shall be, greetinge: Whereas we have been graciously pleased, in con-sideration of service done and to be done unto us by sundry of our musicians, to graunt unto them the severall annuities and yearly pensions hereafter following, (that is to say) to Nicholas Lanier master of our music two hundred pounds yearly for his wages, to Thomas Foord four score pounds yearly for his wages, to Robert Johnson yearly for wages fortie pounds and for stringes twentie pounds by the yeare, to— [sev-eral others, Ferabasco, Lupo, Laurence, Kelly, Cogshall, Taylor, Deer-ing, Drewe, Wornall, Notary, Wrench and] John Laniere . . . . &c.:

These are therefore to will and command [the treasurer to pay the said sums, &c.]

Witness ourself at Westminster, the eleventh day of July.
Per breve de privato sigillo, &c. *

Nicholas Lanier's accomplishments were varied and substan-tial. He was, says Walpole, " musician, painter, engraver, and understood hands," that is, could tell by looking at a picture the name of its painter, from his study of the styles of the masters. Of his pictures I find mention of the following, in various books. " His own portrait in the music-school at Oxford, painted by himself," is (says Sir John Hawkins) " a masterly work." Walpole mentions another work: " as a painter he drew for Charles a picture of Mary, Christ and Joseph." These are all of his paintings specified: but a note in Walpole mentions some of his works in engraving. " Mr. Rose, the jeweller, had all the plates for a drawing-book, by Lanier, etched by himself." On this collection of plates, Nicholas had engraved, in Italian, these words: " First proof

* [John Hawkins, *A General History of the Science and Practice of Music.*— Ed.]

done in aqua forte by N. Lanier in his youthful age of sixty-eight years, 1636." So that here we have record, by his own hand, of his date: his statement that he was sixty-eight in 1636 guiding us to 1568 as the year of his birth.

Of his musical works I have met with the following mention. Dr. Burney says:

> Of Lanier's *musica narrativa* we have several examples, printed by Playford in the collections of the time: particularly the *Ayres and Dialogues* 1653, and the second part of the *Musical Companion* which appeared in 1667 and in which his music to the dialogues is infinitely superior to the rest; there is melody, measure and meaning in it . . . His cantata of Hero and Leander was much celebrated during these times.*

Sir John Hawkins mentions that many of his songs are to be found in the collections published in the time of Charles the First. Walpole says: " a vocal composition for a funeral hymn on his royal master, written by Thomas Pierce, was set by Lanier." I think it quite possible that this is a mistake and that the " vocal composition " referred to was written, not by the Nicholas Lanier of whom Walpole treats, but by a younger Nicholas of whom I shall speak presently. If the elder Nicholas died, according to the *Somerset House Gazette*, in 1646, he could not have written music after the death of Charles the First, which was in 1649; but it may have been the younger Nicholas Lanier, often mentioned by old Samuel Pepys in his Diary—mentioned too, by the way, more than once at evening parties where we find *Mrs. Pierce* and on one occasion the *Mr. Pierce* who probably wrote the words to the funeral hymn for Charles the First. It may be, however, on the other hand, that the date of the death of Nicholas the elder given by the *Somerset House Gazette*—1646—is a mistake, and that he had the melancholy satisfaction of writing this funeral hymn to the memory of his royal patron. This possibility is strengthened by a passage in Anthony a-Wood's *Fasti Oxonienses*, Vol. II, p. 72, which refers to " Nich. Laniere or Laneare, . . . one of the private music to king Charles I, and an excellent painter, (*who died after* 1648,) " this latter date being inserted in place of the statement made in the first edi-

---

* [Charles Burney, *A General History of Music.*—ED.]

tion of the book that he died " about the beginning of the Rebellion."

I am specially interested in finding mention, here and there, of five different portraits of Nicholas Lanier, all of which I sincerely hope may be some day recovered into our family. These are as follows:

1. The portrait of Nicholas Lanier painted by Vandyck, already mentioned. Granger says: " It was the sight of this picture that determined the king to employ that excellent painter." In the account of the sale of Charles the First's pictures after his execution, occurs the following record: " A piece of Nich. Laniere, to the knees, by A. Vandyck, 10*l. purchased by himself.*" Whether this " himself " is the elder or younger Nicholas, I cannot say. Walpole mentions his giving two hundred and thirty pounds for four pictures at this sale, and says " his brothers Clement and Jerome were likewise purchasers." In endeavoring to trace the whereabouts of this portrait I have discovered that it was afterwards at a manor called " The Grange," in Hampshire. Granger, in treating of Nicholas Lanier, says, " At the Grange, in Hampshire, the seat of the Henleys, was a fine portrait of him by Vandyck." In a note to this passage signed " Bindley," it is stated further, with regard to this portrait, that " upon the death of Robert, second earl of Northington, who died in 1772 unmarried, the family house and estate were sold, as was the collection of pictures, by public auction; when *Laniere's portrait* and Vandyck's sketch of the procession of the knights of the Garter were both disposed of." It appears therefore that the picture was in existence in 1772. I have not been able to trace it further, but there seems every reason to believe that it still exists and might be found.

2. Walpole mentions that there was another portrait of Nicholas Lanier " at the late Sir Andrew Fountain's, at Narford, in Norfolk." I have not been able to find any further reference to this picture.

3. A note in Walpole mentions that " there was another portrait " of Nicholas Lanier, " and of Isaac Oliver, in one piece, in the collection of James II "; and refers to the " catalogue published by Bathoe."

4. The portrait painted by himself and now in the music-hall of Oxford University, England. This portrait is mentioned by several writers as the portrait of *Nicholas* Lanier, but the note in Walpole referring to it says that he (Nicholas Lanier) gave a "portrait of himself (*or rather of Jerome, his father*), of his own design and performance, to the music-school at Oxford, &c." It may be, then, that we have here a likeness of the first Lanier who appeared in England.

5. There is an engraved portrait of Nicholas Lanier in the British Museum (Additional *MS.* 15,858, *fol.* 55), as I learn from Lord Braybrooke's notice in his edition of Pepy's Diary. I take this to be the picture also mentioned by Walpole, who says "there is a print of him painted by John Lyvyns, and engraved by Vosterman." (This "John Lyvyns" is *John Lievens*, a celebrated artist of that time.) It is doubtless the same portrait which is found engraved in Walton's *Complete Angler*, in Pepy's Diary, and in Walpole's *Anecdotes.* I sent you a copy of it some time ago, done on plaque by John R. Tait.* It is interesting to note that Lord Braybrooke in mentioning this portrait adds that there is also preserved in the British Museum a letter from Nicholas Lanier, addressed to his niece Mrs. Richards, "at her house in the Old Aumery, Westminster."

Nicholas Lanier died, according to the *Somerset House Gazette* (as quoted by Braybrooke) in the year 1646, aged seventy-eight, and was buried at St. Martin's-in-the-Fields. I have already discussed the possible error in this date.

THE SECOND JEROME LANIER

A note to Walpole says: "Mr. Evelyn notices Jerome, another son" (that is, another son of the elder Jerome, besides Nicholas) as follows, "old Jerome Lanier, of Greenwich, a man skilled in painting. I went to see his collection of paintings, especially those of Julio Romano, which had surely been the king's. There were also excellent things of Polidoro, Guido, Raphael, Tintoret, &c." Evelyn speaks of this Jerome

* [A contemporary artist and friend of Lanier, who was living in Baltimore at this time.—ED.]

as having also been in the household of Queen Elizabeth, and adds: " he showed me her head, an intaglio, in a rare sardonyx, cut by a famous Italian, which he assured me was exceedingly like her." The remark of Evelyn's above, that Jerome Lanier's copies of Romano's paintings " had surely been the king's," agrees with Walpole's statement that at the sale of the king's goods he (*i. e.* Nicholas) gave two hundred and thirty pounds for four pictures, and that " his brothers Clement and Jerome were likewise purchasers."

It is worth while noting in this connection that Evelyn speaks of going to " Greenwich " to see Jerome's collection. In several other notices I find mention of Greenwich in such a way as to indicate that it was the home of the Laniers for several generations. Walpole mentions that Nicholas Lanier deposited the pictures he had bought at the king's sale " *in his father's* apartments in Greenwich palace, where Evelyn saw them in 1652." Again in Pepys' notices of Nicholas Lanier the younger, he is connected with Greenwich, as hereinafter appears.

Jerome Lanier's name is mentioned in the charter hereinafter described in the account of the second Nicholas Lanier. I have not been able to find any particulars of his death.

THE SECOND NICHOLAS LANIER

We now come down to the year 1665, and find the taste for pictures still subsisting among the third generation of Laniers from old Jerome: for under the date of October 31st in that year I find the following entry in the Diary of Samuel Pepys:

> About nine at night I come home, and there find Mrs. Pierce come, and little Frank Tooker, and Mr. Hill, and other people, a great many dancing and anon comes Mrs. Coleman and her husband, and she sung very finely . . . . a pleasant jolly woman and in mighty good humour. Among other things *Laneare did*, at the request of Mr. Hill, *bring two or three of the finest prints* for my wife to see, that ever I did see in all my life.

This " Laneare " would seem to have been Nicholas the younger, from another entry about him in Pepys' Diary. Under date of the evening of Dec. 6th, 1665, Pepys notes:

> And so with my wife walked to *Mrs. Pierce's*, where Captain Rolt and

Mrs. Knipp, Mr. Coleman and his wife, and *Laneare*, ... met, and by and by unexpectedly comes *Mr. Pierce from Oxford.* Here the best company for musique I ever was in in my life, and I wish I could live and die in it . . . . I spent the night in an exstasy almost; and having invited them to my house a day or two hence, we broke up.

Now this " Mr. Pierce from Oxford " is, without doubt, the author Thomas Pierce, of whom Anthony a-Wood gives a full account among the graduates of Oxford, and who wrote, among many other works which Wood specifies, the funeral poem on the death of Charles the First which Wood says was set to music by Nicholas Lanier the elder. It might well be that it was Nicholas the younger who wrote that composition, and this suggests him, rather than either of his brothers (or cousins) John, Andrew, or William, as the Laneare whom Pepys met at the house of Mrs. Pierce.

In response to the invitation mentioned in this entry we find " Laneare " a few nights afterwards at Pepys' house in pretty much the same company. Under date of Dec. 8th, 1665, Pepys records as follows:

By water down to *Greenwich* and there found all my company come— that is Mrs. Knipp and an ill-natured, melancholy, jealous-looking fellow, her husband . . . *Pierce and his wife*, and Rolt, Mrs. Worshipp and her daughter, Coleman and his wife, and *Laneare.* Most excellent musique we had in abundance . . . spending the night till two in the morning, with most complete content as ever in my life.

Pepys had a genuine passion for " musique," and was ambitious to be thought a composer himself, as appears here and there.

A few days before this, Pepys had met Nicholas at church. December 3d, 1665, he says:

It being Lord's day, up and dressed, and to church, thinking to have sat with Sir James Bunce, but was prevented by being invited into Colonel Cleggat's pew. However, there I sat, *near Mr. Laneare*, with whom I spoke . . . "

In a few days we find Nicholas again at the hospitable house of Pepys. The latter writes, January 1st, 1666:

So home, and find all my good company I had bespoke, as Coleman and his wife, and Laneare, Knipp and her surly husband; and good musique we had . . . then to dancing and supper, and mighty merry till Mr. Rolt came in, whose pain of the toothache made him no company, and spoilt ours, so he away, and then my wife's teeth fell of aching, and she to bed. So forced to break up all with a good song, and so to bed.

These lively pictures of the hospitable festivities with which Pepys solaced the grave labors of his active and successful career show us, I think, the same Nicholas Lanier (the younger) who was prominent in obtaining the interesting charter which finally established the corporation of " The Marshall, Wardens, and Cominalty of the Arte and Science of Music in Westminster." Lord Braybrooke, in his edition of Pepys, has a note to the following effect, at the word " Laneare " occurring in the citations I have just given. " The Letters Patent under which the Society of Musicians was incorporated at the Restoration mention a Lanier, possibly a son of Nicholas " (of whom Braybrooke has just given an account in the same note) " as first Marshall, and four others of his name, as wardens or assistants of the company." I have found a copy of these Letters Patent in Hawkins. The instrument dates from just after the Restoration—1660—when it seems that a number of persons—among them Nicholas Lanier and four other Laniers, either his brothers, or cousins, probably—determined to " exert their authority for the improvement of the science and the interest of its professors." I find there had been an old charter of the kind, dating as far back as Edward IV, and renewed in the time of Charles the First. After Charles the First, however, it lay dormant until the Restoration, when these gentlemen determined to avail themselves of it for the purpose of stopping certain practices of unauthorized persons who were bringing the profession into small esteem. The instrument, after some preliminary recitals, goes on to say: " at the prosecution of *Nicholas Lanier, . . . Jerome Lanier, Clement Lanier, Andrewe Lanier, John Lanier*," and several others, " a Scire Facias had been brought in the king's name against the said " obnoxious pretenders " in the high court of chancery," &c., " and that judgment at their said prosecution had been had and given by the said court accordingly," wherefore, " . . . in pursuance of the intent and meaninge of the said King Edward the

Fourth, the King," Charles II, " doth for him his heirs and successors, will, ordain, constitute, declare and grant that the said Nicholas Lanier, . . . Jerome Lanier, Clement Lanier, Andrewe Lanier . . . . John Lanier . . . . William Lanier . . . " and several more, including Henry Lawes and other names held in great esteem then and since, . . . " shall from thenceforth be . . . . a body corporate and politique, in deed, fact and name, by the name of Marshall, Wardens, and Cominalty of the arte and science of musick in Westminster, in the county of Middlesex, and by the same name have perpetual succession, and be capable in the law to implead and be impleaded, and that they have a common seal."

The corporation had important and valuable privileges: the right to examine and license those who professed the art, to summon professors before them for various purposes, and to enforce their determinations by fines which went into their treasury.

The charter goes on to appoint Nicholas Lanier first Marshal for life. This was our Nicholas the younger, the first Nicholas having probably been dead for more than ten years at this time. We are now in 1661, and the latest date assigned for the death of the elder Nicholas is 1649.

I find that the corporation met first on the 22d October, 1661, Nicholas Lanier, the Marshal, presiding; and from this time they proceeded to transact business, of which the following extracts from their minutes will show the nature:

1662, January 20th.   Ordered that Edward Sadler, for his insufficiency in the arte of musique, be from henceforth silenced and disabled from the exercise of any kinde in publique houses or meetings.

July 2d.   Ordered that Richard Hudson, the clerk of the corporation, doe summon all the common minstrels from time to time before the corporation.

July 9th.   Thomas Purcell [whose compositions are still heard with delight], chosen an Assistant in room of Dr. Charles Coleman, dec'd.

These various sources show us Nicholas Lanier the younger, probably in his prime about the years 1661 to 1666 (when Pepys' last notice of him is dated), a man with the tastes of his ancestors for pictures and music, moving in good company, and chosen first Marshal of the corporation which embraced the most solid professors of the time as members.

JOHN LANIER

Besides the mention of him in the above Letters Patent, I find it stated in the works of Lovelace that two of that author's most admired poems were set to music by " Mr. John Laniere." As they were contemporaries, I do not doubt this is the John Lanier mentioned in the charter of the corporation. Of the

JEROME, CLEMENT, ANDREW AND WILLIAM LANIER

mentioned in the charter I know nothing more than the probability that William Lanier gave up his post among the king's musicians in 1660, when John Singleton is mentioned to have been appointed in his place. I do not know whether this Clement and Jerome were the two brothers of Nicholas the elder: Evelyn speaks of " old Jerome Lanier " in 1652, and we are now in 1661; but it is of course possible they may be the same, for they seem to have been long-lived and vigorous men. We have, therefore, probably the following as a correct *resumé* of the family up to this point:

First generation . . . . Jerome Lanier, Sr.
Second generation . . . . Nicholas, Sr., Jerome, Jr., and Clement.
Third generation . . . . Nicholas, Jr., Andrew, William and John.

SIR JOHN LANIER

The John Lanier who terminates the list above given, and of whom we lose sight in 1660, possibly points to some connection with the Sir John Lanier who appears on the scene thirty years afterwards. Since writing my former account of Sir John Lanier, I have seen George Story's *True and Impartial History of the most Material Occurrences in the Kingdom of Ireland during the two last years*, a copy of which, printed in 1693, is in the Peabody Library. This book contains several allusions to Sir John Lanier, and is the authority from which was obtained the first item with regard to that General given in

Macaulay's History of England. I think some important inferences with regard to Sir John Lanier are to be drawn from the
following passages in which his name occurs. Story's book is
in the form of a diary, which he kept while he was engaged in
this stirring Irish campaign of King William against James II.
Under September 1689 he writes: " About the 8th or 9th Sir
John Lanier's (and other) Horse landed at Carlingford, from
Scotland, and were ordered to Armagh . . . and other places."
Carlingford is the port in Ireland where King William is
assembling his forces for a decisive struggle with James; and it
seems from this entry that Sir John with his regiment has been
previously employed in the troubles of the North, for they
come " from Scotland."

The campaign now advances actively towards its crisis at
the Battle of the Boyne. In the next year—1690—Story writes:

on the 15th of February *Sir John Lanier*, with a party of 1000 Horse,
Foot and Dragoons, went from Newry towards *Dundalk*: it was in the
evening when he marched, and next morning early, being *Sunday*, he
appeared before the town. The enemy had fortified it very well . . .
He [*i. e.* Sir John Lanier] drew up his Foot . . . on the side of an Hill,
between the left of our old Horse Camp and the Town, a good musquet
shot from the Bridge; his Horse he sent nearer, somewhat to the right
at the side of the Lane. Whilst the main body was so posted *Major
General Lanier* sent a party of Horse and Dragoons beyond the River
who burnt the West part of the Town from Mortimer Castle to Blake's
House (being a great part of the Suburbs). At the same time a party
of Levison's Dragoons attaqu'd Bedloe's Castle, and took the ensign
that commanded it with 30 prisoners: we lost a Lieutenant and three
or four Dragoons, and had four Horses shot. Our men brought from
beyond the town and about it nigh 1500 Cows and Horses.

The next mention of him, after this foraging expedition, is
on the day before the Battle of the Boyne:

. . . on Monday morning the last of June very early, our whole army
began to move in three lines towards the Boyne, which was but eight
short miles off. The enemy being near, our advance-Guards of Horse,
commanded by *Sir John Lanier*, made their approach very regularly,
and by that time they had got within two miles of Drogheda his
Majesty was in front of them.

On the next day he commands his regiment in battle, then

known as the Queen's Regiment, afterwards as the First Dragoon Guards.

On the 7th and 8th of July following, a muster of the army is had at Finglass, when a severe story of the ravages of sickness and battle is revealed: " Sir John Lanier's Regiment of English Horse " shows " 360 men " in service, and I notice it is one of the four largest in the army, the others being reduced to two hundred or even less, having suffered from a frightful distemper which carried off the men like a plague.

After the Battle of the Boyne Sir John and his regiment remained for some months and assisted in finishing up the campaign.

" Sept. 13th " (1690) " Sir John Lanier, with his own, lord of Oxford's, Langston's, Byerley's Horse, Levison's Dragoons and part of Cunningham's, marches towards *Bir*, which way we heard that Sarsfield was making."

December, 1690. " We had now a part of our Army on their March towards Lanesborough-Pass, commanded by Major-General Kirk and Sir John Lanier."

In May 1691 " Major-General Kirk and Sir John Lanier go for England and land at Neston on the thirtieth."

It would seem that Sir John went home on a short leave of absence and returned. For, about a month afterward, at the battle of Aghrim, it is mentioned that Ruvigny's regiment of horse " and Sir John Lanier's, being both posted on the right, were afterwards part of them drawn to the left where they did very good service." It also appears in the muster after the battle that Sir John's regiment loses twenty-three killed and five wounded.

The last entry concerning him is under date of the 25th July, 1691, when it is stated that " Colonel Mathew's Dragoons were shipped at Belfast, as Sir John Lanier's had been some time before." He then went to the Continent,—as we learn from Macaulay,—and fell gloriously at Steinkirk along with the brave Douglas.

Here we find a gap of twenty-three years between the Lanier whom we left at the house of Samuel Pepys in 1666, and this Sir John who brings his regiment over from Scotland in 1689 to help King William in Ireland; while, on the other hand, a still shorter time intervenes between the death of Sir John Lanier and the emigration of Thomas Lanier to America, which was in or before the year 1716.

With the hope and belief that we will some day be able to fill these two intervals with details satisfactorily connecting Thomas Lanier with Sir John, and Sir John with Nicholas, so as to give us a continuous account of the family back to the year 1568,   I am,

Very truly yours,

SIDNEY LANIER

BIBLIOGRAPHY

BIBLIOGRAPHY

Compiled by PHILIP GRAHAM and FRIEDA C. THIES

I. WORKS BY SIDNEY LANIER

A. COLLECTED PROSE, POETRY, AND LETTERS

Tiger-Lilies. A Novel. Hurd and Houghton. New York, 1867.
Florida: Its scenery, climate, and history. With an account of Charleston, Savannah, Augusta, and Aiken, and a chapter for consumptives; being a
complete hand-book and guide. With numerous illustrations. J. B.
Lippincott & Co. Philadelphia, 1875.
Florida: Its scenery, climate, and history. With an account of Charleston, Sa-
vannah, Augusta, and Aiken; a chapter for consumptives; various papers
on fruit-culture; and a complete hand-book and guide. With numerous
illustrations. J. B. Lippincott & Co. Philadelphia, 1876.
The Centennial Meditation of Columbia, 1776-1876. By appointment of the
U. S. Centennial Commission. A cantata for the inaugural ceremonies at
Philadelphia, May 10, 1876. Poem by Sidney Lanier, of Georgia. Music
by Dudley Buck, of Connecticut. G. Schirmer. New York, 1876.
Poems. J. B. Lippincott & Co. Philadelphia . . . London, 1877.
The Boy's Froissart: Being Sir John Froissart's Chronicles of Adventure, Battle
and Custom in England, France, Spain, etc. Edited for boys with an
introduction by Sidney Lanier. Illustrated by Alfred Kappes. Charles
Scribner's Sons. New York, 1879. (Only the Preface is printed in the
Centennial Edition, since this is the only section of the book written by
Lanier.)
The Science of English Verse. Charles Scribner's Sons. New York, 1880.
The Boy's King Arthur: Being Sir Thomas Malory's history of King Arthur and
his Knights of the Round Table. Edited for boys with an introduction
by Sidney Lanier, editor of " The Boy's Froissart." Illustrated by Alfred
Kappes. Charles Scribner's Sons. New York, 1880. (Only the Preface
is printed in the Centennial Edition, since this is the only section of the
book written by Lanier.)
The Boy's Mabinogion: Being the earliest tales of King Arthur in the famous
Red Book of Hergest. Edited for boys with an introduction by Sidney
Lanier, editor of " The Boy's Froissart " and " The Boy's King Arthur."
Illustrated by Alfred Fredericks. Charles Scribner's Sons. New York,
1881. (Only the Preface is printed in the Centennial Edition, since this
is the only section of the book written by Lanier.)
The Boy's Percy: Being old ballads of war, adventure and love from Bishop
Thomas Percy's Reliques of Ancient English Poetry, together with an
appendix containing two ballads from the original Percy Folio MS.
Edited for boys with an introduction by Sidney Lanier . . . With fifty
illustrations from original designs by E. B. Bensell. Charles Scribner's
Sons. New York, 1882. (Only the Preface is printed in the Centennial
Edition, since this is the only section of the book written by Lanier.)
The English Novel and the Principle of its Development. By Sidney Lanier,

lecturer in Johns Hopkins University. . . . (Edited by W. H. Browne.) Charles Scribner's Sons. New York, 1883.

Poems of Sidney Lanier. Edited by his wife. With a Memorial by William Hayes Ward. Charles Scribner's Sons. New York, 1884.

Poems of Sidney Lanier. Edited by his wife, with a Memorial by William Hayes Ward. New edition. Charles Scribner's Sons. New York, 1891. (Includes seven poems not in the edition of 1884: " A Sunrise Song," " On a Palmetto," " Struggle," " Control," " To J. D. H.," " Marsh Hymns. Between Dawn and Sunrise," and " Thou and I.")

The English Novel: A Study in the development of personality. By Sidney Lanier, lecturer in Johns Hopkins University . . . Revised edition. (Edited by Mary Day Lanier.) Charles Scribner's Sons. New York, 1897.

Music and Poetry: Essays upon some aspects and inter-relations of the two arts. (Edited by Henry W. Lanier.) Charles Scribner's Sons. New York, 1898.

Bob: the story of our Mocking-Bird. With sixteen illustrations in color. (Edited by Charles D. Lanier.) Charles Scribner's Sons. New York, 1899.

Letters of Sidney Lanier. Selections from his correspondence, 1866-1881. With portraits. (Edited by Henry W. Lanier.) Charles Scribner's Sons. New York, 1899.

Retrospects and Prospects: Descriptive and Historical Essays. (Edited by Henry W. Lanier.) Charles Scribner's Sons. New York, 1899.

Shakspere and His Forerunners: Studies in Elizabethan poetry and its development from Early English. Illustrated. (Edited by Henry W. Lanier.) Doubleday Page & Co. New York, 1902. (Two volumes. A limited edition of 102 numbered copies was issued on Van Gelder handmade paper.)

The Lanier Book. Selections in prose and verse from the writings of Sidney Lanier. Edited by Mary E. Burt. Illustrated. Charles Scribner's Sons. New York, 1904.

Select Poems of Sidney Lanier. Edited with an Introduction, Notes, and Bibliography by Morgan Callaway, Jr. Charles Scribner's Sons. New York, 1906.

Hymns of the Marshes. Illustrated from nature by Henry Troth. Charles Scribner's Sons. New York, 1907.

Some Early Letters and Reminiscences of Sidney Lanier. Edited by George H. Clarke, with an introduction by Harry Stillwell Edwards. The J. W. Burke Company . . . Macon, 1907.

Poem Outlines. (Edited by Henry W. Lanier.) Charles Scribner's Sons. New York, 1908.

Selections from Sidney Lanier: Prose and Verse. With an introduction and notes. Edited by Henry W. Lanier. Charles Scribner's Sons. New York, 1916.

Poems of Sidney Lanier. Edited by his wife. With a Memorial by William Hayes Ward. New edition. Charles Scribner's Sons. New York, 1916. (Includes two poems not in the editions of 1884 and 1891: " Our Hills " and " Laughter in the Senate.")

Letters. Sidney Lanier to Col. John G. James. (Edited by Margaret Lee Wiley.) The University of Texas, Austin, 1942.

B. FIRST PRINTING OF POEMS

(Poems marked * were previously uncollected. Numbers in brackets refer to pages in the Centennial Edition, volume I.)

1866

* "To J. L.," in *Round Table* (N. Y.), III, 443, July 14, 1866. [8]
"Spring Greeting," in *Round Table* (N. Y.), III, 443, July 14, 1866. [5]

1867

"The Tournament: Joust First," in *Round Table* (N. Y.), V, 365, June 8, 1867. [6]
"The Tournament: Joust Second," in *Round Table* (N. Y.), VI, 13, July 6, 1867. [6-8]
"A Birthday Song," in *Round Table* (N. Y.), VI, 61, July 27, 1867. [9-10]
"Barnacles," in *Round Table* (N. Y.), VI, 312, Nov. 9, 1867. [11]

1868

"In the Foam," in *Round Table* (N. Y.), VII, 60, Jan. 25, 1868. [12-13]
"Tyranny," in *Round Table* (N. Y.), VII, 124, Feb. 22, 1868. [13-14]
"Laughter in the Senate," in *Round Table* (N. Y.), VII, 236, Apr. 11, 1868. [14]
* *Little Ella* (with music), Montgomery, Ala., 1868. [9]
"Life and Song," in *Round Table* (N. Y.), VIII, 157, Sept. 5, 1868. [16]
The Golden Wedding of Sterling and Sarah Lanier, privately printed, [n. p.], Sept. 27, 1868. [17-18]
"Resurrection," in *Round Table* (N. Y.), VIII, 281, Oct. 24, 1868. [16-17]
"The Ship of Earth," in *Round Table* (N. Y.), VIII, 328, Nov. 14, 1868. [15]
"The Raven Days," in *Scott's Monthly Magazine* (Atlanta), VI, 873, Dec., 1868. [15]

1870

"A Song of Eternity in Time," in *XIX Century* (Charleston, S. C.), II, 708, Feb., 1870. [12]
"Nirvâna," in *New Eclectic* (Baltimore), VI, 294-296, Mar., 1870. [19-21]

1871

"Thar's More in the Man Than Thar Is in the Land," in *Telegraph and Messenger* (Macon), Feb. 7, 1871. [22-23]
"Jones's Private Argument," in *Southern Farm and Home* (Macon), II, 338, July, 1871. [24-25]
"A Song," in *Southern Magazine* (Baltimore), IX, 127, July, 1871. [213]
"A Sea-Shore Grave," in *Southern Magazine* (Baltimore), IX, 127, July, 1871. [214]
* "The Homestead," in *Southern Farm and Home* (Macon), II, 392, Aug., 1871. [25-28]

1874

"On Huntingdon's 'Miranda,'" in *Evening Post* (N. Y.), Mar. 6, 1874. [32]
* "Civil Rights," in *Herald* (Atlanta), Sept. ? 1874. Reprinted in *Daily Telegraph and Messenger* (Macon), Oct. 29, 1874. [40-42]

1875

" Corn," in *Lippincott's Magazine* (Phila.), XV, 216-219, Feb., 1875. [34-39]
" Martha Washington," in *Martha Washington Court Journal* (Baltimore), p. 1,
    Feb. 22, 1875. [46]
" The Symphony," in *Lippincott's Magazine* (Phila.), XV, 677-684, June, 1875.
    [46-56]
" The Power of Prayer," in *Scribner's Monthly* (N. Y.), X, 239-240, June,
    1875. [215-216]
" In Absence," in *Lippincott's Magazine* (Phila.), XVI, 341-342, Sept., 1875.
    [42-43]
" Laus Mariæ," in *Scribner's Monthly* (N. Y.), XI, 64, Nov., 1875. [44]
" Betrayal," in *Lippincott's Magazine* (Phila.), XVI, 711, Dec., 1875. [19]

1876

" Special Pleading," in *Lippincott's Magazine* (Phila.), XVII, 89, Jan., 1876.
    [45]
" To Charlotte Cushman," in *Lippincott's Magazine* (Phila.), XVII, 375, Mar.,
    1876. [58]
" Rose-Morals," in *Lippincott's Magazine* (Phila.), XVII, 587, May, 1876.
    [59-60]
" Uncle Jim's Baptist Revival Hymn," in *Scribner's Monthly* (N. Y.), XII, 142,
    May, 1876. [217]
The Centennial Meditation of Columbia (with music by Dudley Buck), New
    York, 1876. [60-62]
" Psalm of the West," in *Lippincott's Magazine* (Phila.), XVIII, 39-53, July,
    1876. [62-82]
" A Song of the Future," in *Scribner's Monthly* (N. Y.), XII, 543, Aug., 1876.
    [59]
" To ――――, with a Rose," in *Lippincott's Magazine* (Phila.), XVIII, 371,
    Sept., 1876. [82]
" Acknowledgment," in *Lippincott's Magazine* (Phila.), XVIII, 554-555, Nov.,
    1876. [56-57]
" Dedication. To Charlotte Cushman," in *Poems*, Philadelphia, 1877, p. 5. [83]

1877

" Evening Song," in *Lippincott's Magazine* (Phila.), XIX, 91, Jan., 1877. [88]
" To Beethoven," in *Galaxy* (N. Y.), XXIII, 394-395, Mar., 1877. [88-90]
" Tampa Robins," in *Lippincott's Magazine* (Phila.), XIX, 355, Mar., 1877.
    [92-93]
" The Stirrup-Cup," in *Scribner's Monthly*, XIV, 28, May, 1877. [90]
" A Florida Sunday," in *Frank Leslie's Sunday Magazine* (N. Y.), II, 72-73,
    July, 1877. [94-97]
" From the Flats," in *Lippincott's Magazine* (Phila.), XX, 115, July, 1877.
    [97-98]
" The Waving of the Corn," in *Harper's Magazine* (N. Y.), LV, 439, Aug.,
    1877. [83-84]
" The Mocking Bird," in *Galaxy* (N. Y.), XXIV, 161, Aug., 1877. [98]
" The Bee," in *Lippincott's Magazine* (Phila.), XX, 493, Oct., 1877. [91-92]
" To Richard Wagner," in *Galaxy* (N. Y.), XXIV, 652-653, Nov., 1877.
    [102-103]
" A Puzzled Ghost in Florida," in *Appleton's Journal* (N. Y.), III [n. s.], 568,
    Dec., 1877. [99-101]

" A Weather-Vane," in *Dial of the Old South Clock* (Boston), p. 7, Dec. 10, 1877. [112]
" The Hard Times in Elfland," *Every Saturday* (Baltimore), Christmas Supplement, p. 1, Dec. 22, 1877. [105-111]

1878

" Under the Cedarcroft Chestnut," in *Scribner's Monthly* (N. Y.), XV, 380-381, Jan., 1878. [93-94]
" Clover," in *Independent* (N. Y.), XXX, 1, Mar. 7, 1878. [84-87]
" To Nannette Falk-Auerbach," in *Gazette* (Baltimore), Mar. 28, 1878. [117]
" The Harlequin of Dreams," in *Lippincott's Magazine* (Phila.), XXI, 439, Apr., 1878. [112]
" The Dove," in *Scribner's Monthly* (N. Y.), XVI, 140, May, 1878. [99]
" To Our Mocking-Bird," in *Independent* (N. Y.), XXX, 1, Aug. 29, 1878. [117-118]
" The Revenge of Hamish," in *Appleton's Journal* (N. Y.), V [n. s.], 395-396, Nov., 1878. [112-116]
" The Marshes of Glynn," in *A Masque of Poets*, Boston, 1878, pp. 88-94. [118-122]
* " To Miss Charlotte Cushman (With a Copy of ' Corn ')," in Emma Stebbins, *Charlotte Cushman*, Boston, 1878, p. 268. [44]

1879

" To Bayard Taylor," in *Scribner's Monthly* (N. Y.), XVII, 642-643, Mar., 1879. [128-130]

1880

" Opposition," in *Good Company* (Springfield, Mass.), IV, 444, Jan., 1880. [130-131]
" Ode to the Johns Hopkins University," in *Johns Hopkins University Circular* (Baltimore), No. 4, pp. 38-39, Apr., 1880. [133-135]
[" Ireland "], in *The Art Autograph*, New York, 1880, p. 10. [136]
" The Crystal," in *Independent* (N. Y.), XXXII, 1, July 15, 1880. [136-139]
" A Ballad of Trees and the Master," in *Independent* (N. Y.), XXXII, 1, Dec. 23, 1880. [144]

1881

" A Sunrise Song," in *Independent* (N. Y.), XXXIII, 1, Apr. 28, 1881. [143]
" Owl Against Robin," in *Scribner's Monthly* (N. Y.), XXII, 453-454, July, 1881. [131-133]

1882-1935. Posthumously Published

" Marsh Song—At Sunset," in *Our Continent* (Phila.), I, 4, Feb. 15, 1882. [142]
" My Two Springs," in *Century Magazine* (N. Y.), XXIV, 838-839, Oct., 1882. [32-34]
" The Cloud," in *Century Magazine* (N. Y.), XXV, 222-223, Dec., 1882. [139-141]
" Sunrise," in *Independent* (N. Y.), XXXIV, 1, Dec. 14, 1882. [144-149]
" Baby Charley," in *Lippincott's Magazine* (Phila.), XXXI, 58, Jan., 1883. [191]
" Nilsson," in *Independent* (N. Y.), XXXV, 385, Mar. 29, 1883. [196-197]

"Remonstrance," in *Century Magazine* (N. Y.), XXV, 819-820, Apr., 1883.
[122-124]

"Souls and Raindrops," in *Lippincott's Magazine* (Phila.), XXXII, 117, July, 1883. [170]

"At First (To C. C.)," in *Independent* (N. Y.), XXXV, 897, July 19, 1883.
[200-201]

"Strange Jokes," in *Independent* (N. Y.), XXXV, 1281, Oct. 11, 1883.
[167-168]

"Song of the Chattahoochee," in *Independent* (N. Y.), XXXV, 1601, Dec. 20, 1883. [103-104]

"A Song of Love," in *Century Magazine* (N. Y.), XXVII, 559, Feb., 1884.
[58]

"How Love Looked for Hell," in *Century Magazine* (N. Y.), XXVII, 733-734, Mar., 1884. [125-127]

"9 from 8," in *Independent* (N. Y.), XXXVI, 321, Mar. 13, 1884. [194-196]

"Night," in *Independent* (N. Y.), XXXVI, 545, May 1, 1884. [161]

"Night and Day," in *Independent* (N. Y.), XXXVI, 833, July 3, 1884. [160]

"The Wedding," in *Independent* (N. Y.), XXXVI, 1057, Aug. 21, 1884.
[158]

"Wedding-Hymn, To ——," in *Independent* (N. Y.), XXXVI, 1057, Aug. 21, 1884. [155]

"To Willie Clopton," in *Manhattan Magazine* (N. Y.), IV, 380, Sept., 1884.
[158]

"June Dreams, In January," in *Independent* (N. Y.), XXXVI, 1121, Sept. 4, 1884. [29-31]

"To My Class," in *Independent* (N. Y.), XXXVI, 1409, Nov. 6, 1884. [204]

"On Violet's Wafers," in *Independent* (N. Y.), XXXVI, 1409, Nov. 6, 1884.
[205]

"Street-Cries," in *Poems*, New York, 1884, p. 86. [122]

"To Dr. Thomas Shearer," in *Poems*, New York, 1884, p. 112. [207]

"The Jacquerie," in *Poems*, New York, 1884, p. 183. [171-189]

"May the maiden," in *Poems*, New York, 1884, p. 204. [190]

"The hound was cuffed, the hound was kicked," in *Poems*, New York, 1884, p. 206. [189-190]

"To ——," in *Poems*, New York, 1884, p. 222. [153]

"Translation from the German of Heine," in *Poems*, New York, 1884, p. 224.
[154]

"The Dying Words of Stonewall Jackson," in *Poems*, New York, 1884, p. 230.
[156-157]

"Struggle," in *Century Magazine* (N. Y.), XXXI, 572, Feb., 1886. [208]

"To Captain James DeWitt Hankins," in *Century Magazine* (N. Y.), XXXII, 378, July, 1886. [10-11]

* "I said to myself," in *Century Magazine* (N. Y.), XXXIV, 417, July, 1887.
[210]

* "I'll sleep, I'll sleep, and dream a sweet death for trouble," in *Century Magazine* (N. Y.), XXXIV, 417, July, 1887. [210]

"Thou and I," in *Century Magazine* (N. Y.), XXXIV, 417, July, 1887. [210]

* "Water Lilies," on an illustrated Christmas Card by L. Prang, Boston, 1890.
[204]

* [" On the Receipt of a Jar of Marmalade "], in *Record* (New Castle, Va.), Apr. 11, 1891. [202]

[" Between Dawn and Sunrise "], in *Independent* (N. Y.), XLIII, 625, Apr. 30, 1891. [142]

" On a Palmetto," in *Independent* (N. Y.), XLIII, 1265, Aug. 27, 1891. [208]
* [" Beethoven "], in *Independent* (N. Y.), XLIX, 1489, Nov. 18, 1897. [201-202]
* " Oh, Life's a Fever and Death's a *chill!* " in *Independent* (N. Y.), LXI, 1095, Nov. 8, 1906. [153]
* " To G. H.," in *Independent* (N. Y.), LXI, 1095, Nov. 8, 1906. [154]
* " Wan Silence lying lip on ground," in *Poem Outlines*, New York, 1908, p. 37. [209]
* " When bees, in honey-frenzies, rage and rage," in *Poem Outlines*, New York, 1908, p. 85. [162]
* " Ten Lilies and ten Virgins," in *Poem Outlines*, New York, 1908, p. 100. [209]
" To Our Hills," in *Poems*, New York, 1916, p. 222. [166-167]
* " To Mrs. S. C. Bird," in Lincoln Lorenz, *The Life of Sidney Lanier*, New York, 1935, p. 208. [203]
* " Our turkey walks across the yard," in *American Book Collector* (Metuchen, N. J.), VI, 200-203, May-June, 1935. [202]

1945. Previously Unpublished

" As when care-wearied majesty with yet lordly mien " [232-233]
" Burn the Stubble " [169-170]
" The Carrier's Appeal " [197-198]
" Dream of a time when legislatures sit " [209]
" Extravaganza " [227-228]
" Extravaganza—Ode to Coleridge " [225-226]
" Fame " [168]
" Have you forgot how through the April weather " [199]
" Hideous habitants of gloom! " [231]
" Hymn " [234]
" I breakfasted on faith in God " [209]
" In Cubiculo " [162]
" Like a grand water-wheel his life revolved " [168]
" Lines of Devil-giants scowl " [234]
" Lines Tangled about the Round Table " [163-164]
" Love Lost! " [229]
" A Love-Song. To —— " [157]
" Morning on the Thermodoön " [233]
" A Morning-Talk " [156]
" My sweet, bright dreams! *So* sweet! *so* bright! " [229-230]
" Observe yon plumed biped fine! " [203]
" Oh, what if Violet Browne were seen " [205]
" On Reading of One Who Drowned Herself in a Certain Lake, for Love " [5]
" The Poet to the Pennsylvania Board of Pardons " [206-207]
" Pride " [170]
" A Shadow! " [230-231]
" Spring " [222-223]
" Steel in Soft Hands " [169]
" Ten thousand stars were in the sky " [155]
" The earliest songster soonest sees " [203]
" Them Ku Klux " [191-194]
" Then, like the Dove from the dim-hulled Ark " [208]
" There was one fled from the sound of bell's death toll " [232]
" Those Bonds " [199]

"To ——" [213]
"To Carrie Ligon" [159]
"To Idol-Ellie!" [221-222]
"To M. D." [164-166]
["To the Sun"] [143]
"What Is It?" [224]
"Whate'er has been, is, shall be—rind, pulp, core" [200]
"While self-inspection it neglects" [203]
"Wildly the Winter-wind moaneth" [221]
"Will 'All Be Right in a Hundred Years'?" [159-160]
"Yonder Cometh Spring!" [226-227]

C. FIRST PRINTINGS OF SHORT PROSE

(Items marked * were previously uncollected. Numbers in brackets refer to volumes and pages in the Centennial Edition. The Prefaces to the four "Boy's Books," though printed in the present edition as separate essays, IV, 346-400, are listed in this bibliography only under secton I, A. Separate printings of chapters from Lanier's books, in advance of volume publication, are not included.)

1861–1881

* "Flag Presentation at Oglethorpe University," in *Daily Telegraph* (Macon), May 15, 1861. [V, 197-199]
*["The Sherman Bill"], in *Courier and Union* (Syracuse, N. Y.), Apr. 8, 1867. [V, 209-212]
* "The Three Waterfalls," in *Scott's Monthly Magazine* (Atlanta), IV, 599-604, 679-683, Aug., Sept., 1867. [V, 213-230].
* ["Furlow College Address"], *Catalogue of the Trustees, Faculty, Alumnae and Students of Furlow Masonic Female College, Americus, Ga., 1868-9.* Macon, Ga., 1869, pp. 19-30. [V, 247-264]
["Confederate Memorial Address"], in *Telegraph and Messenger* (Macon), Apr. 27, 1870. [V, 267-272]
"Retrospects and Prospects," in *Southern Magazine* (Baltimore), VIII, 283-290, 446-456, Mar., Apr., 1871. [V, 280-305]
"Nature-Metaphors," in *Southern Magazine* (Baltimore), X, 172-182, Feb., 1872. [V, 306-321]
* ["Letters from Texas"], in *World* (N. Y.), Dec. 27, 1872; Feb. 6, Mar. 13, 1873. (Letter I first published entire, as "The Texas Trail in the '70's," in *Outlook* (N. Y.), CV, 582-585, Nov. 15, 1913.) [VI, 187-201]
"San Antonio de Bexar," in *Southern Magazine* (Baltimore), XIII, 83-99, 138-152, July, Aug., 1873. [VI, 202-246]
* "Peace," in *Southern Magazine* (Baltimore), XV, 406-410, Oct., 1874. [VI, 247-253]
"Paul H. Hayne's Poetry," in *Southern Magazine* (Baltimore), XVI, 40-48, Jan., 1875. [V, 322-333]
* "Gounod's *Faust*," in *Gazette* (Baltimore), Jan. 9, 1875. [II, 328]
* "Mayer on 'Sound,'" in *Gazette* (Baltimore), Feb. 5, 1875. [II, 329-330]
"Sketches of India," in *Lippincott's Magazine* (Phila.), XVII, 37-51, 172-183, 283-301, 409-427, Jan.-Apr., 1876. [VI, 254-323]
"The Centennial Cantata," in *Tribune* (N. Y.), May 20, 1876. [II, 266-273]

"The Story of a Proverb, I," in *St. Nicholas's Magazine* (N. Y.), IV, 468-472, May, 1877. [VI, 324-330]

* ["Lanier Genealogy"], as appendices to *Sketch of the Life of J. F. D. Lanier.* New York, 1877 (2nd. edition), pp. 75-87; and 1879 (pamphlet, separately bound), pp. 89-106. [VI, 350-376]

* "The Maryland Musical Festival," in *Sun* (Batimore), May 28-30, 1878. [II, 316-327]

* "Mazzini on Music," in *Independent* (N. Y.), XXX, 3-4, June 27, 1878. [II, 307-315]

* "The Story of a Proverb, II," in *Lippincott's Magazine* (Phila.), XXIII, 109-113, Jan., 1879. [VI, 331-339]

"A Forgotten English Poet," in *International Review* (N. Y.), VI, 284-298, Mar., 1879. [IV, 273-289]

"Rubinstein's *Ocean Symphony* and Emil Hartmann's *Raid of the Vikings,*" in *Sun* (Baltimore), Jan. 31, 1880. [II, 321-322]

"The Orchestra of To-day," in *Scribner's Monthly* (N. Y.), XIX, 897-904, Apr., 1880. [II, 291-306]

"The New South," in *Scribner's Monthly* (N. Y.), XX, 840-851, Oct., 1880. [V, 334-358]

"King Arthur and His Knights of the Round Table," in *St. Nicholas's Magazine* (N. Y.), VIII 89-93, Dec., 1880. [Omitted]

*["Johns Hopkins University"], in *American Cyclopaedia Supplement* (Appleton). New York, 1880, pp. 864-867. [III, 411-419]

1882-1928. Posthumously Published

"Bob: The Story of Our Mocking-Bird," in *Independent* (N. Y.), XXXIV, 1-3, Aug. 3, 1882. [VI, 340-349]

"The Legend of St. Leonor," in *Independent* (N. Y.), XXXVII, 3, Dec. 17, 1885. (Incomplete.) [II, 247-250]

"From Bacon to Beethoven," in *Lippincott's Magazine* (Phila.), XLI, 643-655, May, 1888. [II, 274-290]

"Chaucer and Shakspere," in *Independent* (N. Y.), XLIII, 1337-1338, 1371-1372, 1401-1402, 1748, Sept. 10, 17, 24, Nov. 26, 1891. (Incomplete.) [IV, 304-345]

* "What I Know About Flowers," in *Sunday School Times* (Phila.), XXXVIII, 739, Nov. 21, 1891. [Omitted]

"The Death of Byrhtnoth," in *Atlantic Monthly* (Boston), LXXXII, 165-174, Aug., 1898. [IV, 290-303]

"John Barbour's Bruce," in *Music and Poetry*, New York, 1898, pp. 212-248. [Omitted]

"The Physics of Music," in *Music and Poetry*, New York, 1898, pp. 47-67. [II, 251-265]

"The Doctors of Shakspere's Time," by error as chap. XIX of *Shakspere and His Forerunners*, New York, 1902. [IV, 258-272]

* "Memorial Remarks on Judge E. A. Nisbet," in *Daily Telegraph* (Macon), Feb. 2, 1927. [V, 277-279]

* "Robert E. Lee: In Memoriam," in *Stratford on the Potomac*, Greenwich, Conn., 1928, pp. 5-8. [V, 273-276]

1945. Previously Unpublished

"Bombs from Below: Wanted, Engineers!" (Partially printed, from a variant manuscript, "Devil's Bombs," in Edwin Mims, *Sidney Lanier*, Boston, 1905, pp. 45-47.) [V, 204-208]

["Appendix: On Music"] [II, 333-341]
"John Lockwood's Mill. A Novel" [V, 231-246]
"*Timeo Danaos*! A Voice of the Night" [V, 200-203]

D. UNPUBLISHED MANUSCRIPTS

(MSS and variant drafts of prose and poetry printed in the Centennial Edition are not included; the following items, omitted for various reasons, are more fully described in the several introductions. Approximate dates of composition are given in brackets; initials of owners, in parentheses: "CL" for Charles D. Lanier, "HL" for Henry W. Lanier, "JT" for Mrs. John Tilley—owner of the Clifford A. Lanier Collection. The "Ledger" is a large literary journal in which Lanier wrote much of his early prose and poetry, 692 pp., 1865-1874 (1877?). All are preserved in the Lanier Room, Johns Hopkins University, together with a large number of untitled MSS, mostly miscellaneous notes and fragments, not listed here.)

College Notebook, three fragments of fiction (JT), 9 pp. [1858]
College debates, speeches, essays, and other papers on political and ethical
    subjects (CL), 122 pp.; (JT), 33 pp. [1858-1860]
Debate on Louis Napoleon's Mexican Empire (JT), 25 pp. [1866]
"A chapter on profane swearing" (HL, Ledger, 14-15, 38), 3 pp. [1866-1867]
"Desire and Thought" (HL, Ledger, 74-93; early draft, 45, 50; another version
    entitled "The Oversight of Modern Philosophy," 238-241, 282-284), 29
    pp. [1868?]
"The Error of Cousin and Hamilton" (CL), 32 pp. Final version of above.
    [1868]
"Infinite Solecisms" (HL, Ledger, 384-409; early draft, 58-63, 267-274),
    40 pp. [1868?]
"Formulations of the Infinite" (CL), 28 pp. Final version of above. [1868]
Speech on the meaning of holidays (HL, Ledger, 666-670), 5 pp. [1868?]
Memoranda for a novel (HL, Ledger, 678-683), 6 pp. [1868?]
Speech on Napoleon Bonaparte (HL, Ledger, 684-692), 9 pp. [1868?]
Speech on politics, social life, and religion (CL), 19 pp. [Dated: Marietta,
    Ga., Aug., 1871]
"The Tatler, No. 268" (CL), 6 pp. [1873-1874]
"The Tatler, No. —" (CL), 3 pp. [1873-1874]
"Mr. Query" (CL), 4 pp. [1873-1874]
"The Physics of Poetry" (HL), 266 pp. First "state" of the *Science of
    English Verse*. [1878]
"Shakspere Course," Peabody Lectures II and VI (HL), 36 pp. Second
    "state" of the *Science of English Verse*. [1878-1879]
"English Verse, especially Shakspere's," Johns Hopkins Lectures I-IX (CL),
    444 pp. Another version of matter in the *Science of English Verse*.
    [1879]
Miscellaneous lecture pages (CL), 200 + pp. [1879-1880]
"A Handbook for Home and Village Orchestras," outline (CL), 5 pp.
    [1879-1880]
"On Metrical Tests: or The Rise of Exact Method in Criticism," fragment
    (CL), 17 pp. [1879-1880]
Two drafts of a letter to the *Nation*, replying to a review of the *Science of
    English Verse* (CL), 37 pp. [1880]

E. MUSICAL COMPOSITIONS

(Approximate dates of composition are given in brackets. MSS marked
" HL " are in the possession of Henry W. Lanier, New York City, but photo-
stats are available in the Charles D. Lanier Collection, Johns Hopkins University,
where all the other MSS are preserved. Music merely arranged by Lanier is
not included, except one piece which has been previously published.)

"Orphan's Cradle Song. The Widow Sang the Child to Sleep" (HL), 2 pp.
[A second MS is entitled " Song Without Words: ' The Widow Sang
the Child to Sleep.' For Flute and Piano. Op. 1 "; a fragmentary flute
improvisation in Mary Day's Album is marked by her " From Sidney
Lanier's No. 1 " and dated Oct. 22, 1863.]
" Song of Elaine" (HL), 3 pp. Words by Tennyson. [Mentioned in a letter
from Mary Day, Sept. 16, 1865.]
Little Ella. A Beautiful Ballad. Dedicated to Ella S. Montgomery. By her
Friend S. C. Lanier. May 10, 1866. R. W. Offutt & Co. Montgomery,
Ala., n. d. [Published in Mar., 1868.]
Love that Hath Us in the Net. Words by Tennyson. Music by the Gifted Poet
and Musician Sidney Lanier. A. E. Blackmar & Co. New Orleans, n. d.
[Published May 5, 1884; mentioned in a letter from Mary Day Lanier,
Sept. 20, 1871.]
" Break, Break, Break " (HL), 10 pp. Words by Tennyson. [Mentioned in a
letter from Mary Day Lanier, Sept. 20, 1871.]
" Flow Down, Cold Rivulet " (HL), 5 pp. Words by Tennyson. [*c.* 1871]
" Wind-Song. Flute Solo. To be played without accompaniment " (HL), 1.p.
MS reproduced in A. H. Starke, *Sidney Lanier*, Chapel Hill, N. C., 1933,
facing p. 184. [Fragment with same title dated Dec. 27, 1872.]
" Black-birds: Solo for Flute " (HL), 3 pp. MS, second sheet, reproduced in
the present edition, vol. VIII, facing p. 335. [Mentioned in Lanier's
letter of Sept. 19, 1873.]
" Danse des Moucherons" (HL), 2 pp. MS reproduced in S. T. Williams,
The American Spirit in Letters, New Haven, 1926, p. 256 (first sheet),
and Starke, facing p. 174 (second sheet). [There also survive a second
MS (HL), 10 pp.; and the following fragments: " Theme. Gnats,"
" Tema. Gnats," and " Gnats "—an attempted orchestration. Dated Dec.
25, 1873.]
Il Balen. (From *Il Trovatore.*) Air and Variation for Flute, with Piano
Accompaniment. By the Late Sidney Lanier. A. G. Badger. New York,
n. d. [Published in 1888; mentioned in Mary Day Lanier's letter of
Aug. 26, 1874.]

(The following pieces are known to have been composed by Lanier, but
have not been found; the approximate dates of composition, in brackets, are
taken from the letters, or notes thereto, where they are mentioned: " Wedding
Hymn " and " A Morning-Talk " [Sept. 1, 1865], " Woodlarks " [Sept. 30,
1865], " Le Ruisseau " [June 19, 1867], " Swamp-Robin " [June 28, 1867],
" Sounds from the Army " and " Sea-Spray " [June 12, 1868], ' Field-larks and
Black-birds " [Feb. 28, 1873], " Choral Symphony " and " Symphony of the
Plantation " [Feb. 12, 1881]. Two others are described by A. H. Starke in " Sid-
ney Lanier as Musician," *Musical Quarterly*, XX, 388, 397-398 (Oct., 1934):
" Sacred Memories" and a setting for R. H. Wilde's " My Life Is Like a

Summer Rose "—but a surviving program in the Lanier Room indicates that the former was not by Lanier. In addition, a large number of musical notations and fragments have survived, probably composed between 1867 and 1874, here listed alphabetically: "Aria for Flute," "Bass Flute (To tickle the ears of the groundlings)," "Beowulf's March," "Bird Song," "Concert Stück," "Cradle Song," "Ein Märchen. Song for Flute," "Fantasie on Schubert's 'Des Baches Wiegenlied,'" "For the Princess," "Gnats," "Heimweh Polka," "Indian War Song: Adagio," "Intr. to 'Blackbirds,'" "Jay's Cry," "Lament for Flute," "Miranda," "On Keats's Ode to a Nightingale," "Plantation Symphony," "Quartette," "Romeo and Juliet," "A Sea-Secret, Confidentially whispered to the public," "Sehnsucht," "Serenade," "Soft-Tone Concerts. 'La Reve' for four flutes: air and fantasy," "Song," "The Song of the Lost Spirit," "The Southern Suite. The Corn-Shucking. The Breakdown," "The Spring that feeds the Lake of Dreams," "Subject for Movement in Symphony: Andantino," "The Sweep's Cry: Sweep—ho!" "Symphony Life: Childhood, Youth, Manhood, Age," "Symphony. The Woods," "Trio for Fl., B. F. & 'Cello," "Tuno Religioso. Two Flutes, or Two Violas, or Two Violins & Celli . . . with Orchestra: Obligato," "Wald-Einsamkeit," "A Waltz of Spirits," "What Thoughts So Heavenly," "The Widow, Singing the Child to Sleep. Lullaby, for Flute," "Wind Song," and twenty-odd untitled fragments. These are preserved in the Lanier Room, Johns Hopkins University, in two staff books, on miscellaneous pieces of MSS, on the fly-leaves of volumes in Lanier's library, on the backs of letters and programs.)

II. BIOGRAPHY AND CRITICISM

A. SELECTED BOOKS, PAMPHLETS, AND ARTICLES CONCERNING LANIER

(Printings of Lanier's poetry, prose, and letters are listed only when they contain editorial commentary. Numerous additional items are preserved in the Lanier Room, Johns Hopkins University, including many poems addressed to Lanier by Hamlin Garland, Paul Hayne, Richard Hovey, Clifford Lanier, Lizette Reese, Father Tabb, and others.)

Abernethy, Cecil. A Critical Edition of Tiger-Lilies, Ph. D. Thesis, Vanderbilt, 1941.

Abernethy, J. W. *Southern Poets*, New York, 1904, pp. 3-34.

Adams, Randolph G. "Notes and Queries: Correction by Lanier," in *Colophon* (N. Y.), II, 132, Autumn, 1936.

Akin, John W. *Sidney Lanier: Address Before the Faculty and Undergraduates of Emory College*, Atlanta, 1901.

Alden, H. M. *English Verse*, New York, 1903, p. 392.

Allen, Alfred. "Reminiscences of Sidney Lanier," in *Mid-Continent Magazine* (Louisville), VI, 81-86, May, 1895. (First printed in the Boston *Evening Transcript*, Apr. 13, 1895—copy in the Lanier Room, Johns Hopkins University, with corrections by M. D. Lanier.)

Allen, Gay Wilson. *American Prosody*, New York, 1935, pp. 277-306.

———. "Sidney Lanier as a Literary Critic," in *Philological Quarterly* (Iowa City), XVII, 121-138, Apr., 1938.

Andersen, Johannes C. *The Laws of Verse*, New York, 1928.

Anderson, Charles R. [The Centennial Edition of Lanier], in *Year Book of the American Philosophical Society, 1943*, Philadelphia, 1944, pp. 234-238.

Andrews, C. E. *The Writing and Reading of Verse*, New York, 1918, preface.

Andrews, Maude. [Interview with the Rev. Mr. Reese], in *Constitution* (Atlanta), Feb. 23, 1890.

Anonymous. ["Corn" Critique], in *Evening Bulletin* (Phila.), Jan. 15, 1875. Reprinted in *Telegraph and Messenger* (Macon), Jan. 29, 1875.

———. ["The Symphony"], *Nation* (N. Y.), XX, 362, May 27, 1875.

———. [Review of "Centennial Cantata"], in *Nation* (N. Y.), XXII, 247, Apr., 13, 1876.

———. "The Centennial Cantata," in *Evening Bulletin* (Phila.), May 13, 1876.

———. [Lanier's Cantata], in *Tribune* (N. Y.), May 19, 1876.

———. [*Tribune* letter], in *Nation* (N. Y.), XXII, 336, May 25, 1876.

———. ["Marshes of Glynn"], in *Spectator* (London), LII, 247-248, Feb. 22, 1879.

———. "Shakspere's Doctors. Mr. Sidney Lanier's Lecture," in *Evening Bulletin* (Baltimore), Dec. 16, 1879.

———. [Announcement of Courses and Lectures by Lanier], in *Johns Hopkins University Circulars . . . 1879-1882*, Baltimore, 1882, pp. 1, 2, 18, 30, 51, 61, 89, 99, 151.

———. [Review of "New South"], in *American* (Baltimore), Sept. 22, 1880.

———. [Review of "New South"], in *Nation* (N. Y.), XXXI, 223, Sept. 23, 1880.

———. [Obituary], in *American and Commercial Advertiser* (Baltimore), Sept. 9, 1881.

————. [Obituary], in *Sun* (Baltimore), Sept. 9, 1881.

————. " Sidney Lanier,' 'in *Telegraph* (Macon), Sept. 13, 1881.

————. [Obituary], in *Nation* (N. Y.), XXXIII, 216, Sept. 15, 1881.

————. " Sidney Lanier " (Obituary), in *Harper's Weekly* (N. Y.), XXV, 653, Sept. 24, 1881.

————. " The Death of Sidney Lanier," in *Dial* (Chicago), II, 154, Nov., 1881.

————. [Obituary, with notice of Johns Hopkins commemorative meeting of Oct. 22, 1881], in *Nation* (N. Y.), XXXIII, 394, Nov. 17, 1881.

————. " The Death of Sidney Lanier," in *Johns Hopkins University Circulars . . . 1879-1882*, Baltimore, 1882, p. 168.

————. " Report of Sidney Lanier Memorial Fund and . . . Tablet," in *Johns Hopkins University Circular* (Baltimore), II, 88, Apr., 1883.

————. " The Lanier Memorial," in *Critic* (N. Y.), XII, 224, May 5, 1888.

————. [Lanier family] in *Biographical Souvenir of Georgia and Florida*, Chicago, 1889, pp. 501-504.

————. " The Marshes of Glynn," *Telegraph* (Macon), Oct. 17, 1890.

————. [Unveiling of Keyser Bust, Macon], *Constitution* (Atlanta), Oct. 19, 1890.

————" Lanier's Birthday," in *Sun* (Baltimore), Feb. 4, 1891.

————. " Recent Recognition of Sidney Lanier," in *Johns Hopkins University Circular* (Baltimore), X, 49-50, Feb., 1891.

————. [Review of " How to Read Chaucer "], in *Independent* (N. Y.), XLIII, 1748, Nov. 26, 1891; XLIII, 1786-1787, Dec. 3, 1891.

————. " The Sons of Sidney Lanier and ' Hard Times in Elfland,' " in *Young Southron* (Atlanta), I, 26-31, Christmas, 1896.

————. [Sidney Lanier], in *Critic* (N. Y.), XXI, 45, July 24, 1897.

————. " Lanier and Music," in *Reader* (Indianapolis), VIII, 218-220, July, 1906.

————. " Sidney Lanier," in *Johns Hopkins Alumni Magazine* (Baltimore), V, 1-2, Nov. 1916.

————. " Sidney Lanier, the South's Greatest Poet," in *Westminster Magazine* (Oglethorpe Uinversity), Mar., 1918.

————. [Reminiscences of Lanier], in *Evening News* (Macon), Feb. 22, 1925.

————. (Gadda Boute, pseudo.). " Sidney Lanier's Affection and Admiration for Charlotte Cushman," in *Telegraph* (Macon), June 7, 1925.

————. " Sidney Lanier Commemoration," in *Johns Hopkins Alumni Magazine* (Baltimore), XIV, 482-505, June, 1926.

————. " Sidney Lanier," in *Times* (N. Y.), Feb. 3, 1929.

————. " Sidney Lanier," in *Johns Hopkins News Letter* (Baltimore), pp. 3-4, Feb. 12, 1929.

————. " Widow of Sidney Lanier Dies," in *Telegraph* (Macon), Dec. 30, 1931.

————. " The Last Days of Sidney Lanier," in *News* (Macon), Feb. 3, 1932.

————. " Poet-Soldier," in *Telegraph* (Macon), Feb. 4, 1932.

————. " Sidney Lanier's Romance," in *News* (Birmingham), Nov. 12, 1933. Reprinted in *Advertiser* (Montgomery), Nov. 19, 1933.

————. " One Hundredth Anniversary," in *Musician* (N. Y.), XLVII, 35, Mar., 1942.

Apthorp, W. F. " The Centennial Cantata," in *Atlantic Monthly* (Boston), XXXVIII, 122, July, 1876.

Atkinson, C. Prescott. " Clifford Lanier," in *Library of Sotuhern Literature*, Atlanta, 1907, VII, 3021-3039.

Avery, I. W. *History of Georgia*, New York, 1881, pp. 626-627.

Avery, Myrtha L. "Lanier Urged for Hall of Fame," in *Journal* (Atlanta), Apr. 30, 1933.

Baskervill, William M. "Southern Literature," in *Publications of Modern Language Association* (Baltimore), VII, 89-100, 1892.
———. *Southern Writers*, Nashville, 1897, I, 137-298.
Bassett, Jonn Spencer. "The Struggles of Sidney Lanier," in *Methodist Review* (Nashville), XLIX, 3-17, Jan., 1900.
Bates, Katharine Lee. *American Literature*, New York, 1898, pp. 188-190.
Beeson, Leola S. "New Light on the School Days of Sidney Lanier," in *Journal* (Atlanta), May 17, 1935.
———. *Sidney Lanier at Oglethorpe University*, Macon, 1936.
Benjamin, Mrs. Walter R. [Early draft of Lanier's "Power of Prayer"], in *Collector* (N. Y.), LVIII, 106-107, June-July, 1945.
Bentzon, Therese (Mme. Blanc). "Un Musicien Poete. Sidney Lanier," in *Revue des Deux Mondes* (Paris), CXLV, 307-341, Jan. 15, 1898. Reprinted in *Choses et Gens d'Amerique*, Paris, 1898, pp. 171-233. Translated into English in *Littell's Living Age* (Boston), CCXVII, 411-423 and 517-524, May 14 and 21, 1898.
Bikle, Lucy L. Cable. *George W. Cable: His Life and Letters*, New York, 1928, pp. 94, 214.
Billing, Beatrice Mary. "On Wings of Song," in *Southern Literary Messenger* (Richmond), II, 13-18, Jan., 1940.
Birss, J. H. "A Humorous Quatrain by Lanier," in *American Literature* (Durham, N. C.), V, 270, Nov. 1933.
Black, G. D. "Sidney Lanier," in *Antiochian* (Yellow Springs, Ohio), XI, 4-6, Feb., 1886.
Blair, Gordon. *Father Tabb*, Richmond, 1940, pp. 55-65.
Blankenship, Russell. *American Literature as an Expression of the National Mind*, New York, 1931, pp. 430-432.
Blitch, Lela. Sidney Lanier, Artist, Critic and Human Being, M. A. Thesis, University of Maryland, 1935.
Bocock, Macklin. "Life of Sidney Lanier in Music and Poetry," in *Virginia Gazette* (Williamsburg), VIII [n. s.], No. 7, p. 6; No. 8, p. 3, Feb. 12, 19, 1937.
Boifeuillet, John T. "The Diploma of Sidney Lanier," in *Journal* (Atlanta), Mar. 22, 1925.
———. "Robert E. Lee and Sidney Lanier," in *Journal* (Atlanta), March 15, 1929.
———. "Lanier's Growing Reputation," in *Journal* (Atlanta), Oct. 24, 1933.
Bopes, Charles Francis. "A Lost Occasional Poem by Sidney Lanier," in *American Literature* (Durham, N. C.), V, 269, Nov., 1933.
Bourgeois, Yves R. "Sidney Lanier et Le Goffic," in *Revue Anglo-Americaine* (Paris), VIII, 431-32, June, 1931.
Bowen, Edwin Winfield. *Makers of American Literature*, Washington, 1908, pp. 348-363.
Bowman, Isaiah, "Remembering the Beauty," *Program of a Meeting Held in . . . the Peabody Institute*, Baltimore, 1940, pp. 10-23.
Boykin, Laurette Nisbet. *Home Life of Sidney Lanier*, Atlanta, 1888.
———. *A Study of Sidney Lanier*, Atlanta, 1889.
Boynton, Percy H. *American Poetry*, New York, 1918, pp. 670-675.
———. *History of American Literature*, Boston, 1919, pp. 349-358.

———. *Literature and American Life*, Boston, 1936, pp. 57, 409, 577-585, 678, 891.

Bradford, Gamaliel. "Portrait of Sidney Lanier," in *North American Review* (Boston), CCXI, 805-817, June, 1920. Reprinted in *American Portraits, 1875-1900*, Boston, 1922, pp. 59-83.

———. *Letters* (Ed. by Van Wyck Brooks), Boston, 1934, p. 237.

Brenner, Rica. *Twelve American Poets Before 1900*, New York, 1933, pp. 296-320.

Brevard, Caroline. *Literature of the South*, New York, 1908.

Brown, Pearl Elizabeth. A Study of Sidney Lanier's Verse Technique, M. A. Thesis, University of Chicago, 1921.

Browne, William Hand. *Sidney Lanier. Memorial Address*, Baltimore, 1881.

———. "Sidney Lanier," in *From Dixie*, Richmond, 1893, pp. 40-51.

Buck, Paul Herman. *The Road to Reunion, 1865-1900*, Boston, 1937, *passim*.

Buckham, James. "In Honor of Lanier," in *Literary World* (Boston), XIX, 56-57, Feb. 18, 1888.

Burt, Mary E. "The Genius of Sidney Lanier," in *Symposium* (Northampton, Mass.), I, 9-13, Oct., 1896.

———, ed. *The Lanier Book*, New York, 1914, pp. vii-x, 127-143.

Burton, Richard E. (A bibliography appended to D. C. Gilman's *The Forty-Sixth Birthday of Sidney Lanier*), Baltimore, 1888, pp. 53-56.

———. "An Account of the Hopkins Meeting of February 3, 1888," in *Critic* (N. Y.), XII, 63, Feb. 11, 1888.

———. *Literary Leaders of America*, Chautauqua (N. Y.), 1903, pp. 296-309.

Butts, Sarah Harriet. *The Mothers of Some Distinguished Georgians . . . ,* New York, 1902.

Cady, Frank W. "Writings of Sidney Lanier," in *South Atlantic Quarterly* (Durham, N. C.), XIII, 156-173, Apr., 1914.

Callaway, James A. "The Imprisonment of Sidney Lanier," in *Telegraph* (Macon), Feb. 3, 1916. Reprinted in *Confederate Veteran* (Nashville), XXIV, 558, Dec., 1916.

Callaway, Morgan, ed. *Select Poems of Sidney Lanier* (with introduction and bibliography), New York, 1895.

Reviews:

Bookman (N. Y.), I, 45, Feb. 1895 (H. W. Mabie).

Dial (Chicago), XVIII, 299-301, May 16, 1895 (W. M. Baskervill).

Union and Advertiser (Rochester, N. Y.), Feb. 16, 1895 (G. N. Lovejoy).

———. "The Poetry of Sidney Lanier," in *Methodist Review* (Nashville), XLIV, 147-157, Nov., 1895.

Calvert, George H. "Sidney Lanier," in *Golden Age* (N. Y.), V, 4-5, June 12, 1875.

Calverton, V. F. *The Liberation of American Literature*, New York, 1932, pp. 138-142.

Carroll, Armond. [Father Tabb and Sidney Lanier], in *Westminster Magazine* (Oglethorpe University), April, 1920.

Carroll, Charles C. *The Synthesis and Analysis of the Poetry of Sidney Lanier*, Owensboro (Ky.), 1910.

Christy, Arthur. "The Orientalism of Sidney Lanier," in *Aryan Path* (Bombay), V, 638-641, Oct., 1934.

Clark, Harry Hayden. *Major American Poets*, New York, 1936, pp. 903-913.

Clark, Thomas Arkle. *Sidney Lanier, Biography and Selections*, Taylorville (Ill.), 1914.

Clarke, George Herbert. "Some Early Letters and Reminiscences of Sidney
    Lanier," in *Independent* (N. Y.), LXI, 1092-1098, Nov. 8, 1906.
    Reprinted as pamphlet, Macon, 1907.
Clay-Clopton, Virginia. *A Belle of the Fifties*, New York, 1904, pp. 197-199,
    201.
Coleman, Charles W. "The Recent Movement in Southern Literature," in
    Harper's Magazine (N. Y.), LXXIV, 837-855, May. 1887.
Conway, Moncure D. "Washington-Lanier-Ball Tradition," in *William and
    Mary College Quarterly Historical Magazine* (Williamsburg, Va.), III,
    137-139, Oct., 1894.
Cottman, George S. "James F. D. Lanier," in *Indiana Magazine of History*
    (Indianapolis), XXII, 194-202, June, 1926.
————. *The James F. D. Lanier Home, An Indiana Memorial*, Indianapolis,
    1927.
Coulson, Edwin R., and Richard Webb. *Sidney Lanier, Poet and Prosodist*,
    Athens (Ga.), 1941.
Credo, Ethel. The Use of Figures of Speech in Lanier's Longer Poems, M. A.
    Thesis, University of Texas, 1938.

Dabney, J. P. *The Musical Basis of Verse*, New York, 1901, *passim.*
Dabney, Virginia. *Liberalism in the South*, Chapel Hill, 1932, pp. 220-221, 224.
Davidson, James Wood. *Living Writers of the South*, New York, 1869, pp.
    319-324.
Day, Edward. "The Religion of Sidney Lanier," in *Christian Register* (Boston),
    pp. 373-375, Apr. 5, 1906.
Dewey, Thomas Emmett. *Poetry in Song, and Some Other Studies in Literature*,
    Kansas City (Mo.), 1907, pp. 46-73.
Dixon, Amzi Clarence. *Sidney Lanier, the Johns Hopkins Poet: an Appreci-
    ation*, Baltimore, 1925.
Dobbin, Isabel L. "Lanier at the Peabody," in *Peabody Bulletin* (Baltimore),
    pp. 4-5, Apr.-May, 1911.
Doyle, T. A. "Indomitable Courage of Sidney Lanier," in *Catholic World*
    (N. Y.), CLVI, 293-301, Dec., 1942.
Dutcher, Salem. (Tyrone Power, pseudo.). "Georgia Poets—The ' Symphony '
    of Sidney Lanier," in *Chronicle and Sentinel* (Augusta), June 11, 1875.
Dutton, Sister M. Agatha. A Comparative Study of Sidney Lanier and Francis
    Thompson, M. A. Thesis, Boston College, 1932.

Edwards, Harry Stillwell. "Sidney Lanier," in *Telegraph* (Macon), Sept. 13,
    1881.
————. "Lanier the Artist," in *Journal* (Atlanta), Mar. 19, 1929.
————. "Romance of an Old Desk," in *Journal* (Atlanta), Feb. 15, 1934.
Ellerbe, J. E. "Sidney Lanier," in *Confederate Veteran* (Nashville), XXXI,
    210-211, June, 1923.
Ellis, Theo. W. "The Macon Archers," unidentified newspaper clipping in
    Washington Memorial Library (Macon, Ga.).
Ellsworth, William Webster. *A Golden Age of Authors*, New York, 1919, pp.
    111-112.
Emmett, Chris. *The General and the Poet, Albert Sidney Johnston and Sidney
    Lanier*, San Antonio, 1937.
Ethridge, Willie Snow. [Reminiscences of C. M. Wiley], in *Telegraph* (Macon),
    July 30, 1926.

————. "Stories of a Fair-Haired Lad," in *Telegraph Sunday Magazine* (Macon), Feb. 3, 1929.

Fagin, N. B. "Sidney Lanier: Poet of the South," in *Johns Hopkins Alumni Magazine* (Baltimore), XX, 232-241, Mar., 1932. Reprinted, with revisions, in *Poet-Lore* (Phila.), XLIII, 161-168, 1936.

Finley, John. "A Poet-Musician," in *Times* (N. Y.), Sec. 3, p. 1, Sept. 20, 1931.

Flournoy, M. H. *Essays: Historical and Critical*, Baltimore, 1928, pp. 89-96.

Foerster, Norman. "Lanier as a Poet of Nature," in *Nation* (N. Y.), CVIII, 981-983, June 21, 1919.

————. *Nature in American Literature*, New York, 1923, pp. 221-237.

Forsythe, Gladys May. Sidney Lanier, the Man, M. A. Thesis, University of Maryland, 1928.

Franklin, Fabian. *Life of Daniel Coit Gilman*, New York, 1910, pp. 241-244.

Fraser, A. M. "James Woodrow: 1828-1907," in *Library of Southern Literature*, Atlanta, 1907, XIII, 5957-5963.

French, John C. "Sidney Lanier's Life in Baltimore," in *Sun* (Baltimore), Sept. 6, 1931.

————. "First Drafts of Lanier's Verse," in *Modern Language Notes* (Baltimore), XLVIII, 27-31, Jan., 1933.

————. "New Lanier Letters," in *Ex Libris* (Johns Hopkins University Library), IV, No. 4, 3-4, May, 1935.

French, Samuel G. *Two Wars: An Autobiography*, Nashville, 1901, p. 157.

Furst, Clyde. "Concerning Sidney Lanier," in *Modern Language Notes* (Baltimore), XIV, 197-205, Nov., 1899.

Garber, Blanche Goode. "The Lanier Family and the Lanier Home," in *Indiana Magazine of History* (Bloomington), XXII, 277-284, Sept., 1926.

Garland, Hamlin. "Roadside Meetings of a Literary Nomad," in *Bookman* (N. Y.), LXX, 403-406, Dec., 1929.

————. *Roadside Meetings*, New York, 1930, pp. 144-153.

Gates, Merrill E. "Sidney Lanier's Moral Earnestness," in *Critic* (N. Y.), VI, 227, May 9, 1885.

————. "Sidney Lanier," in *Presbyterian Review* (N. Y.), VIII, 669-701, Oct., 1887.

————. "A Note on Sidney Lanier," in *Critic* (N. Y.), XII, 245, May 19, 1888.

————. "On the Ethical Influence of Lanier," in *The Forty-Sixth Birthday of Sidney Lanier*, Baltimore, 1888, pp. 31-36.

Gilman, Daniel Coit. "Personal Recollections of Sidney Lanier," in *Our Continent* (Phila.), I, 130, Apr. 12, 1882.

————, ed. *The Forty-Sixth Birthday of Sidney Lanier*, Baltimore, 1888.

————. "The Launching of a University," in *Scribner's Magazine* (N. Y.), XXXI, 327-336, Mar. 1902.

————. "Pleasant Incidents of an Academic Life," in *Scribner's Magazine* (N. Y.), XXXI, 614-624, May, 1902.

————. "Sidney Lanier: Reminiscences and Letters," in *South Atlantic Quarterly* (Durham, N. C.), IV, 115-122, Apr., 1905.

————. "Reminiscences of Sidney Lanier," in *Pathfinder* (Sewanee, Tenn.), I, 2-5, Sept., 1906.

Goodnow, F. J. "Lanier and the University," in *Johns Hopkins Alumni Magazine* (Baltimore), XIV, 503-505, June, 1926.

Goodwin, Grace Duffield. "Lanier and Keats," in *Independent* (N. Y.), XLVII, 1154, Aug. 29, 1895.

————. "Two Singers of Sunrise: Lanier, Gilder," in *Poet-Lore* (Phila.), IX, 407-410, Summer, 1897.

Gosse, Edmund. "Has America Produced a Poet?" in *Forum* (N. Y.), VI, 176-186, Oct., 1888. Reprinted in *Questions At Issue,* London, 1893.

Gottlieb, Frederick H. [Lanier as a Flutist], in *Flutist* (Ashville, N. C.), May, 1926.

————. [Letter About Lanier as a Musician], in *Telegraph* (Macon), Feb. 3, 1929.

Graham, Philip. Lanier's Thought in Relation to That of his Age, Ph. D. Thesis, University of Chicago, 1927.

————. "Lanier's Reading," in *Studies in English* (Austin), XI, 63-89, 1931.

————. "James Woodrow, Calvinist and Evolutionist," in *Sewanee Review* (Sewanee, Tenn.), XL, 307-315, July, 1932.

————. "Lanier and Science," in *American Literature* (Durham, N. C.), IV, 288-292, Nov., 1932.

————. "A Note on Lanier's Music," in *Studies in English* (Austin), XVII, 107-111, 1937.

————, and Joseph Jones. *A Concordance to the Poems of Sidney Lanier,* Austin, 1939.

Green, E. M. "College Days in Old Oglethorpe," in *Westminster Magazine* (Oglethorpe University), Jan., 1915.

Greenlaw, Edwin. "A Sidney Lanier Professorship at Johns Hopkins," in *Johns Hopkins Alumni Magazine* (Baltimore), XVIII, 136-141, Jan., 1929.

Greenslet, Ferris. *Life of T. B. Aldrich,* Boston, 1908, pp. 213-215.

Griggs, Edward Howard, ed. *Sonnets to Sidney Lanier and Other Lyrics by Clifford Anderson Lanier,* New York, 1915, pp. 9-13.

Griswold, Frances Catherine. Sidney Lanier: His Theories of Verse in Relation to his Practice, M. A. Thesis, University of Illinois, 1927.

Grove, George. *Dictionary of Music and Musicians* (American Supplement), Waldo S. Pratt, ed., New York, 1930.

Hankins, J. DeWitt. "Unpublished Letters of Sidney Lanier," in *Southern Literary Messenger* (Richmond), II, 5-11, Jan., 1940.

Hankins, Virginia W. "Some Memories of Lanier," in *Southern Bivouac* (Louisville), II [n. s.], 760-761, May, 1887.

Hanna, Elizabeth H. "Georgia's Poet of Nature," in *Journal* (Atlanta), Mar. 27, 1932.

Harman, H. E. "Sidney Lanier—A Study," in *South Atlantic Quarterly* (Durham, N. C.), XIV, 301-306, Oct., 1915.

————. "A Study of Sidney Lanier's 'The Symphony,'" in *South Atlantic Quarterly* (Durham, N. C.), XVII, 32-39, Jan. 1918.

Harris, Joel Chandler. [Lanier's Death], in *Constitution* (Atlanta), Sept. 12, 1881.

Harrison, John M., and Aubrey Starke. "Maternal Ancestors of Sidney Lanier," in *Virginia Magazine of History and Biography* (Richmond), XLIV, 73-80, 160-174, Jan. and Apr., 1936.

Hartwick, Harry. Bibliography in Walter F. Taylor's *A History of American Letters,* Boston, 1936, pp. 550-553.

Hayden, Horace E. "Lanier-Washington-Ball," in *William and Mary College*

Quarterly Historical Magazine (Williamsburg, Va.), III, 71-74, July, 1894.

Hayne, Paul Hamilton, ed. "A Poet's Letters to a Friend," in *Critic* (N. Y.), VIII, 77-78, 89-90, Feb. 13 and 20, 1886. Reprinted in Lanier's *Letters*, New York, 1899, pp. 219-245.

Hazen, Charles Downer, ed. *The Letters of William Roscoe Thayer*, New York, 1926, pp. 26, 34, 36.

Hearn, Lafcadio. *History of English Literature*, Tokyo, 1927, II, 870-871.

Hendrick, Burton Jesse. *The Training of an American; the Earlier Life and Letters of Walter H. Page, 1855-1913*, Boston, 1928, p. 325.

Henneman, John Bell. "The National Element in Southern Literature," in *Sewanee Review* (Sewanee, Tenn.), XI, 345-366, July, 1903.

———. "The Biography of Sidney Lanier," in *Sewanee Review* (Sewanee, Tenn.), XIV, 352-357, July, 1906.

Higginson, Thomas Wentworth. "Sidney Lanier," in *Chautauquan* (Meadville, Penn.), VII, 416-418, Apr., 1887.

———. *Women and Men*, New York, 1888, pp. 296-300.

———. *Contemporaries*, Boston, 1899, pp. 85-101.

Hill, Walter B. "Sidney Lanier," in Appendix to Lucian Knight's *Reminiscences of Famous Georgians*, Atlanta, 1907, pp. 712-716.

———. "Poet of Passionate Purity," in *Telegraph* (Macon), Feb. 3, 1933.

Holden, Florence P. "A Study of Sidney Lanier's Poem 'Sunrise'," in *Werner's Magazine* (N. Y.), XX, 476-510, Jan., 1898.

Hollar, Rosita Holdsworth. "Lanier, Agrarian Poet-Prophet," in *Southern Literary Messenger* (Richmond), III, 71-73, Feb., 1941.

Holliday, Carl. *A History of Southern Literature*, New York, 1906, pp. 343-355.

———. *Three Centuries of Southern Poetry (1607-1907)*, Nashville, 1908, pp. 173-182.

Horder, W. Garrett. "Sidney Lanier and His Poetry," in *The Quarto . . . For 1896*, London, 1896, pp. 15-27.

Hubbell, Jay B. "A Lanier Manuscript," in *Library Notes* (Duke University), II, No. 2, 2-3, Nov., 1937.

———, ed. "A Commencement Address by Sidney Lanier," in *American Literature* (Durham, N. C.), II, 385-404, Jan., 1931.

———. *American Life in Literature* (with bibliography), New York, 1936, II, 209-228.

Hubner, Charles W. *Representative Southern Poets*, New York, 1906, pp. 15-54.

Huckel, Oliver. "The Genius of the Modern in Lanier," in *Johns Hopkins Alumni Magazine* (Baltimore), XIV, 484-503, June, 1926.

Ives, Ella Gilbert. "Sidney Lanier," in *Transcript* (Boston), Dec. 19, 1900.

Jackson, Lena E., and Aubrey Starke. "New Light on the Ancestry of Sidney Lanier," in *Virginia Magazine of History and Biography* (Richmond), XLIII, 160-168, Apr., 1935.

———. "Sidney Lanier in Florida," in *Florida Historical Society Quarterly* (Tallahassee), XV, 118-124, Oct., 1936.

Jacob, Cary F. *The Foundations and Nature of Verse*, New York, 1918, pp. 31, 114, 117.

Jacobs, Thornwell, ed. [Facsimile of Lanier's B. A. Diploma], in *The Oglethorpe Book of Georgia Verse*, Oglethorpe, 1930.

James, John G. *Southern Students' Handbook of Selections for Reading and Oratory*, New York, 1879, p. 18.

Johnson, Gerald W. " Shin Bone Players," in *Evening Sun* (Baltimore), Dec. 26, 1935.
————. " Baltimore and Her Poets," in *Evening Sun* (Baltimore), Jan. 16, 1936.
————. " Flower of Pratt Street," in *Evening Sun* (Baltimore), Feb. 20, 1936.
Jones, Howard Mumford. " Sidney Lanier," in Percy H. Boynton's *American Poetry*, New York, 1918, pp. 670-675.
Jones, Joseph, and Philip Graham. *A Concordance to the Poems of Sidney Lanier*, Austin, 1939.
Jones, Mary Callaway. *Sidney Lanier: A Chronological Record of Authenticated Facts*, Macon, 1940.
Jones, Walter B. " Clifford Lanier," in *Advertiser* (Montgomery), Jan. 30, 1928.
Jones, Weimar. ." Sidney Lanier's Visits to Old Asheville Citizen," in *Citizen-Times* (Asheville, N. C.), Feb. 27, 1944.

Karsten, E. Pickard. " Sketches of Sidney Lanier and His Life in Macon," Clippings from *News* (Macon), 1926, and bound as pamphlet by Washington Memorial Library, Macon.
Kaufman, Matthias S. " Sidney Lanier, Poet-Laureate of the South," in *Methodist Review* (Nashville), LXXXII, 94-107, Jan., 1900.
Kaufman, Paul. " A National Psalm by a Southern Singer," in *Christian Science Monitor* (Boston), Feb. 10, 1925.
Kell, J. M. *Recollections of a Naval Life*, Washington, 1900, pp. 296-297.
Kellogg, Clara Louise. *Memoirs of an American Prima Donna*, New York, 1913, pp. 50-51. Passages reprinted in *America Through Woman's Eyes*, New York, 1933.
Kelly, Frederick. " Sidney Lanier at the Peabody Institute," in *Peabody Bulletin* (Baltimore), pp. 35-38, Dec., 1939.
————. " Lanier's House on Denmead Street," in *Maryland Historical Magazine* (Baltimore), XXXVI, 231-232, June, 1941.
Kent, Charles W. " A Study of Lanier's Poems," in *Publications of the Modern Language Association* (Baltimore), VII, 33-63, Apr., 1892.
————. *Southern Poems*, Boston, 1913, pp. 73-74.
Keyserling, Hermann. " The South—America's Hope," in *Atlantic Monthly* (Boston), CXLIV, 605-608, Nov., 1929.
Kilpatrick, Helen. [Recollections of Lanier], in *Telegraph* (Macon), July 8, 1928.
King, Fred Alvin. " Sidney Lanier: Poet, Critic, and Musician," in *Sewanee Review* (Sewanee, Tenn.), III, 216-230, Feb., 1895.
King, Grace. *Memoirs of a Southern Woman of Letters*, New York, 1932, pp. 110-112.
Kirkus, William. [Obituary], in *American Literary Churchman* (Baltimore), I, 34, Nov. 1, 1881.
Klemm, G. " Sidney Lanier: Poet, Man and Musician," in *Etude* (Phila.), LIX, 299-300, 342, May, 1941.
Knight, Lucian Lamar. *Reminiscences of Famous Georgians*, Atlanta, 1907, pp. 533-537; 712-716.
————. *Georgia's Landmarks, Memorials and Legends*, Atlanta, 1914, II, 604.
Kreymborg, Alfred. *Our Singing Strength*, New York, 1929, pp. 160-171.
Kuhl, E. P. " Sidney Lanier and Edward Spencer," in *Studies in Philology* (Chapel Hill), XXVII, 462-476, July, 1930.

Lamar, E. Dorothy Blount. *Sidney Lanier, Musician, Poet, Soldier*, Macon, 1922.
———. *A Brief in Behalf of Lanier for the Hall of Fame*, Macon, 1934.
———. *A Brief Addressed to the Electors of the Hall of Fame*, Macon, 1935.
———, ed. *Correspondence Promoting the Centennial Edition of the Writings of Sidney Lanier*, Macon, 1943.
Lane, Mary. "Macon: an Historical Retrospect," in *Georgia Historical Quarterly* (Macon), V, 20-34, Sept., 1921.
Lanier, Charles Day. Preface to Lanier's *Bob: The Story of Our Mocking Bird*, New York, 1899.
———. Preface to Lanier's *Letters*, New York, 1899.
———. Preface to Lanier's *Retrospects and Prospects*, New York, 1899.
Lanier, Clifford A. *Thorn-Fruit*, New York, 1867.
———. "Reminiscences of Sidney Lanier," in *Chautauquan* (Meadville, Penn.), XXI, 403-409, July, 1895.
———. "Some Reminiscences of Sidney Lanier," in *Christian Advocate* (Raleigh, N. C.), Apr. 20, 1899.
———. "Sidney Lanier," in *Gulf States Historical Magazine* (Montgomery), II, 9-17, July, 1903.
Lanier, Henry Wysham, ed. "A Poet's Musical Impressions, from the Letters of Sidney Lanier," in *Scribner's Magazine* (N. Y.), XXV, 622-633 and 745-752, May and June, 1899. Reprinted in Lanier's *Letters*, New York, 1899, pp. 65-116.
———, ed. "Letters between two Poets," in *Atlantic Monthly* (Boston), LXXXIII, 791-807 and LXXXIV, 127-141, June and July, 1899. Reprinted in Lanier's *Letters*, New York, 1899, pp. 119-215.
———, ed. Preface to Lanier's *Music and Poetry*, New York, 1898.
———, ed. *Letters of Sidney Lanier: Selections from his Correspondence, 1866-1881*, New York, 1899.
———, ed. Preface to Lanier's *Shakspere and His Forerunners*, New York, 1902.
———, ed. "In a Poet's Workshop. Poem Outlines by Sidney Lanier," in *Century Magazine* (N. Y.), LXXVI, 847-850, Oct., 1908.
———, ed. *Poem Outlines of Sidney Lanier*, New York, 1908.
———, ed. Introduction and Notes to *Selections from Sidney Lanier, Prose and Verse*, New York, 1916.
Lanier, J. F. D. *Sketch of the Life of J. F. D. Lanier*, New York, 1877.
Lanier, Mary Day, ed. *Poems of Sidney Lanier* (with a memorial by William Hayes Ward), New York, 1884, *et seq.*
———. "George Westfeldt, the Friend of Lanier," in *Symposium* (Northampton, Mass.), I, 13-14, Oct., 1896.
———. Preface to *The English Novel*, New York, 1897.
Lanier, Robert Sampson. A Poet Facing the World, B. A. Thesis, Princeton University, 1931.
Lantz, Emily Emerson. "Point Lookout Prison," in *Sun* (Baltimore), June 30, 1929.
Lanz, Henry. *The Physical Basis of Rime*, Stanford University, 1931, pp. 178-180.
LeConte, Joseph. *Autobiography of Joseph LeConte*, New York, 1903, pp. 60, 112.
LeConte, William. "A Bedfellow of Sidney Lanier," in *Westminster Magazine* (Oglethorpe University), July, 1912.
Le Gallienne, Richard. "Sidney Lanier," in *Academy* (London), LVIII, 147-148, Feb. 17, 1900. Reprinted as "Poetry of Lanier," in *Living Age*

(Boston), CCXXIV, 840-843, March 31, 1900, and in Le Gallienne's *Attitudes and Avowals*, New York, 1910, pp. 342-350.

———. "Sidney Lanier," in *Evening Transcript* (Boston), May 26, 1900.

Leisy, Ernest E. *An Interpretative History of American Literature*, New York, 1930, pp. 144-146.

Lewisohn, Ludwig. *Expression in America*, New York, 1932, 88-89.

Lind, W. Murdock. "A Dead Poet's Library. Sidney Lanier's Literary Treasures," in *Sunday News* (Baltimore), July 24, 1892.

Link, S. A. "Sidney Lanier," in *New England Magazine* (Boston), X [n. s.], 14-19, March, 1894.

———. "Sidney Lanier," in *Christian Advocate* (Raleigh, N. C.), Mar. 13, 1902.

Litz, Francis A. *Father Tabb*, Baltimore, 1923, pp. 140-141, 164-168, *passim*.

Long, Francis Taylor. "The Life of Richard Malcolm Johnston in Maryland, 1867-1898," in *Maryland Historical Magazine* (Baltimore), XXXIV, 305-324, Dec., 1939.

Lorenz, Lincoln. *The Life of Sidney Lanier* (with bibliography), New York, 1935.

Reviews:

American Literature (Durham, N. C.), VIII, 232-233, May, 1936 (C. R. Anderson).

Evening Sun (Baltimore), Jan. 11, 1936 (G. W. Johnson).

Evening Transcript (Boston), Dec. 21, 1935 (J. W. Maury).

Herald-Tribune (N. Y.), Feb. 15, 1936 (E. L. Walton).

Saturday Review of Literature (N. Y.), Jan. 25, 1936.

Times (N. Y.), Jan. 25, 1936 (J. Cournoz).

Lovell, Caroline Couper. *The Golden Isle of Georgia*, Boston, 1932, pp. 272 f.

Lovett, Howard Meriwether. "Macon in the War Between the States," in *Confederate Veteran* (Nashville), XXXII, 20-22, Jan., 1924.

———. "Georgia's Intellectual Center in the Sixties," in *Confederate Veteran* (Nashville), XXXII, 97-98, Mar., 1924.

Lowell, James Russell. [Letter to D. C. Gilman], in *The Forty-Sixth Birthday of Sidney Lanier*, Baltimore, 1888.

Mabie, Hamilton Wright. "The Poetry of the South," in *International Monthly* (Burlington, Vermont), V, 201-223, Feb., 1902. Reprinted as "Sidney Lanier," in *Outlook* (N. Y.), LXXI, 236-239, May 24, 1902.

MacClintock, W. D. [Lecture on Sidney Lanier], in *Critic* (N. Y.), XX [n. s.], 95, Aug. 5, 1893.

McCowan, Hervey Smith. "Sidney Lanier, the Southern Singer and His Songs," in *Self-Culture* (Akron, Ohio), X, 398-400, Jan., 1900.

McMahon, G. W. "Samuel Knox—A Patriot," in *Confederate Veteran* (Nashville), XXXII, 89, Mar., 1924.

McNaspy, Agnes T. "Sidney Lanier, Bard of the South," in *Signet* (N. Y.), XII, 16-20, Oct., 1931.

Macy, John. *The Spirit of American Literature*, New York, 1913, pp. 309-323.

———, ed. *American Writers on American Literature*, New York, 1931, pp. 327-341.

Magruder, Mary Lanier. "The Laniers," in *Southern Literary Messenger* (Richmond), II, 26-27, Jan., 1940.

Malone, Kemp. "Sidney Lanier," in *Johns Hopkins Alumni Magazine* (Baltimore), XXI, 244-249, Mar., 1933.

Manly, Louise. *Southern Literature*, Richmond, 1895, pp. 394-398.

Marble, Earl. " Sidney Lanier," in *Cottage Hearth* (Boston), IV, 141, 142, June, 1877.

Matthews, Brander. *A Study of Versification*, Boston, 1911, pp. 74, 87, 267.

Mayfield, John S. " Lanier's Trail in Texas," in *Texas Monthly* (Ft. Worth), III, 329-337, Mar., 1929.

――――. " Lanier in Lastekas," in *Southwest Review* (Dallas), XVII, 20-38, Oct., 1931. Reprinted as pamphlet, *Sidney Lanier in Texas*, Dallas, 1932.

――――. " Sidney Lanier's Immoral Bird," in *American Book Collector* (Baltimore), VI, 200-203, June, 1935.

――――. " Sidney Lanier's Friendship with Charlotte Cushman," in *Journal* (Atlanta), July 21, 1935.

――――. *Some New Facts Concerning Sidney Lanier in Florida*, Baltimore, 1935.

――――. " Sidney Lanier's War Experiences," in *Telegraph* (Macon), Jan. 31, 1937.

Meader, John Richard. " The Genius of Sidney Lanier," in *Globe* (Chicago and Phila.), IV, 675-688, Apr.-June, 1894.

Melton, Wightman F.: "Sidney Lanier in Baltimore," in *Daily News* (Griffin, Ga.), June 20, 1935.

――――. " Dewing Woodward Knew Sidney Lanier," in *Daily News* (Griffin, Ga.), Dec. 8, 1938.

Mencken, Henry L. *Prejudices—Third Series*, New York, 1922, pp. 152-153.

Miles, Dudley. " The New South: Lanier " (with bibliography), in *Cambridge History of American Literature* (New York, 1918), II, 313-346.

Miles, J. Tom. " Lanier," in *Southern Literary Messenger* (Richmond), I, 599, Sept., 1939.

Miller, C. W. E. " The Relation of the Rhythm of Poetry to that of the Spoken Language," in *Studies in Honor of B. L. Gildersleeve*, Baltimore, 1902, pp. 502 f.

Mims, Edwin. [Sidney Lanier], in *North Carolina Journal of Education* (Raleigh), pp. 5-8, June, 1898.

――――. *Sidney Lanier*, Boston, 1905.
    Reviews:
        Critic (N. Y.), XLVIII, 355, Apr., 1906 (J. L. Gilder).
        Current Literature (N. Y.), XL, 36-38, Jan., 1906.
        Dial (Chicago), XL, 119-122, Feb. 16, 1906 (W. E. Simonds).
        Independent (N.Y.), LX, 109-110, Jan. 11, 1906.
        Nation (N. Y.), LXXXII, 60, Jan. 18, 1906 (E. L. White).
        News (Baltimore), Dec. 2, 1905 (Frances L. Turnbull).
        Outlook (N. Y.), LXXXI, 650-652, Nov. 18, 1905.

――――. *The Advancing South*, New York, 1926, pp. 51-53.

――――. " Sidney Lanier," in *Dictionary of American Biography* (New York, 1933), X, 601-605.

Monroe, Harriet. *Poets and Their Art*, New York, 1926, pp. 268-284.

Moore, Elizabeth Haley. " Sidney Lanier," in *Alabama Historical Quarterly* (Montgomery), V, 35-46, Spring, 1943.

More, Paul Elmer. *Shelburne Essays, First Series*, New York, 1904, pp. 103-121.

Morris, Harrison S. " The Poetry of Sidney Lanier," in *American Weekly* (Phila.), XV, 284-285, Feb. 18, 1888.

Moses, Montrose J. *Literature of the South*, New York, 1910, pp. 358-383.

Moulton, Charles Wells. [Sidney Lanier], in *Magazine of Poetry* (Buffalo, N. Y.), II, 253-259, 1890.

————. "Sidney Lanier," in *Library of Literary Criticism*, Buffalo, 1904, VII, 325-332.

Myers, Jay Arthur. *Fighters of Fate*, Baltimore, 1927, pp. 174-181.

Myers, Sallie Jemison. [Lanier at Oglethorpe], in *Journal* (Atlanta), Sept. 25, 1927.

Myrick, Susan. [Reminiscences of Lanier], in *Telegraph and News* (Macon), Mar. 29, 1931.

Newcomer, Alphonso G. *American Literature*, Chicago, 1908, pp. 272-275.

Newell, A. C. "Lanier's Life at Oglethorpe College," in *Constitution* (Atlanta), Feb. 27, 1894. Reprinted in part in Baskervill's *Southern Literature*, Nashville, 1897.

Newell, T. F. "Sidney Lanier," in *Recorder* (Milledgeville, Ga.), Mar. 17, 1896.

Noble, Charles. *Studies in American Literature*, New York, 1898, pp. 268-277.

Northen, Mattie Traylor. "Sidney Lanier as I Knew Him," in *Journal* (Atlanta), May 19, 1929.

Northrup, Milton Harlow. "Sidney Lanier," in *Daily Courier* (Syracuse, N. Y.), Sept. 10, 1881.

————. "Sidney Lanier: Recollections and Letters," in *Lippincott's Magazine* (Phila.), LXXV, 302-315, Mar., 1905.

————. "Some Early Recollections of Sidney Lanier," in an unidentified newspaper clipping, Lanier Room, Johns Hopkins University.

Oehser, Paul H. "The Poet Who Sang a Song," in *Light and Life Evangel* (Chicago), XXXVIII, 1, Feb. 4, 1934.

————. "Sidney Lanier, Nature Poet," in *Nature Magazine* (Washington), XXXV, 468, 500, Nov., 1942.

Oliphant, Jean. "Wesleyan College Presents Sidney Lanier, Flutist," in *Wesleyan Alumnae* (Macon), I, 4-9, Jan., 1925.

Olney, Clark. "Archaisms in the Poetry of Sidney Lanier," in *Notes and Queries* (London), CLXVI, 292-294, Apr. 28, 1934.

Omond, Thomas Stewart. *A Study of Metre*, London, 1903, p. 22.

————. *English Metrists*, Oxford, 1921, pp. 195-202.

Orgain, Kate A. *Southern Authors in Poetry and Prose*, New York, 1908, pp. 9-23.

Orr, Oliver. "Sidney Lanier's Fame and Memorials," in *Southern Literary Messenger* (Richmond), II, 28-32, Jan., 1940.

Ortmann, Otto. "Musical Baltimore in the Seventies," in *Evening Sun* (Baltimore), July 8, 16, 1935.

Oxnam, G. B. "Sidney Lanier, A Prophet of the Social Awakening," in *Methodist Review* (N. Y.), XCIX, 86-90, Jan., 1917.

Page, Curtis Hidden. *Chief American Poets*, Boston, 1905, pp. 691-695, 650-651.

Painter, F. V. N. *Poets of the South*, New York, 1903, pp. 81-101, 227-234.

Pancoast, Henry S. *An Introduction to American Literature*, New York, 1898, pp. 275-283.

Parker, John. [Lanier at the Peabody], in an unidentified newspaper clipping, Lanier Room, Johns Hopkins University.

Parks, Edd Winfield. *Southern Poets*, New York, 1936, pp. cxiii-cxix, 168-170.

————. *Segments of Southern Thought*, Athens, Ga., 1938, pp. 63-69, 104-110.

Parrington, Vernon L. *Main Currents in American Thought*, New York, 1930, III, 334.

Pattee, Fred Lewis. *A History of American Literature Since 1870*, New York, 1915, pp. 274-288.

Payne, L. W., Jr. *Southern Literary Readings*, Chicago, 1913, pp. 209-226.

Payne, William Morton. *American Literary Criticism*, New York, 1904, pp. 29-30.

Peacock, Gibson. "Sidney Lanier," in *Evening Bulletin* (Phila.), Sept. 9, 1881.

Perine, George C. *Poets and Verse-Writers of Maryland*, Cincinnati, 1898, pp. 263-267.

Perry, Bliss. *The American Mind and American Idealism*, Boston, 1913, p. 63.

———. *A Study of Poetry*, Boston, 1920, pp. 171, 172, 210, 211.

Phelps, William Lyon. "Fifty Years of Lanier," in *Journal* (Atlanta), July 6, 1931.

Phillips, W. B. "Barrett Wendell [on Lanier]," in *Harvard Alumni Bulletin* (Cambridge, Mass.), pp. 986-988, May 10, 1925.

Pickett, LaSalle Corbell. "The Sunrise Poet," in *Lippincott's Magazine* (Phila.), LXXXVIII, 851-858, Dec., 1911.

———. *Literary Hearthstones of Dixie*, Philadelphia, 1912, pp. 41-65.

Pollard, Edward B. "The Spiritual Message of Sidney Lanier," in *Homiletic Review* (N.Y.), LXXIV, 91-95, Aug., 1917.

Pope, John Collins. *The Rhythm of Beowulf*, New Haven, 1942, pp. vii-viii.

Pressly, Thomas J. "Agrarianism—An Autopsy," in *Sewanee Review* (Sewanee, Tenn.), XLIX, 145-163, Apr.-June, 1941.

Pullen, Sister M. Consuella. The Imagery of Sidney Lanier's Poetry. M. A. Thesis, Catholic University of America, 1940.

Ransom, John Crowe. "Hearts and Heads," in *American Review* (N.Y.), II, 554-571, Mar., 1934.

Rede, Kenneth. "Lanier's 'Owl Against Robin,'" in *American Collector* (Metuchen, N.J.), III, 27-30, Oct., 1926.

———. "The Sidney Lanier Memorial Alcove," in *American Book Collector* (Baltimore), III, 300-304, May-June, 1933.

Reese, Lizette Woodworth. "The Spirituality of Lanier," in *Johns Hopkins Alumni Magazine* (Baltimore), XIV, 482-484, June, 1926.

Roberts, Frank Stovall. "The Lanier Brothers, of Georgia," in *Confederate Veteran* (Nashville), XXVII, 376, Oct., 1919.

Roquie, Margaret B. "Sidney Lanier," in *Times* (Georgetown, S.C.), Feb. 12, 1937.

———. "Sidney Lanier, Poet-Musician," in *Etude* (Phila.), LV, 576, 617, Sept., 1937.

Royce, Josiah. *Spirit of Modern Philosophy*, Boston, 1892, pp. 442-445.

Russell, Charles Edward. *The American Orchestra and Theodore Thomas*, New York, 1927.

Rutherford, Mildred Lewis. *American Authors*, Atlanta, 1894, pp. 368-375.

———. *The South in History and Literature*, Atlanta, 1906, pp. 485-496.

———. "The Poets of the South, 1865-1906," in *Rutherford's Scrap Book* (Atlanta, 1926), IV, 1-13.

Ryan, W. Carson. "Johns Hopkins: University Pioneer," in *Studies in Early Graduate Education*, New York, 1939, pp. 15-46.

Ryan, W. E. "Sidney Lanier," in *Post* (Washington), Nov. 5, 1933.

Saintsbury, G. E. B. *History of English Prosody*, London, 1910, III, 493-497.

Sapir, Edward. "The Musical Foundations of Verse," in *Journal of English and Germanic Philology* (Urbana, Ill.), XX, 213-228, 1921.

Sargent, Epes. *Harper's Cyclopaedia of British and American Poetry*, New York, 1881, pp. 916-917.

Scharf, J. Thomas. *History of Baltimore City and County*, Philadelphia, 1881, pp. 655-656.

Scherer, James S. B. *The Holy Grail*, Philadelphia, 1906, pp. 73-114.

Scott, W. J. "Life and Genius of Sidney Lanier," in *Quarterly Review of Methodist Episcopal Church, South* (Nashville), V [n. s.], 157-171, Oct., 1888.

Scudder, Horace E., and Marie H. Taylor. *Life and Letters of Bayard Taylor*, Boston, 1885, *passim*.

Semple, Patty. "Sidney Lanier," in *Southern Bivouac* (Louisville), II [n. s.], 661-667, Apr., 1887.

Shackford, J. Atkins. "Sidney Lanier as a Southerner," in *Sewanee Review* (Sewanee, Tenn.), XLVIII, 153-173, 348-355, 480-493, Apr., July, Oct., 1940.

Shadman, W. H. "The Lanier Oak," in *Pilot* (Brunswick, Ga.), Mar. 1, 1920.

Sharp, William, ed. *American Sonnets*, London, 1889, pp. 118-125.

Shepherd, Henry E. "Sidney Lanier," in *Current Literature* (N. Y.), XXXII, 108-111, Jan., 1902.

———. *The Representative Authors of Maryland*, New York, 1911, pp. 5-87.

Short, J. Saulsbury. "Sidney Lanier at Johns Hopkins," in *Johns Hopkins Alumni Magazine* (Baltimore), V, 7-24, Nov., 1916.

———. "Sidney Lanier 'Familiar Citizen of the Town,'" in *Maryland Historical Magazine* (Baltimore), XXXV, 121-146, June, 1940.

Sillard, P. A. "Sidney Lanier and His Poetry," in *American Catholic Quarterly Review* (Phila.), XLIV, 33-39, Jan., 1919.

Simonds, Arthur B. *American Song*, London, 1894, pp. 122-125.

Sladen, Douglas B. W. "Sidney Lanier," in *Independent* (N. Y.), XLII, 806, June 12, 1890.

———. *Younger American Poets*, New York, 1891, pp. 635-655.

———. "An American Rossetti," in *Literary World* (London), XLVIII [n. s.], 378-379, Nov. 17, 1893.

Smith, Bridges. [Lanier and M. H. Northrup], in *Daily Telegraph* (Macon), Aug. 25, 1918.

———. [Reminiscences of Frank Stovall Roberts], in *Daily Telegraph*, Dec. 8, 1918.

———. [The Composition of Lanier's "The Carrier's Appeal"], in *Daily Telegraph*, Nov. 10, 1926.

Smith, Charles Forster. "Sidney Lanier as Poet," in *Methodist Review* (N. Y.), LI, 196-210, Mar.-Apr., 1902.

———. *Reminiscences and Sketches*, Nashville, 1908, pp. 136-163.

Smith, C. Alphonso. "The Possibilities of the South in Literature," in *Sewanee Review* (Sewanee, Tenn.), VI, 298-305, July, 1898.

Smith, Egerton. *The Principles of English Metre*, London, 1923, pp. 54, 71.

Snoddy, James S. "Color and Motion in Lanier," in *Poet-Lore* (Phila.), XII, 558-570, Autumn, 1900.

———. "Sidney Lanier: The Poet of Sunrise," in *Poet-Lore* (Phila.), XV, 89-94, Winter, 1904.

Snyder, Henry Nelson. *Modern Poets and Christian Teaching. Sidney Lanier*, Cincinnati, 1906.

———. "The Matter of Southern Literature," in *Sewanee Review* (Sewanee, Tenn.), XV, 218-226, Apr., 1907.

——. "Sidney Lanier," in *Library of Southern Literature*, Atlanta, 1907, VII, 3041-3045.

Spann, Minnie. "Sidney Lanier's Youth," in *Independent* (N. Y.), XLVI, 789, June 21, 1894.

——. "Sidney Lanier's Manhood," in *Independent* (N. Y.), XLVI, 821-822, June 28, 1894.

Spencer, Thomas Edwin. *Sidney Lanier, A Study in Personality*, St. Louis, 1930.

Squires, W. H. T. *The Land of Decision*, Portsmouth, Va., 1931, pp. 104-128.

Starke, Aubrey H. "Sidney Lanier and Paul Hamilton Hayne . . . ," in *American Literature* (Durham, N. C.), I, 32-39, Mar., 1929.

——. "William Dean Howells and Sidney Lanier," in *American Literature* (Durham, N. C.), III, 79-82, Mar., 1931.

——. "Lanier, the Unknown Man," in *Journal* (Atlanta), Sunday Magazine, pp. 6, 18, Aug. 20, 1933.

——. "Sidney Lanier: Man of Science in the Field of Letters," in *American Scholar* (N. Y.), II, 289-397, Oct., 1933.

——. "Lanier's Appreciation of Whitman," in *American Scholar* (N. Y.), II, 398-408, Oct., 1933.

——. "More About Lanier" (See Allen Tate), in *New Republic* (N. Y.), LXXVI, 337-338, Nov. 1, 1933.

——. *Sidney Lanier: A Biographical and Critical Study*, Chapel Hill, 1933.

Reviews:

American Literature (Durham, N. C.), V, 275-279, May, 1933 (C. R. Anderson).

Commonweal (Boston), XVIII, 192-193, June 16, 1933 (G. N. Shuster).

Herald-Tribune (N. Y.), Apr. 23, 1933 (H. Brickell).

Times (N. Y.), Apr. 9, 1933 (H. Gorman).

Times Literary Supplement (London), Aug. 24, 1933.

Transcript (Boston), May 13, 1933.

(See also articles by Ransom, Tate, and Warren.)

——. "The Agrarians Deny a Leader," in *American Review* (N. Y.), II, 534-553, Mar., 1934.

——. "An Omnibus of Poets," in *Colophon* (N. Y.), IV, part 16, Mar., 1934.

——. "Sidney Lanier as a Musician," in *Musical Quarterly* (N. Y.), XX, 384-400, Oct., 1934.

——, and Lena E. Jackson. "New Light on the Ancestry of Sidney Lanier," in *Virginia Magazine of History and Biography* (Richmond), XLIII, 160-168, Apr., 1935.

——. "An Uncollected Sonnet by Sidney Lanier," in *American Literature* (Durham, N. C.), VII, 460-463, Jan., 1936.

——, and John M. Harrison. "Maternal Ancestors of Sidney Lanier," in *Virginia Magazine of History and Biography* (Richmond), XLIV, 73-80 and 160-174, Jan. and Apr., 1936.

——. "Annulet Andrews: Poet," in *South Atlantic Quarterly* (Durham, N. C.), XXXV, 194-200, Apr., 1936.

Stebbins, Emma. *Charlotte Cushman*, Boston, 1879, pp. 268-269.

Stedman, Edmund C. "The Late Sidney Lanier," in *Critic* (N. Y.), I, 298-299, Nov. 5, 1881. Reprinted in *Genius and Other Essays*, New York, 1911, pp. 250-253.

——. *Poets of America*, Boston, 1885, pp. 449-451.

——. *Nature and Elements of Poetry*, Boston, 1895, pp. 195-196, 282.

Stedman, Laura, and George M. Gould. *Life and Letters of Edmund Clarence Stedman*, New York, 1910, II, 115, 154, 279.

Strong, Augustus H. *American Poets and Their Theology*, Philadelphia, 1916, pp. 371-418.

Sutton, Maude Minish. "Sidney Lanier's Home in the North," in *News and Observer* (Raleigh), Oct. 2, 1927.

Swayne, Egbert. "The Poet, Sidney Lanier, As a Musician," in *Music* (Chicago), XVI, 125-131, June, 1899.

Swiggett, Glen Levin. "Sidney Lanier," in *Conservative Review* (Washington), V, 187-192, Sept., 1901.

——, ed. "To the Memory of Sidney Lanier," Lanier issue of *Pathfinder* (Sewanee, Tenn.), I, No. 3, Sept., 1906.

Tabb, Jennie Masters. *Father Tabb: His Life and Work*, Boston, 1921, pp. 17-20.

Tate, Allen. "A Southern Romantic," in *New Republic* (N. Y.), LXXVI, 67-70, Aug. 30, 1933. (See John T. Boifeuillet and A. H. Starke.)

——. "More About Lanier," in *New Republic* (N. Y.), LXXVI, 338, Nov. 1, 1933. (See A. H. Starke.)

Taylor, Bayard. "The Centennial Cantata," in *Tribune* (N. Y.), Apr. 12, 1876. Reprinted in *Telegraph and Messenger* (Macon), Apr. 18, 1876.

——. "A Picture of the Opening Ceremonies [of the Centennial Exhibition]," in *Tribune* (N. Y.), May 11, 1876.

Taylor, Marie Hansen, and Horace E. Scudder. *Life and Letters of Bayard Taylor*, Boston, 1884, *passim*.

——. *On Two Continents*, New York, 1905, pp. 258-259.

Taylor, Walter F. *A History of American Letters* (with Hartwick's bibliography), Boston, 1936, pp. 271-281.

Thayer, William R. "Sidney Lanier and His Poetry," in *Independent* (N. Y.), XXXVI, 742-743, June 12, 1884.

——, ed. "Letters of Sidney Lanier to Mr. Gibson Peacock," in *Atlantic Monthly* (Boston), LXXIV, 14-28, and 181-193, July and Aug., 1894. Reprinted in Lanier's *Letters, New York*, 1899, pp. 3-61.

——. *The Letters of* (ed. by Charles Downer Hazen), Boston, 1926, pp. 26, 34, 36.

Thirkield, Wilbur P. "Sidney Lanier," in *Times* (Chattanooga), Jan. 23, 1926.

Thom, Helen Hopkins. *Johns Hopkins, A Silhouette*, Baltimore, 1929, p. 79.

Thomson, Eunice. "Sidney Lanier's Courtship," in *Journal* (Atlanta), Sunday Magazine, p. 10, Feb. 3, 1935.

Thomson, William. *The Basis of English Rhythm*, Glasgow, 1904, pp. 26, 36-38.

——. *The Rhythm of Speech*, Glasgow, 1923, pp. 271, 273, 287, 289, 291.

Thorpe, Harry Colin. "Sidney Lanier: A Poet for Musicians," in *Musical Quarterly* (N. Y.), XI, 373-382, July, 1925.

Tolman, Albert H. "Lanier's *Science of English Verse*," in D. C. Gilman's *The Forty-Sixth Birthday of Sidney Lanier*, Baltimore, 1888. Reprinted in *Views About Hamlet and Other Essays*, Boston, 1904.

Traubel, Horace. *With Walt Whitman in Camden*, New York, 1906, III, 207-209.

Trent, William Peterfield. *Southern Writers*, New York, 1905, pp. 404-407.

——. *The South in the Building of the Nation*, Richmond, 1909, XII, 53-55.

Trout, John M. Sidney Lanier, Ph. D. Thesis, Princeton University, 1928.

Turnbull, Francese L. *The Catholic Man*: A Study, Boston, 1890.

———. "Sidney Lanier: A Study," in D. B. W. Sladen's *Younger American Poets*, New York, 1891, pp. 645-655.

Tyler, Lyon G. "Washington and his Neighbors," in *William and Mary College Quarterly Historical Magazine* (Williamsburg, Va.), IV, 35-36, July, 1895.

Varnedoe, J. O. "Oglethorpe's Greatest Graduate," in *Westminster Magazine* (Oglethorpe University), Aug., 1912.

———. "Sidney Lanier: An Appreciation," in *Georgia Historical Quarterly* (Savannah), II, 139-144, Sept., 1918.

Voigt, G. P. *The Religious and Ethical Element in the Major American Poets* (Bulletin of the University of South Carolina), Columbia, S. C., 1925, pp. 139-149.

———. "Sidney Lanier," in *Saturday Review of Literature* (N. Y.), XIII, 9, Apr. 4, 1936.

Von Sturmer, H. H. "A Soldier-Poet," in *Excelsior* (Barbados), I, 233-236, Oct., 1890.

Walker, George W. "A Poetical Genius," in *Quarterly Review of the Methodist Episcopal Church, South* (Nashville), VII, 193-206, Apr., 1885.

Wann, Louis. *The Rise of Realism . . . 1860-1888*, New York, 1933, pp. 168-198, 770-772.

Ward, William Hayes. "Lanier's Essay, 'Mazzini on Music,'" in *Independent* (N. Y.), June 27, 1878.

———. "Sidney Lanier, Poet," in *Century Magazine* (N. Y.), XXVII, 816-821, Apr., 1884.

———. "Memorial," Introduction to Mary Day Lanier's *The Poems of Sidney Lanier*, New York, 1884, pp. xi-xli.

———. "Four Poems," in *Independent* (N. Y.), XLIX, 933, July 22, 1897.

Warren, Robert Penn. "The Blind Poet: Sidney Lanier," in *American Review* (N. Y.), II, 27-45, Nov., 1933.

Watkins, Mattie A. "Sidney Lanier, Poet, Musician, Soldier of the Confederacy," in *Confederate Veteran* (Nashville), XL, 426-427, Dec., 1932.

Wauchope, George Armstrong. "Dr. Woodrow and Sidney Lanier," in *State* (Columbia, S. C.), Jan. 18, 1907. Reprinted in Marion Woodrow's *Dr. James Woodrow*, Columbus (S. C.), 1909, pp. 156-165.

Wayland, John W. *Sidney Lanier at Rockingham Springs*, Dayton (Va.), 1912.

Webb, Richard, and Edwin R. Coulson. *Sidney Lanier, Poet and Prosodist*, Athens (Ga.), 1941.

Weber, William Landor. *Southern Poets*, New York, 1903, pp. xxvii-xxxii.

Weirick, Bruce. *From Whitman to Sandburg in American Poetry*, New York, 1924, pp. 73-84.

Wendell, Barrett. *Literary History of America*, New York, 1900, pp. 495-499.

West, Charles N. *A Brief Sketch of the Life and Writings of Sidney Lanier*, Savannah, 1888.

Westfeldt, Gustaf R. *Fifteen Minutes With Sidney Lanier*, New Orleans, 1915,

Westfeldt, Jenny Fleetwood. "The Last Days of Sidney Lanier," in *Evening News* (Macon), Feb. 3, 1932.

White, Edward Lucas. "Reminiscences of Sidney Lanier," in *Johns Hopkins Alumni Magazine* (Baltimore), XVII, 329-331, June, 1929.

White, William. "Lanier, A Poet for Musicians," in *Daily Trojan* (Los Angeles), Dec. 18, 1937.

Whiteside, Mary Brent. "Lanier and the Path to Fame," in *Westminster Magazine* (Oglethorpe University), XVI, 57-61, Sept., 1931.

Wiggins, Robert Lemuel. *Life of Joel Chandler Harris,* Nashville, 1918, pp. 70, 80, 127.

Wilkens, F. H. "Early Influences of German Literature in America," in *Americana Germanica* (N. Y., 1900), III, 110-136.

Wilkinson, William Cleaver. "One More Homage to Sidney Lanier," in *Independent* (N. Y.), XXXVIII, 1261, Oct. 7, 1886.

Willard, Frances E. "Notes of Southern Literary Men and Women," in *Independent* (N. Y.), XXXIII, 3-4, Sept. 1, 1881.

Willcockson, Ruth. Rhythmical Principles and Practices of Sidney Lanier, M. A. Thesis, University of Chicago, 1928.

Williams, Stanley T. *The American Spirit in Letters,* New Haven, 1926, pp. 255-257.

———. "Sidney Lanier," in John Macy's *American Writers on American Literature,* New York, 1931, pp. 327-341.

Wills, George S. "Sidney Lanier—His Life and Writings" (with bibliography) in *Publications of the Southern History Association* (Washington), III, 190-211, July, 1899.

Wilson, Heileman. "The Genius of Sidney Lanier," in *Fetter's Southern Magazine* (Louisville), II, 11-16, Feb., 1893.

Wood, Clement. *Poets of America,* New York, 1925, pp. 68-81.

———. "The Influence of Poe and Lanier on Modern Literature," in *Southern Literary Messenger* (Richmond), I, 237-240, Apr., 1939.

———. "Lanier's Religion Was Unorthodox," in *Southern Literary Messenger* (Richmond), I, 641, Sept., 1939.

Woodberry, George Edward. "An Introductory Note," in John S. Mayfield's *Lanier in Texas,* Dallas, 1932.

Woodrow, Marion. *Dr. James Woodrow,* Columbia, S. C., 1907, pp. 156-165.

Woolf, Winfield P. "The Poetry of Sidney Lanier," in *Sewanee Review* (Sewanee, Tenn.), X, 325-340, July, 1902.

Wray, J. E. "Sidney Lanier's 'Song of the Chattahoochee '," in *Quarterly Review of the Methodist Episcopal Church, South* (Nashville), XVI [n. s.], 157-163, Apr., 1894.

Wysham, Henry Clay. "Sidney Lanier," in *Independent* (N. Y.), XLIX, 1489-1490, Nov. 18, 1897.

Young, Barbara. "Memoria," in *Times* (N. Y.), Sept. 7, 1926.

Young, Eleanor. "The Trail of a Silver Flute," in *Christian Science Monitor* (Boston), Sept. 12, 1931.

B. SELECTED REVIEWS OF LANIER'S PUBLISHED VOLUMES

BOY'S FROISSART

Academy (London), XVII, 194, Mar. 13, 1880.
Appleton's Journal (N. Y.), VIII, 96, Jan., 1880.
Atlantic Monthly (Boston), XLV, 130, Jan., 1880 (H. E. Scudder).
Harper's Magazine (N. Y.), LX, 474, Feb., 1880.
Literary World (Boston), X, 402, Dec. 6, 1879.
Nation (N. Y.), XXIX, 392, Dec. 4, 1879.

BOY'S KING ARTHUR

Academy (London), XIX, 7, Jan. 1, 1881.

Atlantic Monthly (Boston), XLVII, 122-123, Jan., 1881 (H. E. Scudder).
Harper's Magazine (N. Y.), LXII, 315, Jan., 1881.
Literary World (Boston), XI, 441, Dec. 4, 1880.
Scribner's Monthly (N. Y.), XXI, 322, Dec., 1880.

BOY'S MABINOGION

Dial (Chicago), II, 182-183, Dec., 1881.
Harper's Magazine (N. Y.), LXIV, 316, Jan., 1882.
Literary World (Boston), XII, 449, Dec. 3, 1881.

BOY'S PERCY

Academy (London), XXIII, 237-238, Apr. 7, 1883.
Harper's Magazine (N. Y.), LXVI, 316, Jan., 1883.
Independent (N. Y.), XXXIV, 10, Nov. 23, 1882.
Nation (N. Y.), XXXV, 468, Nov. 30, 1882.

ENGLISH NOVEL

American Literary Churchman (Baltimore), II, 206-207, Aug. 1, 1883 (William Kirkus).
Century Magazine (N. Y.), XXVII, 957--958, Apr., 1884 (Brander Matthews).
Critic (N. Y.), III, 228-229, May 19, 1883.
Daily Tribune (N. Y.), Feb. 28, 1897.
Dial (Chicago), IV, 40-41, June, 1883.
Evening Bulletin (Phila.), May 17, 1883.
Evening Transcript (Boston), May 19, 1883.
Harper's Magazine (N. Y.), LXVII, 798-799, Oct., 1883.
Independent (N. Y.), XXXV, 12, Sept. 6, 1883.
Literary World (Boston), XIV, 204-205, June 30, 1883.
Nation (N. Y.), XXXVII, 38, July 12, 1883.
New Englander (New Haven), XLIII, 97-104, Jan., 1884. (F. H. Stoddard).

FLORIDA

Literary World (Boston), VI, 116, Jan., 1876; XII, 215, June 18, 1881.
Nation (N. Y.), XXI, 277, Oct. 28, 1875; XXII, 63, Jan. 27, 1876.
Telegraph and Messenger (Macon), Jan. 26, 1876.
Tribune (Chicago), Dec. 18, 1875.

LETTERS

Dial (Chicago), XXVIII, 55, Jan. 16, 1900.
Nation (N. Y.), LXIX, 416, Nov. 30, 1899.
Press (Phila.), Dec. 10, 1889.
Sewanee Review (Sewanee, Tenn.), VIII, 346-364, July, 1900 (W. P. Woolf).
Transcript (Boston), May 26, 1900 (Richard LeGallienne).
Times, Saturday Review (N. Y.), Dec. 9, 1899 (Joel Benton).

MUSIC AND POETRY

Book Buyer (N. Y.), XVIII, 144-145, Mar., 1899 (R. E. Burton).
Critic (N. Y.), XXXIV, 365-366, Apr., 1899.
Dial (Chicago), XXVI, 338-339, May 16, 1899 (W. M. Payne).
Nation (N. Y.), LXVIII, 228, Mar. 23, 1899.

POEM OUTLINES

Century Magazine (N. Y.), LXXVI, 847-850, Oct., 1908.
Independent (N. Y.), LXV, 1249, Nov. 26, 1908.
Poet-Lore (Phila.), XIX, 482-487, Winter, 1908.
South Atlantic Quarterly (Durham, N. C.), VIII, 97-98, Jan., 1909
   (Edwin Mims).
Times, Saturday Review (N. Y.), XIII, 606, Oct. 24, 1908 (Bliss
   Carman).

POEMS, 1877

Daily Graphic (N. Y.), Jan. 22, 1877 (R. H. Newell).
Evening Post (N. Y.), Nov. 23, 1876 (G. C. Eggleston).
Harper's Magazine (N. Y.), LIV, 617-618, Mar., 1877.
Herald (N. Y.), Jan. 21, 1877.
Nation (N. Y.), XXIV, 16, Jan. 4, 1877.
Times (N. Y.), Dec. 2, 1876.
Tribune (N. Y.), Nov. 21, 1876 (Bayard Taylor. Reprinted in *Critical
   Essays and Literary Notes*, N. Y., 1890, pp. 312-314).

POEMS, 1884, *et seq.*

American (Phila.), IX, No. 228, 167-168, Dec. 20, 1884 (W. R.
   Thayer).
Atlantic Monthly (Boston), LV, 288, Feb., 1885.
Critic (N. Y.), III [n. s.], 3-4, Jan. 3, 1885.
Dial (Chicago), V, 244-246, Jan., 1885 (F. F. Browne).
Evening Bulletin (Birmingham), Dec. 1, 1884 (W. R. Burton).
Independent (N. Y.), XXXVI, 1609, Dec. 18, 1884 (W. R. Thayer).
Lippincott's Magazine (Phila.), XXXV, 525-526, May, 1885.
Literary News (N. Y.), VI [n. s.], 9-10, Jan., 1885.
Literary World (Boston), XVI, 40-41, Feb. 7, 1885.
Nation (N. Y.), XXXIX, 528, Dec. 18, 1884.
New Englander (New Haven), XLIV, 227-238, Mar., 1885 (D. H.
   Chamberlain).
Quarterly Review of the Methodist Episcopal Church, South (Louisville),
   VII, 193-206, Apr., 1885 (G. W. Walker).
St. John Globe (St. John, New Brunswick), April 25, 1885 (C. G. D.
   Roberts).
Saturday Union (?), Jan. 14, 1885 (F. R. Whitten).
Spectator (London), LXV, 828-829, Dec. 6, 1890.
Times (Chicago), Dec. 6, 1884.
Tribune (Minneapolis), Mar. 5, 1885 (R. MacDonald).

RETROSPECTS AND PROSPECTS

Chautauquan (Meadville, Pa.), XXIX, 512, Aug., 1899.
Independent (N. Y.), LI, 1763, June 29, 1899.

SCIENCE OF ENGLISH VERSE

Constitution (Atlanta), May 20, 1880 (J. C. Harris).
Courier (Boston), June 6, 1880.
Critic (N. Y.), I, 14, Jan. 15, 1881.
Dial (Chicago), I, 55-58, July, 1880 (F. F. Browne).
Evening Post (N. Y.), May 24, 1880.

Globe and Democrat (St. Louis), May 24, 1880.
Harper's Magazine (N. Y.), LXI, 796-797, Oct., 1880.
Literary World (Boston), XI, 227, July 3, 1880.
Nation (N. Y.), XXXI, 310-311, Oct. 28, 1880.
New Englander (New Haven), III [n. s.], 566-567, July, 1880.
News and Courier (Charleston, S. C.), May 20, 1880.
Scribner's Monthly (N. Y.), XX, 473 f., July, 1880.
Times (N. Y.), June 18, 1880.

SHAKSPERE AND HIS FORERUNNERS

Athenaeum (London), No. 3943, 649-650, May 23, 1903 (W. Heinemann).
Atlantic Monthly (Boston), XCI, 266-267, Feb., 1903 (Ferris Greenslet).
Dial (Chicago), XXXV, 165-169, Sept. 16, 1903 (Albert H. Tolman).
Dial (Chicago), LI, 245-246, Oct. 1, 1911 (C. F. Tucker Brooke).
Nation (N. Y.), LXXVI, 401, May 14, 1903.
Outlook (N. Y.), LXXIV, 476-477, June 20, 1903.
Sewanee Review (Sewanee, Tenn.), XI, 452-462, Oct., 1903 (L. W. Payne, Jr.).
South Atlantic Quarterly (Durham, N. C.), II, 157-168, Apr., 1903 (W. P. Few).
Sun (N. Y.), Dec. 21, 1902.
Tribune (Chicago), Jan. 17, 1902 (Elia W. Peattie).

TIGER-LILIES

Atlantic Monthly (Boston), XXI, 382, Mar., 1868.
Courier and Union (Syracuse, N. Y.), Feb. 25, 1868.
Daily Courier (Charleston), Feb. 4, 1868 (W. G. Simms).
Daily Telegraph (Macon), Dec. 17, 1867.
Evening Mail (N. Y.), reprinted in *Georgia Journal and Messenger*, Dec. 18, 1867.
Georgia Journal and Messenger (Macon), Dec. 18, 1867.
Peterson's Magazine (Phila.), LIII, 237, Mar., 1868.
Picayune (New Orleans), Mar. 19, 1868.
Round Table (N. Y.), VII, 396, Dec. 14, 1867.